D1203565

WITHDRAWN

SUTTER

The Man and His Empire

CALVIN T. RYAN LIBRARY
KEARNEY STATE COLLEGE
KEARNEY, NEBRASKA

John Augustus Sutter

From the painting by Frank Buchser, 1866
Museum of the City of Solothurn, Switzerland

SUTTER
The Man and His Empire

BY

J. PETER ZOLLINGER

GLOUCESTER, MASS.

PETER SMITH

1967

CALVIN T. RYAN LIBRARY
KEARNEY STATE COLLEGE
KEARNEY, NEBRASKA

Copyright, 1939, by Oxford University Press, Inc.. New York
Reprinted, 1967 by Permission of
Oxford University Press

110973

979.454
Z 75

DEDICATED TO MY WIFE

ANNA R. ZOLLINGER

IN GRATEFUL TRIBUTE TO

HER UNTIRING ASSISTANCE

PREFACE

In the summer of 1839 the Fates cast upon the shores of California a homeless wanderer from foreign parts, an erring Ulysses in search of a land where he might prosper and live in peace. It was this pioneer who a little later created our first firm foothold on 'the Coast' and built the catwalk bridging the immense gulf of wastes and rocks between the Missouri and the Pacific. The man was Johann August Sutter.

It throws a curious light on our 'scientific age' that a historic figure whose name once shone like a flaming comet in the skies of fame and whose accomplishments touched every hamlet of the globe has never to this day been honored by an impartial study. In his own time accounts of his life were published only by pronounced worshipers or enemies and to no better purpose than to produce a distorted effigy either of a haloed martyr or of a perfect rascal.

Within the last decade and a half a number of sketchy portraits of the penny-shocker type have been given out on paper and on celluloid. Sutter's name, therefore, requires no introduction. Yet behind all these adventurous and fantastic yarns the true nature of this strange man has always remained hidden.

The main obstacle in the way of a basic study of the life of Sutter always was the impenetrable darkness shrouding his European years. Recently, however, thanks chiefly to Rudolf Bigler and through the author's own efforts, the fundamental data concerning Sutter's early years have been brought to light. They furnish not only a solid basis to build on, but also a standard by which to *judge him and the fanciful tales which he spread about his origin.*

But it was not Sutter's pre-American years alone which have so long been hidden in darkness. Of the seventy-seven years of his life, the ten most important ones, his historic phase, were amply documented; the others practically unexplored. It was imperative, therefore, to trace his footsteps not only in the country of his origin, but through the American Continent from New York to St. Louis, to Santa Fe, along the Oregon Route, all over California, and back to Pennsylvania where he lies buried.

Everywhere this field-work has yielded abundant new material. The suspicion which furnished the original incentive for this study— that behind the machine-made film hero (or villain) there was awaiting the discoverer a vital, fascinating personality—was fully justified. A new, at times scarcely expected image thus arises before our eyes: a bewitching double personality overly endowed with brilliant gifts and lamentable weaknesses; a man both shrewd and naive, plain and opalescent, ebullient and quixotic of temperament.

Many of Sutter's fantasies assumed astoundingly concrete form. His California Empire for instance. All were attempts to give shape in one way or another to a mysterious, visionary urge. For his inner as for his outer life his fantasies were of enormous functional importance. Some of his fictions, however, were palliatives, endeavors to shield behind an opalescent smoke-screen certain stretches of his life. For this reason it must be obvious that his own memoirs and other autobiographical fragments can be of only limited value to the biographer, that they may be used only with utmost precaution and only when they are substantiated by more objective evidence.

All the sources used are authentic documents. The chapters covering Sutter's youth in Switzerland are based on material in official Swiss archives, libraries, newspapers and historical publications, supplemented in many essential points by unpublished American sources. The chapters on Sutter's life in Missouri and New Mexico

are derived from data contained in American public records, con-
temporary memoirs, letters and publications in German-American
and American newspapers and historical periodicals.

For the California phase of the story, most of the published sources
of the period have been consulted: histories, memoirs, letters, news-
papers and periodicals. Most of the sources, however, are manu-
scripts in the Bancroft Library of the University of California at
Berkeley, the California State Library in Sacramento, and the
Henry E. Huntington Library in San Marino. Among these docu-
ments there are numerous letters of Sutter's in English, Spanish,
French and German; the New Helvetia Diary, and at least a hun-
dred memoirs of California contemporaries of Sutter, many of them
long known. Most valuable among the new material concerning this
period were the letters of Sutter to John Bidwell, Pierson B. Read-
ing, John Marsh, and William A. Leidesdorff, and the 'State-
ment' by John A. Sutter, Jr. But above all, this portrait of Sutter
has been enriched by the original manuscript of over 1,000 pages
(folio) of Henry Lienhard's memoirs.

The main part, naturally, of every life of Sutter must be devoted
to the years which secure him a place in American history: his years
of pioneering which prepared the way for the American conquest of
the Pacific Coast and culminated in the gold discovery. Entirely new,
and perhaps one of the chief contributions to our lore of Sutter, is the
section of the book devoted to Sutter's path from New York to Cali-
fornia, that amusing road of metamorphosis on which the pitiful
shopkeeper from Burgdorf changed into the glamorous 'ex-captain of
the Royal Swiss Guard of France'—a fiction which may well be said
to have served him as a spring-board to success. New, no less, is the
presentation of the last thirty years of Sutter's life and the digest of
the famous lawsuit of the United States vs. Sutter, which hitherto
have always been dismissed in a few words.

The aim to achieve objectivity and a certain comprehensiveness naturally forbade the elimination of anything of moment, pleasant or unpleasant about certain aspects of Sutter's private life. Now there are aspects of the private life of a historic figure which are entirely unrelated to his public career. Nelson and Grant may illustrate the point. On the other hand it is possible for a man's private life to encroach upon his public one to the extent of becoming a directional momentum. Edward VIII has furnished the most recent and most remarkable example. The ruinous conflict between Sutter and his eldest son is another. As if by silent agreement all predecessors in this field have suppressed it, although it contains perhaps the main key to the enigmatic Sutter. At all events it imparts to his story an uncanny depth often reminiscent of antique tragedy. In brief, the naked facts of Sutter's life seem to present a tale more unusual, more fantastic, more stirring than anything literary speculation has hitherto been able to suck from its thumbs, or anything brought to light by the squabbles of California local historians.

I am indebted to a great many more persons than space permits me to mention here. In California the following, by their aid and courtesy, have furthered my undertaking: Dr. Herbert E. Bolton, Director of the Bancroft Library and his staff; Miss Mabel R. Gillis and Miss Caroline Wenzel of the California State Library; the officers of the Henry E. Huntington Library; Mr. Douglas S. Watson of the California Historical Society; the Society of California Pioneers, and Mr. Allen Lane of Santa Rosa.

I am obliged to Mr. A.H. Lienhard of Minneapolis for the loan of his father's memoirs, to Mrs. Van Rensselaer Wilbur of Pasadena for interrupting her translation of that manuscript for my benefit, and to Mr. H.M. Lydenberg, Director of the New York Public Library, for making possible the transfer of this document to New York.

In Switzerland I owe thanks above all to Herr Rudolf Bigler, Municipal Librarian of Burgdorf; to Dr. Otto Gass and the late

Dr. Carl Gauss in Liestal; to the late Dr. Hermann Escher in Zurich; to Frau Marguerite Walser and Herr Gerold Walser in Basle. In Kandern, Baden, Herr Albert Eisele has been of great help to me.

Most deeply, however, I am indebted to my wife who, from beginning to end, has shared with me the happy and exacting labor of research.

J.P.Z.

New York, May 1, 1939.

CONTENTS

Part I : One of God's Gentlemen

1. POLITICAL HOROSCOPE   I

2. CHILDHOOD AND YOUTH   3

3. TRAGIC OVERTURE   8

4. A GREENHORN IN MISSOURI   17

5. SANTA FE AND WESTPORT   27

6. BRILLIANT IMPERSONATION   39

7. THE PROMISED LAND   48

8. RECOMMENDATIONS   53

Part II : The Empire-Builder

9. RIO SACRAMENTO   63

10. NEW HELVETIA   68

11. CONQUISTADOR AND MISSIONARY   73

12. DON JUAN AUGUSTO SUTTER   79

13. FOREIGN AFFAIRS   84

14. THE LORD OF NEW HELVETIA   89

15. THE WHITE ELEPHANT — 93

16. GROWING-PAINS OF A PRIVATE EMPIRE — 103

17. THE GOOD SAMARITAN — 108

18. LIFE AT SUTTER'S FORT — 115

19. NO END OF TROUBLE — 122

Part III : Arms and the Man

20. WAR CLOUDS — 129

21. SKIRMISHES — 137

22. THE ACTOR'S FAVORITE ROLE — 142

23. CAHUENGA — 149

24. ALL FOOLS' DAY — 156

25. THE LIFE-BLOOD OF EMPIRE — 161

26. THE NOOSE — 170

Part IV : Tool of Destiny

27. PROVIDENCE AND THE DEVIL — 181

28. SUBTLE CHANGES — 184

29. PIG AND PETTICOAT — 191

30. STARS AND STRIPES — 200

31. TRANSITION — 212

32. AN INTIMATE PORTRAIT — 218

CONTENTS

33. MILLS, MORMONS, AND ANASHE'S DAUGHTER   225

34. LIGHTNING IN THE MOUNTAINS   232

35. SECRETS WILL OUT   240

36. ORGIES OF DRUNKENNESS   248

Part V : Tragic Dawn

37. FATHER AND SON   261

38. A SAGA OF TWO CITIES   270

39. THE PEAK OF LIFE   281

40. A PEER'S BOURGEOIS FAMILY   286

41. SHORTCUTS TO RUIN   292

42. THE SPIRIT OF CONQUEST   300

43. THE SQUIRE OF HOCK   305

44. THE LUXURY OF JUSTICE   317

45. A NEW CAMPAIGN   324

46. THE LAST RETREAT   329

47. THE SHADOW OF THE CAPITOL   335

NOTES   343

SOURCES   353

INDEX   365

ILLUSTRATIONS

John Augustus Sutter   *Frontispiece*

The Kandern Papermill. Sutter's
    Birthplace   *Opposite page*   10

Window at Burgdorf with Sutter's
    Signature   "   "   10

Mrs. Anna Dübeld Sutter   "   "   16

John Augustus Sutter, Jr.   "   "   16

Santa Fe, 1849   "   "   36

Monterey, 1841   "   "   36

Sutter at the Time of the Founding of
    New Helvetia   "   "   70

Juan Bautista Alvarado   "   "   70

Mariano Guadalupe Vallejo   "   "   70

Manuel Micheltorena   "   "   70

Sacramento from the Foot of J Street,
    1849   "   "   210

San Francisco, 1849   "   "   210

Sutter in His Early Seventies   "   "   336

PART ONE

ONE OF GOD'S GENTLEMEN

1. POLITICAL HOROSCOPE

THE Mississippi still marked the western boundary of the United States. Beyond it all land was held by Spain. Part of it, though— those immeasurable prairie stretches later known as the Louisiana Territory, between the Mississippi, the Rocky Mountains and Canada—had recently been ceded to France; but the Spaniards still governed it. Now the Spanish Intendant in New Orleans had tried to bottle up the Mississippi Valley and block the export of agricultural produce from those western American states bordering on the eastern bank of the great river and on the Ohio. Result: Hectic turmoil. Western demagogues loudly demanded that a reply be given at the point of the bayonet to the Spanish autocrat in New Orleans. The Government in Washington had a hard task trying to prevent a filibusters' march on New Orleans. With dramatic intensity and amidst the pangs and spasms of parturition, the West had suddenly forced itself upon the public mind. The West was born.

There are moments in the theater of history which make one think of a great master of the stage, secretly plotting, co-ordinating and timing the actions so as to make things 'click.' Such a moment was February 15, 1803. On that day a number of things occurred between the Alps and the Potomac, the effects of which were subsequently to merge and interweave into a dynamic pattern which, to this day, has left its mark upon the map of the world.

February 15, 1803. In the House of Representatives in Washington a bill was delivered providing for an appropriation for the purchase of Louisiana. On this day, also, as throughout the month, Thomas Jefferson and his two disciples, Madison and Monroe, were cloistered among the books and charts of the President's study. The document over which their heads bent gravely was the draft of the instructions with which Monroe was to depart for Paris to negotiate the acquisition of Louisiana. 'On the event of this mission depend the future destinies of the Republic,' said Jefferson. He foresaw that only the possession of that vast wild territory of the West could guarantee the free, unhampered development of the young nation.

February 15, 1803. Napoleon had just completed the 'Act of Mediation,' through which he tried to perpetuate in all form his *de facto* protectorate over Switzerland. Until now he had been completely deaf to all proposals of the American Ambassador Livingston concerning the wish of the American Government to acquire Louisiana by treaty. But presently English criticism, carping at his Swiss protectorate, incited the tyrant's wrath. Two days later, on February 17, a historic conversation took place at the Tuileries between the First Consul and Lord Whitworth. Napoleon, in words fit for 'the mouth of a hackney coachman' intimated that he would henceforth stand for no more British criticism, even if his actions were not in accord with the terms of the peace of Amiens. These words opened renewed warfare.

Because England was bound to seize upon New Orleans, and because Napoleon could not hope to defend it against Britain's naval power, he, with a sudden about-face, now jumped at the chance to sell Louisiana to the United States. Thus Switzerland's temporary loss of her independence became one of the prime agents of the Louisiana Purchase. And from a Jeffersonian vision the American West had become an overawing reality.

February 15, 1803. On this day also was born the Swiss who,

more than any other individual, helped push the western boundary of the United States even farther west to the Pacific, and who was to tie the new coast to the old one with ties of gold. His name was Johann August Sutter. He might well have said with Napoleon, 'I was born when my fatherland died;' and he might have added, with even better reason, 'born also on the day when my new fatherland was born,' the great American West.

All these far-reaching and dramatic events between the Alps and the Mississippi were profoundly to influence the life of Sutter. Europe was arming to the teeth to fight out the issues of medieval feudalism, of imperialism and of democracy. In the United States a bloody fight was waged between the champions of Jeffersonian democracy and the royalistic principles embraced by the Federalists. Everywhere the stars of feudalism, of imperialism and of democracy loomed threateningly in the political skies at the hour of Sutter's birth, and throughout his long life the three-cornered fight between the three principles for which they stood was to continue in him.

2. *CHILDHOOD AND YOUTH*

THE name of Sutter or Suter is frequent and widespread throughout the southernmost range of the German tongue. And not without good reason. It derives from one of the oldest crafts, one of the most useful among those brought north of the Alps by the conquering Romans: the *sutor*, the cobbler. Johann August's immediate forbears, however, were peasants and ribbon-weavers, native to northwestern Switzerland, and citizens of the village of Rünenberg in the magnificent hills of the Basle Jura, where they have been traced as far back as 1574.

About the middle of the eighteenth century Sutter's grand-father left the village for the city. There he learned the paper-maker's trade and married. Being an intelligent and reliable work-man, apparently, his employers, the old Häussler family of Basle paper-makers, transferred him to Kandern, a tiny townlet thir-teen miles north in what was then the Margravate of Baden, where he became supervisor or foreman of the firm's papermill. Sutter's father, Johann Jakob Sutter, Jr., born at Basle in 1776, followed in his sire's footsteps and at an early age inherited the foreman's position in that little outpost of Swiss industry.

In August 1801 the younger Johann Jakob Sutter married Christine Wilhelmine Stober, daughter of Pastor Johann Adolf Stober of Grenzach, and of this union Johann August Sutter was born at five o'clock in the morning of February 15, 1803. His father having already advanced to the master's position, the child was born right at the mill,[1] and therefore virtually on Swiss terri-tory, a spot, at least, which almost enjoyed the status of a Swiss enclave and which during the Thirty Years' War had sometimes been respected as neutral territory even by roving and pillaging bands of Swedes.

Not until five years later, November 27, 1808, was the little family augmented by a second and last child, Jakob Friedrich.[2] The births of both these sons were recorded in Rünenberg, the village which their forefathers had called native for centuries and where they possessed inalienable citizenship. Johann August him-self was baptized in Kandern on February 23, 1803.

Being the only child of his parents until he had well advanced into his sixth year, the boy no doubt was the spoiled and pampered little darling of his mother. The mental characteristics of an only child (too often an ill-starred heritage) remained among the most constant determinants of his personality throughout his life. It was probably from his mother, the pastor's daughter, that he inherited many of the unusual traits which lifted him right out of his paternal peasant ancestry; namely, beauty and charm, versatility, the gifts of conversation, of handling people and of making friends; and the love of books which was his to the end of his days.

Apart from its charming location at the foot of the Black Forest, there was nothing venerable in Kandern's local atmosphere. Its reputation was based pre-eminently on its beer-pretzels and its marked bibulous tradition, which, according to Johann Peter Hebel, the poet of that region, became crystallized in the legend of a ghost who haunted all drunkards at midnight. To this day a large tankard is all that Kandern carries in its coat of arms.

The personal circumstances determining Sutter's earliest years are shrouded in darkness. But life as a whole, as young August eagerly observed and imbibed it, was as colorful as any boy could desire. His formative years fell into the heyday of Napoleonism. Kandern, situated but a few miles from the one bridge far and wide which allowed armies to cross the Rhine easily, was rarely devoid of uniforms. Towards the end of 1813, after the battle of Leipzig, Basle, owing to its bridge, became the concentration point of the largest of the allied armies of Germany, Austria and Russia, and the headquarters of the campaign against Napoleon. For weeks troops poured in through all the roads of Baden.

There is every reason to believe that these armies and officers in their resplendent uniforms stirred young August's ambition. They must have kindled to a blazing fire his hopes of playing one day an important military role himself. The desire to be a military somebody constituted half his life and became the mother of his unbridled urge for palming off anecdotes of a military career as fictitious as any Münchhausen tale.

Witness some of the things he wrote even in his old age: In a petition addressed to the United States Congress in 1866, this son of a factory foreman insisted that he 'was born of a respectable family enjoying independent circumstances,' and that he 'received a good education, literary and military.' He could never repress such fables. In his Reminiscences he states that, after having moved to Switzerland in 1819 and attended school in Neuchâtel, he became 'associated with Weber, now publisher of the *Illustrated News* at Leipzig. After which I entered as cadet at Berne, Switzerland, and served in the army until I went to America in 1834. Was officer in the Swiss Army at the time Napoleon [III] was a refugee in Switzerland and captain of artillery.' And a few days before his death he told listeners at an evening party in Washington that he 'frequented the military academy at Thun, Switzerland, and was the fellow student of Louis Napoleon, later Emperor of France.'

These and other self-glorifying tales which Sutter told credulous admirers have been retold and reprinted in good faith a thousand times. Indeed they have become so much a part of his legendary self that they impose upon the biographer the necessity of integrating them, vague as they are, into his life. For in them, as much as in anything he did and said, is revealed the mettle of the man, that lovable liar and captivating dreamer, the brilliant actor on the stage of life and the self-made gentleman.

What in reality was the youth of this self-styled friend of Louis Napoleon and business partner of one of Europe's foremost publishers?

He was a brilliant and fascinating youngster, much too talented in his father's eyes to waste his days as a worker, or even as the foreman of the papermill. So, his elementary education having been completed in Kandern, he was sent to French Switzerland in 1819, where, according to his own admission, he enjoyed a year's tuition in a private school in Neuchâtel or St. Blaise. After that he came to Basle, there to be apprenticed to the firm of

Emanuel Thurneysen, printers, publishers and booksellers, who had just acquired the papermill at Kandern.

Basle, one fears, was obviously an uncongenial city for a young man of Sutter's restless spirit and irreverence. Since the days of the Ecumenical Council of 1431–48, when Basle was the hub of the Christian world, since the days when Erasmus of Rotterdam had taught in the university and the city had been one of the centers of learning, of literature and art, it had sunk gradually into the smug spiritual sterility of stark Puritanism. What if its burghers were prosperous? What if the show of riches of Basle's silk barons roused in young Sutter a life-long fondness for wealth and a desire to display himself in style? His own chances of partaking of the wealth of the world, of commercial success were minute. For the world which at his birth still received him with fanfares of *Liberté! Égalité! Fraternité!* had since collapsed and given way to one of the darkest periods in European history. Among the Swiss cities Basle was one of the most reactionary, and its rural subjects, of which Sutter was one, were once more disfranchised. Semi-serfdom politically, and semi-serfdom as a commercial clerk seemed to be Sutter's lot.

Add to this the sanctimonious spirit of the city, dominant, most likely, also in the house of Thurneysen, and it is easy to visualize Sutter in an uncomfortable straitjacket. His aptitude for subordination was always nil, his mind being independent and teeming with vast, vague dreams. The ritual of the counting-house never held out any comforts to his yearning soul, and the sacrosanct solemnity of double-entry remained to his heart a mystery closed with seven seals.

Is it any wonder, then, that at the end of his apprenticeship in 1823, we find him discharged by Thurneysen, although his friend and fellow-apprentice, Johann Jakob Weber, continued there as a clerk and later became one of the leaders of continental publishers? Weber is the only European besides Napoleon III, whose name appears in the few lines with which, in his Reminiscences, the old Sutter dismissed the pre-American phase of his life. But by sleight of hand he turned his fellow-apprenticeship with Weber into a reputable business partnership.

Needless to say, after his 'association' with the famous Weber, Sutter did not enter the Military Academy at Berne (for there was no such academy). Nor did he serve as captain in the Swiss Army (for there was no Swiss Army at the time, there were only the militia troops maintained by each of the twenty-two cantons). Moreover, service as an officer was a prerogative of the upper classes, and Sutter, the son of a mill foreman from a disfranchised rural domain, was emphatically not of this privileged stratum. The plain truth is that probably Sutter never did any military service in his native country, not even as a militiaman. For his name has never been found in any muster-roll. [3]

What did he do? Alas, his own fictions palliate that period of his life which, apart from the misfortune following upon the gold discovery in California, was his most painful.

3. *TRAGIC OVERTURE*

INTO the autograph album of his friend Weber, J. Aug. Soutter (thus he frenchified his name at the time) wrote on March 26, 1823 the prophetically pathetic words of farewell: 'Hope not to have found a friend, save in him who has found one in thee. All yearn for such a treasure; few mean to pay for it, and that is why friends on earth are such marvels.' He added the motto: '*Aime, bois et chante.*'

Then, from the booktrade's realm of prestige, Sutter descended to clerkdom in a draper's shop in the little town of Aarburg. The change was not without significance. Perhaps the daily preoccupation with articles of dress offered him a substitute for the forbidden military life that was more satisfactory and more congenial than books, though he continued to love these.

It was in Aarburg that Sutter's real tale began, that epic which took for its scope the breadth of two oceans and the expanse of a continent—all the space between the Alps and Honolulu. As usual it began with a woman. In Aarburg Sutter met Annette Dübeld, his future wife. Soon he followed her to her hometown Burgdorf, in the canton of Berne, a jewel of a medieval town, situated in a poetic, fertile landscape, in the face of the snow-clad Alps, and bedded snugly in the saddle of a hill, between castle and church, the symbols of temporal and spiritual power. In this quite unusual setting Sutter first earned his living as a lowly grocery clerk in the store of Salzfaktor Aeschlimann.

But for Annette, the world might never have heard of Sutter. In the summer of 1826 he applied to the elders of his native Rünenberg for a marriage licence, or, more exactly, petitioned for their gracious consent to his marriage. A Swiss at that time was in no way a citizen of Switzerland, nor even of his canton. His civic rights, if he possessed any, were strictly confined to the one town or village which he called *heimat*, home. But the benevolent tyranny of patriarchal supervision extended over all the native sons, even if they lived 'abroad,' i.e., beyond the bailiwick. Indeed, the exercise of a sort of marriage censorship over those who had strayed beyond the fold seemed particularly needful, because, if any of them failed to support himself and his family, he was invariably deported to his native place and there became a public charge.

Very wisely, therefore, Sutter supplemented his application for a marriage permit with letters of the Reverend Samuel Jäggi of

Burgdorf and the attorney Dr. Carl Schnell. The clergyman assured the village elders of Rünenberg that Sutter's bride-to-be was of good character, of good family, that she had received the blessings of Christian baptism and 'from the earliest childhood had enjoyed the benefits of a careful education.' Lawyer Schnell testified that the bride's mother, the widow of Samuel Dübeld, possessed assets free of all liability in the amount of 20,000 Swiss francs and that she continued to operate the remunerative bakery and restaurant of her late husband. Her house, one of the finest and largest, occupied the most prominent corner of the town square.

Under these reassuring circumstances the village patriarchs of Rünenberg declared in writing that as far as they were concerned there was no obstacle in the way of a marriage between 'Johann August Sutter, citizen of Rünenberg, domiciled as a clerk in Burgdorf' and Anna Dübeld of the said city of Burgdorf. A month later, on October 24, the marriage was solemnized in Burgdorf. It was, alas, an emergency wedding, forestalling by but one day the birth of a son, named after the father Johann August.[4]

Sutter was now twenty-three years old, husband and father within twenty-four hours, and employed as a clerk in the grocery store of Salzfaktor Aeschlimann in the Schmiedengasse. How boyish he still was may be guessed from the fact that to this day his name is preserved in that store as he scratched it boyishly into a little vine-framed window-pane of a storage room—perhaps in a moment of despair, when he needed a visible symbol upon which to pin his hopes. For his position was in no way enviable. The circumstances of his marriage prove with what reluctance he entered upon the state of matrimony. Although his mother-in-law was a woman of means, he had but lean chances of bettering his condition in the near future, since all remunerative crafts, trades, and professions constituted as yet privileges of the native burghers.

The Kandern Papermill. Sutter's birthplace
Photograph by the author

*Window at
Burgdorf with
Sutter's signature*
Photograph by the author

As a non-native resident Sutter was merely tolerated, disfranchised, and his technique of making himself an in-law of a prominent old Burgdorf family cannot at first have impressed the watchful city fathers very favorably.

However, by dint of Frau Dübeld's money and influential connections, perhaps also on the strength of his own magnetic personality, he was officially permitted, two years after his marriage, to embark on his first independent venture. On August 28, 1828, he bought from the heirs of the Widow Trechsel-Grimm a house in the Schmiedengasse (Burgdorf's Main Street), on the upper story of which he lived with his growing family, while on the ground-floor he opened a draper's and drygoods store, in which, between 1831 and 1833, his brother Jakob Friedrich and one Benedikt Seelhofer, an irresponsible youth and a consumptive, also owned interests.

But the firm of Johann August Sutter & Company did not prosper. For three years its business was carried on under special permit and the condescending benevolence of the Burgdorf city elders, until, in 1831, the repercussions of the Paris July Revolution brought about a number of minor revolutions in Switzerland, as a result of which the old order was definitely buried. The freedom of trade was proclaimed and all restrictions on commerce were removed. At once a speculative mania seized the country, a rage of expansion, a struggle for elbow-room, a short, sky-rocketing boom paid for with many a terrific crash.

All of which led to Sutter's undoing. For years he had borne the drudgery of men in subordinate positions. He had suffered the fate of those without civic rights, of one merely tolerated, wherever he had lived since childhood, now suddenly to find himself elevated into equal rights with the once privileged. He had the very temperament which thrives on booming and boosting. His visionariness always went beyond his capacity of fulfilment. He was

110973

extremely liberal, open-handed; he trusted himself and his fellow-men too much; he lived extravagantly, far beyond his means. And he was ever more ready to yield to his impulses pressing towards the enjoyment of life than eager to know at the end of a month whether or not he could strike a satisfactory balance in his ledgers.

The consequences were not long in making themselves felt. In May, 1832, the little firm of Sutter & Company was forced to ar-range a settlement with its creditors, and these had to be satisfied with twenty-five per cent of their dues. Soon Seelhofer took ad-vantage of Sutter's temporary absence 'on the road' to escape with more than half the stock-in-trade. Yet Sutter, careless as he al-ways was about the details of business, did not even bother *legally* to dissolve the partnership; he merely announced its breaking-up in the local press. And thus it came about that, when Seelhofer died a little while later, all he left to his deserted partner was the heritage of their joint debts. To meet the demands of his credi-tors, Sutter sold the house he lived in to his mother-in-law for the sum of 11,000 francs, but continued to occupy it as her tenant. Hard as he worked, though, he sank deeper and deeper into the morass of debts. His business correspondence reached as far as Nuremberg, Germany, and Lyon, France. Personally he combed the countryside, the villages and hamlets far and wide, to obtain orders on cloth and yarns and whatever finery the age-old fashion books prescribed for the rural belles—only to find that there were obstacles more formidable than all the restrictions of trade under the old order. Under the new regime the old spirit which held that a man was a citizen only of his native village, but a foreigner everywhere else, survived. And among the slow, stodgy and sus-picious Bernese, only thirty miles from Sutter's native Rünenberg, his lively manners, his dialect, perhaps the very goods he sold, pro-claimed him a foreigner. Against such deep-rooted prejudice and passive resistance, the liberalism stirred up by the new freedom of trade broke ridiculously.

Meanwhile he and his family had to live, and living, as Sutter understood it meant living in style. That he owed to himself, he owed it to the prominence of his wife's family. He therefore spent freely and lived far beyond his means, thus establishing for himself a pattern of life from which, the longer he followed it, the less he could deviate—except in scope. On a scale ever larger he was later to repeat over and over again the adventure of Burgdorf, always starting from scratch and with his personal fascination as his only capital, always the victim of a strange ecstasy of growth and expansion, and also of a type of man whose modest foreshadowing in Burgdorf was Benedikt Seelhofer. There seems to have operated in Sutter an innate rhythm which had to assert itself as long as his heart beat. This was his art of living. His creditors complained that, instead of reducing his debts, he bought a mass of fine clothes and even books, paying on one occasion as much as 25 livres for the complete works of Walter Scott. For he was very fond of fiction and of travel literature.

And he had also become the father of five children.

To make matters worse, his relations with his wife's family grew strained. His only brother, Jakob Friedrich, had also come to Burgdorf and in March 1831 had married a sister of Annette, Marie Sophie Dübeld. This marriage proved a complete failure. Jakob Friedrich, a compositor by trade, was a thorough good-for-nothing, whom his wife divorced after two years of childless marriage. The young outcast then went to Geneva, whence he was to be deported to his native Rünenberg, a physical and moral wreck, and a public charge until his death in 1844.

The shadow of this catastrophe was bound to make itself felt also in August Sutter's domestic life. His own matrimonial existence, founded as it was on an emergency wedding, was none too

happy, and Annette happened to be of a rather domineering nature. Heinrich Lienhard, who, in 1849, escorted her to California, describes her as harsh, rude, narrow-minded, 'not bad-look-
ing,' full of the vain conceit of the small-town élite, purseproud
and parsimonious. She could probably never forgive herself for
having been forced to marry this penniless stranger and thus to
have brought disgrace upon her family in more than one way.

Nor was this all. Sutter himself, as developments of later years
were to prove with shocking clarity, was unable to shake off his
resentment, an abysmally profound resentment, against this marriage, into which he had been thrust by the impending birth of a
child. Indeed, as will be seen, there was buried in him a deep, primordial, and largely unconscious hatred against this fatal child.
And this enmity, perhaps, contained the very seed of his tragic
old age.

Thus the situation had become fraught with conflict and threatening doom. During the six years of the existence of his firm, Sutter had piled up an incredibly heavy debt—not altogether through
his own fault. His financial security, meanwhile, still depended on
the credit advanced him, so it seems, on the strength of the backing of his mother-in-law, who was now no longer well disposed
towards him. It needed but the wreck of his brother's marriage to
supply the spark that brought about the explosion of his own affairs. Actually, soon after that divorce, in the spring of 1834,
Frau Dübeld severed her financial relationship with her son-in-
law by selling the house he lived in and for which he neglected to
pay rent.

Without her backing he was lost, forced to face one of two unpleasant alternatives: either he publicly declare himself completely bankrupt and resign himself to being ruined physically and
spiritually behind the bars of debtors' prison, or else seek salvation
from all this in flight. We can readily understand why he chose

this latter way out. The prospect of years of prison life was unbearable to a man of his mettle, who, with his spirit already straitlaced by the petty-bourgeois narrowness of Burgdorf, rebelled against the fetters of matrimony. He therefore gathered what cash he could secretly raise, procured a passport on May 13, 1834 and then, abandoning his wife and five children and his huge debt, he took French leave. His wife, apparently, made no objections; rather she helped him escape. Two weeks after his departure he notified her from Havre that he did not intend ever to return. Immediately upon this news, bankruptcy proceedings were started against the fugitive, and on the demand of one of his chief creditors, the Savings Bank of Sumiswald, to which he owed 4,224 francs, a belated warrant of arrest was issued against him by the Chief of Police at Berne:

J.A.Suter, merchant from Rünenberg, Canton of Baselland, whose last address was Burgdorf, Canton of Berne, has secretly liquidated his assets, disappeared on May 8 or 9 from his residence, and is said to be on his way to America. He is 31, provided with a passport written in French, issued by the Clerk of the District of Burgdorf, and dated May 13, 1834, in which America is given as his destination.

Said Joh.Aug.Suter owes the *Privat Ersparnis Kasse* Sumiswald, in the District of Trachselwald of this canton, the main sum of 6,000 francs in two bonds and has caused this bank a total loss through the removal of his assets and his secret departure.

For which reason this formal request is issued, and addressed to all Hon. Authorities of Police, to arrest, upon meeting him, and safely secure said fugitive Suter, to relieve him of all drafts, cash, and other valuables he may carry on him, and to notify the authorities here, so that they may be able to start extradition proceedings against his person or recover his assets.

Berne, June 12, 1834.

Half a year later Frau Dübeld died and left what was considered a handsome fortune of 25,000 francs. But Sutter's debts—

CALVIN T. RYAN LIBRARY
KEARNEY STATE COLLEGE
KEARNEY, NEBRASKA

not fully paid off until twenty-eight years later, in 1862—were more than twice as high—51,183 francs. ' Of the many clothes and books which he owned,' we read in the Burgdorf bankruptcy records, ' none were found when his inventory was taken.' With these, apparently, he could not part. Of his wardrobe, at any rate, we shall hear more. On the other hand he left behind a ' house-book ' (journal) of 1831 ' in which nothing was written and in which many pages were cut out,' and a few bolts of cloth, aprons, slippers, handkerchiefs, neckties, gloves and similar store goods, a trumpet, a piano, a sign reading ' Joh.Aug.Sutter Tuchhandlung,' and some outstanding credits, worth, all together, about 15,000 francs.

Frau Annette Sutter and her five young children moved into an exile of shame, the *stöckli*, grand-parents' retreat, of an old farmhouse a mile beyond the city. Her share of her mother's estate was confiscated to serve as bond against her husband's obligations, and so she remained dependent on the benevolence of her sisters and on what meager earnings she could procure. In such pitiful circumstances she lived for sixteen years.

Not so her fugitive and handsome husband.

John Augustus Sutter, Jr.

Mrs. Anna Dübeld Sutter

4. *A GREENHORN IN MISSOURI*

SUTTER landed in New York in July 1834.

The country he now came to was no longer the primitive farmers' republic of the war of independence. The old order lay on its deathbed, and a new civilization was rising. King Cotton had become the tyrant of the nation. All over the world the cheaply-working mechanical looms had created an insatiable demand for cotton, and nowhere could this commodity be grown as well as in the Southern States of the American Union. It was King Cotton which pushed American settlements farther and farther west, King Cotton which tore up the treaties with the Indians, burnt down their forests, tilled their soil, and demanded the importation of new masses of black slaves, or else their breeding—like stock—in the land itself.

The North, no less, was being transformed by King Cotton. Factory towns bristling with chimneystacks rose everywhere under everlasting blankets of black smoke. There was a mushroom growth of spinning and weaving mills, from which mechanization spread to all other crafts. A whole new world of soot-wrapped settlements, river-steamers, railroads, foundries, and coal-mines originated and reached out towards the west. Already, two states of the Union, Louisiana and Missouri, had been organized west of the Mississippi, in the territory acquired at the time of Sutter's birth. Of these two Missouri was the youngest, the wildest, and the most romantic, touching as it did directly upon the Indian territory.

Immediately after landing, Sutter, too, made for this romantic border state of the then Far West, counting within an area of 69,000 square miles a mere 300,000 inhabitants, most of them living in St. Louis, on farms and little villages of the vicinity, and along the Mississippi and Missouri rivers. The rest was primeval forest.

What drew Sutter there? For one thing, though he was the son and grandson of a factory foreman, the smoke-bound, young industrial east of the United States could not be to his taste. He never felt at home in cities and was essentially a romantic. Perhaps, also, he had as yet too much respect for the police of orderly and civilized communities. From the fugitive's viewpoint the virgin forests certainly were safer. Like any goat off the tether he preferred the farthest distance which it was possible to reach.

But there was still another reason why he went west. At the very time Sutter had indulged in his dangerous and too ardent courtship of Annette Dübeld, an impractical and romantic German gentleman out of Rousseau's school of nature-worship put down on paper in the remote wilderness of Missouri strangely catching words, letters to his friends in Germany full of ecstatic descriptions of this enchanting Eden:

'I wish that you could but for a moment see my present surroundings. To be true, the hills and valleys are all covered with tall trees, but in such a manner that you might think an artist had here been at work creating a park.' Then again he writes: 'It is unusually tempting to settle in regions where nothing hampers one's choice and where, with a map in your hand, you may roam through beautiful nature for hundreds of miles, to study to your heart's content the condition of the soil and its vegetation in woods and meadows. Here, if anywhere, it is possible to combine pleasure with utility. . . . And what is more, you can have your choice of climate.' In short, the propagandist exclaims in one of his most seductive passages: 'I cannot help telling you that the lives of the inhabitants of these regions at first transported me into reverie, and even now, having had three months' time to study things, I seem to be facing a mirage as often as I consider what Nature here offers to man.'

The writer's name was Gottfried Duden. He had much more to say in these letters to his friends at home on the conspicuous advantage of life in the romantic freedom of Missouri. But then, having decided that as far as he was concerned he had had enough of it, he returned to Germany, published his American correspondence, and thus became the cause of the first great wave of German immigration into Missouri. To the naive Germans, to those dissatisfied with political conditions in their own land, and to the romantic hankering after an unmitigated *Gemütlichkeit*, Gottfried Duden had shown the way to Paradise. Soon Duden's farm in Warren County, Mo. (perhaps the original 'Dude ranch' of the holiday-maker's West?) became a little shrine of pilgrimage and the intellectual center of a group of Teutons as romantically impractical as their absent inspirer. A great many of these Duden disciples were men of excellent breeding, who had abandoned lucrative positions and promising careers to grapple with the virgin soil and make themselves believe that they liked it.

Certainly, the fact that Sutter, too, now set his eyes on Missouri cannot be termed an accident. For in his own country, as well as in Germany, Duden's best-seller was widely advertised in the most popular papers, and only two years before Sutter's departure from Burgdorf an unauthorized reprint of the book had been published under the auspices of the Swiss Emigration Society. It would be strange if Sutter, the former publisher's apprentice and a voracious reader, had overlooked it.

Thus, with his superbly acute sensorium for elect society, he, too, now bent his way towards that gathering-place of the elite of immigrants, Duden's Missouri. With four other greenhorns, two Germans and two Frenchmen, he traveled through Pennsylvania and Ohio to Cincinnati. There, he says, they separated, because they would never have learnt any English if they had remained together.

Sutter stayed in Cincinnati for two or three months, but late in the autumn of 1834 he made his appearance in the German colony of St. Louis. Lodging at the Hotel Schwyzerland kept by a *landsmann* of his on Front Street, he became acquainted with another greenhorn who had just arrived from Westphalia. This scurrilous fellow, Johann August Laufkötter, was for a while Sutter's most constant companion, and it is to his fondness for belittlement and calumny that we are indebted for most of our knowledge of Sutter's life in the Middle West.[5] For from these slanderous writings of the old Laufkötter—inspired by the discovery, years later in California, that his former fellow-greenhorn and bed-fellow had become a semi-heroic and legendary figure, while he himself had remained unknown—it is easy enough to sift a good many credible and pertinent facts corroborated, in part at least, by other contemporaries. But other details which we must take on Laufkötter's sole authority fit well enough into the jig-saw puzzle of Sutter's personality.

Sutter's grand fiasco in Burgdorf—scrupulously kept secret, of course—had not left him unscathed. Now that his flight had carried him to the outermost fringe of white man's land, and now that the solace that lies in wandering had given out, he felt uprooted, spiritually at sea, and for a long time rather afraid to engage in any new venture, lest he fail again. No doubt the discovery, spared none of these immigrants, that the real Missouri hardly resembled the paradise of Duden's promises, was not exactly helpful in the effort of getting settled. According to Laufkötter, the Swiss of this Missouri colony in particular became victims of homesickness to such a degree that not one of them, from the learned professor to the humble mechanic, could or would try to make use of his knowledge and ability. Sutter was no exception, and if he was no sufferer from pathologic nostalgia, he at least was driven to seek oblivion of his deplorable past in wild dreams of adventure. He 'wanted to strike out,' says Laufkötter, he had 'his eyes constantly on various projects of an adventurous character.' For a while he toyed with the idea of founding a settler's colony of his own, but as he was known to have been a shopkeeper in the old country and rather romantically disposed, no-one considered him to have enough leadership for such an enterprise. 'A man who had never handled an implement save the yardstick would make a poor person to lay out plans for a colony,' they said. Meanwhile, loath to try his hand at some humdrum business, the shopkeeper from Switzerland indulged in his favorite pastime of playing the gentleman.

Together with Laufkötter he joined the German Club of St. Louis. 'By dint of his vivacity, his gentle and winning manners, and his manly personality he soon assembled a circle of friends about him,' writes another member of the club, Gustav Ph. Koerner, a man who later played an important role in Illinois politics, became a close friend of Lincoln, and United States Minister to Spain. The German Club presented an odd assembly of recent immigrants. Some members were merchants, some professional men, younger sons of the nobility, ex-officers or mechanics. Most of them had been lured into the romantic wilds of Missouri by Duden's freakish book. Some had taken a fling at the back-breaking task of turning virgin forests into arable fields. But many of these *lateinische Bauern*, farming scholars, as they were jokingly called by the more humble populace, soon drifted back to the city, after having found out that their prophet Duden had 'written too well and worked too little' himself. Others were wise enough from the beginning not to try to wrench farm produce from their knowledge of Greek and Latin. Some were already established in business or in their old professions as lawyers, doctors, teachers, clergymen, or in the Government Land Office. But all the latest arrivals, notably those of the Giessen Immigration Society, also an organization inspired by Duden, felt as uprooted and unsettled as Sutter himself. To make things even worse for Sutter, they all had ample means, whereas he had very little. At least those who had something spent very liberally at the club, so that there was a constant and free flow of wine and liquor. And there was whist playing and noisy discourse on intellectual and political topics and vast impractical schemes.

Now it so happened that at the beginning of winter an imposing looking individual from Prairie du Chien in the Wisconsin territory popped up in this colorful German circle and caused a tremendous stir. He let it be known that he had been a Russian officer with the rank of colonel and military attaché to the Prussian Crown Prince. At once these floundering German immigrants, who had but recently fled from the petty tyranny of little princes, bowed before this nearest approach in their midst to a crowned head.

Bourgeois-gentilhomme Sutter, though a republican, did as the others did. Indeed, it seems that he was the first and staunchest of the colonel's enthusiastic admirers, and soon also his creditor to the amount of $50, which, in his own penury, meant quite a lot to him. It was Sutter who, ahead of all, took such pride in introducing the brilliant newcomer into the club and in securing his enrolment as an honorary member. They all adored him, lionized him, revered him, heaped liberal loans upon him in the hope of being repaid royal interests, as soon as dividends were thrown off by the magnificent projects with which the colonel was teeming. But what overwhelmed Sutter in particular was not so much the reflected splendor of royal serenity, as the immaculate courtliness of the new luminary's manners.

For a few weeks, then, club life was one continuous revelry. When news arrived that the colonel's ships were coming up the Mississippi and that the distribution of vast profits was at hand, he invited all his friends to a gigantic champagne party of several days' duration at a roadhouse, the Prairie House, a few miles outside St. Louis. But when finally the bill was presented by the innkeeper, the 'Colonel' had mysteriously vanished. His angry guests, forced now to pay for their own champagne, hunted him down; the impostor was found out and imprisoned. However, reports Laufkötter, the dazzling brilliance of his exquisite appearance still lingered on and left upon the ambitious young Sutter an indelible impression. It pointed out new untold possibilities. . . .

The idle winter of riotous club life left many of the immigrants, including Sutter, in straitened circumstances. Sutter had meanwhile moved out to St. Charles, where rents were cheaper, and where his friend Laufkötter had opened a store from which victuals and drinks could be procured gratis. It is not apparent from the St. Charles county records that Sutter himself had a farm there, as he maintained in later years. Nor do the records bear out his contention that at St. Charles 'he made before the proper tribunals his declaration of intention to become a citizen of the United States.' Laufkötter's declaration is preserved, and Laufkötter doubts whether Sutter ever filed his.[6]

In the precarious situation in which Sutter now found himself at St. Charles, it became imperative to do something. There had been frequent talk of organizing, or participating in, a trading expedition to Santa Fe. This highly interesting and often remunerative form of American trade was then at its apex. But none of the Missouri Germans were sufficiently informed to warrant a venture in this direction, eager as were those who had some money left to invest it in such trade, and eager as were the unemployed of the colony to do something. Under such circumstances it happened that Sutter was introduced to a few French merchants of St. Louis, who went to Santa Fe every spring. As he spoke French fluently (though with a heavy *accent bâlois*), and as the Frenchmen were very much impressed by his charming personality and by his plight as well, they consented to take him along to Santa Fe as their companion. Glowing with joyous anticipation he came back to St. Charles to say good-bye to his friends there. His friend-in-need Laufkötter supplied him with a little pocket-money. This he invested in old pistols, cheap trinkets, and old German students' jackets bought in a St. Louis pawnshop. He added a few pieces of his own very large wardrobe, and with these things as his stock-in-trade, Sutter, in the spring of 1835, set out on his first trip to Santa Fe.

Of his own *experiences* during this excursion nothing is known beyond the fact that he seems to have been ill at Santa Fe and spent most of his time in the room of one of his French patrons. But the *results* of the trip were nevertheless startling.

The adventurous life of the trail was much to his liking. The caravan of 1835 in general marked one of the high points in the history of the Santa Fe trade. Sutter's own little investment threw off a large profit. For the first time since his arrival in the New World he was no longer adrift, his life was again full of purpose, his self-confidence was completely restored, and so it is not surprising that in the autumn he returned to Missouri brimming with enthusiasm for Santa Fe and the fabulous profits to be made there in trade. As proof of his contentions he brought back seven mules received in exchange for his old pistols and clothes, and also a barrel of fiery El Paso wine. The cask was soon drained in the service of friendship. But the animals were first pastured for a few weeks on the farm of a comely German widow and then sold. Then, with the proceeds from the sale of these mules, Sutter began an itinerant trade among the farmers in the vicinity of

St. Charles and embarked on a lively propaganda campaign for a Santa Fe caravan of his own.

These activities also brought him in contact with that group of faithful disciples of Gottfried Duden, who were scattered around the old Duden farm, and whose spiritual leader now was Pastor Friedrich Münch. And here it was that the most startling issue of Sutter's first successful venture in the new country was brought to light: 'Sutter appeared in 1835 . . . in the so-called Duden Settlement in Warren County, Mo.,' reports Pastor Münch, 'and informed us . . . that he had been an officer in the Swiss Guard of Louis Philippe, but had been forced to flee from Paris in the July Revolution of 1830.' (The name of Louis Philippe is Münch's mistake. Sutter himself always maintained that he had served under Charles X.)[7]

The fruitful example of the dazzling 'colonel' from Prairie du Chien and the inspirational benefits of adventurous travel had resulted in the birth of the famous 'Captain' Sutter.

Sutter's first edition of the fictitious story of his military past was launched with due precaution. His old friends in St. Louis and St. Charles knew him only as a merchant, but it looks as if not only the gentlemen of the Duden Settlement, but all Sutter's new acquaintances from now on were initiated into his invented soldierly existence, even the farmers among whom he traded. And that explains an observation of Laufkötter's (tallying admirably with Pastor Münch's statement) which he correctly reported, although interpreted quite differently: In pursuing his course as a trader among the farmers, he writes, Sutter used liquor freely, and the farmers, therefore, 'thought him a capital fellow and gave him the name of "Captain" by which he was afterwards known.'[8] The farmers evidently knew more than Laufkötter.

Thus everything points to the fact that henceforth each step of Sutter's seemed calculated to build up the legend of his glorious military career. And was this not, after all, the thing to do in this Eldorado of impostors? Had not almost every immigrant come under one false pretence or another ever since Columbus had posed as a God before the Indians? The country swarmed with men of self-imposed titles of every description, from the humble captain to the swaggering count or prince. Even famous German officers of George Washington's army, Kalb and Steuben, for instance, had nonchalantly raised themselves into the nobility by pulling their own bootstraps, i.e., by putting a 'von' before their names.

Logically, Sutter's next step now was to establish his right to his title even before his oldest Missouri friends. This could be achieved by the simple device of becoming the captain of a caravan to Santa Fe. In a double meaning he therefore fostered, as Pastor Münch says, 'the fondest hopes and expectations for such an enterprise. . . . His engaging nature and his art of persuasion soon succeeded in uniting with him a number of our German friends . . . who failed to derive satisfaction from life in the primeval wilderness, for the purpose of organizing a trading caravan for New Mexico, with himself as their captain. Voluminous purchases were made in St. Louis (on credit). . . .'

The preparations for the trip filled a good part of the winter of 1835–6 and helped to pass it away pleasantly. 'Everybody gathered about my store,' writes Laufkötter, 'to hear Sutter talk of the prospects of the coming expedition. They were mostly young men with money, and this fact so deeply impressed Sutter that he was profuse in his assurances of the fortunes they would surely realize.' Laufkötter himself had no doubts on this point, for he readily sold out his share in the little firm of Wiese & Laufkötter of St. Charles, in order to return a wealthy man from Santa Fe.

5. *SANTA FE AND WESTPORT*

SUTTER's second Santa Fe expedition has hitherto remained the darkest and most mysterious chapter of his life. What was known were scathing rumors, the defamations of a hectic whispering campaign, and the stains and smears on him produced by a great volume of vitriolic ink. Laufkötter made himself the standard-bearer of these incriminators, whose activities towards the close of Sutter's life were no doubt partly to blame for his failure to obtain justice before the United States Supreme Court and before Congress. Laufkötter took particular and sadistic pleasure in broadcasting the story, fortified by a good deal of lurid detail, that the expedition was one continuous orgy of embezzlements and rogueries on the part of Sutter. Others went still further and made him a murderer. But Sutter never expressed himself on this mysterious episode of his life, a sure sign that at least he was deeply ashamed of it.

Happily, there are other witnesses outside the chorus of calumniators, men whose testimony deserves all the more credence as it was not given during that long and poisonous period of Sutter's public trial following the gold-rush, and not in California, where the quarrel was hottest. They are the historians of the Santa Fe trade, and Sutter's contemporaries of the Duden circle in Missouri. Outstanding among these latter is an anonymous but obviously very cultured participant in the Santa Fe venture who, as 'E' (possibly Dr. Engelmann, a physician and botanist), soon after the return of the caravan to St. Louis, published an extensive account of the trip in the *Anzeiger des Westens*,[9] the newspaper of the Missouri Germans. Looking at these unbiased reports, one really wonders how all the rumors could survive so long!

But for his unfortunate marriage with Annette Dübeld, Sutter might never have seen America. Without the experience of Santa Fe he probably would not have come to California, and without California his name most likely would have remained unknown. Santa Fe, therefore, and the following station, Westport, belong to the most important turning points in Sutter's life.

The caravans to Santa Fe owed their origin to the discovery of a few Americans that that provincial capital lay only at a distance of 700 miles from St. Louis, while the only Mexican harbor, Vera Cruz, was separated from it by 1,000 miles. Land freightage on goods from St. Louis was therefore one third lower than on merchandise brought in from Vera Cruz. Moreover, there were ways and means of obtaining from the customs officers of the north certain reductions on the official tariff rates, whereas the regular rates charged at Vera Cruz amounted to sixty per cent ad valorem. For a gratuity equivalent to about one third of the established duties, these Mexican officials of the north were usually willing to reduce the tariff by two thirds. Thus it became possible to sell American imports, such as textiles, shoes, hardware, and cheap fancy articles, to the people of Santa Fe at prices which appeared to them extremely low, although the Missouri traders made a profit on them twice as high as the gain they could have realized in the home markets. Both parties were, therefore, exceedingly well satisfied.

On April 15, 1836, the fifteen members of Sutter's group left St. Charles, their headquarters, and with their merchandise, valued at $14,000, half of which was bought on credit, they proceeded to Independence in western Missouri. There the provisions for the long trip were bought, chiefly bacon and cornmeal and liquor. The caravan itself, however, assembled about 200 miles west of Independence at Council Grove, a very beautiful prairie spot, famous for the splendor of its huge old trees and its crystalline brooks, so full of fish as to allow making the richest catches with the wagon covers. The train assembling here consisted of about eighty wagons, drawn by ox-teams and mules. As a rule each trader had his own wagon, but Sutter's group of fifteen or sixteen partners possessed only four carts and was composed, to quote Laufkötter, of 'bankers, doctors, colonels, captains, merchants, mechanics, farmers, single and married men.'

Another hundred miles to the west, at Diamond Springs, the captain of the whole caravan was elected and the corporals were appointed. The election was accompanied by all the tumult which in those days went with the vote, but after a short and heated brawl a drink of whisky quickly established peace. The captain elected was Mr. Carr.

On the whole the trip was easy and rather pleasant, twelve or fourteen miles representing the average daily advance. Shortly before sunset camp was established and the wagons were arranged into a square, shafts pointing outward. Outside the camp were the guards of the day, appointed by the captain and his corporals, and the horses, tethered up. Within the square remained the other members of the caravan and the oxen, which were let out for grazing only an hour before daybreak.

There were few notable adventures. Only the fording of the Little Arkansas caused great difficulties, because of a change in the weather and because of the steepness of the river banks and the treacherous bottom sands. The resultant bad tempers and over-indulgence in whisky led to the first real diversion, a free-for-all in Sutter's German camp. There was even a pretence of dueling. 'We clearly saw,' observes the critical Laufkötter, 'that our captain [Sutter] was not accustomed to weapons and had probably never handled any.' But after this dark interlude, another member of Sutter's group reports, 'the first ray of sunshine put every one again on the right track.'

Soon they passed Pawnee Rock, which rose precipitously from

the level plain. Many inscribed their names on the rock. The first detached groups of buffalo made their appearance in this neighborhood. Then, crossing the Big Arkansas with its flat borders, the caravan left the territory of the United States and came into northernmost Mexico.

Now began that 'disconsolate region that does not even bear a bush, where one is forced to maintain camp fires with buffalo dung, a feat not so easy on a rainy day.' This was the land of buffalo grass, of cacti, of palmettos, rattlesnakes and prairie vipers, the horned toad (used by the Mexicans as an aphrodisiac), of the gazelle, and the miles upon miles of the black streaks of buffalo. Thus they reached the sandy desert of the Cimarron, whose dry zig-zag course they crossed fifteen times. But even this arid stretch held no adventure and demanded no unusual exertion from the travelers. Not a word of complaint is heard about suffering through lack of water, for barrels of wine and whisky formed the chief bulk among the provisions of these fifteen desert-wise Germans.

As they crossed the divide between the Cimarron and the Canadian River, the country again became greener, and after a slow, seven weeks' journey the traders reached Santa Fe.

The arrival at Santa Fe of the American caravan was always the paramount event of the year. It was as if Santa Claus and Prince Carnival came to the citizens of that little provincial capital in the midst of summer and in the guise of bearded American merchants from Missouri. The caravan of the previous year, the first in which Sutter participated, had brought the volume of trade to a new high record and there had been every reason for his overbrimming with enthusiasm when he returned to St. Charles.

But what happened now, in 1836? What lies behind all those rumors of later years concerning Sutter's doings in Santa Fe?

To the dismay of all, they found that the situation in New Mexico had markedly changed. The authorities had saddled the trade with new and more diversified duties. Traders from the newly born Republic of Texas had launched a rival caravan. A few Americans who were established permanently in Santa Fe and owned large stocks of goods tried their utmost to demoralize the business of the visiting dealers. Moreover, a severe crisis had unsettled the chief industry of the people of Santa Fe: their gold mines. And on top of it all, an insurrection of the wild Apaches and Navajos had called most of the able-bodied men of Santa Fe into battle. In brief, New Mexico was in the very pit of a business slump.[10]

Trade, therefore, was extremely dull. There were very few buyers. The tariff laws, being rather new still, were more strictly enforced by the officials, and the customary bribing ritual could easily become a boomerang for novices in the business. Laufkötter may be stating the truth when he maintains that Sutter was arrested as a smuggler and kept in the *juzgado* for a few days, although the very objective correspondent of the *Anzeiger des Westens* knows nothing of this. Add to this that not one member of Sutter's little German company had any real experience in this sort of trade, that many of them knew no Spanish, that the years they had spent at school or on the drill-grounds of little provincial garrison towns can hardly have sharpened their bartering instincts, and it is easy to see that their enterprise was bound to fail completely under circumstances that proved too much even for the more seasoned traders.

For failure was by no means confined to Sutter's little German company; it was pretty general. So disheartening, for the most part, was business, that the leaders of the groups composing the Missouri caravan found it advisable to issue a joint statement. This they dispatched by courier to St. Louis, in order to prepare their friends and silent partners for the fiasco. The statement was published in the *Missouri Republican* on October 22, and in the *Anzeiger des Westens* of the same date. It reads:

SANTA FE, AUGUST 22, 1836

To all those whom it may concern: permit us to say, that Santa Fe, Province of New Mexico, is at this time in a dilapidated state, in consequence of Indians, the failure of Gold Mines, and many other things too tedious to mention, as we are in a hurry. But the undersigned, pledge our word and honor, that we believe it will be improper for the Merchants of Missouri, on any account, to sustain a Company the ensuing year. Those here at present are compelled to lose money, and if goods are again sent to this place, they possibly may never get what they have heretofore credited.

Twenty-six signatures are affixed to this. The twentieth, signed by the only man who insisted on giving his title, reads 'J.A.Sutter, Capt.'

Meanwhile, the dullness of trade did not keep the visiting dealers from enjoying themselves. Pleasure and dissipation was an essential part of every trip to Santa Fe. Concerning this side of the business, the correspondent of the *Anzeiger* writes illuminatingly:

The fandango, a dance modified here the better to suit the voluptuous character of the country, formed the general entertainment every night, as long as we were here. The Germans were not seldom involved, and on such occasions were the favorites among the women, who derived a quite particular and very obvious pleasure from the unaccustomed sight of ornate young beards.

Others hint that some men were too eagerly bent on pleasure to have any time left for business. And Laufkötter completes the picture by adding that among the stock-in-trade of the Germans only 'fancy articles diminished rapidly, on account of the gallantry of the members, who vied with each other in winning the esteem of the ladies, and Mr. Sutter even competed for the prize.'[11]

Here, then, was some manner of reward for the troubles of a

seven weeks' journey. Besides, the caravan was not an entire
failure. At least the correspondent of the *Anzeiger* insists that
'business is not quite so bad.' Some still made a little money, and
to these belonged Sutter. Though it may seem somewhat puzzling
that individually he succeeded where the company enterprise
which he had organized failed, the matter is not hard to explain.
Even Laufkötter admits (though elsewhere he contradicts himself) that Sutter had no stake, or only a very insignificant one, in
the venture of his German companions. He had only done the
drumming to get them together and acted as their captain during
the trip. But, rugged individualist that he was, he traded on his
own account at Santa Fe. And as he was easily the shrewdest
among his own group, probably spoke Spanish better than any of
them, had been in Santa Fe before and was no doubt the most
imposing and most charming personality, his individual success is
not surprising. Nor need we be astonished that petty, rancorous
minds like Laufkötter, extremely angered over the loss of their
investment, now tried to make Sutter responsible for their own
fiasco. But it is significant that the *Anzeiger* correspondent, in his
whole long report, does not by as much as one syllable hint at the
possibility of foul play. On the contrary, he definitely lays the
blame for the general failure upon the unfortunate political and
economic circumstances dominant in 1836 at Santa Fe. Moreover, if at the time there had been a general outcry among those
who suffered losses against any particular malefactor, the matter
would undoubtedly have been aired in the *Anzeiger*. But nothing
of the sort happened.

Individually, then, Sutter did not fare badly at Santa Fe. His
profits were invested in about 100 mules and mustangs entrusted
to the care of a faithful Mexican servant, Pablo Gutierez. They
were wild things and most of them escaped before the Missouri
border was reached. The others were sold to the settlers about

St. Louis and St. Charles. Pastor Münch has left us a little humorous account concerning Sutter's mustang business and at the same time a rather favorable description of his personality. The wild beasts, he writes, 'were almost impossible to manage. I myself bought one, bothered with it a whole long winter, and in the spring was forced to shoot it. Others let the indomitable animals roam about freely and never saw them again.' But while Sutter succeeded in making a good profit for himself, 'the company enterprise proved a complete failure. The sale of the [company] mules brought difficulties, winter forage caused great expenses, and at last the animals were disposed of under the hammer, for a lump sum, far below their value. The claims in St. Louis [$7,000 —for trade goods bought on credit] were partly satisfied out of the private resources of resident participants, for the other part remained a dead loss.' Sutter himself, Münch writes, 'was then still a young and sturdy man, blond and well-nourished, jovial, somewhat adventurous, and shrewder than one might have suspected one of his apparently cordial nature to be; he was agile to an eminent degree and full of rare spirit of enterprise. For such a one America was the proper soil for unusual success.'[12]

However, even if Sutter was in no way guilty in a legal sense of the failure of his German traveling companions, his enterprise nevertheless had brought heavy losses to several of his friends and their acquaintances. His standing in St. Louis and St. Charles was bound to suffer, and it is natural that as soon as he had sold his mules and horses he preferred to settle elsewhere. He was ashamed of this new failure. But there was still another consideration which caused him to put a little more distance between himself and the circle of old friends. His removal from eastern Missouri was a shrewdly calculated step in the scheme of building up his 'military past.' In the interest of this scheme he had to leave the men to whom the greenhorn had naively confessed that he was a shopkeeper. Naturally, it could not suffice him to derive his title from the captaincy of the little German group of the Santa Fe caravan. He wanted to be taken for a dyed-in-the-wool soldier. And so the man who at Santa Fe had for the first time signed himself 'J.A.Sutter, Capt.' now introduced himself to the people of his next abode as 'Captain John A. Sutter, formerly of the Royal Swiss Guards of Charles X of France.'[13]

As such we find him in the spring of 1837 residing at Westport, now a residential section of Kansas City, and then a settlement but four years old. A new outfitting and starting point for trading caravans, Westport bade fair to become a dangerous rival of Independence and to have a great future. For, unlike Independence, it enjoyed the advantage of having a very good landing-place on the Missouri. In addition, it bordered on the reservations of the Delaware and Shawnee Indians west of the Missouri. It was the market-place for the natives' hunting yield, furs and peltries, and —important even more—the place where they spent most of their yearly $300,000 in Government subsidies. All these were potent motives for any merchant to establish himself at Westport. Here Sutter first came into close contact with the American Indians and acquired that intimate knowledge of their nature which, a few years later, was to prove one of his chief assets as a colonizer.

Very little that is trustworthy is known regarding Sutter's life in Westport. The slanderous Laufkötter would have it that Sutter had so enriched himself by leading his friends into the Santa Fe fiasco as to be able to buy 'the whole town of Westport,' three farms in the vicinity, one of them with a sawmill, and to build a large hotel. But the chronicles of Westport know nothing of all this. The plain truth is that, as in Burgdorf, he was now again a simple storekeeper, having acquired the firm of Lucas & Cavenaugh—most likely without sufficient ready cash. As usual, he lived extravagantly and kept too many irons in the fire to forge

any. So, only a year after his removal to Westport, he was confronted with another bankruptcy. (Even Laufkötter admits that
when he visited the 'owner' of the town of Westport in the fall of
1837, he had to share the bed with Sutter.) Failures seemed to become chronic with him. In Burgdorf he had a wife and five young
children, living in need, probably clinging desperately to the vague
hope of his success in the New World, and pining for the day
when his remittances would relieve their poverty. Yet, again, he
had failed. He was completely discouraged and at the end of his
tether. To his best friend, John Calvin McCoy, the founder of
the town, he talked of suicide. . . .

It was probably not till now that something Sutter had heard in
New Mexico began to germinate in his mind, opening new vistas
and pointing a way out. Down in Taos he had met the *alcalde*
Charles Beaubien,[14] a French-Canadian by birth, a renegade
priest and naturalized Mexican citizen. In his younger years
Beaubien had been in California and was lavish and eloquent in
his descriptions of that remote country with its delightful climate
and 'perpetual summer.' It was later Sutter's pleasure to attribute
to Beaubien's tales his indomitable desire to see that arcadian land.
The few facts, however, that have come down to us regarding his
experiences in Westport, make it appear almost certain that such
a trip came to him only as a desperate afterthought born of his
Westport fiasco.

There exists a touching description of his departure for the Far
West. The eye-witness was none other than his good friend John
Calvin McCoy, whose account of the event has been preserved in
a transcription by his daughter, Nellie McCoy Harris:

Early one misty morning in the spring of 1838 a piteous looking procession moved slowly westward. This little procession consisted of two
men riding Indian ponies, one leading an old sorrel packhorse, the living
image of Rosinante. The rider at the head of this little van looked as for-

Santa Fe, 1849
Stokes Collection of Historical Prints, New York Public Library

Monterey, 1841
From De Mofras' 'Exploration'

lorn as the 'Knight of the rueful countenance;' yet there was an air of determination about him and a gentle mien that marks the aristocrat. This
was Captain John A. Sutter, at whose mill on the American River gold
was discovered in 1848. His fellow-traveler, the only one of Captain Sutter's long retinue left was a fellow-countryman named Wetler.

The raconteur then glances back upon Sutter's failure as the
successor to Lucas & Cavenaugh and his inability to pay his employees' wages, and then continues:

Other complexities arising, he went to my father in desperation, saying
he was going to take his life. He was reasoned with and at length abandoned his intention. My father offered to lend him money to pay off his
indebtedness, though his own purse was a slender one, at the same time
offering to help him to continue his proposed journey onward. He and
others of the merchants procured a modest outfit for him and my father
gave Captain Sutter a horse, Allen McGee at the same time providing
one for Wetler. Captain Sutter insisted upon leaving with Colonel Mc-
Coy a lot of fashionable toggery, if I may so designate the court apparel
of a Swiss gentleman. Among the lot, I remember a long black silk velvet
circular coat, satin lined; some knee-breeches, a silk vest or two, and a
gold fob of curious design that a grand-daughter of Colonel McCoy's
now wears as a bracelet.

Who can doubt but that this magnificent gentleman's wardrobe represented the very 'many clothes' authenticated by the
Burgdorf bankruptcy records, the removal of which had made his
creditors so angry?

This, then, was 'Captain' Sutter's departure for California, the
promised land. But whether this excursion into the farthest west
came to him as a welcome inspiration in times of distress, or
whether it was the realization of a long-cherished plan, this much
is certain: his leave-taking from Westport, the last outpost of
American civilization, bears a striking resemblance in manner to
his adieus to Burgdorf. With this remarkable difference however:

whereas Burgdorf had sent its curses after him and preserved its grudges even beyond his death, the memories he left in Westport appear to have been the friendliest. The shopkeeper of Burgdorf had evolved into a bird of such exotic plumage as to remain unforgettable to all. Even John C. McCoy, who seems never to have been repaid for what he lent Sutter, nevertheless is said to have always spoken of his distant debtor as of a 'personage of lofty ideals and of the highest integrity,' a perfect and exceedingly charming gentleman.[15]

Indeed, in this captivating nature which, in the boundlessness of the American horizon, had begun to unfold amazingly, lay the true seed of Sutter's destiny. He may have failed again: he may at times have been devoid of all self-confidence and in despondency have talked of suicide, he may have set out on his overland trip literally on an old gift-horse and without a penny which he could call his own. Still, as will be presently apparent, he carried with him values which proved immeasurably higher than any tangible ones: his ever buoyant, indefatigable nature, a wealth of visions, inventiveness, irresistible charm, sparkling conversation, persuasiveness, the manners of a perfect court gentleman, the self-imposed title of captain, and an invented military past replete with glory.

Ex-captain of the Royal Swiss Guards of Charles X of France! That was to prove a masterful stroke of fiction, in itself worth to him a little kingdom in royalties.

6. BRILLIANT IMPERSONATION

SUTTER departed from Westport about April 1, 1838, and spent the next three weeks among his friends, the Delaware Indians, waiting for an opportunity to 'hitch-hike' across the continent. Hitch-hiking west in 1838 meant appending oneself to the caravan of the American Fur Company as far as the Rocky Mountains, and from there to reach the Pacific with one of the trains of the Hudson's Bay Company. Every summer the caravans of both companies used to meet in the mountains to bring supplies to their hunters and trappers and to collect from them the season's yield of peltries.

The caravan of Captain Drips set out on April 22, a Sunday. Typically enough, Sutter could not stay in Westport until this date, the ground there having become much too hot under his feet. He joined the caravan about May 1, when it crossed the Delaware Reservation. The whole train consisted of about 200 horses and mules, 17 carts, all covered with black oil-cloth, and each drawn by 2 mules tandem. Only the vehicle of Captain Drips had 3 animals, and a Scotsman, Sir William Drummond Steward, who traveled for his pleasure, had 6 mules to his wagon. There were about 60 men.

Sutter and his companions were not the only 'deadheads.' Trailing in the wake of Captain Drips was also a little band of American missionaries on their way to various mission stations among the Indians of Oregon. They were not a very companionable and encouraging lot. In fact, their own superior, the Reverend William Henry Gray, describes them as a pitiful group of spiritually dwarfed, blinker-wearing, and rather conceited little Puritans. No wonder, then, that Mrs. Myra Eells, the wife of one of these missionaries, to whom we owe most of our knowledge of this

adventurous trip, almost completely ignored in her detailed journal her heathen fellow-traveler, the genial, sport- and drink-
loving foreigner John A. Sutter.

They followed the usual Oregon route, across rolling prairies
varying between gladed grasslands and more sandy stretches. For
weeks the Platte River, then its northern arm, prescribed their
course, leading them now over vast flats, now between awe-
inspiring bluffs, resembling a skyscraper city in ruins, 'with streets
just narrow enough to walk in,' as Mrs. Eells says. Thus, on
June 2, they reached Fort Laramie.

And still they followed the North Platte, over high plains, between distant hills covered with snow, across sage-covered wastes,
through pelting hail-storms and gales that carried off their hats.
Always there was a pungent chill in the air, so that the women,
with all their winter clothes on, could not 'keep comfortable.' In
the worst of weather they made ready to cross the North Platte,
at a point south of the mouth of foaming Sweetwater River. Boats
had to be made of buffalo hides and willow branches. The buffalo
had to be hunted first and the skins dried, a task which required a
long time in the pouring rain. The wagons were then taken apart
and ferried across in sections. Meanwhile the camp was flooded
by the rising waters. The baggage was reared in steep piles, on top
of which the trembling and shivering missionary women were
put. At last, on June 11, after three days of desperate toiling, everything was shipped across to the western bank, while snow was
continually falling on the mountain slopes just a little above.

Soon after, with the unparalleled abruptness typical of the mountains, the weather changed. The prickly pear burst into blossom
on the flat table-lands north of Sweetwater River, and so, in the
blazing heat of summer, on June 23, eight weeks out of Westport, they reached the terminus of the caravan: Wind River Rendezvous, near the fork of Wind and Popoagie Rivers.

And here our travelers' blind trust in the leadership of Captain Drips came in for a painful disappointment. They had not been told that the caravan would avoid the customary rendezvous, several days' trips beyond the Continental Divide, on Green River, because the Hudson's Bay Company had driven her rival, the American Fur Company, out of the territory west of the mountains, causing considerable ill-feeling between them. Only the trappers of the American company had been informed about the shifting of the summer camp.

The transcontinental travelers therefore failed to connect with the Hudson's Bay train, and no connection, under ordinary circumstances, meant no onward journey and return to the east. Already the missionaries were resigned to the inevitable.

But not Sutter. For him there could be no retreat. For $100 in 'beaver orders' (worth $130 at the rendezvous) he bought an Indian boy guide from one of the trappers, Bill Burroughs, who had purchased the youngster from the famous Kit Carson. A hundred dollars was a high price, but then the boy spoke a few words of Spanish and English.

Apparently the trip across the prairies had acted on Sutter like a marvelous tonic. No longer did he look like one intent on suicide. His conviviality, the charming fellow in him had completely gained the upper hand over the Knight of the Rueful Countenance, and it is not surprising that he became a favorite with the hunters and trappers. Many of them, hearing that he was bound for California, were ready to accompany him. Nor did he miss the opportunity to augment his following by a few recruits. Beside the German cabinet-maker whom McCoy calls Wetler,[16] the Mexican mule-driver Pablo Gutierez, whom Sutter had brought from Santa Fe, the Indian boy he had just purchased, at least two mountaineers went to make up his following. They were Niklaus Allgeier, a Bavarian, and the Tyrolese Sebastian Keyser.

With the thermometer at 100 degrees Fahrenheit, they had in
every respect a 'hot time' at the rendezvous. The Fourth of July
was celebrated with orgies of drunkenness. Even on the fifth, remarks Mrs. Eells in her diary, 'twelve white men came dressed
and painted in Indian style and gave us a dance. No pen can describe the horrible scene they presented.' The Puritan souls were
deeply shocked to see that 'white men, brought up in a civilized land' could 'appear so much to imitate the devil.' Whisky
was thirty dollars a gallon, 'yet on some days nearly the whole
camp of the trading companies was unfit for business because of
its use.'

Then something quite unexpected happened. On July 8, who
should appear at this improvised camp of the American Fur Company but Captain Francis Ermatinger of the Hudson's Bay Company, a Canadian of Swiss ancestry. He knew of the coming of the
American missionaries because their Superior, William Henry
Gray, had gone east from Oregon the year before to bring reinforcements to his field of work. Having waited in vain for them at
the old rendezvous, a chalk inscription on one of the locked doors
of the abandoned camp had at the last moment told Ermatinger
where to look. The legend read: 'Come to the Popoazua on
Wind River and you will find plenty of trade, whisky, and white
women.' And so the vital connection with the farthest west was
established.[17]

With Captain Ermatinger, Sutter, his little following and the
missionaries traveled as far as Fort Hall, where Ermatinger was
stationed. He then provided them with a new guide to the next
western stronghold: Fort Boise, on the middle course of Snake
River, which they reached on August 15.

The three days' rest at Boise remained memorable to the entire
party. 'How glad we were,' says Sutter in his memoirs, 'to come
to a resting place where we could get something to eat.' For

months they had retched at the mere thought of buffalo meat. But here at Boise they now were treated to such luxurious titbits as milk, butter, turnips, pumpkins and salmon. At Boise, also, the strict Mrs. Eells at last condescended to notice her strange fellow-traveler, Captain Sutter, and to mention him in her extensive travel journal, after having taken tea with him at the residence of M. Payette, the commander. [18]

At Fort Boise, at last, the motley company of transcontinental wayfarers broke up. The missionaries dispersed to their stations; Sutter and his little party continued at their own risk, though with a guide provided by M. Payette.

They crossed the Blue Mountains to Fort Walla Walla and from there went to the American mission of Perkins and Lee at the Dalles. Asking for a new guide to the Willamette Valley, Sutter was told that Mr. Lee was about to go there himself with a band of horses which he wanted to exchange for cattle. But after a few days' trailing after Mr. Lee, Sutter's companions became exceedingly impatient of the missionary's course, 'so impatient,' reports Sutter, 'that they rebelled. . . . So we struck out over the mountains through the wildest country I ever saw, climbing up one side and letting the horses down the other side by ropes and climbing down on our hands and feet. In crossing streams we were obliged to throw a rope across. The torrent carried away my horse, which would have been lost but for my Mexican servant. . . .'

The perilous shortcut brought them to the Willamette Mission eight days ahead of Mr. Lee, but they made up for the exhausting travail by resting almost three weeks, and without overstaying their welcome. On the contrary: Sutter at least was something of a star guest, if we correctly interpret the record-book of the Willamette Mission, which, on November 1, 1838, chronicles as follows: [19]

Have been favored at this Mission lately with visits from several Ladies and Gentlemen from Vancouver, also with a tarry two or three weeks of Capt. Sutter, a Swiss gentleman who has crossed the Continent from the U.S. this season and is on his way to California intending to return with cattle, leave them here, go to Switzerland and return with his family and friends to found a Swiss settlement—his visit among us has been of a truly pleasant character.

Sutter was building up his stature not only by reconstructing a regrettable past. He was already rehearsing his future role of colonizer and empire builder.

Canoes then took him down the Willamette Valley to the terminal of the overland route: Fort Vancouver, Pacific headquarters of the Hudson's Bay Company. This was a settlement of considerable size commanded over by James Douglas. A stockade 750 feet long and 450 feet wide encircled over 30 buildings, including workshops, offices, and living-quarters for the chief officials. About 50 out-houses served as quarters for the employees.

By all appearances the Captain Sutter who arrived at Vancouver toward the middle of October 1838, was an even more glamourous personality than the one who had impressed the hunters and trappers of Wind River Rendezvous. The curative and tonic effects of the long journey over the plains and mountains, often advised by doctors and extolled by patients who had taken the advice, seems to have brought to a magnificent showing all of his splendid qualities. Undoubtedly he had had time to spin out an impressive store of yarns glorifying his romantic experiences as a captain in the Royal Swiss Guard of France; stories he may have read or heard and ingeniously adapted for his own use. As a matter of fact, while he resided at Burgdorf, there had lived there a former officer of the Royal Swiss Guard by the name of Suter, whose name appears in a paternity case on the records of the court for matrimonial matters, and it may almost be taken for granted that from this fellow our hero borrowed most of the trimmings which endowed his assumed role with so much convincing authority.

But he also came exceedingly well recommended. A letter of introduction written by Sir William Drummond Steward, who had traveled with Drips' caravan to Wind River Rendezvous, formed the nucleus of a collection which increased at every fort and at every mission. No wonder that James Douglas would have liked to retain the colorful stranger, at all events during the coming winter. Such visitors were all too rare in the crude wilderness of Oregon. But Sutter, too impatient to reach his destination, declined.

From Vancouver he had intended to wend his way south along the coast. But the trails were represented to him as impassable at this season and the Indians as too hostile and warlike for a small party like his. On the other hand, many vessels were said to ply between the Sandwich Islands and the California coast, and since the Hudson's Bay bark *Columbia* was just setting sail for those mid-Pacific Islands, Sutter took passage on her, hoping to reach the land of his desire a little sooner by way of this considerable detour.

James Douglas supplied him not only with more letters of introduction, but also with his passage and that of two of his companions. They sailed about November 11, and after a stormy voyage of twenty-eight days the *Columbia* (Captain Humphreys), on Sunday, December 9, arrived at the port of Honolulu on the Island of Oahu, just as the native Islanders were solemnly going to Church in silk dresses—and barefooted.

Irrepressibly, lustily, Sutter's stature was growing. At Honolulu he arrived as a minor celebrity, with letters of introduction addressed to the most eminent foreign settlers of the islands: Mr. Pelly (later Lord Pelly) the British Consul; John C. Jones, the

American Consul, and Mr. French, a prominent American merchant. The *Sandwich Island Gazette* took due notice of the arrival of 'Capt. Shuiter.'

Before long, if Sutter's own word deserves our trust, King Kamehameha III offered him 'strong inducement to remain and take command of his military department.' Very wisely Sutter declined the honor. At this early hour of the gay masquerade, a practical test of his military science might have prematurely spoiled the fascinating fiction to which he was only just beginning to give flesh and blood.

Still, it was at Oahu that the shrewd Sutter first proclaimed in print the basic fact of his invented military past. In a letter to the editor of the *Gazette* he protested politely against an item in the *Hawaiian Spectator* to the effect that Mr. Gray, the head of the missionary party with which Sutter had traveled to Walla Walla, had been attacked the year before by a party of Sioux headed by a Frenchman. 'As I was formerly an officer of the Swiss Guard in the French service,' wrote the shopkeeper from Burgdorf, 'I consider it my duty to defend the honor of the French nation; hence I am compelled to correct the accusation that a party of Sioux had been commanded by a Frenchman. . . .' The charming fabulist was in fine form!

Unfortunately, the reputed frequency of ships sailing from the Islands to California also proved a fiction. Shortly before Sutter's landing the old trading-ship *Bolivar* had left for the coast. But four months passed and there was yet no prospect of a sailing. Sutter was getting impatient. The only ship then in port was a British brig, the *Clementine*; she rode at anchor—for sale.

In this dilemma, Mr. French came to Sutter's aid. He chartered the *Clementine*, freighted her with goods for the Russian colony at Sitka, Alaska, and offered Sutter a free trip there as supercargo with the privilege of taking the vessel south along the coast to California. Thus, on April 20, 1839, Sutter sailed north again, a bigger man than ever. New and weightier letters of introduction to eminent personalities in Russian Alaska and in Mexican California were bulging his pockets. But beyond that, Honolulu's lords of trade, like Mr. Douglas of Vancouver, had demonstrated so much confidence in the imposing little Swiss as to enable him to purchase on credit cannon and other armament, for which he hoped to find use in California. With his stature, his following, too, had grown. Ten native Islanders, Kanakas, two of them women, one or two more white men, and a large bulldog now formed his retinue. So vague, apparently, were Sutter's ideas about California that he believed that with this motley crew he could found a settlement there!

But first he now came to Sitka, seat of the Governor of Russian Alaska, consisting of a citadel and a few other buildings, and in its civil aspects mainly a whaling station on barren rocks, where not even enough grass would grow for the Governor's two milch cows.

Yet, somehow, life in those frigid latitudes seemed full of zest and glee to Sutter. Those days at Sitka! Even a few months before his death he still spoke nostalgically of the pomp and brilliance which surrounded him there. 'A magnificent reception was given me by the authorities, and Princess Menschikoff, the Governor's lady, paid me particular honors,'[20] he—a tottering old man of seventy-seven—told an admiring audience of friends in Washington. And in his Reminiscences he elaborates: 'I had the privilege to dance with her. There were many feast days, sometimes three in a week, and there I had use for my knowledge of languages. With the chief clerk I had to speak Spanish, with the storekeeper German, and with the Governor, his lady and officers French. I was obliged to dance Russian dances which I had never seen before.'

In moments when festivities made no claims upon this busy social luminary during that month at Sitka, one may perhaps presume, he attended to the sale of the goods shipped from Honolulu. Then, this rather prosaic duty halfway discharged (he sold but part of those goods), and Governor Kouprianoff's letters of introduction made out and signed, the *Clementine* bore this newest idol of the Pacific down south, through a choppy sea, towards the goal so patiently, tenaciously, and circuitously striven for: the Golden Gate, which, however, was not yet known under this name.

7. *THE PROMISED LAND*

AT last Sutter was in California.

To get here he had traversed the American Continent and crossed the Pacific Ocean in three directions. Since his departure from Westport fifteen months had passed. But even if he had only wandered over the Continent alone, the consciousness of having reached a new world could not but have overwhelmed him here. Standing at the Golden Gate today, one feels separated from New York by an entire ocean. And an ocean it is; if not of water, at least of immense stretches of sands and stones. How much more so this was in Sutter's time! Here, at last, was his real New World.

California. What did it mean in those times? Among a hundred persons not many could have told you where to look for it. It was a land as far removed from civilization as any wonderland of the fairy-tales. It might have been on the moon—at any rate not 'on the map.' It had not dawned yet upon that somnolescent region that horses could draw a wagon; only oxen qualified for that task. Spoke-wheels were unheard of; a slice of a tree-trunk more or less circular, one foot thick and pierced by a smaller tree was the only thing known there as a wheel. The sturdy limb of an oak was called a plow, and the most modern tools available were those discarded as unserviceable by some ship's carpenter.

Politically California formed the northwestern corner of the Republic of Mexico. Tradition, population and language therefore were Spanish as far as the white man was concerned. But that immense and God-forsaken province was settled by only about 5,000 whites; there were from six to ten times as many natives. From San Diego to Yerba Buena the 'Spanish' population was spread out thinly along a very narrow surf-washed ribbon of land. To this they clung as though sight and sound of the breakers insured them eternal salvation. The whole vast interior of the country, everything that lay beyond the coastal range, particularly the fertile valleys of the Sacramento and the San Joaquin, was still the exclusive hunting-grounds of wild Indians.

California had seen happier days. Not many years before Sutter's arrival, the chain of eighteen Franciscan missions stretching from San Diego to Sonoma had stood in their glory. They formed the real centers of population, all lying along the *Camino Real*, each one day's journey on foot from the other. In these missions Franciscan monks spread Christianity among the Indians and taught them the wisdom of agriculture and the skill of the crafts. These fathers were the actual conquerors of the land and at one time their native, christianized wards numbered some 30,000; the animal wealth of the missions was counted by the hundred thousand and large areas of land were under cultivation.

Most of that was gone now. The military officials and soldiers who, as a matter of form, governed and protected the province, who never worked and lived at the expense of the missions, had become more and more indebted to these. But instead of paying these debts, the Mexican Government had chosen the simpler

expedient of secularizing the missions. Their buildings, lands and
herds were auctioned away, which usually meant only that they
were pocketed by a handful of superior officials. The mission Indians themselves were set free, most of them joining their wild
brethren of the woods to teach them the vices they had learned
from the Spaniards.

The soldiers and officials, however, understood neither agriculture nor craft and, parasites that they were, they succeeded
within a few years in reducing the province to somewhere near
its aboriginal state. Soon the secularization of the missions, being
an outstanding example of official plundering, became the prime
cause of numerous political intrigues, for plundering whetted the
appetite of those who had benefited, and sowed the seed of dis-
content among the less favored. But these internal frictions were
not dangerous. The minute white population constituted one
large family; each branch was related to the other by ties of marriage, and this intimate relationship inspired the whites with a
holy fear of bloodshed. Even the few foreigners who had already
become settled in the land were united with the native sons
through marriage.

Yet, in spite of the rapid decline, California was still a happy
country. All work was done by the few Indians who, after the
secularization of the missions, had chosen to remain civilized. The
'Spaniards,' as they still liked to call themselves, had little else to
do but propagate their kind in order that there might be no end
to baptizing, betrothing, marrying and giving away in marriage,
to burials and birthday parties, and every other cause for merry
feasting.

A happy land: living was as free as air, though luxuries were
unknown. It was not necessary to own a house or patch of soil.
If you needed shelter, anybody's house was yours. You knocked
on the door, and as in a fairy-tale it was opened for you with a sin-

cere '*Pase, Usted, es su casa*'—'step in, this is your house.' You could travel for a thousand miles, and your polite request for food and shelter, together with the new face and the morsel of gossip you brought, would liberally pay your host for what he unstintingly offered.

Two things only the country was pining for: diversion to break up the monotony of this arcadian life, and independence from Mexico. Many of the little revolutions were born of the desire for a change. Then the joyful rush of men to arms was usually far in excess of the ability of the opposing leaders to maintain them; for of bloodshed there was no danger. Only for fighting the horse-thieving and cattle-killing Indians no volunteers could ever be obtained!

Such was human existence in the Department of Alta California, whose head was Governor Juan Bautista Alvarado, a son of the country. Mexican authority meant little enough to the Californians. Because less Indian blood flowed in their veins than in those of the Mexicans, they deemed themselves a nobler race and dreamed of complete independence. For that, however, the armed power of the little population was not sufficient; but since the province was far removed from the City of Mexico, nothing prevented them from at least behaving rather independently.

Monterey was the capital of the Department, though capital is perhaps too good a word for the twenty mud-walled houses, without glass windows, scattered about the idyllic shores of a little bay. But the climate made four walls and a roof a very minor item in the business of living. The usually smiling skies and the tradition of Spanish pride had made of California a land completely self-sufficient, economically and spiritually.

The *presidio* or citadel lay in ruins but was still formally guarded by one old soldier and an absentee officer. Government consisted chiefly in diverting the revenues from the custom-

house—almost the only source of income for the department—
into restricted private channels. The exorbitant duties, however,
levied on all imports by Mexican law, instead of producing revenues, had only given rise to an unconcealed smuggling industry
at every seaport.

Governor Alvarado, a debauched young man of thirty-one
when Sutter came to California, had risen to his high station from
a simple clerkship and through a little revolutionary pastime. But
he was forced to share his powers with his equally young revolutionary helpmate and uncle, Mariano Guadalupe Vallejo, the
comandante general. And each of the two strove hard to be the
only one of consequence.

This rivalry for supremacy between the governing nephew
Alvarado and the commanding uncle Vallejo now became the
vise between whose jaws the newcomer from Switzerland in-
truded.

Vallejo was one of the few pure-blooded Spaniards in the
country and exorbitantly proud of his 'untainted Spanish blood.'
In 1832 he had been ordered by the Mexican Government to
establish a military post at Sonoma as a means of checking the
advance from the north of the Russian-American Fur Company,
whose nearest settlement was at Bodega. Soon Vallejo considered
his exalted person the real ruler in northern California. He lived
in greater splendor than anyone else. As a sign of his serene presence he always kept around his house a guard whose task was to
let no-one, friend or stranger, pass by without taking off his hat.
Even when he traveled, this guard accompanied him and enforced
the ceremony of hat-lifting before whatever house the little tyrant chose for the night's or day's rest.

History knows of no California William Tell with enough
courage or curiosity to see what would happen if the capping
formality were disregarded. Vallejo's nephew, the Governor,

could but grin and bear it. But when unexpectedly a brave little fellow with a glamorous military reputation arrived from the very land of Tell, it looked to Alvarado as if the day of his revenge had come.

8. RECOMMENDATIONS

THERE is something in omens. Certainly Sutter's arrival in California was indicative of all the trouble awaiting him there. After having led by the nose and bewitched shrewd businessmen, diplomats and courtiers into writing letters of recommendation for him and granting him credit, he now came to grips with hostile realities.

Trouble had developed on the *Clementine*. Progress was slow and provisions were at the vanishing point. But at last the ailing ship, helped by a copy of Belcher's Survey of the Pacific Coast, which Kouprianoff had had the foresight to have traced for Sutter, located the narrow entrance to the bay of California. Tucked away there against the foot of bare but lovely hills, on a little inner bight, lay a half dozen primitive huts known by the name of Yerba Buena. But the little harbor itself was dedicated to the most personable of all saints: San Francisco. Under his patronage the distressed *Clementine* cast anchor on July 1, 1839.

Yerba Buena at the port of San Francisco was not an official port of entry. The Mexican officers who boarded the *Clementine* would not allow Sutter to land. Protestations that he was in distress, out of provisions, and driven to shelter by pitiless weather seemed to avail nothing. 'Not a port of entry,' the officers insisted, and fifteen soldiers stood by to give silent emphasis to the pompous recitation of the law by their superiors. Fortunately,

Sutter had letters of introduction to all the important inhabitants of Yerba Buena. Some of these came presently on board, and by dint of unrelenting argument succeeded at last in obtaining for the weary voyagers a term of grace of forty-eight hours.

Carpenters and sailmakers were immediately put to work repairing the vessel. Fresh provisions were taken on board, and as soon as possible the *Clementine* sailed south again. Leaving Yerba Buena on July 2, Sutter arrived at Monterey early the following day.

Of the neat parcel of letters of introduction which had carried the former shopkeeper to the coast of California, those addressed to Vallejo have been preserved. The American Consul at Honolulu, for instance, had written:

HONORED SEÑOR AND FRIEND:
It is with great pleasure that I introduce to your acquaintance the bearer of this, Captain John A. Sutter, a Swiss gentleman and a person of the first class among men, honored for his talents and his reputation, and I recommend him to you for his fine character.

Captain Sutter goes to California with the intention of settling there if the country meets with his expectations, and you shall do me a great favor if you will assist him with all the means at your command. I desire nothing less than that you treat him as if he were

Your most obedient servant,

JOHN C. JONES

Sutter lost no time in making use of such words of gold. Arrived at Monterey, he proceeded at once to the house of David Spence with the letters addressed to this son of Scotland, reputable prince of smugglers, and Justice of the Peace.

The following day Mr. Spence could do no less than introduce in person to Governor Alvarado a visitor of such rare charm and excellence. Apparently, in the midst of the Fourth of July festivities, celebrated at the house of Thomas Oliver Larkin, Spence slipped Sutter's letters of introduction into the Governor's hand. So overwhelmed was Alvarado that he retired from the feast in order to devote himself in his official capacity to the stout little Swiss so imposingly recommended. 'He had never seen a man with so many letters of recommendation,' says Sutter.

The role which he had come to play in this almost virgin country was that of an *empresario de colonizacion*. Somewhere he must have heard of such a thing, but he did not know that such a large-scale colonizer was required to bring with him many adherents. His own following, however, consisted of only three white men and ten Kanakas, and so the Governor saw himself obliged to expound to him the practical and legal difficulties confronting his scheme. Even if he had the necessary people, these colonists could, after ten years, demand of an *empresario de colonizacion* that he divide all land and movable property equally among them. This news, says Alvarado, made Sutter 'rather pensive.'

The Governor then proposed that Sutter take up residence as an individual only, east of the Sacramento, where he could select whatever lands appealed to him; that after a year he should return to Monterey, to receive his citizenship, and in due time the legal title to the lands he had chosen. These would then forever constitute the patrimony of his family, and no-one could interfere with his possessions.

Alvarado, Sutter relates, 'was very glad that someone had come who wanted to settle in the wilderness of the valley of California, where the Indians were very wild and very bad.' This may be so. The first thought in Alvarado's mind, however, was not of the wild Indians whom Sutter was going to subjugate. He thought of the newcomer chiefly as a log or stumbling-block, to be placed gently but annoyingly between the spurred boots of his strutting uncle Vallejo at Sonoma. He therefore warned Sutter on no account to settle 'within the territory belonging to the jurisdiction of Sonoma, in view of the fact that that frontier was commanded over by the *comandante general* M.G.Vallejo, who kept it subject to *ciertas ordenanzas militares* that could not agree with an adventurous nature coming to the country to live independently.' Thus writes Alvarado in his account of this epochmaking interview.

On July 7, Sutter, provided with a passport for himself and his following, returned to Yerba Buena.

The traders of this little pueblo at the beautiful harbor were practically all naturalized citizens. Messrs. Spear and Hinckley, both from Massachusetts, had a store there. William Antonio Richardson, by birth an Englishman, operated ships between Yerba Buena and the Sandwich Islands and served as captain of the port. The Frenchman Victor Prudon occupied a little cubbyhole where he dispensed drinks, did a little trading and, being an excellent Spanish scholar, drafted many an official document.

Immediately upon Sutter's second landing at Yerba Buena the accounts with French & Co., the charterers of the *Clementine*, were settled and a week later she sailed back to Honolulu under Captain Blinn, who had accompanied Sutter.

Sutter then hastened to pay his respects to the grandee of Sonoma, upon whose favor or disfavor almost everything seemed to depend in northern California. Together with Captain Richardson and Captain Wilson he was brought to the Sonoma landing, whence Vallejo's horses carried him into the village. From Sonoma he intended to visit the Russian settlement at Ross.

At Yerba Buena everybody had done his best to keep the lively and entertaining newcomer within easy reach. Vallejo, restrainedly polite, also suggested that it was not necessary for Sutter to go as far inland as the Sacramento Valley, there being vast stretches of unoccupied land nearer the bay. But Sutter pretended not to care for the bay; his preference, he said, was for a navigable river. Captain Wilson offered to sell him his farm in the Sonoma Valley for a very low price. Again Sutter declined and provoked Wilson to exclaim: 'Well, my God, I would like to know what you do want!'

Whether Sutter knew exactly what he wanted remains doubtful. But Alvarado's warning to keep out of the jurisdiction of Sonoma had not fallen on deaf ears. Perhaps, also, Sutter remembered not without pain that whenever and wherever he had tried to give concrete form to any of his schemes within established communities, he had failed. And then, 'I had information that the people of that valley had a way of marking other people's calves that I did not like. I noticed also the hat must come off before the military guard, the flag-staff, and the church, and I preferred a country where I could keep mine on, in other words, where I should be absolute master.'

Vallejo, of course, could not like the air of independence about this stranger. And the fact that the charming guest was so excessively recommended could only stiffen the *comandante*'s reserve. But it was particularly impolitic of Sutter to debase Sonoma to a mere stepping-stone on his way to that Russian settlement which had necessitated the military station of Sonoma. Sutter's trip to Fort Ross could not but appear as an act of hobnobbing with Vallejo's enemy. It was bound, in the *comandante*'s eyes, to stamp the adventurous Swiss a rather suspicious subject.

Still, the following day Vallejo obligingly loaned Sutter horses and a *vaquero* for a guide. By sundown, over prairies white with sun-bleached wild oats and through magnificent forests of redwood, he reached the first Russian farm, halfway between Bodega and Ross.

Not infrequently, residents of the bay region took clandestine trips into the 'enemy's' territory and risked the ire of Vallejo to supply themselves with articles produced by the skillful craftsmen of the Russian establishments. For such bootleggers a room with excellent beds was always ready at this midway station of two farm houses. Sutter, too, spent the night there. In the morning the guide from Sonoma was replaced by a Russian escort, fresh horses were again supplied, and Sutter left with words of praise for this free hostelry.

Ross itself was magnificently situated on a sheer cliff above the Pacific. Broad bands of rolling meadows and gently sloping wheat-fields extended up and down the rocky, cragged coast above the cliffs. Behind them rose dark wooded hills of enthralling beauty. On a level stage formed by the projecting cliffs the fort was erected. A square palisade flanked by two log bastions enclosed the principal buildings, among which there was also a pretty wooden chapel.

This unique and busy colony was presided over by Alexander Rotscheff, a writer and prolific translator for the Russian theater, urbane, elegant and highly educated. In Rotscheff and Sutter two kindred spirits met. Both were amateur soldiers, adventurous, fond of travel, and full of fashionable romanticism. If one was a *littérateur*, the other was at least one of those rare raconteurs whose genius, defying the written word, is essentially bound up with their living sparkling selves.

At Sonoma, Sutter's exuberance had laid the foundation for Vallejo's jealousy and hostility. At Ross it won the friendship of the Governor, and thus, during the first trip into the country, Sutter unwittingly made two slings for himself. For Fort Ross, which the Russians sold to him eighteen months later, was to become more troublesome to him than even the envy of Vallejo.

Back at Yerba Buena, Sutter at once began with the prepara-tions for his advance into the wilderness. From Spear & Hinckley he chartered the schooner *Isabella* and from William S. Hinckley the yacht *Nicolas*. A four-oared pinnace completed the little fleet. Provisions were laid in, agricultural implements and seeds were bought, tools of all kinds, muskets and rifles, lead and powder for these and for the cannon which had come from the Islands. So firm was the reputation of Captain Sutter that everything was furnished him against his verbal promise to pay in beaver furs and deer-fat, which the optimistic colonizer expected to send down to the bay in great quantities.

At Yerba Buena Sutter also augmented his crew from whatever stray folk were available there. When everything was ready, a farewell dinner lasting all night was given him on board the ship *Munsoon* from Boston, the only vessel then at anchor in the bay. 'All were there to bid me good-bye as to one they never expected to see again,' says Sutter with habitual exaggeration. Undoubtedly, Spear & Hinckley and his other creditors thought differently. Surely they did not let their goods and money go astray for the mere fun of seeing him depart? They had infinite trust in this self-made, living fiction. They, as much as Sutter himself, hoped for tangible returns on their liberal investment.

PART TWO

THE EMPIRE–BUILDER

9. *RIO SACRAMENTO*

THE grand, joyful masquerade was over. Beginning with pushing a little figurative ribbon through a buttonhole, Sutter had step by step added to the realism of his martial fiction. He had then dramatized it, cast himself in the title-role and taken it on a successful try-out tour of the Pacific.

So far, so good. But now he was to prove to himself that he really was the man others believed him to be.

The Sacramento Valley as the scene of his future activities had been fastened upon his mind from the very outset. He had heard from a ship's captain, Meiggs, of the beauty and fertility of those vast bottomlands, uninhabited save by wild Indians and countless animals. Doubtless he had also heard tales of the beautiful valley at the Hudson's Bay settlement in Vancouver, whose trappers visited it every winter. And it may be assumed with reasonable certainty that in Sitka he had a chance to read the accounts of the German-Russian Otto von Kotzebue and of Sir Edward Belcher, who had both navigated the Sacramento as far up as the mouth of the American River.

The approaching dawn of August 1, 1839, bade halt to the wassailing on board the *Munsoon*. Sutter climbed down into the pinnace manned by his Kanakas and with them led the procession of boats up the long, wide bay bedded within hills of sublime repose and beauty. The declining sun found them about thirty miles farther northeast, where the Straits of Carquinez gave into Suisun Bay. There, camp was set up on shore, while Sutter called on Ygnacio Martinez at the *El Pinole* ranch and negotiated the purchase of cattle and horses which were to be delivered to him as soon as a site for his settlement had been chosen.

The following morning the explorers pushed up Suisun Bay imperceptibly narrowing down into the mouths of both the Sacramento and the San Joaquin Rivers. The hills around them had receded. Only solitary Monte Diablo with its two peaks beckoned over the starboard gunwales, bedeviling the vessels into veering to the right and entering the San Joaquin. Not until after two days did they become aware of the mistake. Thus, by taking another two days for their return to the bay and exploring all the sloughs there, they lost the better part of a week.

But at last the mouth of the Sacramento was found and they entered upon what was virtually virgin territory. They found themselves in the midst of a wide placid river bordered on both sides by vast jungles of trees, bushes and tules, framing numerous sloughs. High mud-coats at the bottom of the tree-trunks betokened terrible winter floods.

Always Sutter and his Kanakas, excellent oarsmen, were at the head of the little fleet, entering into all the sloughs and setting up navigation signals for the two larger vessels by attaching slips of paper to trees and bushes. All along there were other and stranger tree decorations—Indian prayers, bunches of white feathers swaying from overhanging boughs, placed there in order to coax the spirits into supplying an abundance of fish and other sustenance.

In spite of a wealth of Indian signs, the savages themselves remained invisible until the explorers reached a point about twelve miles below the present City of Sacramento. Here 200 warriors in gaudy paint and feathers had gathered in a clearing by the river. The shrieking garishness of their make-up and their deafening noise left nothing to be guessed about their purpose. Sutter's men immediately wanted to open fire, but he bade them stay their attack. His intimate contacts with the Delawares had taught him how to deal with savages. Unarmed he stepped on land after having instructed his men to stand by with their arms. Presuming that some of these Indians were former mission subjects, he greeted them with a loud and friendly *'Adios, amigos!'* Immediately two of the warriors stepped forward and addressed him in Spanish.

Sutter explained to them that he had not come to make war upon their people, but to live among them as their friend. He showed them his agricultural implements and assured them that there were no 'Spaniards' among his followers (the Hispano-Californians were particularly hated); he invited them to visit him and receive, as soon as he had chosen the location for his settlement, tokens of his friendship.

The Indians were well pleased when the white chief's message was translated to them and they dispersed quietly. Most of them belonged to the Walagumne tribe, whose chief, one of the two who spoke Spanish, was Anashe, destined to become tied to Sutter by bonds of a touching friendship. He now boarded Sutter's pinnace and served as his pilot, while the other Spanish-speaking Indian was dispatched down the river with a message for the larger vessels.

Frequent stops were now made to explore the surrounding country. Thus they penetrated slowly up the Sacramento, past the mouth of the American River and into Feather River which, being wider at that point than the Sacramento, they mistook for the latter. They returned, however, the same evening to the fork of the two waters, where in the meantime the *Isabella* and the *Nicolas* had arrived.

The Kanakas were greatly fatigued from rowing, and so was Sutter. The crew made themselves as comfortable as they could on shore or on deck, and Sutter retreated to his little cabin on the *Isabella*. 'As I was entering,' he relates in his Reminiscences, 'the men called out to me, demanding how long I was going to take them about the wilderness in this manner. I told them I would give them an answer in the morning. During the night I thought the matter over. I wished to explore the country further up; but I knew I could do nothing with mutinous men. I concluded to return and so told the men the next morning.'

Descending a few miles, he turned into the American River and up it as far as it was navigable. There he gave orders to land everything, pitch the tents and mount the cannon. Then, calling all hands together, he announced that the next morning the boats would return to Yerba Buena, and that all who wanted to go back were free to do so.

The moment for this decision was wisely chosen. Sutter's chief purpose in returning the vessels to their home port was to secure fresh provisions before the original supplies were exhausted. But it afforded him a welcome opportunity to test the mettle of his men and to weed out those who showed no liking for a trying existence hedged in by all the stark discomforts of primeval wilderness. The real hardships were yet to come—but with them already were clouds of mosquitoes so thick that one could cut them with a knife. Six of the white men decided to return with the boat crews.

The parting provided a memorable scene. Already the young camp was surrounded by hundreds of curious Indians. As the boats slipped from their moorings, noses downstream, a parting salute of nine guns was fired, throwing the assembled savages into a frenzy of confusion. 'A large number of deer, elk, and other animals of the plains were startled,' writes William Heath Davis, the captain of the *Isabella*, 'running to and fro, stopping to listen, their heads raised, full of curiosity and wonder, seemingly attracted and fascinated to the spot, while from the interior of the adjacent woods the howls of wolves and coyotes filled the air, and immense flocks of water fowl flew wildly about the camp. . . .

The salute was the first echo of civilization in the primitive wilderness so soon to become populated and developed into a great agricultural and commercial center.'

The three white men who had chosen to cast their lot with Sutter were Friedrich Hügel, Louis Morstein and Henry King, a German, a Belgian and an Irishman, all recruits from Yerba Buena. Then there was the Indian boy-servant bought at the Wind River Rendezvous, eight male Kanakas and the bulldog from the Islands. There were also the two Kanaka women. It is not to be supposed that Sutter was quite serious when he said, 'two of the Kanakas brought their wives with them.' They were there essentially for his benefit. Sutter's favorite among the two belles was Manaiki or Manuiki.

The spot where he had landed corresponds approximately to the foot of Twenty-eighth Street, Sacramento City. The day was the thirteenth or fourteenth of August; for on the latter date, before dispatching his superfluous retinue back to the coast, he wrote the following illuminating letter:

AUG.14,1839
'RIO SACRAMENTO'

Señor Dⁿ Ignatio Martinez

en el Pinole.

Dear Sir!

Please to send me the Horses and Cattle so quick as possible, for help tribe them I send you two of my Indiens which are in my Service for show you the Road on my new place, I hope your Son will come himself, it is very necessary that I have the Oxen for move on another place, then the Musquitos eat us nearly up here, and without the Oxen we can do not anything. I take one yoke of Oxen more, which you offert me for $16.–, also I take two good Milk Cows more, and 10 or 12 Taurau's or Bullocks for meat and several Horses and Mares from you or Señor Castro for Goods, with which you will be very much pleased. I would take also som more young Cows, like I have from Capt. Wilson.

Please to send me also 2 or 3 Sadles which I need very bad, the two Indiens have no sadles, please to give them some old Saddles. If Mr. Octave Custot the french Gentleman will come with you I shall be very well pleased to receive him, and also the young Gentleman who wanted to come with me for show me the Country which could not come because his Mother died.

With the Lunch [launch] of Mr. N.Spear please to send me 6 fanegas de Trigo and 6 fanegas Beans, 1 bag of Mantega, 8 arobas dried meat and some Indien corn for seed if you please.

Excuse my bad writing and receive my sincere Respects.

Your

Most Obt Servant

J.A.SUTTER

The letter is of prophetic importance. Here was struck the keynote of the whole voluminous correspondence soon to burst forth from that isolated wilderness camp and to cover half of California with its almost stereotyped appeals, 'please to send me,' 'it is very necessary that I have,' 'I take,' and 'please to send me also,'—all against equally stereotyped vague promises to pay in 'Goods, with which you will be very much pleased.'

Here, in a nutshell, is the story of years of a fantastic, titanic struggle to conjure out of nothing a little private empire, to launch a kingdom on a shoestring.

10. NEW HELVETIA

THE site which Sutter had selected belonged to the territory of the Ochecame Indians, whose chief, Narciso, a former neophyte of the mission San José, soon made himself and his people friendly to the curious intruder. The natives were given the customary presents: beads and colorful handkerchiefs for the multitudes, shirts and blankets for the chiefs. An exhortation to keep the treaty of friendship was then emphasized by a demonstration of the artificial thunderbolt of the white chief's cannon, which the Indians confessed they 'did not care to have tried on them.'

During the next few days the neighborhood was explored. A knoll about a mile south of the landing-place with its stormclouds of mosquitoes suggested itself as the most suitable site for a permanent camp. Here, on the highest elevation of the neighborhood, two huts were constructed in the Kanaka fashion. Sutter himself first lived in a tent. Soon a more permanent building was begun; an adobe structure forty feet long, containing a blacksmith's shop, a kitchen and Sutter's own room. One of the first tasks, also, was the cutting of a road down to the landing-place. This settlement he dedicated to the land of his ancestors and called it *Nueva Helvecia*—New Switzerland.

Three dismal failures—Burgdorf, Santa Fe and Westport—had neither shaken Sutter's buoyant vitality nor broken his will to succeed in the face of all obstacles. He was now about to begin again from the very beginning. The unclaimed primeval forests and savannahs, untamed savages, a handful of willing followers, and the credit advanced him on the strength of his fascinating personality, these were the raw materials from which he hoped to fashion his own empire. The tools and weapons he was able to procure were tantalizing. The coastal settlements of California were nothing but dead chips, deteriorated cuttings of sixteenth century Spain.

But now the unusual happened: Sutter, the charming vagabond, the elegant drawer-of-the-long-bow, here revealed himself a man of impassioned practical visions, one possessing the gift of imparting his visions to a hundred others, so that they worked for him for no better pay than food and shelter, and the hope of a little more substantial reward in the event of his success. There was no lack of tasks. And yet those few henchmen who knew the ropes, the tools and grips, had to devote most of their own precious time to teaching the Indians to work.

For a time the venison supplied by Indian hunters was the staple food of the colony. Deer, elk and gazelle roamed the valley in immense herds. Along the waters black clouds of fowl would rise at every shout or report of a gun. Brooks, rivers and sloughs were thick with fish. A little later dried and fresh beef was added to this meaty fare. But everything else, even the coarsest bread, remained for a long time a luxury.

Not many weeks passed before Sutter learned what it meant to depend on the Hispano-Californians. In spite of the two Indians he had dispatched down the river to help Ygnacio Martinez and his men drive the cattle to the Sacramento, Martinez, with Spanish indolence and mulish stubbornness, bided his time until it suited him to live up to the agreement. Meanwhile he employed Sutter's Indians for his own benefit. A month passed, six weeks. Sutter sent a second messenger, a third. At last, with the return from Yerba Buena of Nathan Spear's launch, Martinez sent some supplies: dried meat, a tub of fat and a bushel of beans. But not till late in October did the cattle arrive—and with them unending trouble! Instead of the 10 tame cows Sutter was charged for in the bill, only 9 were delivered, and instead of the 35 heifers or calves promised, he received 33.[1] Hospitable and liberal as were the Californians in social intercourse, in trading they were given to the deceitful tricks of all primitive people. In a sharp letter to Martinez, Sutter complained not only of the short delivery of cattle; Martinez had also failed to pay the two Indians he had exploited for two months. Furthermore, Sutter protested, 'the wheat you sent me is so full of maggots as to have filled my whole house with their stench and made me lose all my flour. I would never have thought that you were capable of selling me such

Sutter at the time of the
founding of New Helvetia

Juan Bautista Alvarado

Mariano Guadalupe Vallejo

Manuel Micheltorena

wheat!!!!' He told Martinez, *con bastante dolor,* that such treatment was not what he 'would expect from a gentleman.' He accused him of having 'failed in good faith and loyalty,' for which reason he, Sutter, did not see why he himself should now be obliged to fulfill the terms of their pact. A petty, if heated, altercation; but one of far-reaching consequences.

For behind Martinez, of course, the whole Hispano-Californian clan was forthwith massed, and thus, before the year closed, Sutter was embroiled in a hot skirmish with the native sons. Vallejo particularly made it his business to molest Sutter's men when they came down to Sonoma on business. He insisted on demanding their passports. That was provoking to Sutter and in his letters to the *comandante general* he began to use the same bold tone that characterized his epistles to Martinez. Only the feeling of safety in the remoteness of his settlement and the certainty of Governor Alvarado's backing can have inspired such a major blunder. That the strutting little tyrant of Sonoma had badly knocked his shin against the stumbling-block which his mischievous nephew, the Governor, had placed at his door, presently became apparent. For within a few months New Helvetia assumed unmistakable importance.

The friendship Sutter managed to maintain with the savage Indians, and the many roving elements attracted to the new settlement, gave the *comandante general* reason to pause. Sailors deserted their ships at Yerba Buena to join Sutter. Hunters and trappers from the Rocky Mountains strayed into his camp and asked for employment. This was all highly suspicious in Vallejo's eyes. Above all there was one man, well known to Vallejo, who had cast his lot with Sutter: Octave Custot. Hailing from Nancy in Lorraine, he claimed to have occupied the chair of Professor of Agricultural Science and to be an expert on beet sugar. On these pretexts Vallejo had once employed him. But it was not long before the 'first beet sugar produced in California' turned out to have been stolen from Vallejo's Peruvian supply—which was more a matter for laughter than anything else.

For about a year Custot proved extremely useful as Sutter's secretary. Better than Sutter himself with his thick Swiss accent, Custot could win the confidence of the French-Canadian trappers, and induce them to enter Sutter's service. But these activities of the French factotum served only to sow more discord between the Californians and Sutter. For among the chief causes of the country's animosity towards foreigners were the Rocky Mountain trappers, uncivilized half-brigands appearing in the wildest of Indian arrays, with rifles and pistols and bowie knives, and sometimes raiding the herds of cattle and droves of horses of the inhabitants.

By the end of 1839 the Californians were definitely on their guard. The rapid growth of the new settlement in the Sacramento wilderness, the courage and rare spirit of enterprise of its leader, his military reputation (however fictitious), his ability to marshal whole tribes of savage Indians—all seemed to the Californians omens of a storm gathering in their very backyard. No wonder Vallejo wrote in an order issued December 26 to his brother, Captain José Jesus Vallejo: 'It is imperative not to lose sight of a new colony of foreigners which has arisen in the region of the Sacramento River and which, though founded with the permission of the Departmental Government, is in conflict with existing laws. This establishment with its treacherously venomous exudations is extremely suspicious.'

As yet no open rupture occurred. Vallejo in particular did his best to maintain decorum. Nevertheless it was undeniable: four months after the quickly rising settler had occupied his chosen territory, a powerful whispering campaign against him was well under way.

11. CONQUISTADOR AND MISSIONARY

As regularly as wind and weather permitted, Sutter sent his pinnace, manned by inexperienced Indians and with a Kanaka at the helm, on shopping-trips to Yerba Buena and the ranches around the bay. These were hazardous ventures, especially as in November the torrential winter rains set in. Under favorable circumstances the round trip could be accomplished in eight or ten days. But at one time, when Sutter himself accompanied his crew, the current of the river was so powerful that the homeward journey alone required seventeen days, during which nearly all the provisions purchased perished.

Most of the food had to be bought on credit, time having as yet been too short to grow crops of any kind at New Helvetia. Indeed, for almost two years Sutter made no serious attempts in agriculture at all. The hunt for beaver and otter skins (besides cattle hides almost the only currency of the country) seemed still the easier way of realizing quick profits. But the returns of his first trapping expeditions were quite unsatisfactory. His Indians lacked experience, and their outfit was too poor to assure even a modest yield. His creditors, therefore, all had to wait.

Ygnacio Martinez was the first to become impatient. Presently he pestered Sutter with such brash demands for immediate payment that he provoked the master of New Helvetia to burst out in one of his brief notes: 'Dear and respected Sir, . . . if you have forgotten the laws of trade I can still teach you, and do not think you frighten me with your threats. Not having anything else to say to you, I sign myself,—Yours truly, J.A.Sutter.' Martinez then took his complaint to Vallejo who, however, being a military and not a civil officer, declared himself powerless in the matter. In fact, Vallejo even maintains that he prevented a forceful seizure of New Helvetia which Martinez plotted with his (Vallejo's) Indian guard. This was in April 1840.

At the same time the Indians of the Sacramento became troublesome, possibly because they had been inveigled by just such men as Martinez to revolt against Sutter. Once, in the middle of the night, as Sutter was conferring with Octave Custot, a shout of terror, 'Oh, Señor!' rent the stillness. Custot rushed out and found an Indian struggling between the jaws of Sutter's bulldog. While the would-be assassin's wounds were tended by Sutter, there was another shout of panic. A second savage, gripped by the dog's teeth, writhed convulsively. Sutter sewed up the wounds with silk thread and dismissed the attackers with the sharp warning that another such surprise would be repaid with swift punishment.

This did not prevent further attacks. In truth, Sutter's efforts to befriend, to educate and civilize these savages first earned him nothing but hostility. Though for a brief moment certain kinds of work seemed to appeal to them as a novel pastime, they quickly tired of labor and then hated it wholeheartedly. Yet it was on their co-operation that Sutter depended for the realization of his ambitious plans. He therefore had to use coercion. He had to threaten. And they, in return, revolted. Some began to shoot at his cattle and to steal his horses. Then, in May 1840, the Mokelumnes, as a definite indication of beginning hostilities, withdrew from their villages and massed together on the Cosumnes River.

But Sutter did not wait for their attack. Leaving a small armed guard to watch the houses, he, with six of his men, surprised the Indians in a night attack, and after they had lost half a dozen of their warriors, they were willing to sue for peace. Again Sutter showed himself merciful, promising that everything would be forgiven and forgotten if they returned to their villages and attended to their work as before.

Undoubtedly his Indian policy was effective and sagacious. Many testify that they had never seen a man so skillful and tactful in dealing with and taming Indians. These latter, on the other hand, were usually quick to see that kindness was the better part of Sutter's nature. Against his superior weapons and novel tactics they were helpless, whereas much was to be gained by their unconditional submission.

For a year, then, they gave him no further trouble. Many now showed themselves willing to learn the ways of the white man. Their pay, of course, was small but adequate. A sheet-iron coin stamped with a number served as the Indian's work-record and, according to the number of star-shaped holes punched into it, indicated the size of his pay-envelope.

The feeding of these half-savages presented a scene which shocked many a white visitor. At meal times, long wooden troughs, V-shaped and standing on short legs, were brought into the court of the settlement. Into these the cook poured a half-solid gravy, consisting mainly of bran-mush and spiced with some meat scraps and occasional vegetable remnants. Then the overseer led the Indians in file to their feeding troughs. There, kneeling down on both sides of them, they scooped out the mush with the spoons they were born with, and with as much gusto and clamorous smacking as though they were a herd of hogs they cleaned out the troughs.

Sometimes, on a clear spring day, the cook could save himself a lot of work by simply turning out the Indians into the meadows, where they were told to feed on a species of sweet clover which had always constituted a favorite item in their native fare. Roots, berries, but above all acorns and grasshoppers were the staple foods of these Indians in their natural state, the grasshopper-hunt forming the chief occupation of their summers. By the method of encirclement the huge swarms of these insects were driven into large funnel-shaped pits, then deprived of their legs to prevent escape, and roasted alive on hot cinders. When ground to powder, they were mixed with acorn meal and then baked into cakes and loaves.

Polygamy was the rule (and not a happy one) among the Sacramento Indians. Because the chiefs monopolized many of the squaws, the young bucks remained wifeless. But now they complained to Sutter, and because they were more docile workers than the old ones, their gain, most naturally, was Sutter's gain. Therefore, at a pow-wow one Sunday morning he solemnly decreed a more equitable distribution of squaws as paramount for the welfare of his peoples. He had the men lined up in a row and the women in another, facing the men; then he bade girl after girl step forward to make her own selection. Only the most important chiefs were graciously permitted to keep two wives—a very wise exception, considering that the supreme white chief himself could not well pretend to be vowed to strict monogamy.

With the help of the friendly tribes of his neighborhood, Sutter gradually made subservient the other Indians of the Sacramento and of the lower San Joaquin Valley. He conquered by good example as well as strength of arms. Many natives were quick to perceive that Sutter was their best protector against hostile tribes of their own race.

In the autumn of 1840, for instance, Chief Acacio and a group of former mission Indians from San José called on Sutter and requested his permission to trade at the village of the Yalesumnes, whose men were at the time working in New Helvetia. Reluctantly—for the visitors hinted that they might trade in a few women—Sutter consented and ordered Julian, his second *alcalde*, to accompany them and to supervise the bartering. But when Acacio and his men came to the village of the Yalesumnes, they attacked it, killed five men and abducted the women and children.

At once Sutter called together his white companions and pursued the rapers. And as it now appeared that his own man Julian was far from being innocent, he, with several others who confessed guilty of the crime of murder, was taken to the settlement and fusilladed, 'for show the others an example more to see what bad actions get for recompense,' as Sutter wrote to José Jesus Vallejo at San José. 'If I would let go all this things I could not more existe here.'

It was ruthless executions such as these, judiciously resorted to at wide intervals, besides Sutter's usual paternal kindness, which quickly commanded the respect of the savages. He was the most lenient of masters as long as his word was obeyed. But in anger he was terrible. In all these Indian campaigns he made it a rule to gather the widows and orphans of the warriors killed in battle. The squaws were then given other husbands; the children were brought to the settlement and trained to become domestic servants.

A valuable reinforcement of five men was received in the middle of August 1840. Captain Josiah Spaulding of the ship *Lausanne* had brought them out of Oregon and, being forbidden to land at Yerba Buena, had disembarked them at Bodega. At Fort Ross, then, they were in detail instructed how best to reach the Sacramento without attracting the attention of Vallejo at Sonoma. Among the five was Pablo Gutierez, the mule-driver from Santa Fe; the Bavarian Nicolaus Allgeier and the Tyrolese Sebastian Keyser who had fallen in with Sutter at the Wind River Rendezvous. The two others were Peter Lassen, a Danish blacksmith and hunter, and the eccentric William Wiggins from New York.

The white population had now increased to about twenty. A

member of the original ship's crew of the exploring expedition had subsequently joined the colony for good. This was Robert Ridley, a jovial Cockney who signed up as master of the pinnace. Perry McCoon was overseer of stock. Another Irishman, John Chamberlain, spent some of his time (when he was not meddling with the squaws) as a blacksmith, and an Englishman, Bill Daylor, a sturdy ex-seaman, looked after the kitchen.

An independent neighbor had also arrived and proved excellent company. This was John Sinclair, a Scotsman who, as *major-domo* on the new ranch of Captain Eliab Grimes, made his home a few miles above New Helvetia on the American River. Apart from Sinclair, however, the nearest settlers were still Ygnacio Martinez and John Marsh, 75 and 100 miles away respectively.

John Marsh: the name identified a miserly New-Englander with an odiously colorful past, a fine Harvard education, a dirty squaw for a bedmate, and a squalid mud hut at the foot of Monte Diablo for shelter. As he had done a little snooping among medical subjects, he posed as a full-fledged physician and so formed a truly congenial trio with 'Captain' Sutter and 'Professor' Custot. Sutter, by the way, had already met him in 1835 at Independence. A cranky hermit, Marsh cared for nobody, and no-one cared for him. But as the only medicine-man in the country he was a powerful one-man racket, demanding on occasion as much as 100 head of cattle for a bed-side visit. He, too, contributed to Sutter's herds, incidentally trying, of course, to overcharge him. They lent books to each other, French and Spanish novels, and newspapers. But the one priceless medical book in all California, which was among Sutter's possessions, he carefully withheld from Marsh. This Sutter needed himself to cure the ailments cropping up among his colonists and Indians. Only when John Chamberlain became afflicted with a certain 'fearful disease' and Perry McCoon was 'suffering with an equal complaint,' was Sutter compelled to turn over to his rival Marsh the two patients—but not the medical book.

12. *DON JUAN AUGUSTO SUTTER*

A YEAR had now gone by since Sutter first set foot upon the virgin soil of the Sacramento Indians. Within this year fantastic scribes have succeeded in boosting his wilderness into a paradise of 'tropically gigantic size.' Alas, Sutter was no match for such fellows. He could not do it. In reality the settlement of New Helvetia at this time still presented to a visitor its original primitive sight and resembled more than anything else a South Sea village of perhaps a dozen tule huts in which the trappers and Kanakas lived and in the midst of which, like a hen among her chickens, sat the one story adobe house of three rooms.

A year's residence was the prerequisite for Mexican citizenship, and a year almost to the day after his landing at the American River, Sutter, punctuality personified, appeared before Governor Alvarado in Monterey in order to receive the promised citizenship; at the same time Martinez tried to bring to bear on his reluctant debtor of New Helvetia as much official pressure as he could mobilize.

At the capital the mills of officialdom were at once set in motion to convert John Augustus Sutter, alias Johann August, into Don Juan Augusto Sutter, *naturalizado de Mexico.* The kindly Scotsman David Spence, esteemed gentleman smuggler, host to Sutter, and Justice of the Peace, testified that a year previously the petitioner had made his declaration of intention to become a Mexican citizen and also the deposition that he was '*Suizo, Catolico Apostolico y Romano*' (Protestants were not tolerated at that time in Mexico). A few other witnesses subscribed to this and attested that the applicant was *de buen conducto*.

On August 29, 1840, the naturalization papers were delivered to Sutter.

Governor Alvarado had reasons to be well pleased with this newest citizen. He could afford to laugh up his sleeve for having assured his uncle Vallejo a perennial nuisance in the shape of this adventurous Swiss. In addition to citizenship he now endowed him with official power, authorizing him 'to represent in the Establishment of New Helvetia all the laws of the country, to function as political authority and dispenser of justice, in order to prevent the robberies committed by adventurers from the United States, to stop the invasion of savage Indians and the hunting and trapping by companies from the Columbia.' If necessary, he was entitled to 'make use of arms' in the observance of these duties.

No less than Alvarado, Jimeno Casarin, the Secretary of State, took a lively interest in Sutter and the colony of New Helvetia. The financial difficulties Sutter labored under had not been hidden from the capital; for the hue and cry, the gossip and the whispering campaign severely hurt his credit. Yet, more than ever, further credit was a crying need, the only thing that could save the exposed colony from being wiped out by Indians or jealous Californians.

In this quandary Jimeno Casarin now tapped new credit sources for Sutter in the person of the amiable Sub-Prefect Antonio Suñol at San José. Suñol, a native of Spain who had deserted from the French navy, was to remain for many years one of the most reliable purveyors, and Sutter's letters to him, written almost without exception in French, form one of the most illuminating sources of information regarding New Helvetia.

Unquestionably, good fortune had been with Sutter on this trip to Monterey. Only one thing was lacking to satisfy his momentary ambitions, namely, an official confirmation of his self-imposed military rank. No doubt he did not fail to ask even for this favor; but, says he, Alvarado 'was afraid to give me a military title for fear of Vallejo.'

Nevertheless, Don Juan Augusto Sutter, *representante del gobierno y encargado de la justicia en las terrenas del rio Sacramento*—that was no mean achievement for a new-fledged citizen. Indeed, it was almost a miracle. Throughout the country feeling against foreigners was rampant because large powers then had their greedy eyes pinned on this helpless province. It was exactly this general dread of foreigners, especially Americans, which in Sutter's instrument of office had inspired the clause concerning 'adventurers from the United States.' The United States' 'manifest destiny' was California's most dreadful nightmare. But almost every foreigner was suspected as a potential traitor, whether he was naturalized or not, single or married to a native woman. Yet Sutter was treated with the greatest official regard in Monterey. Here, as always, he was a law unto himself.

Back at New Helvetia, he threw himself with fresh vigor into his ever increasing activities. During his absence disorders had cropped up among the Indians and had to be stamped out. But chiefly he now had to forge his various irons while they were red-hot. The new high tide of credit was to be harnessed quickly; for fortune, Don Augusto knew, was fickle under the Mexican emblem.

Almost every week now, or as often as the boat and its popular Cockney skipper went down the river, Sutter treated Suñol to one of his French exercises, incidentally asking for 'as much corn, peas, and beans as the messenger, Robert Ridley, can get into the launch.' Or for 'a pair of geese, male and female, and a pair of turkeys.' He acknowledged the receipt of whatever Suñol was kind enough to send and then asked for 'more . . . more . . .

more. . . .' And it worked like magic. For variety's sake he occasionally promised to send 'a quantity of beaver the next trip.' But usually the good Suñol had to content himself with promises and for a long time showed no displeasure over this unbalanced exchange of sometimes doubtful French for excellent values—a state of affairs unquestionably very flattering to Don Augusto.

At this time already the decision must have matured in Sutter to fortify New Helvetia. The extemporized South Sea village was in no way fit to guarantee life and limb against all hazards of the wilderness. Moreover, to be the commander of a fort, and from the walls and bastions of the fort to rule the Sacramento Valley, was an ambition dear to Sutter's adventurous heart. To realize it, however, he needed considerably larger means, and these in turn forced him to consider how to meet his increasing obligations.

During the second winter he therefore expanded his trapping operations. As an entirely new enterprise, on which he set great hope, he began with the distillation of brandy from the wild grapes growing in profusion along the borders of the Sacramento. Nor could a definite agricultural program be put off much longer, even for strategic reasons, if New Helvetia was to become a self-sustaining domain.

And lumber, too, in which the Sacramento Valley was deficient, became a crying need. In the spring of the year already a party had been dispatched into the mountains to locate a source of lumber. Some timber had been rafted down the American River for twenty-five miles—but not enough of it. For years lumber remained one of the most pressing problems.

During the winter adobes were now made in large quantities by Sutter's Indians. A few fields were broken and wheat and corn sowed. Corrals were built for the milch cows, the working oxen and horses; the wild stock grazed in the open country according to the custom of the ranches. Because of large purchases from

Suñol and others, and the natural increase, the herds [2] had grown considerably, and as cattle were constantly being killed for food, a tannery was the logical outgrowth. It was established at the point on the American River where Sutter had first landed.

In the second winter the first adobe house with its thatched roof burned down. This little catastrophe, like the dramatic close of an act, terminates the first period of New-Helvetian history. Meanwhile Sutter had had time to assure himself that at last the place was found where nothing could stop him from attaining the success and worldly position which he never doubted he deserved. Indeed, in the Sacramento Valley all the circumstances seemed to favor his making a small but precious world dance to his pipe.

Yet, the decision to stay rooted was not reached without an inner struggle. For throughout the year Martinez had waged a tenacious fight for immediate payment of Sutter's debts and given Sutter a bitter foretaste of what might be expected if his difficulties should again get beyond control. The case was finally settled to Martinez' satisfaction. Nevertheless, the animosity against Sutter which it had stirred up would not subside. Not without reason he wrote to his distant neighbor John Marsh: 'It is a great trouble to make a new Establishment in the Country and if I had not commenced I would no more begin.' And then he added, most characteristically: 'but now I do my possible to make it at once so large and so extensive as possible.'

In other words, was he not, even as he wrote this, vaguely wondering whether he did not take upon himself more than he could carry?

13. FOREIGN AFFAIRS

It has been pointed out at the very beginning how strangely circumstances seemingly independent of each other could sometimes work together to mould Sutter's destiny. This now happened here. Suddenly event began to dovetail with event.

Sutter, with 'a great deal of *persévérance*,' had just begun to carve out of the Indian hunting-grounds a domain of personal supremacy 'so large and so extensive as possible.' This, one would think, was a decision springing from himself alone. Yet at that precise moment events in general also rose with his ambitions. 1841 became in many respects one of the most momentous years in Sutter's life. Many a seed was here sown that did not sprout or bear fruit—or turn into poisonous nettles—until much later.

A year heavy with events: it began with new hostilities among the Indians. Periodic waves of resentment against Sutter's rule and its enforced labor were natural with the aborigines, to whom work was an abomination reserved for squaws. Early in February Sutter was compelled to undertake a new campaign. And since open resistance against him was of no avail, the Indians resorted to treachery. Immediately following the campaign, three plots to take his life came to light. Even Chief Anashe, who had first spoken to Sutter when he ascended the Sacramento and who now supervised the salmon fisheries, was a party to the last of these conspiracies. However, in this as well as in the two other cases Sutter refrained from any punishment. It may well be because of this show of mercy that Anashe became, as is frequently mentioned later, a particularly faithful servant of his master.

But it was the tide of politics which in 1841 brought matters to a head.

Sutter's earliest official act had been a proclamation forbidding the trappers of the Hudson's Bay Company from operating in the valleys of the Sacramento and the San Joaquin. This step was in strict conformity with his instrument of power, which expressly enjoined him to 'prevent the hunting and trapping by companies from the Columbia.' To be sure, this order contradicted a certain agreement, concluded in 1837 between the Provincial Government and the Hudson's Bay Company, giving the latter hunting privileges in those valleys. Standing on this treaty, the Hudson's Bay Company paid no attention to Sutter's edict and as usual sent its trappers south for the winter.

To Sutter, who probably knew nothing of that agreement and who could not be blamed for the ambiguity of the Government, the Hudson's Bay men were a cause of considerable irritation. Their presence meant not only a flagrant disregard of his official power; above all they interfered with his own trapping expeditions and curtailed their yield. Therefore, as he could not by force eject the intruders, he tried subtler methods.

Practically all Hudson's Bay trappers were French-Canadians. By treating them liberally from his newly installed brandy-still, Sutter hoped to lure these men into his service or to induce them occasionally to deliver their catch of beaver to him instead of to their regular employers. Business cared less about morals than it does today. The Hudson's Bay Company itself had never shrunk from any means to dispose of a competitor. True, Sutter was deeply in debt to the company and to James Douglas, its Vancouver representative, and for this reason perhaps ought to have twice reflected before he acted. But on the other hand his ability to pay depended on nothing as much as on his trapping operations, which his chief creditor tended to render fruitless.

However, whether we side with him on ethical grounds or not, Sutter was unfortunate in selecting the moment for this warfare. James Douglas happened to be in Yerba Buena to establish a

Hudson's Bay post there, and to his diplomatic acumen it was an easy matter to obtain from Governor Alvarado a renewal of the trapping concessions of the treaty of 1837.

Now it was Sutter's turn to be amazed at the double-dealing of the Government. So—tit for tat. Not long before this a Frenchman, Pierre Dubosc, had been killed by the Suisun Indians of the Sonoma district, and the authorities had not raised a finger to punish the murderers. Sutter, therefore, now sent his *agent provocateur* Custot to all the camps of the Hudson's Bay trappers, reminding them of their duty as patriotic Frenchmen to avenge the death of their brother. This, he no doubt hoped, would drive them to a rash act, which again would be swiftly followed by the expulsion of every Hudson's Bay man. But nothing of the sort happened. Douglas strictly forbade his trappers to maintain any kind of contact with Sutter, and there the matter ended.

At least Sutter succeeded again in having all California on its toes, and the affair served mainly to increase still more the general fear of great foreign powers and of every foreigner in the land.

The very establishment of a Hudson's Bay Company station at Yerba Buena was a symptom of danger overlooked by no-one. British armies always followed in the wake of commercial and Bible missionaries. Not Douglas alone, but Sir George Simpson, Governor-in-chief of the Hudson's Bay Company, was then in California, and it was precisely in his capacity as British empire-builder that he was bound to perceive in Sutter an obstacle to be reckoned with. Not in vain he wrote in his Journal: 'The Americans, as soon as they become masters of the interior through Sutter's establishment, will soon discover that they have a natural right to a maritime outlet; so that whatever may be the fate of Monterey and the more southerly ports, San Francisco will, to a moral certainty, sooner or later fall in the possession of the Americans'—unless, his innuendo is, the British take it first.

Simpson and Douglas were not the only foreign agents who came to California in 1841. The United States, too, sent its pathfinders: the great exploring expedition of Charles Wilkes, a first detachment of which reached New Helvetia on August 23 under Lieutenant Ringgold. The Indian fishermen notified Sutter of the approaching little fleet in advance and so gave him time to don his splendid uniform and to prepare an exuberant welcome, putting out the flags and loading the cannon. It was an imposing visit, and even the Indians began to understand that to the outside world their white overlord was an important man. A second detachment of the Wilkes exploring expedition under Lieutenant George F. Emmons arrived at Sutter's on October 18, completely down-at-heel, famished and exhausted through deprivations and sickness. The wrecking of one of the expedition's ships on the bar of the Columbia River had forced this group to travel all the way from Oregon on foot.

Finally France was not to be missing in this great international race of spies. She sent Eugène Duflot de Mofras, young attaché of her legation in Mexico City, the acme of French *élégance*, pleasantry and superficiality. He had landed in May, and his visit to the Sacramento three months later became one of the high spots in the annals of New Helvetia. What was more natural than that Sutter's legendary service under Charles X should now become the tie which seemed to secure *la Nouvelle Helvétie*, and with it California as a whole, for France? It is fairly obvious from the official report of De Mofras that Sutter, in the congenial company of men and liquor, was as usual in the mood for polite buffoonery. 'M. Sutter still considers himself a Frenchman,' writes De Mofras. 'He has with him and tries to attract Canadians and Frenchmen.' He is convinced that within a few years 'New Helvetia will be an important establishment, through which pass the caravans coming from Canada, Oregon, and the United

States.' More important still, he believes that California will belong to that nation which can win Sutter for herself and has the courage to send there 'a *corvette* and 200 men.' For 'it is the lot of this province to be conquered, and we do not see why France should not collect her part of this magnificent heritage.'[3]

Naturally, why all these foreign lords of trade, ambassadors-at-large, and officers were coming to the country could not remain hidden from any Californian. But for Sutter the visit of De Mofras was soon to become especially significant. His hob-nobbing with the sensational French agent was presently to reveal to him far-reaching practical potentialities. In his hands it became a whip with which he held the inimical Californians at bay. De Mofras had obligingly put him into a position to threaten them with French intervention!

It did not take long before Sutter made use of this weapon. For the greater the number of foreign visitors, the higher their station, the less the Californians were inclined to trust the latest Mexican official. Sutter's energy, his daring, perseverance, his Indian conquests, the manysidedness of his enterprises soon became to the native sons symptoms of an evil spirit dangerously like the spirit of the dreaded Yankees. And since, opposite all this, they were completely helpless, they at least opened the floodgates of their small talk, the quintessence of their provincial life. They nagged at him and spat at him and endowed him with every sinful vice. They accused him of doing a thriving business in stolen horses. They did not fail to make the best of the fact that he was 'living in open concubinage with two black [!] women from the Sandwich Islands,'—no matter if in their own conduct they could not rise above him. Even in Sutter's method of making adobe bricks they smelled stark heresy, and their evil tongues sneered that instead of kneading straw into the clay, 'he merely took earth and covered it with cow or horse dung.' Such was their impotent defence. José Castro, however, the *comandante* at San José, would be seized by sporadic attacks of furious rage and threaten the complete destruction of New Helvetia.

But before things could come to a head, three more events were necessary, each one of such far-reaching importance as to require a detailed account.

14. *THE LORD OF NEW HELVETIA*

W HILE the Californians were warring against Sutter, Governor Alvarado remained unshaken in his support of his *protegado suizo*. Indeed, at this very time he bestowed upon him the most magnificent favor.

In June 1841 Sutter traveled again to Monterey to request of his chief the formal grant of the land he occupied. The last preliminary condition had been fulfilled when, in January, a sketchy survey was made by Jean-Jacques Vioget, another genial Swiss living at Yerba Buena.

The Governor, in endorsing Sutter's petition, did not mince his words. The applicant, he says 'has sufficiently accredited his laboriousness, good conduct, and other qualifications required in such cases' and demonstrated his 'truly patriotic zeal in favor of our institutions by reducing to civilization a large number of savage Indians.' Therefore, on June 18, 1841, Sutter received from Alvarado what was later to be known as the *New Helvetia Grant*, a title deeding to him 11 square leagues of land (48,818 acres), contingent upon the fulfilment of a few minor conditions, among them the settlement on the land of 12 families.

As soon as Sutter returned from Monterey with the baronial land-grant in his baggage, the work of fortifying New Helvetia began. Once it was well under way, he did not hesitate to advertise the new state of affairs by changing his address from 'New Helvetia' to 'Fort of New Helvetia.'

The new residence was probably completed by this time. This, too, was an adobe building with main floor, attic and basement, designed to serve as a last stronghold of defence and also as the mansion in which all the representative functions were to take place.

About this central structure and the spacious courtyard, 300 feet long and 160 feet wide, was thrown a wall reinforced with timber, 18 feet high and 3 feet thick throughout. The northwest and southeast corners were strengthened by bastions underneath which were the dungeons. By and by a second, thinner wall was built within the outer one, leaving an even distance of 17 feet between the two. This intermural space was then roofed over and divided into numerous compartments serving as workshops, storerooms and as sleeping quarters for the garrison and laborers.

From among his Indians Sutter then selected the most stately and intelligent ones to form a guard. Military discipline was henceforth maintained at the Fort. The gate—in the south wall—was constantly guarded. Every half hour of the night, when the sentry's sandglass had run down, a bell was struck, and the man on duty called out, so that Sutter heard it: 'All's well!'

Until the protective outer wall was up, Sutter, side by side with his Indians and Kanakas, made adobe bricks during as many hours as he could wrench from his numerous other duties.

His own working day usually began at four o'clock in the morning. At sunrise the general reveille was sounded. Then, except for the siesta during the hot noon hours in summer, work continued until sundown. After supper there was for the indefatigable lord of the wilderness more work: the planning of the next day; letters full of requests for articles and raw materials needed for the fort structure, for tools, for seeds, provisions and a hundred other things. There was hope to be held out for early payments. Regrets were to be sent and explanations tendered if he could not pay. So on many a day the midnight candle flickered to the accompaniment of the scratching pen, the periodic watchbells, and the slightly ironic calls of 'All's well!'

The erection of Fort New Helvetia was one of the three events which served quickly to bring the excitable blood of the Californians to the boiling-point.

And presently a new cause for suspicion fanned native feeling already rampant. It so happened that the commencement of Sutter's fortifications coincided with the beginning of American mass immigration to California. In the middle of October 1841 three families arrived from Oregon with Lieutenant Emmons' exploring party. Two weeks later there came a single man direct from Missouri: James John, who had run ahead of his overland companions. These, known as the Bartleson party, numbering about thirty members, arrived at John Marsh's farm on November 4, and about the same date another American immigrant company reached Los Angeles by way of a southern route.

Sutter did his utmost to swell the ranks of New Helvetia's population by recruits drawn from these newcomers. 'I have plenty to do for 60 or 80 men,' he wrote to John Marsh. Sixty or 80 men were a small army in those days. All in all the American immigrants of the year numbered about 200. And Sutter's Fort was designed to accommodate 1,000! The idea of such numbers alone was sufficient to make all California shudder.

But even more startling was another fact which was now moved into the spotlight of public consciousness by these dramatic events. All of a sudden the Californians discovered that Sutter, accidentally, intuitively or purposely had selected for his settlement the most strategic point of the interior. Nor could any of the eminent foreign visitors refrain from commenting upon this fact. The remarks of De Mofras have already been quoted. Sir George Simpson wrote:

'If he [Sutter] really has the talent and courage to make the most of his position, he is not unlikely to render California a second Texas. For fostering and maturing Brother Jonathan's ambitious views, Captain Sutter's establishment is admirably situated. Besides lying on the direct route between San Francisco on the one hand and the Missouri and Willamette on the other, it virtually excludes the Californians from all the best parts of their own country.' With their present force they would never penetrate beyond the narrow and comparatively barren coastal strip of land, 'if Sutter or any other adventurer can gather round him a score of such marksmen as won Texas on the field of San Jacinto.'

No-one could have brought home the shocking truth more pointedly. Suddenly Sutter's Fort now stood before the Californians' eyes as a bolt before the interior of their own land, the key-point of the most important routes, lock and door to all that was vital for the possession of California. And as such it had already drawn upon itself the eyes of greedy powers. With the dramatic vigor that characterizes all signal moments of Sutter's life, a situation had here developed far larger than anything he had probably dreamed of. This was a far cry from the little drygoods store in far-off Switzerland. But if the situation was only partly of his own making, the sense of power to be derived from it was none the less intoxicating. Indeed, Sutter was now so firmly saddled on the high horse as to foster no doubts of being able to sit astride two mounts at the same time—even if one should happen to be an elephant.

And when the elephant was offered to him, he promptly bought it.

This purchase brought the exciting events to a head. For in the eyes of the Californians it was an even greater affront than the erection of Fort New Helvetia.

For Sutter, however, the elephant turned out to be a white one.

15. THE WHITE ELEPHANT

Ross and Bodega, southernmost settlements of Russian America, had been established in 1812 to provide the mother colony at Sitka, where nothing would grow, with agricultural produce. During the first few years a lucrative seal and sea-otter hunt, carried on at the expense of agriculture, had seemed to justify the erection of extensive buildings and fortifications. But so zealous were these Russian hunters that within five years they had about exterminated the seals and otters. Nothing else they tried their hands at thereafter, neither ship-building nor the growing of wheat and fruit, would yield a return substantial enough to pay for the upkeep of the overexpanded settlements. Incessant friction with the Mexican authorities, who had always hotly disputed the right of the Russians to settle within their territorial claims, added to the knotty problem, so that at length, on April 15, 1839, an imperial order was regretfully signed at St. Petersburg to liquidate these establishments. A whole year passed before the order reached the Russian Governor at Sitka, who then took immediate steps to dispose of the old white elephant.

The Hudson's Bay Company, to which it was first offered, declined it. Then Sutter was approached. But as at this time he was not inclined to purchase more than the Russian live-stock and the movable property of Ross and Bodega, Commandant Rotscheff, on July 26, 1841, informed him that his offer could not be considered. Meanwhile negotiations had been opened with Vallejo and Alvarado very much to Sutter's annoyance who, considering himself the favorite of the Russians, already saw himself double-crossed by his friends and by his chief adversary. He was so peeved that when he seized the pen to vent his anger in a letter to Suñol, he wrote what was probably the worst French piece of his whole life and which, as he alone could translate it into equivalent English, is best given in the original:

Les Messieurs Russe ont trouvé des acheteurs pour toutes leurs Maisons et Ranchos, et pour cette raison cela ne me pouvait pas convenir; mais en même tems on peut voir le Character de Russe, ils parlaient très hautement qu'ils prefereraient de brûler toutes les maisons avant de les vendre à un homme du païs, et surtout à Mr. Vallejo qui avait insulté le pavillon Russe etc. etc. et aprésent pour recevoir quelque 1000 Piastres de plus, ils n'ont pas honte de faire des telles arrangements. Seulement des Russe peuvent agir come cela.

Haughtily the Russians had talked of burning all their buildings rather than sell them to a native of the country, but now, for a shabby thousand piasters more than Sutter had offered, they were not ashamed to go back on their word. There's Russian character for you; only Russians could act like that!

About a year before these events animosity between Vallejo and the Russians had climaxed in the affair of the *Lausanne*. Its American skipper, Josiah Spaulding, had coolly avoided paying duties at San Francisco by landing at Bodega which, he claimed, was a free Russian port. When, therefore, towards the end of 1840, news first reached Vallejo of the imminent withdrawal of the Russians from his vicinity, he was quick to arrogate unto himself all the credit and boastfully to write to Mexico that their retreat was the direct result of his own firm patriotic stand in the *Lausanne* affair.

Now, towards the end of July 1841 the Russian agent, Peter Kostromitinoff, appeared rather unexpectedly at Sonoma with a formal sales offer. To a patriot of Vallejo's mettle here was cause for rejoicing, and he at once made known his elation to Alvarado, with whom he managed to keep up a united front against the Russians. 'The news I have for you,' he wrote, 'is too good not to convince me that you will share my exultation. *Se van por fin los Rusos! se van,*—the Russians are going at last, they are going! and truly and unalterably Cape Mendocino will now mark the northern boundary of California, for although Geography always said so, our jurisdiction never reached beyond the American Creek.' Vallejo happened to be in bed and very ill when Kostromitinoff arrived. But as a bringer of happy tidings the Russian mediator revealed miraculous powers. 'His appearance proved a more effective remedy than all the science of Aesculapius, Hippocrates, and Gallian together.'

Vallejo's gloating over the collapse of the Russian colonies was not all patriotism pure and simple. He, too, envisaged the body of his beloved nation as a patient milch cow. There was private profit to be scooped out of this Russian liquidation and with this gain, he confided to Alvarado, he might extend his mercantile enterprises from land to the seven seas. He thought of acquiring a sea-going vessel, possibly a Yankee clipper. The strategy to follow was simple enough. All he and nephew Alvarado had to do was to block the sale of Ross and Bodega. Neither of them believed that there was a man in California wealthy enough to buy what the Russian-American Fur Company offered for sale. Vallejo and Alvarado therefore could hope that sooner or later the Russian property would simply fall into their own lap.

Accordingly, Vallejo's answer to the Russian agent was that the Mexican Nation must have the first option and that, while personally he was willing to buy the live-stock for $9,000, the *land*, as belonging by right to Mexico, could not be sold. Neither could the buildings of Ross and Bodega be disposed of by the

Russians, because they were constructed of timber grown on Mexican soil. In other words, 'the Mexican Nation could not without loss to its dignity *purchase* what already and unquestionably *belonged* to her.'

For safety's sake Governor Alvarado wrote to Mexico for guidance. However, he received no authorization to buy, but instructions to occupy the Russian settlements as soon as they were vacated. For lack of soldiery he could not follow this instruction. Nor could he, for the very same reason, prevent the sale of the settlements in case a buyer should unexpectedly be found.

Overtures to the Californians having led into a blind alley, the Russians renewed their negotiations with Sutter, who immediately informed Suñol that this time he would present a stiffer front to them—'*mais aprésent je seroi un peu plus difficile.*' But on September 4, the day Lieutenant Ringgold of the Wilkes' exploring expedition returned from the upper Sacramento, Commandant Rotscheff of Ross unexpectedly appeared at New Helvetia and hurried Sutter off to Bodega, where Kostromitinoff, the sales-agent, was waiting for them.

After supper, and probably after the 'stiffer front' had been pleasantly dissolved in wine, the formal offer of sale was submitted to Sutter. He was asked $30,000 for the Russian possessions. It was intimated that even now there were a few others reflecting upon the purchase, but that Governor Kouprianoff at Sitka, he with whom Sutter had spent such glorious weeks two years before, preferred him to be their successor at Ross, as he considered him a far safer debtor than anyone else, including the Mexican Government.

It was a shrewd argument, going straight to Sutter's heart, so helpless in the face of flattery. It raised him on a well-anointed pedestal, and from it he slipped into the trap, thus making himself the keeper of this big white elephant, Ross and Bodega.

A *contrat de vente* was drawn up in French. Its substance was this: The Russian-American Fur Company, abandoning its southernmost settlements with the consent of His Majesty the Emperor of all the Russias, cedes to Monsieur Sutter all its posts from Port Bodega north to Fort Ross, '*except only the land,*' and Sutter pledges himself to pay within four years the sum of $30,000, *plus* a cash down payment of $2,000. The payment shall be in produce of the country and divided in the following instalments: $5,000 the first and second years and $10,000 the third year. The fourth and last instalment of $10,000 shall be in coin. The kind and quantity of produce to be delivered the first and second years shall be:

1,000 *fanegas* [1,600 bushels] of wheat	$3,200
100 *fanegas* of peas	250
25 *fanegas* of beans	75
50 *quintales* of soap [5,000 lbs.]	700
200 *arrobas* of suet [5,000 lbs.]	400
250 *arrobas* of tallow	375

Sutter is bound to deliver these goods f.o.b. San Francisco on September 1 for three years beginning with 1842. He is to pay all harbor and tonnage dues for the Russian ship collecting the goods and, in case of his failure to deliver the instalments according to agreement, he shall be liable to defray the company's expenses of sending a ship to the port of San Francisco. But perhaps the most important part of the contract is this: Until the payment of the entire sum of $30,000, the establishment of New Helvetia 'together with all his [Sutter's] movable and fixed property shall serve as a guarantee.'

The conviction fairly assails one, in reading this contract, that it was a severe imposition on Sutter, and one cannot help wondering how the Russians made him sign it. He must have known that he could not succeed where a company as strong and rich as the

Russian-American Fur Company had failed, and indeed he never thought of trying to develop these abandoned Russian colonies. As settlements they were of no use to him. What he chiefly wanted was the Russian cattle, the store-goods, tools and implements which he needed for the construction and equipment of Fort New Helvetia. Now if Vallejo had been willing to pay $9,000 for the cattle alone, and Sutter was required to pay $2,000 cash down for the movable goods, what was the additional $21,000 for? This vast sum (in those days it was probably much more than twice its value today) can only be rated as the lumber value of some forty-odd houses, barns, sheds, fences and stockades, some of which Sutter was not allowed to touch, as they, too, were to stand intact as security. Even if one allows that lumber was expensive in California, the price which Sutter paid still seems exorbitant in view of the labor involved in dismantling the Russian structures and of the great distance the material had to be hauled before it could be used at New Helvetia. Yet Sutter agreed to mortgage New Helvetia to provide security for this most doubtful acquisition.

What prompted Sutter to buy these settlements? To begin with, he would not have obtained the things he badly needed and wanted if he had not bought all that the Russians had to sell. Secondly, no price may have seemed too high to him if the transaction served to snub Señor Vallejo. And finally there was the question of the lands belonging to Ross and Bodega. No doubt the notion of being known to the world as the overlord of yet another little principality was nectar and ambrosia to him. And although the lands were expressly excluded from the purchase, Sutter, given sufficient time, apparently hoped to establish a good claim on them. At any rate, he procured from Commandant Rotscheff a separate deed (not registered with the authorities), whereby Ross and Bodega were 'delivered to his [Sutter's] indisputable possession *with all the lands.*'

Sutter having agreed, informally as yet, to accept the conditions of the sale, the deal was celebrated at a banquet on board the Russian schooner *Helena*, which lay at anchor at Bodega. 'Champagne flowed freely,' reports Sutter, 'the emperor's health was drunk and the health given of the new owner of Ross and Bodega.'

But the transaction did not become final until he had paid down $2,000 in cash. The task of raising so much money absorbed three months, thus furnishing an early indication that, in assuming these liabilities towards the Russians, he was overtaxing his ability to pay. Not until December 13 was he ready to appear before the Justice of the Peace at Yerba Buena and to put his hand to the fatal *contrat de vente*. His compatriot Jean-Jacques Vioget and Vallejo's American brother-in-law, Jacob Primer Leese, were witnesses.

Already in October Sutter had begun to transfer the Russian cattle to New Helvetia. About 100 head were lost in crossing the Sacramento River. However, since the chief value of the stock lay in the hides, and the hides of most of the drowned animals could be saved, the damage was not great. The herds taken over from the Russians comprised 1,700 oxen, cows and calves; 940 horses and mules, including 100 plow horses and 20 pack mules; and 900 sheep. So that Sutter's entire fortune in animals now amounted to about 4,500 head of cattle, 1,500 horses and mules, and close to 2,000 sheep. A herd of hogs of unknown size was kept four miles below the fort on the Sacramento River.[4]

For the cash down payment of $2,000, Sutter received a 22 ton launch, re-christened *Sacramento*, and 4 smaller boats, 49 plows, 29 rakes, 43 harnesses, 15 halters, 20 reins, 5 four-wheeled carts, 10 two-wheeled carts, a machine for winnowing wheat— all far from being new, of course, and largely useless.

Sutter was now Lord not only of New Helvetia, but also of

Ross and Bodega. The personal consequences from this transaction were not to be revealed until a few years hence. But the meaning it assumed for the Californians became unmistakably clear at once.

Throughout the year events had succeeded each other with precision. At the beginning of the year the feelings of the Californians towards Sutter had not been any too kindly. Then, to their regret, Governor Alvarado had presented to the Swiss a little private empire on the Sacramento. Immediately thereupon Sutter had begun to fortify himself in his wilderness lair. There came the foreign spies and emissaries, and with them the increasing dread of a foreign invasion. Moreover, these eminent visitors all delighted in rubbing it into the skin of the Californians that Sutter's Fort occupied the most strategic location of the hinterland. All that was oil in the fire of local patriotism. But not enough: as if on the mysterious cue of some sinister demon, there arrived now the vanguards of American mass immigration. And finally, at the very moment when Alvarado and Vallejo thought they had forced the Russians to leave Ross and Bodega behind as a parting present to them, Sutter, 'the ungrateful villain!' (these are Alvarado's words) snatched the coveted prize away from them.

Tension seemed to have reached the breaking-point. The Californians' blood was seething. Threats poisoned the air already befouled by bad temper. Vallejo took revenge on Sutter for his snub by pestering his cattle-drivers when they came through Sonoma. But most voluble of all was José Castro, the *comandante* of San José, who again threatened the complete annihilation of New Helvetia.

Things came to such a pass that Sutter considered the time ripe for a generous counter-blow in the form of a menacing proclamation. He released only one copy of it; but as the addressee was judiciously selected, he did not have to worry about its circulation, in his own broken English or in Spanish. He sent it to Jacob Primer Leese, Vallejo's American brother-in-law.

'Very curious Rapports come to me from below,' the broadside began,[5] and then dispensed with decorum. 'The poor wretches don't know what they do.' Did they mean war? Very well then: 'The first french fregate who came here will do me justice. The people don't know me yet, but soon they will find out what I am able to do. It is to late now to drive me out the country.' Let them take one step and he would 'make a Declaration of Independence and proclaim California for a Republique. . . . I am Strong now, one of my best friends, a German Gentleman came from the Columbia with plenty people, another party is close by from the Missouri. . . . ' His garrison is large enough to hold the fort until his couriers bring reinforcements from the Willamette, from 'the Hunters and Shawnees and Delawares with which I am very well acquainted,' and 'about 2 or 300 more' from the Missouri. Indeed, 'that is my intention, Sir, if they let me not alone.' He 'will be a faithful Mexican' just as long as he is left in peace and given guarantees for his security. But if 'this Rascle of Castro' should venture within speaking distance of New Helvetia's cannon, 'a very warm and hearty welcome is prepared for him.' Ten guns and five field-pieces are ready to protect the fortress, and he has 'also about 50 faithful Indians which shot their musquet very quick. . . . '

When and where in the world was there ever another usually sociable and genial immigrant, after but two years in a new country, put in a position to issue words like these? What other citizen of but fifteen months could thus be bullying his government, publicly playing with the thought of revolt, and with impunity thumbing his nose at his adopted nation?

Whatever Castro had intended to do, he now stayed away from New Helvetia. Vallejo, however, grievously incensed, immediately demanded of Governor Alvarado a large armed force to check those '*Individuos del Missouri*' who flocked to the '*Gobernador de la Nueva Helvecia*' and were received by him with open arms. And presently he also sent a spy to the dangerous settlement in the person of Rudesindo Berreyesa. This man, deeply impressed by what he found, reported that Sutter issued numerous passports to foreigners, especially trappers of the Hudson's Bay Company, and that these might '*al improviso y de noche*' attack Sonoma. He was filled with dismay also at the sight of the many Indians at New Helvetia. 'All are provided with good horses. Should it be possible that these Indians . . . are conspiring to help the Swiss to hoist the French flag in our country?'

And Alvarado?

The cumulative effect of all the dramatic happenings of the year was the abrupt collapse of the friendship between the Governor and Sutter. Alvarado, by using Sutter as a tool of intrigue against Vallejo, had only succeeded in defeating his own purpose. Henceforth he, too, fostered nothing but scorn for his ex-protégé who, as he later put it, 'conceived the idea of making the Californians believe that he was fate and providence to them.'[6]

Yet, whether Sutter actually made any such conscious endeavors or not, and whether Alvarado liked it or not, Sutter, in more than one respect, proved to be exactly that: Fate and providence personified of California.

16. GROWING–PAINS OF A PRIVATE EMPIRE

With the end of 1841 or the beginning of 1842 Sutter's life and the history of New Helvetia enter upon a new phase. Alvarado's land-grant had raised the settler in the unclaimed wilderness to the status of a grand-seigneur. The primitive tule village was about to transform itself into a mighty fortress. But of even greater consequence perhaps was Sutter's acquisition of Ross and Bodega and the financial burden he had thus taken upon his shoulder.

Through the contract concerning Ross he had pledged himself to furnish the Russians during each of the next two years 1,600 bushels of wheat, 160 bushels of peas, 400 bushels of beans and various other produce, to double these quantities in the third year, and in the fourth year to pay the equivalent of the third instalment in cash. These obligations now made imperative an adaptation of all means to this one end. They forced Sutter to promote farming as his foremost enterprise. Only now, in this struggle with the virgin soil, his real pioneering began.

The task, as was soon to become apparent, would have befitted a Titan. Were there men available to help him? And with what kind of tools was the gigantic labor to be achieved?

A few of the immigrants who had arrived with the Bartleson party of 1841 proved very useful. Ahead of all others was John Bidwell, the man who was the answer to Sutter's prayers, a youth who, because of his gentleness and intelligence, immediately and completely captured Sutter's confidence. He was the very antithesis of everything a superstitious fear taught the Californians to expect in an 'adventurer from the Missouri.' Modest, well-behaved, God-fearing, this boyish Chautauquan and ex-school-teacher had just come of age, and the spontaneous friendship that sprang up between master and servant forms one of the touching episodes in the colorful tale of New Helvetia.

Then there was that 'German Gentleman' mentioned in the famous proclamation of November. His name was Carl A. Flügge. In St. Louis, where Sutter had known him, he had kept a stationery-store and circulating library. He sported a pair of spectacles—provoking in the frontier—and wore an ostentatious air of German *Kultur* to the disparagement of the humbler members of the community. To Sutter, however, he proved for a while to be very useful as secretary and ambassador-at-large.

Another German arrival of 1841 was Henry Huber, who for many years was superintendent of agriculture and master of the still. But he looked as tart as the wild grapes from which he distilled brandy, and his name, as mispronounced by the natives, sounded exactly like the Spanish name for the grape: *uba*.

Besides these men there were, of course, always a few for whom the name 'adventurer' was rather too fine a feather in the cap. But Sutter, having such large aims, was not in a position to discriminate. He welcomed all. In the main, however, he had to depend on the lazy and inexperienced Indians. As soon as a tribal chief recognized Sutter as his and his people's overlord, he took upon himself the obligation to furnish, according to the size of the tribe, up to 200 men to work for two weeks at a time in Sutter's fields or on his fort. But these labor quotas were rarely delivered unless called for. For this purpose, domesticated natives, former mission Indians, were sent on horseback into the villages to drive their wild brethren in herds towards the fort. And no-one could have done this job more expertly and with greater relish than these 'Christian' servants who, through continual breathing in the atmosphere of their great white lord, had become infested with a supreme contempt for their naked and filthy blood-relations of the woods and mountains.

Apart from food and shelter the remuneration for a two weeks' period of labor consisted of a muslin shirt or a pair of muslin pantaloons to each laborer. Yet, more frequently than on the Indians' bodies, these shirts and pantaloons were later to be found as ornaments on shrubs and trees, serving as 'prayers' to the gods and spirits for an abundance of fish, grasshoppers and acorns.

Need one add that under these conditions it was a wonder if any results were achieved at all?

And what about the agricultural implements? For never yet had the hand of man broken a furrow in the soil of this valley. Sutter found his chief reliance in the Californian plow, which, John Bidwell says, was nothing but 'the crooked limb of a tree with a piece of flat iron for a point and a pole for a tongue to hold by.' True, there were also forty-five plows of Russian origin, but these were so complicated and difficult to manage that they were useless in the hands of the Indians.

Sickles were practically unknown. Anything with a semblance of an edge had to be used for harvesting: hunting and kitchen knives, split willow sticks, fragments of old rusty barrel-hoops, and then most of the grain crop was still left to be pulled up simply with the roots. Efficiency was achieved only in the threshing. Once cut or pulled up, the wheat was piled a yard or two deep into large *eras* (threshing floors) surrounded by high clay walls. A band of wild horses was then driven in and chased about in a circle by war-whooping Indians, and in an hour the entire harvest of the year was trampled out under impenetrable clouds of dust. The system, however, proved efficient only as far as time was concerned, and the cleanliness of the wheat always left a great deal to be desired. The winnowing again was extremely tedious, as it could be done only on days when a good breeze was fanning.

In spite of all handicaps Sutter fared not badly as a farmer in 1842; at least for a beginning—for the crops fell short of the quantity he was committed to deliver to the Russians. This might not have been embarrassing if the deficiency could have been supplied from one or the other of the many enterprises of New Helvetia, not one of which, however, as yet threw off the slightest profit. The fur trade brought much annoyance and little reward this season, because the foreman of the trappers, one McVickers, defrauded Sutter of part of the catch, and the Hudson's Bay men again encroached upon his territory. As yet no leather reached the market from Sutter's tannery. The crude flourmill was barely sufficient for the needs of the settlement. The men working as blacksmiths in the fort were mostly bunglers. The attempts at distilling brandy from wild grapes did not succeed. And even the horses taken over from the Russians, about 1,000, proved largely useless. Some were finally given away to the Indians, but most of them were good enough only to be killed so that ropes could be made from their manes and tails.

The reason for these many failures was chiefly the lack of efficient labor. Numerically, there were enough men. 'If any chose to work, Sutter would pay them, or if they did not, he would feed them to keep them with him,' says Joseph B. Chiles, who visited the settlement in 1841. In May 1842 Sutter was compelled to discharge a number of these good-for-nothings and botchers. But new ones always came with new pretensions, and Sutter, who himself had made his way largely on the strength of an elegant fiction, would naively believe in any newcomer until experience taught him another sad lesson.

He was caught in a vicious circle. Because all his possessions remained pledged to the Russians until the fulfilment of his obligations towards them, he naturally tried to satisfy them first. But he owed many others. 'In fact,' says Bidwell, 'he seemed to be owing everybody.' He worked desperately with all the resources at his command, but everything seemed to work adversely. His expenses continually outran his income. Happily Sutter was not easily discouraged. He had long since become used to that, having scarcely ever known the world to conform to any other pattern. And as the walls of his fort were gradually rising, there also rose with them the consolation that at least his lesser creditors would not dare knock at his portals seeking collection.

His little empire had its vulnerable point though, depending entirely as it did for its communication with the outside world upon the launch *Sacramento* acquired from the Russians. This vessel, in August 1842, was embargoed at the instigation of a few creditors, among them the Frenchman Euloge Célis in Yerba Buena and Sutter's fellow-Swiss Jean-Jacques Vioget. Presently Sutter's other creditors sucked courage from this first public show of strength against the mighty debtor. Even the good Suñol lost his patience. Rumors reached Sutter that Suñol's partners and brothers-in-law, the Bernals, were planning to descend on New Helvetia to drive away the cattle. To appease them, Sutter offered some of his 'good Russian horses.' But Suñol and the Bernals insisted on being paid in cattle. Their threats developed into a country-wide agitation most injurious to Sutter's credit. He had to plead with Suñol and to entreat him not to resort to desperate measures. He grew outraged at the unnamed person, the 'infamous liar' who spread the tale that Sutter 'wrote letters just for pastime' and would pay just when it pleased him. He sent his envoy Flügge to San José; but the suggestions for a settlement thus submitted were refuted, and Sutter finally saw himself obliged to borrow cattle with which to pay Suñol from Robert Livermore, who owned a farm near San José.

Why borrow? What of his own large herds? He wrote to Suñol that 'most of them no longer exist,' that he had 'but a few' head. He had in fact given away large numbers to some of the men who had stayed with him from the beginning and worked without pay. That most of his cattle were gone was correct also as far as the original settlement was concerned. But they still did exist— forty-five miles away on Feather River, on a newly established ranch named Hock, or Hock Farm, after a tribe of Indians located in the vicinity. The removal of the stock to the north had become imperative because of the necessity of cultivating large tracts of land near the fort; and also because the land between the fort and the Sacramento was subject to dreadful inundations during the rainy season and therefore unsuitable for the wintering of cattle. At Hock, moreover, they were much safer before the greedy hands of impatient creditors, none of whom had courage enough to penetrate so far into the Indians' world.

These were some of the stones in Sutter's hard-earned daily bread, the snares that constantly beset his course; and it is scarcely to be imagined that the book on practical agriculture which he had loaned from John Marsh could offer him much help in all this trouble. The truth is that from the moment he signed the sales contract concerning Ross, he was tightly cornered.

In this distress he finally hit upon the device of hiring out his Indians and selling the Indian children which his wars had reduced to orphans. This sort of trade was very common among the Californians, and many were Sutter's regrets that his supply could not keep step with the demand.

17. *THE GOOD SAMARITAN*

HAND in hand with Sutter's troubles at home there went certain political difficulties, also partly growing out of his Russian deal.

None of the Californians was as profoundly and lastingly peeved at Sutter's purchase of Ross and Bodega as the *comandante general* Vallejo, his neighbor of Sonoma. Soon after that startling proclamation of November 1841, Vallejo had dispatched a vitriolic denunciation of Sutter's activities to Mexico, and in it he had summed up his own fervent wishes in a sly recommendation. He urged the Central Government to fortify its position in California by uniting in one person the highest civil and military authority of the department and to give this man a very large army. He did not miss the opportunity to couple this advice with a tarring and feathering (on paper) of his dear nephew, Governor Alvarado. And then he effectively capped his report by submitting his resignation as *comandante general*. This, he no doubt thought, would make it easy for the Government in Mexico to appoint him to the new high office whose creation he had proposed.

His messenger, however, the Frenchman Victor Prudon, arrived a little too late in Mexico. The Superior Government had already anticipated his advice and appointed a young Mexican colonel, Manuel Micheltorena, Governor of California and *comandante general* in one. And even the army which was to support him in office had been authorized.

Thus Vallejo with his cabals now saw his fondest hopes frustrated in various ways. Instead of being promoted he found himself debased to a mere 'commander of the northern frontier.' Instead of the splendid army with which the prospective Governor Vallejo had hoped to dictate terms to his undesirable neighbor of New Helvetia, the new Governor brought troops from Mexico recruited chiefly from prison inmates.

But the worst was this: the proud Californians had always taken offence whenever Mexico imposed on them a governor of its own choice. Without exception these Mexican chiefs had sooner or later been chased out of the department, a fact which could not have remained hidden from Governor Micheltorena. It was a foregone conclusion that, to prepare himself for the inevitable day of revolt against him, he must ally himself with the non-native element in California and sue for their support. Among those most unlikely to join hands with the native sons the Lord of New Helvetia unequivocally stood first. And this, reduced to the plainest terms, meant simply that with the arrival of Micheltorena and the removal of Alvarado, Sutter's newest enemy, there was again a man ruling in Monterey who could not but earnestly seek Sutter's friendship.

No wonder Vallejo grew envious beyond words. He tried to make impossible all co-operation between Sutter and Micheltorena by warning the new Governor, immediately he arrived, against the Swiss. He accused him of a '*marcada tendencia de conspirar*' and of threatening 'every day' to call in French warships which, it was said, 'awaited only his signal to take possession of California.' But it proved a fruitless endeavor. Sutter himself, through his envoy Flügge, had already sent the new Governor a very diplomatic message of felicitation, together with his pledge of cooperation and thus gained a pre-emption of his chief's goodwill. So, in the end, nothing was left to Vallejo but to vent his anger on Sutter directly by sending him arrogant letters and by incessantly molesting his men when they came through Sonoma on their frequent trips between the Sacramento and Ross.

It was about this time also that one clause in Sutter's New Helvetia grant began to reveal itself as a pernicious snag. He could regard his little empire as his and his heirs' inalienable property only after he had settled twelve families on the land. And as everything was mortgaged to the Russians, his ultimate possession remained staked on two main factors: immigration, which alone enabled him to comply with the settler clause, and the weather, on which his crops, the ransom for his Russian mortgage, depended.

In 1842 rainfall and crops were good, but there were only a few sporadic settlers. From the Sandwich Islands, in May, came

Theodore Cordua, a German of Spanish descent who, after varied adventures in all parts of the world, was drawn to California by tales of Sutter's famous settlement. In exchange for $8,000 in merchandise he was given cattle, horses and a square mile of land on the Yuba River, where he established his ranch New Mecklenburg. A squaw was soon on hand to make, according to the letter of the Mexican law, a perfect family.

About the same time Nicolaus Allgeier, Sebastian Keyser, David Dutton and a few others were given sub-grants, horses, sheep and cattle, in return for services. Their squaws they had already. That made a few more families, but not yet twelve.

In 1843 the tables turned. No rainfall and no crops, but immigrants. Some forty Americans who had gone to Oregon the year before came to the fort early in July under the leadership of Lansford Hastings, a preposterous lawyer from Ohio. He came with the avowed purpose of proclaiming California an independent republic after the Texan model and himself as President. But the scarcity of American settlers fell like a chill on his heroic intentions, whereupon he went back east over the southern route, promising, however, to return within a year with an army of 1,000 followers.

More newcomers, the Chiles-Walker party of some two-score men, reached New Helvetia on November 10 after a troublesome crossing of the mountains and many a bloody fight with hostile Indians. With Chiles came some of the best men that were ever to enter Sutter's service. Pierson B. Reading, a native of New Jersey, was engaged as clerk and chief of trapping operations. Samuel Hensley, a Kentuckian, became super-cargo of the launch.

Simultaneously with the arrival of the Chiles-Walker party at Sutter's, another company of immigrants reached the valley near the present town of Stockton, and of these, too, many came to the fort.

From now on immigration never ceased. Newcomers kept pouring in in seasonal waves, one coming from Oregon in spring or summer, and the high tide washing over the sierras in the autumn, or even after the first snow had fallen on the mountains. 'Sometimes,' says Sutter, 'my houses were full of immigrants, so much so that I could scarcely find a place to sleep myself.' And he fed them all, clothed them out of his unpaid-for stores, and during the inclemencies of the winter season housed them under his mortgaged roof. Then, when fine weather returned and they had recuperated and regained strength, they moved again. They thought of New Helvetia more as of a God-given temporary refuge than as a place to stay; especially those with families.

Almost every one of the many hundreds of immigrants to California before the gold-rush spent some time at Sutter's settlement, and the many testimonies of his benevolence towards these pitiful wanderers are overwhelming. One of the most touching is the report of Lieutenant Emmons who in October 1841 had arrived on foot from Oregon with a detachment of the Wilkes' exploring expedition. Their path had been beset with untold hardships and deprivations. But in New Helvetia 'everything that heart could wish was supplied from the bountiful storehouse of this large-hearted, generous man. . . . Fresh provisions were sent to the camp daily, including fresh baked bread, milk, fish, groceries, and the delicacies our sick and feeble men so much required.' The sick were brought to Yerba Buena in Sutter's launch, the others were supplied with horses, yet 'for all this the noble man declined any compensation.'

Of Sutter's personal appearance, Emmons says that 'in his brilliant uniform of a Mexican officer and his magnificent presence' he 'looked as I have in fancy pictured Cortez in his palmiest days.'

The day after his arrival at the fort, Pierson B. Reading wrote in his diary: 'What could be more gratifying after we had been for nearly six months traveling among hostile Indians, half starved as we were, than to reach a haven such as this castle proved to be?'

No sacrifice was here too great. John Bidwell relates that sometimes Sutter ground some of his precious seed-wheat so as to provide bread for newcomers. And he adds: 'Because of his magnanimity he could not refuse employment to anybody who asked for it. As long as he had anything he trusted everybody with everything,—friends and strangers alike. . . . Always liberal and affable, no man could be more obliging than he, especially to strangers. . . . His establishment was a home to all Americans, where they could live as long as it suited them without charge.'

These and numerous other reports praising Sutter in a hundred ways, open to us the very heart of this strange man. True, in later years, when, under the crushing mountain of his debts, Sutter was forced to think more realistically of his financial obligations, it could happen that immigrants who had heard fabulous tales and who expected miracles of him were sorely disappointed and remained unforgiving.

But in these early years it was different. How ridiculous, therefore, is the theory propounded by a California historian that Sutter's immigration policy sprang solely from a crafty scheme to make a quick fortune one way or another! No-one whose sole purpose in life is monetary gain could ever act as Sutter did. No-one would have been in a better position to exploit the immigrants ruthlessly. And John Marsh, for instance, the miserly hermit of Monte Diablo, did make it his practice to take a toll from every immigrant coming to his habitation. Why not Sutter?

'He was not a Yankee,' some of his contemporaries answered. Until his dying day Sutter remained an utterly exotic creature on this continent, mainly, perhaps, because there was in his scale of values something which stood high above the assets of the ledger. Hard as the former draper had to struggle to make ends meet, charity with him did not begin at home. The opportunity of 'cutting a figure' in his resplendent uniform, of posing as a soldier among soldiers, or to stand before the immigrants as the father of the country, their protector, to him seemed worth the cost of large stocks of provisions not yet paid for.

Pierson B. Reading hit the nail on the head when he began his characterization of Sutter, 'it gives him pleasure to administer to the wants of the wayworn, weary traveler.' Sutter himself once confessed: 'Everything I have done in my life I have done for my own pleasure.' He was one of those Falstaffian creatures that live for the sensation and the tickle of being alive. His entire physique was a radiating mass in which the joy of life became contagious. Therein rested the fascination of his personality which, in its best moments, was a marvel of nature, a lusty phenomenon like an enchanting cataract, a geyser or a magnificent thunderstorm.

Happily this love of pleasure was coupled with a tenderness of heart very easily moved to tears. And had not he himself once been the underdog, disfranchised, merely tolerated? All this combined to produce the extremely rare phenomenon of a parvenu dispensing favors with such simplicity and sincerity of heart as to leave the recipients wholly unaware that they were merely supernumeraries in a delightful spectacle.

But there was yet another side to the matter. To Sutter immigration was also synonymous with progress. More keenly than anyone else he saw the possibilities inherent in large numbers of these immigrants. They were worth coddling. But less than anyone else he thought of making the passing moment pay its due to him. Only his senses had this miraculous gift. His mind seemed always to be living in the future.

And therein, alas, part of his misfortune lay hidden.

18, *LIFE AT SUTTER'S FORT*

TOWARDS the end of 1843, after a building period of two years, the fort was now so far advanced as to impress one as a thing completed. Visitors coming up the valley would approach it by the two-mile road leading from the *Embarcadero* on the Sacramento over the well-timbered plain to the wooded knoll crowned by the fortress.

With its high walls and bastions loopholed and armed, it presented a rather imposing sight. The cannon frowned defiantly at the enemy. Two pieces stood beside the gate in the south wall, constantly guarded by vigilant sentinels. Entering through the gate, one came into a vast court, along the walls of which there were the sleeping quarters of the fort population, storage rooms and workshops of practically every trade. Here blacksmiths were busy at the forge or the anvil, there gunsmiths took care of the garrison's rifles and those of the hunters. There was a carpenters' shed, a shop for the shoemakers. In one corner of the court a primitive gristmill was kept going; in another corner there stood a shady oak-tree. The center of the large rectangle was occupied by the mansion or main building and close by were the kitchen and the still. A mile away from the fort, on the American River, lay the tannery. And later there was added to these manufactures a spinning and weaving shop and a hat factory.

Although only the principal buildings were covered with shingles, all others with tule thatch, yet the whole impressed most visitors rather powerfully, all the more since they knew that only a few years previously this place had been haunted only by wild animals and savage Indians.

But the sight of the rare figure who ruled here sufficiently explained the wonder of this wilderness fortress. 'It is almost impossible,' writes Reading,

to conceive in what manner and in so short a time Capt. Souter has made such extensive and permanent improvements. But when you read the character of this gentleman you will at once conceive that with his intelligence he is remarkable for his perseverance, industry and enterprise, No one could have laboured under more disadvantages than he has in carrying forward the improvement of this beautiful property, so far removed from where he could obtain the necessary articles . . . labourers . . . and different kinds of mechanics; all this, however, he has most certainly overcome.

All visitors, of course, were regaled with the old legend of Sutter's service in the glorious Royal Swiss Guard of France; they all report it faithfully and without a shade of doubt in their memoirs. Nor could the clever showman refrain from treating eminent guests to impressive demonstrations of his regal powers. A Swedish naturalist, 'Doctor' Waseurtz de Sandels, who in 1843 came to the Sacramento from South America (one of those who were rather shocked at the methods of Indian mass-feeding) has left us the following colorful description of a scene:

Hundreds of Indians had again resorted to work and to acknowledge the authority of the white chieftain. Only the chiefs of these Indians came armed with bows and arrows, all others came unarmed and after having gone through their customary graceful movements in file, in square, in flank, and in body, the chief made a long speech which seemed very eloquent. He then laid down his bow and arrow at Sutter's feet, saying: 'Take these, and with them puncture this heart if I or my tribe betray the trust you now put in us and which we now solemnly promise to keep.'

Yet, seen at close quarters, life in Sutter's Fort was often devoid of most of the romantic atmosphere with which passing visitors and newly arrived settlers were fond of endowing it. Tongue in cheek, James Clyman, a trapper who arrived in 1845, remarks that it 'has an imposing appearance at a distance . . . but on nearer inspection it is found that the whole Fort, houses and all, are built of doba or mud walls and covered inside and out with dust and fleas, which grow her[e] to the gr[e]atest perfection.'

Nor were the fleas the only undesirables. There were mosquitoes! 'I should like to have your company up here a week or two,' John Sinclair once wrote to William H. Davis, in Yerba Buena, 'that you might know the pleasure of letter writing in the midst of myriads of mosquitos, while every line you wrote, you would be obliged to lay down your pen and enjoy the luxury of scratching for a while. I write with one hand, my other is employed in that most vulgar of all occupations, scratching. . . . N.B. This letter is nothing but scratching.' Fleas and mosquitoes! This was the plaintive refrain of innumerable letters and descriptions. But happily it was possible to get acclimatized to their society. Even scratching became smooth routine and assumed its more or less orderly place in the more or less orderly pattern of life at New Helvetia.

In this little rural kingdom, Sutter was everything: ruler absolute, the law in person, administrator, Justice of the Peace, physician, matchmaker, bread-giver, parson and patriarch. Theoretically some sort of military discipline regulated the empire of this enthusiastic amateur soldier, to whom the beat of drums and the burst of cannon were like love songs. Drum, fife and bell made life real to this strange visionary. Drums called his Indians to their feeding-troughs, drums accompanied the clang of their sickles and barrel-hoops when they were dispatched into the wheat-fields. But for variety's sake the little Russian chapel-bell installed in a turret above the residence rang out cheerily over the serene fields and woods, to count the hours of the day and night and to rouse the sleepers at day-break.

From morning till night and sometimes through the night, the monotonous screeching of a gristmill driven by four mules would invade the neighborhood. The flour ground was of the coarsest and the bread hard to distinguish in color and consistency from the adobe bricks; but, in the opinion of at least one witness, it was 'nevertheless sweet and wholesome and preferable to any other to be met with in the country.' Others objected to the pebbles occasionally found in it or complained that it was often sour.

Nor was there always bread. In times of drought they lived on beef exclusively. Sporadically the scarcity of credit eliminated from the daily fare all things that had to be bought. 'Sometimes we could not get coffee and sometimes no sugar,' says Sutter in his Reminiscences. But: 'We found peas a good substitute for coffee and acorns still better. Indeed, it was difficult always to tell acorn coffee from genuine coffee.'

News trickled slowly into this remote colony. California could not boast of a single newspaper of her own. As often as boats touched the coast from Honolulu, copies of the *Polynesian* would reach New Helvetia with news that had come around Cape Horn or from the East Indies. Sometimes a friend of a settler had the thoughtfulness to send a package of discarded Boston or New York papers around the Horn or with one of the immigrant trains across the plains and mountains. At best the latest news was six months old; more often a year. But still the precious papers made the circuit of the country until they were too frayed to be legible.

Sutter's own letters to his family first had to travel north to the Columbia, thence with the couriers of the Hudson's Bay Company through Canada, from there to England, and then to Switzerland. Later the Russian agent who came to collect the wheat in autumn would take a letter to Sitka, whence it traveled to the coast of Siberia, across the Continent of Asia to Russia, Germany and Switzerland.

As regularly as wind, weather and intervening creditors permitted, Sutter's launch *Sacramento* plied between New Helvetia and the bay of San Francisco. Down the river went beaver and otter skins, deer-tallow, hides, wheat, peas, and beans after the harvest. Up the river came beads, cotton and all sorts of trinkets with which the Indians were paid; the innumerable articles Sutter needed for new buildings and the equipment and operation of his workshops; foodstuffs, tobacco, nails, tools, boarding, shingles, iron for the blacksmiths, lead and powder secretly bought from merchant-ships under the cover of night or brought to him from Sitka by the Russians. And even books purchased from mariners in Yerba Buena.

Most of the armament of Sutter's Fort had come to the Sacramento as contraband from the Hawaiian Islands or from South America. The Russians had left him only one good brass field-piece, cast in St.Petersburg in 1804 and said to have fired upon Napoleon's armies in 1812. But dozens of old flintlocks had come into Sutter's possession with the Russian purchase—arms which Napoleon had left behind on his retreat from Moscow. The garrison uniforms of blue or green cloth with red trimmings were likewise Russian liquidation stock and filled with savage pride the hearts of the Indians elected to wear them.

Almost every evening after supper the garrison was put through its paces to delight the soldierly heart of August Sutter. Usually there was available some old soldier, a German or a Swiss, to act as drill-sergeant, and it was but one of the colorful touches of this heterogeneous colony to see the Indian garrison fall in, goose-step, and go through all sorts of motions and formations—on German words of command.

Beside the regular garrison there was also a little Indian cadet corps with uniforms of blue drill pantaloons, white cotton shirts and red bandanas. These boys were drilled on Sunday mornings.

Underneath the cloak of military discipline, the rule of the Lord of New Helvetia was not severe. Jovial and kind-hearted, courteous towards everybody, and sensualist that he was, he could not be a strict disciplinarian. How could he have been hard and ruthless with the employees whose pay was usually months in arrears? In the beginning Sutter had tried to enforce a modicum of discipline by withholding all intoxicants from his men. But with the distillery working, and with Sutter never more than an arm's reach from the bottle, it was impossible to prevent the liquor from seeping into unauthorized channels. Indians as well as white men and Kanakas would risk anything for a drink.

Once the whites threatened quitting Sutter's employ *en masse* if he continued to refuse them an occasional barrel of liquor, particularly on a holiday. He had to relent, and, following the advice of a wise old sailor, he gave them the dangerous drink, departed for a few days' hunting trip, and arranged to return at a time when 'all the trouble would be over.'

But perhaps the greatest obstacle to smooth routine and efficiency was the insular cohabitation of Indians, Kanakas, Negroes, and white men. And such white men! Only one in a score was of the pioneer type. The rest were vagabonds, untrained and incapable of learning.

Almost without exception they went to bed with squaws and cheerfully littered the fort with a rabble of naked half-castes. But, with his own two Kanaka women and sundry squaws, what could Sutter do? How could he have stopped this interference of nature with his desire to keep up appearances? He knew too well that to effect a change here he would have to begin with himself, and to him the cost was prohibitive. Alas, there was no remedy as simple as a few days' hunting trip! The best he could do was to see that each of the little brats had a shirt on hand when guests of note were expected. Even this was not always practicable. Guests would occasionally come unannounced, and there were times when the supply of shirting even for the adult Indians ran low.

By nature the Indians were completely amoral. Their squaws were chattel which they would willingly lend to any stranger for a paltry consideration. For one of the squaws to find favor in Sutter's eyes was to her native husband an honor equal to attaining court rank, and often it meant being raised to the nobility of well-dressed, well-fed loafers. Sutter tolerated a number of such native gentlemen about his citadel, and they did not inspire their less favored brethren and their white task-masters to hard, self-denying discipline.

Occasionally Sutter would give an even more salient demonstration of *caprice de grand seigneur*. Nicolaus Allgeier lived on Feather River with a young squaw who suddenly got tired of him and began to rebel. He brought her to Justice Sutter, asking him to throw her in the calaboose until she repented. But as soon as Allgeier had returned to his ranch, the tender-hearted Justice to the great amusement of the colony, accommodated the prisoner in his own household. As often as Allgeier came near the fort, the young squaw was locked up again, and he was told that she had not reformed. She soon became one of the favorites at court, and the boorish German was at last obliged to take another wife.

It was a pretty thorough state of promiscuity. He who had not brought along with him a white woman had no choice but to satisfy himself with squaws. There were none but squaw-men in the interior of California. John Chamberlain, for instance, Sutter's Irish blacksmith, was said to have been successively 'married' to no less than nineteen Indian women. He was the prize buck of the settlement, and at least once, when Sutter went to Yerba Buena, he left his *majordomo* specific instructions 'to have a sharp eye on Chamberlain' to prevent him from 'entering the appartment of the girls.'

As for Sutter, he was in some ways remarkably constant in his devotions. For five or six years Manaiki, one of the two Kanaka women, remained his favorite and was regarded as his wife proper. We have it on the authority of Henry Lienhard, his *majordomo* of later years, that she bore her master several children, and that beside her a number of squaws were delighted whenever some one recognized in their half-white infants the image of their great white chief. But all these wild sprouts succumbed to the frequent epidemics of small-pox and typhoid fever.[7]

The frontier was never half so romantic as those who sought it first imagined. It was more often stark tedium, and all the laws of civilized life soon were reduced to hurdles to be taken in an effort to break down the monotony and drudgery of frontier life.

Here, as elsewhere, the price of conquest was submission to the spirit of the vanquished.

19. *NO END OF TROUBLE*

THERE were long periods when squaw love was about the only comfort of the wilderness-dweller, and it was earned and paid for with no end of trouble. As yet Sutter's efforts to settle the Sacramento Valley with permanent ranchers had met with little success. Too many of the men who came to California were inveterate rovers, and the voices that warned against him buzzed like the undying chorus of the crickets. They called him a fool for trying to live in the interior and so they had to do their best to prove him a fool.

It is doubtful, therefore, whether by 1843 Sutter had complied with the settler clause of his land-grant. John Sinclair, 'a talented man and capital company where grog and cards were stirring,'

lived outside of New Helvetia. On his own land Sutter had settled Pablo Gutierez, Theodore Cordua, John Smith, Nicolaus
Allgeier, Sebastian Keyser and a few others. But some of these
soon tired of their lonely ranches and returned to work at the fort.
Sutter's Hock Farm on Feather River was now in charge of John
Bidwell, and a German, William Benitz, looked after Sutter's interest at the former Russian settlements. Charles Flügge parted
company with Sutter at the end of 1843, having lost faith in the
success of the settlement and in Sutter's ability to pay.

For Sutter's difficulties were incredible. He was sorely in need
of credit. Though he did everything in his power to forge ahead,
circumstances invariably turned against him. Ross and Bodega he
had bought as a source of ready lumber otherwise hard to obtain.
Yet the best of the Russian structures defied dismantling—the
immense *eras*, threshing floors, for instance, built most substan-
tially of handhewn redwood planks, 6 inches thick and so perfectly matched together that they would hold water. Their sides
were about 8 feet high. Their diameters varied from 200 to 300
feet. But they were so well joined with huge Russian nails that it
was quite impossible to break them apart without ruining the lumber. Sutter tried to raft one of these giant threshing arenas whole
down the coast, across the bay, and up the Sacramento, but it
foundered on the rocks before it reached the entrance to the bay.

The best of the Russian houses were equally well made. Hence
the greater part of this vast store of lumber, which should have
gone into the buildings of New Helvetia and for which Sutter had
mortgaged all he had, remained for the weather to play havoc
with and a prey to wild fires. Such was generally Sutter's luck.

Because of the lack of proper equipment he had been unable to
pay the Russians a full instalment of wheat in 1842. In 1843 he
doubled his efforts, only to find that the very heavens turned
against him. The Russians received no wheat at all this year. The

shadow of sadness began to spread over Sutter's usually optimistic correspondence. His debt to the Russians had increased not only because interest on it was accumulating, but also because the cost of sending a ship and crew in vain from Sitka to Yerba Buena was charged against him.

In 1844 the skies played even worse pranks on the ever hopeful Swiss. Intent on making good all his obligations, he put into the ground no less than 2,000 bushels of wheat. But for months after there was no rain and the sky gleamed like polished steel. The settlers watched, they almost prayed for rain. Hope rose again in spring when they observed that the next change of the moon was to take place at midnight—a sign of rain which had never been known to fail. And actually—a little fleecy cloud appeared, another, the sky turned grey, there was a little pleasant patter on the hard caked soil and shingled roofs. But that was all. The sight of the sun became hateful. Of the 2,000 bushels of seed only 150 pushed through the soil, bringing a harvest of again 150 bushels. But where the seed had been good plump kernels, the harvest yielded dwarfed shrunken wheat.

Still the pioneer kept up his faith. With his clear blue eyes pinned on the far horizons of hope, he started again right from the beginning. Sending out to various places along the coast and around the bay, he 'picked up,' as Bidwell says, 'a little seed-wheat here and there to sow for another harvest.'

There was no scarcity of other trouble in 1844. In April Sutter was sued by William G. Rae, Yerba Buena agent of the Hudson's Bay Company, for the sum of $3,322 which Sutter owed the company. In June another claim was filed; but as all Sutter's property was already mortgaged, nothing could be done.

Then, because Sutter still owed the tonnage dues for the Russian ship which in the fall had come from Alaska on a wild goose chase, the harbor authorities put an embargo on his launch. Only after some pitifully frantic writing did Sutter succeed in redeeming the vessel. But in the autumn, when the Russian ship made its second vain voyage to Yerba Buena, he could only extricate himself from the severe embarrassment arising out of new tonnage dues by boldly making out a check on the Custom House at Monterey! *'Un grande impostura'* the customs chief at the capital termed the move in his rebuke to the subordinate at Yerba Buena who had accepted Sutter's draft.

Eulogio Célis, who once before had caused an embargo to be put on Sutter's launch, proceeded anew against him. And Vallejo was prompted to write to him, 'not officially, but as a private individual' that, as long as this affair with Célis remained unsettled, Sutter could never send his launch to the bay without risking another embargo. Henceforth the *Sacramento* sailed armed like a man-of-war.

In June the troublesome launch was washed on the rocks at Bodega and caused great damage to Sutter and a few of his men. It took two weeks to get her afloat and repaired.

There was other trouble at Bodega. Stephen Smith from Baltimore, a former sea-captain, had come to California with the first steam-engine and the first three pianos. He had obtained permission to settle at Bodega, where, towards the end of 1844, his steam grist- and sawmill began operating. On the strength of his doubtful deed to the former Russian lands given him by Alexander Rotscheff, Sutter made some ineffective demonstrations against Smith and a few other settlers who had been given grants by the government in the Bodega region. How desperate he must have felt! Once more he resorted to utterly naive, impotent threats: if Bodega was not given back to him, a Russian man-of-war would come to his assistance.[8]

His situation became increasingly critical. The meager rivulets of credit were drying up and there were times when he had to stoop to humiliatingly beseeching letters for mere morsels of credit. His rich but undeveloped empire was in danger of being starved out of existence by drought and personal enemies.

More often than before, Sutter now resorted to turning his Indians into cash by hiring them out and by selling orphan children. In California this was no uncommon business. Antonio Suñol, among others, was always glad to accept Indian labor in trade. Sutter sent him some in June and wrote: 'When you no longer need the Indians, kindly notify me so that I can send the launch to bring them back. Some of these Indians have no shirts and I have not an ell of *Manta* left to have some made. You will greatly oblige me by providing them with shirts and charge me with the cost.'

In return, the good Suñol again advanced credit for 400 *arrobas* (10,000 lbs.) of dried meat and was promised payment in leather and hides. But when the next batch of leather came from the tanning vats of New Helvetia, 'it was not so good.' Suñol was asked to wait for the next batch, 'which will be the best that was ever tanned in California.' Suñol must receive the best 'for the sake of the *bon renomé*[!] that fine leather is produced on the Sacramento.'

Thus went on ad infinitum the tragicomedy of trying to maintain sufficient credit without paying too many debts.

Sutter's Cattle Brand

PART THREE

ARMS AND THE MAN

20. WAR CLOUDS

WHILE Sutter was thus wrestling with drought and debts, he was unnoticeably drawn upon a wider stage. East and west of the mountains, north and south of the Rio Grande, things were stirring. The great span of empire conceived at the very time of Sutter's birth by the father of American democracy was about to receive its concluding link. And Sutter was to be instrumental in its forging.

One day in early March 1844, while he was walking outside the fort over the hard-baked crevassed soil through which the wheat had never pushed, two human skeletons wearing Scotch caps (and little else) rode up to him on phantom horses. They were John Charles Frémont, the leader of a United States exploring expedition, and his mountain guide Kit Carson. Trying to find a road to California practicable for immigrant trains and military columns, Frémont and his party had become snow-bound in the region of Lake Tahoe. He knew that just beyond the forbidding barrier of ice and snow lived Sutter, 'the possessor of a principality.' After weeks of horrid battling with the elements, fatigue, cold and starvation, he had succeeded in winning his way 'to the perpetual spring of the Sacramento.' An Indian had that morning shown him the way to Sutter's Fort.

Captain Sutter, Frémont reports, 'gave us a most frank and cordial reception—conducted us immediately to his residence—and under his hospitable roof we had a night of rest, enjoyment, and refreshment, which none but ourselves could appreciate.'

After Frémont's corps had caught up with him, they made their camp at the mouth of the American River, availing themselves of all the opportunities New Helvetia offered for rest, recuperation, refitting and repairs. 'An impetus was given to the active little population by our arrival, as we were in want of everything,' continues Frémont. 'Mules, horses, and cattle were to be collected; the horse-mill was at work day and night, to make sufficient flour; the blacksmith's shop was put in requisition for horse-shoes, and bridle-bits and pack-saddles, ropes, and bridles, and all the other little equipment of the camp, were again to be provided.'

What Sutter lacked in his own store-houses—especially flour—he sent for. His couriers flew off in all directions. The launch made a special trip to Yerba Buena in order that nothing should be lacking. In the hands of any other man, this visit of the little host of explorers reduced to skeletons, and the thousand things they were in need of, might easily have been conducive to a boom. But, as at the time of Lieutenant Emmons' visit, the Lord of New Helvetia was but too apt to forget the urgent needs of the debt-ridden trader of the Sacramento. To be sure this time he could not afford to make presents of all the things furnished to the American party; but he supplied them at cost, if not below. Frémont paid him in drafts on the United States Topographical Bureau. But these drafts Sutter was later forced to dispose of at a discount of one fifth of their face value, after the newly appointed United States Consul in Monterey, Thomas Oliver Larkin, had apparently been willing to cash them for even less.[1]

Altogether, Sutter was to get scant reward for all he did for Frémont. This son of a French immigrant and of an American mother was a fair epitome of everything unflattering other nations said about the Americans of those days. He was arrogant, ambitious, taking a thousand favors for granted, while his long memory tenaciously hugged unpleasant trifles and little adversities.

Frémont departed on March 24 after a three weeks' stay. Sutter, in compliance with his official duties, had notified Governor Micheltorena of Frémont's presence in the department. However, he had diplomatically put off his report long enough to avoid difficulties between the trigger-tempered Mexicans and the mulish Frémont, and by the time a military command under Lieutenant-Colonel Rafael Tellez came kicking up the dust of New Helvetia to inquire about the American officer's business, the latter was well on his way back to the United States.

For these were the days when the relations between Mexico and the United States were almost ruptured by the events in Texas, that one-time Mexican province wrenched loose and declared independent in 1836 by American settlers. Just now, in 1844, Congress in Washington openly discussed whether the Republic of Texas should or should not be invited to join the Union as a state, the result being, of course, that from coast to coast the atmosphere became saturated with talk and threats of war. Not only that. On the Mexican side arose intense fear that the foreigners in California, that remote and unprotected province, might repeat the example of their Texan compatriots. For this reason, in July Governor Micheltorena received instructions from Mexico to organize a California auxiliary army, the *defensores de la patria*. Soon after Sutter was made commander of the Sacramento troops with the rank of Captain and thus, at last, received his first genuine military title.

Without delay he went to work pressing the men of his valley into his new corps. Two trained old soldiers in his employ attended to the drill. One was Ernest Rufus, a German, the other a fellow-Swiss from Basle, Jacob Green, alias Jacob Dürr, who had actually served in the Royal Swiss Guard of France of which

Sutter had so much to tell, although, one suspects, never in Dürr's presence.

In the midst of these warlike preparations, on August 5 or 6, 1844, arrived the first immigrants of the season, the Kelsey party from Oregon, numbering thirty-six men, women and children. Sutter now hoped for a much larger contingent of newcomers in the fall. Quite unreasonably, stubbornly disregarding the impossibility of accomplishing a round trip within a year, he counted on the return of Lansford Hastings with a train of wagons and the promised army of 1,000, including artisans, lawyers and physicians.

Sutter's fervid expectations are easily understood. For more and more the continued existence of New Helvetia depended on the question whether good artisans were obtainable or not. Bitter experience had taught him that only a small percentage of all arrivals was of some value to him or to anybody else. There was always much that the immigrants found not to their liking in California: the Spanish-Mexican population, the lack of timber and rainfall, and the unsettled political future of the land. Every spring, therefore, many of these malcontents journeyed north again to Oregon, only to be met somewhere on the trail by a similar band of paradise hunters who had failed to find what they were looking for in Oregon. That territory (still jointly managed by England and the United States) was too rainy, too British and in general too raw to offer sinecures. For it was an obsession with many of these rovers that the inhuman hardships of the overland trip conferred on them a brief for a lifetime of ease and abundance.

In the Department of Alta California itself political trouble was secretly brewing. For some time, dissatisfaction with Micheltorena had been rife and rankling in the blood of native sons. Not by any means because of any of the Governor's shortcomings, but simply because he was a Mexican—practically a foreigner to them. But they were hostile chiefly because his presence in the seat of power deprived the Californians of the opportunity of dipping their hands to their hearts' content into the trough of departmental revenues. Moreover, the 'bastard army,' the *cholos*, which the Governor had brought from Mexico, was particularly and rightly irksome to local pride and now furnished a convenient excuse for starting one of those artificial quarternary fevers in the body politic.

Of this nascent conspiracy Sutter remained ignorant. After having for almost two years maintained a friendly correspondence with the Governor, he, now, in October 1844, at last prepared to undertake the long-delayed trip to Monterey for his first interview with Micheltorena. For some time the thought of rounding out his possessions had been on his mind. The day might come, and was conceivably quite near, when land-grants could no longer be so easily procured. What Sutter desired above all was a supplementary deed to his New Helvetia grant. This latter entitled him to regard as his, within certain natural boundaries, eleven square leagues of his own choice. The supplementary title which he coveted was to grant him *all* the land within those boundaries, some of these marginal or *sobrante* lands to be reserved for his children in Switzerland, some to compensate him for his losses at Bodega.[2]

John Bidwell accompanied him on this trip, and they were followed by an escort of armed servants. No caballero would travel otherwise. But they did not gallop *ventre à terre*, the only way a Californian ever rode a horse. Their mounts were reined; for Sutter never was a dashing equestrian. And he must not stir up too much dust either, especially at San José, lest Suñol become aware of his debtor's presence. For as soon as rumors went abroad that Sutter had left the fort for any destination, his creditors were likely to follow him.

Sutter did call, though, on the British Vice-Consul James

Alexander Forbes at San José. From him he first heard of the impending revolt against Micheltorena, and the news proved a severe shock to Sutter. He cared intensely only for the pomp and splendor of military life, but not for the strictly professional side of war, of which he understood nothing. At once he poured forth his sorrows and apprehensions in a long letter to his *majordomo* Pierson Reading,[3] the essence of which was: 'Do not deliver anything to nobody, and not even respect an order of the Government, and if you see that it will be necessary, send all the Cattle and Horses, Manadas etc. up to P.Lassen or even further, and in the case they should keep me, raise all the foreigners you can and a strong body of Indians and make a Mouvement toward here. . . . Be on your Guarde. . . .'

It is by no means the letter of a thoroughbred man of arms, but that of an over-anxious civilian whose business affairs stand little chance of surviving the shocks of a revolution.

The matter had its compensations. Being the first to inform the Governor of the plot against him, Sutter was doubly well received at the capital. Micheltorena, a tall stately man, was of an urban mind, liberal and very obliging, and he had the gift of regarding his secret fun at the ridiculous pettiness of the Californians as ample reward for the many troubles of his office. It was natural, therefore, that the spontaneous friendship between the two worldly foreigners in the self-sufficient, stagnant atmosphere of California quickly consolidated into a gentlemen's agreement: Sutter pledged himself to render military assistance to the Governor whenever he should call for it, and Micheltorena promised to repay such support with a new land-grant.

Sutter spent most of his few days in Monterey in making numerous purchases from armaments to a new wardrobe. He recruited a little band of artisans to take back to New Helvetia: a pump-maker, a cooper and a cook (both Negroes), a German brewer, a 'German blacksmith which is a great Mécanique,' and others; a motley crew which no-one, when it was lined up in front of Mr. Spence's house, would believe he could ever hold in check.

With particular delectation Sutter steeped himself in the honors paid him by the Governor. 'The Governor invited me several times to the Caffé,' he wrote home to Reading,[4] 'and the last Sunday I was invited with about 6 of his first Officers to a splendid Diner, and the troups was mustered on my account etc. and [he] visited me in Mr. Spences house.' And in his Reminiscences he adds that 'everywhere it was regarded as extraordinary that a foreigner should be so intimate with him.'

During one of these days Micheltorena and his official retinue, including Sutter, paid the officers of the U.S. man-of-war *Savannah*, then at anchor at Monterey, a formal visit, concerning which the surgeon of the ship, William Maxwell Wood, has left a remarkable little thumbnail sketch. He writes:

Among the persons in the suite of General Micheltorena, when he visited the ship, was a man of medium or rather low stature, but with a marked military air. He wore a cap, and a plain blue frock coat, a moustache covered his lips. His head was of a very singular formation, being flat and wall-shaped behind, and rising high over the crown, with a lofty and expanded forehead. His manners were courteous, but displayed great precision. Such was Captain Sutter, a Swiss by birth. . . . He controls all within the extent of several hundred miles. . . . The Mexican Government became exceedingly jealous of his powers and influence; but not having sufficient power to suppress him, made virtue of necessity, and acknowledged his authority as military governor of the neighborhood . . .

So great was the personal fascination of the imposing little Swiss that the trained eye of a U.S.N. surgeon, which so keenly analyzed the ill-proportioned cranium of the man, could yet mistake him for a martial blue-blood and military paragon.

Meanwhile, Sutter received impressions no less profound. The utter ceremoniousness of formalities, the solemn diplomatic toasts at table, but above all the ship's band were, as he wrote, to him 'an overwhelming pleasure.' He was, in fact, so spellbound that he missed his boat, the *Sterling*, on which, to avoid falling into the hands of Micheltorena's enemies after having so publicly hob-nobbed with the Governor, he had booked passage for Yerba Buena. She sailed without him, but not without his baggage and armaments. After a futile attempt to overtake the *Sterling* in a rowboat, he returned to the *Savannah*, on which he spent the night, and sailed the following day on the *Don Quixote*. His escort, meanwhile, and his newly recruited working gang he sent back to New Helvetia on the land route. Only Bidwell stayed at the capi-tal a few weeks longer to attend to business.

But already the hornets were buzzing. Having evaded Suñol at San José on his trip south and given him a wide berth on his way home, Sutter, on his arrival at Yerba Buena, found the Bernal brothers, Suñol's in-laws and partners, lying in ambush for him. They had anticipated tricks and would not miss this chance to voice their sentiments in the face of their elusive debtor. Staunch new promises, however, pacified them once more. Sutter prom-ised to pay his entire debt in beaver-skins, the most coveted tender; or, if the season's yield of beaver should be insufficient, in cattle. 'This is all I can do,' he then wrote to Suñol, 'and not even the Government will compel me to do otherwise.'

Then he transferred his baggage from the *Sterling* to his own launch. But barely had he set sail on his little craft when an order for his arrest reached Yerba Buena from José Castro, one of the leaders of the insurrection. By a hair's-breadth Sutter escaped.

With this abortive attempt to capture the unpopular *Suizo*, the revolt against Micheltorena began.

21. SKIRMISHES

ALL internal bouts in California were in the nature of an *opéra bouffe*. Soon after Sutter's return to his fort, the insurgents fell upon Monterey and drove away the cavalry horses belonging to the government. Micheltorena pursued the robbers for several days without success, and then returned to his capital.

This first coup of the insurgents, the horse capture, resulted in the Treaty of Santa Teresa. Micheltorena had to agree to remove the chief eyesore, his *cholos*, by sending them back to Mexico. In return the Californians promised to give him no further trouble. Suspicion and animosity, however, once aroused, would not subside in spite of the peace treaty. Micheltorena had strong reasons to believe that the disbanding of his army could only mean sawing off the branch he sat on. So he deferred disbanding, with the result that presently the ugliest names rose from both camps like swarms of croaking ravens.

New Helvetia, too, was thrown into a feverish turmoil. This was the season for plowing and sowing. The last two crops had failed. A military campaign at this moment, therefore, meant the almost certain forfeiture of a large part of next year's harvest—a burdensome cost for a doubtful victory. No wonder Sutter, who had never hesitated to swing the cudgel of foreign intervention over California, was at first deeply alarmed over the possibility of actual war.

Yet he decided to enter the arena as Micheltorena's ally. No matter what might be said in favor of the Californians, they rebelled; not for any ideal cause, but simply for the departmental loaves and fishes. Moreover, they were not Sutter's friends. On the other hand he had received from Mexico a little empire, and since he had also been made a captain of the *defensores*, his boyish heart was not devoid of pride or thankfulness towards his superior government. A life-long ambition had been fulfilled. And had he not, since his earliest youth, been passionately day-dreaming of the military life? So the lure was great to indulge for once in the glamor, the romanticism, the adventurousness and perhaps even the heroism of battle.

And there was more to it. After two years of drought Sutter was wading deeper than ever in debts. Who knows but that for this reason he did not welcome war as a relief from the dull, painful stringency at home and possibly expected a victory over the Californians to annihilate the crushing burden of his obligations?

At all events his sense of realism could not but be warped under these various affections. He overlooked the fact that the other foreign settlers, above all the Americans, upon whose support he depended, could not be enthusiastic for a government with which their own country might at that very moment be at war.

There was now daily drill at the fort. Agents were sent out all over the country to sign up the settlers far and near. And this presently led to an epistolary duel between Sutter and Vallejo. The latter had long made it a rule to embrace neutrality whenever war threatened to shake him up from his comfortable armchair or when the possibility of choosing the wrong winner might endanger his possessions. Now it was Sutter's propaganda among the settlers of the Sonoma district which stung Vallejo. Though he himself had often enough tried to meddle in the internal affairs of New Helvetia, he would not think of suffering any like attempt on Sutter's part. Here at last was presented to him the long-hoped-for, unparalleled opportunity to fall over his rival and undesirable neighbor, this *Suizo*, this foreign upstart! Not physically, of course; only on paper. If the *comandante* had completely forgotten the use of the sword, he at least had never stopped practice with the goose-quill.

So now he lunged forward with a grandiloquent snub which, as yet, was not too unfriendly: 'I am forced to assume,' he wrote to Sutter, 'that the rebels exist only in your feverish imagination; but even if there were a rebellion, I, who occupy the first place on this frontier and consider myself a patriot, could never tolerate that a subaltern of mine assume the initiative where I alone have to give orders.'

His martial indolence, however, did not prevent Vallejo from defending the right of his fellow-countrymen to clear the department of the Mexican convict army and in general to abet them. 'Or do you believe, Señor Sutter, that the wolf and the tiger can be trusted with the guarding of the sheep and the lambs? *Cierta-mente que no!* Likewise have I always believed, and still do believe, that the criminals and assassins which, to our disgrace, form the pretorian cohort of the señor general are not the people best suited to educate, enlighten, and protect the inhabitants of California!'

Sutter could but blunderingly parry Vallejo's broadsides. In Spanish, as in French and English, he was far from perfection. All the more reason there was for him to make ethics and not style the issue. The alternative was, he insisted, between supporting the legitimate government and becoming a rebel.

'Rebel?' Vallejo flared up. He would advise Sutter not to use this word and in its stead say 'a multitude of persons who in good faith demand of their government the remedy of its evils.' But his chief sorrow was the disgrace to the *gloria nacional* in the impending spectacle of a governor's marching against the country at the head of *'una banda de estrangeros.'*

Sutter replied bluntly: 'Your expressions are very strong! . . . and I have the honor to tell you that three fourths of those you call foreigners are Mexican citizens by naturalization and I think we have the same rights as the sons of the country. . . . We are not as sanguinary as you imagine . . . and the same native sons will yet thank us for the good we mean to do for California. . . .'

Thus, on December 21, the verbal skirmish ended.

Meanwhile, the eagerly awaited immigrants from the United States, the Elisha Stevens party, had arrived on the thirteenth of the month. There were about fifty men, a few women and many children. And they had brought the first wagons. It was these wagons whose tires marked the trail which henceforth was to be *the* emigrants' road from Fort Hall to Sutter's Fort.

Many of these newcomers were quickly pressed and coaxed into the creaking military machine of New Helvetia. Men who had been in the country for only two weeks now became *defensores de la patria*. But so powerful was the lure of the lands which Micheltorena promised to all his supporters that few could resist and many were brought into the net.

Sutter then made the first offensive move by sending out his men to drive the government horses stationed at Sonoma to the Sacramento. Too late: Vallejo had already delivered the *manada nacional* into the hands of the insurgents; so Sutter's raiders satisfied their lust for plunder by shooting one of Vallejo's cows and improvising a barbecue.

Blood, though only bovine blood, had flowed now, and speedily the tales of the 'atrocities of Sutter's band of foreigners' spread south like a nation-wide nightmare. From San José and Sonoma a vast outpour of lies, of which the Californians were past masters, was disseminated. Sutter, it was given out, intended to devastate the land 'with 150 adventurers and 2,000 savage Indians.' Or again that 'several thousand dangerous immigrants' had arrived at Sutter's Fort with families and such an outfit of arms as to render vain all thought of resistance.

When these tales of terror reached José Castro, he demanded

of Micheltorena an explanation of Sutter's activities, making it clear that war was inevitable if Sutter made any attempt to 'execute his sinister intentions.' The answer he received was perspicuously devious. Micheltorena had already sent Sutter the final order to march.

Sutter at once signaled his readiness and reported on the state of his army by a special courier, his trusted Mexican servant Pablo Gutierez from Santa Fe. The message was enclosed between the double soles of Pablo's boots especially designed for such service. But near San José the messenger was captured by Castro's men. Sutter's dispatches were found within the boots, and that day Pablo was dangling at the end of a rope on a tree.

Enough bad blood had now accumulated and events had to take their course. In vain did Charles M. Weber, Sutter's former employee who lived at San José, undertake a trip to the Sacramento with the intention of putting the insurgents' case before Sutter in his own language. He was at once thrown into the calaboose, and so were the two Hernandez brothers who had come with him. The hint was understood by others and even the most reluctant now enlisted.

When Vallejo saw that nothing would stop the clash between the two parties, he gave further evidence of his neutrality by discharging his command, so that they could augment the insurgent forces. Some of them, however, did join Sutter. Or was it rather those elements in Sutter's army which trotted along against their will and were determined to get on an even score with him at the first opportunity?

22. *THE ACTOR'S FAVORITE ROLE*

FEW actors of Napoleon's perfection in the art of make-believe were his equals also as soldiers and as statesmen. For five long years Sutter had deeply impressed the world in his imposing martial role. Indeed, he had perhaps begun to overlook the fact that he wore his tunic, rattled his sabre and threatened with his cannon merely as a brilliant actor. Now he was suddenly expected to give proof of his soldiership in a realistic test. Fortunately for him, California realities were as flimsily theatrical as anything behind footlights. The stage was thus set for a fine piece of comic warfare.

The total strength of Sutter's forces was about 200 men. Beside his duties as Commander-in-Chief he took charge of the artillery of one shining brass field-piece. A company of about 100 Indians, 'all armed with something,' was captained by the German Ernest Rufus, whose two lieutenants were the Swiss Jacob Dürr and Chief Rufino of the Mokelumne tribe. But the unit before which all California trembled was the company of mounted foreign riflemen commanded by Captain John Gantt, a loud-mouthed mountaineer who had been dismissed from the United States Army for 'knowingly signing false certificates with regard to pay.'

The fort was left in charge of Pierson B. Reading, a garrison of fifteen white men and thirty Indians.

On New Year's Day, 1845, *Comandante* Juan Augusto Sutter took leave of Manaiki, his exotic love. Then, having dispatched cavalry and artillery to the mouth of the San Joaquin River, he, with the infantry, embarked on his launch.

It was anything but a happy beginning. At the outset the martial spirit deserted Sutter. Only three miles from the fort, the civilian and farmer Sutter started pouring out his thoughts in letters to his *majordomo*.[5] And what, of all things, on the eve of his first war-like venture, should have monopolized his mind for several days? Victory? Glory? The stirring drumtaps? Not at all. First, domes-tic trifles which he ought to have attended to before departing. But above all Manaiki. It now occurred to him that he ought never to have left without having the lock on her door repaired. (His misgivings were not unfounded.) Her future kept on worry-ing him. He desired her to continue the enjoyment of her privi-leged position, even if he should never return. 'In case I should be killed,' he wrote to Reading from the camp on the San Joaquin, 'you will see that Manaiki receive her wages comming to her until the last day of her being at the Establishment.' Manaiki was the one thing or person whose possible loss filled him with concern. He wrote of her with the tenderness of a peasant and almost in the language of elementary symbols: 'Every year Manaiki make a Garden of her own, . . . she have always the best and largest Melons and Watermelons. . . .'

But while his paramour kept him preoccupied, his armed strength was being diligently undermined. John Gantt, the cap-tain of his foreign riflemen, allowed a message brought by Cas-tro's emissaries to circulate freely among the men. Worst of all, Sutter himself bit off his nose to spite his face by forcing John Marsh to join the ranks. Marsh, miser, squaw-man, misanthrope, Harvard graduate and the most formidably well-read man in Cal-ifornia, knew but two gods: Money and Privacy. Yet, when the *defensores de la patria* were organized, Sutter could not refrain from making it plain to Marsh[6] that he, too, would be 'called upon to bear arms and in case of delinquency . . . made to serve ten years in the regular army.' He knew, of course, that this must irk Marsh the Yankee and the hermit. Still, he continued: 'Of course, we are all good citizens and ever ready to *obey* the man-dates of the glorious Mexican Republic.'

After preliminaries such as these, there arrived, on January 3, 1845, a courier at Marsh's with the following message:

Sɪʀ

I hereby order you to deliver to Salinez (the bearer) two bullocks to kill, also one yoke of oxen to assist me in leaving this place.
Landing at the San Joaquin Jan 3rd 1845.
I have the honor to be

Yours

J.A.Sᴜᴛᴛᴇʀ

Comander in Chief of the
Forces of the River Sacramento

It is not recorded with what feelings these lines were received by the same John Marsh who, two years later, wrote under the signature of a high United States naval commander who sent him a similar scrap of paper, 'a most unequivocal jackass.' The fact is that on the same day the animals required of him arrived at Sutter's camp.

Two days later Marsh himself was ordered to report, and, remembering that his friend Charles M. Weber sat in the dungeon of New Helvetia, he promptly appeared and enlisted—and, like the Pope's mule, bided his time to kick. His impressment was to prove Sutter's greatest blunder.

About January 9 Sutter's army joined the regular troops of General Micheltorena at Salinas. Castro and ex-Governor Alvarado and a handful of their followers had fled south to Los Angeles. (Los Angeles was situated, as Sutter once explained in a letter, 'near San Pedro and San Diego.') There they spread more of their gargantuan lies about the 'atrocities of Sutter's foreign legion' and his ferocious Indians, although as a matter of form they had notified Sutter's men through Suñol and Forbes that they would refuse to fight them.

All this was in the orthodox tradition of California, where wars and revolutions were humane affairs, staged with all due regard to potential comedy, and where the final clash seldom amounted to more than a laying on the table of all the cards, in order that it could be argued who would win if the game were really played.

In Los Angeles, meanwhile, a quorum of the *Junta* or Assembly was convoked. Micheltorena was 'deposed' and Pio Pico, the chairman of the gathering, proclaimed Governor. The election of this old, bombastic individual with the appearance of a shriveled clown constituted the first major casualty of this comic warfare. 'Ye Gods!' exclaimed a resident of Santa Barbara when he heard the news, 'The idea of Pio Pico being dignified with the title of Excellency is almost too ridiculous to be true.'

Micheltorena, although determined to stamp out the insurrection, was not in a hurry; for he was ailing. All the more thoroughly could the subversive elements in Sutter's army indulge in their activities. Sutter's report on this ramshackle force was anything but rosy. There was constant friction between him and the *comité* or soldiers' council, and the camp heard 'a great deal of Grumbling and growling . . . about some Comforts which cannot be secured.' [7]

Within a month, Micheltorena's army had at the rate of seven miles a day advanced as far as Santa Barbara. Most of the time the weather was dismally cold and incessantly rainy, relieved, happily, by frequent comical interludes. Spies were caught and obligingly released again and told to go home to mother. Mission larders and cellars were treated unsparingly after a few lean days on the road.

It was during the short stay at Santa Barbara that Sutter approached Micheltorena again about the grant for which he had petitioned in October. And because he had since the beginning of the war preparations already accumulated new debts to the amount of $8,000 for equipment and maintenance of his army, the Governor, on February 5, gave him those marginal or *so-brante* lands for which he asked.[8] This new *Sobrante grant* made Sutter the legal owner of all the territory within the natural boundaries mentioned in his first or New Helvetia grant, all in all 33 square leagues or 229 square miles. No doubt the most pleasant interlude of the whole campaign!

Near Buena Ventura the first 'encounter' with the enemy's forces occurred. Sutter sent out a reconnoitering party of twenty-five riflemen who, the following day, returned with the stunning intelligence that they had all been captured by Castro, 'treated well, given drink . . . and released on giving their word not to take up arms again against the Californians.' Some of Sutter's men did not even wait to be captured and released on parole; they walked straight home without asking for leave. And others, remembering that in war, as in the cockpit, the only thing that matters is to pick the winner, deserted to the enemy.

Sutter, however, was apparently convinced that the great day of his first actual battle had now arrived. There was to be a devastating night attack on Buena Ventura. At sunset and in a torrent of rain he set out across the mountains, over ground so slippery as to cause men and horses to fall into ravines. Besides, about half of the men decided to linger behind and to sleep in the woods, and many of these absented themselves for good. Was it surprising, then, that at daybreak, when at last they approached Buena Ventura, Sutter's staff found it neither convenient nor advisable to follow him farther on the road to glory? 'Captain Gantt said he did not believe half the guns [would] go off,' reads Sutter's own description of this episode. 'Commandante Valdez did not think we were strong enough to make the attack; Estrada said he considered it no more a night attack, for it was now daylight.' Only Ernest Rufus, the German captain of the Indians, reported his natives ready and their powder dry.

By and by, some of the stragglers began to trickle in again and slowly to swell Sutter's following to somewhere near its former numeric strength, and he decided to risk an attack on the *pueblo* of Buena Ventura. He had been informed that the night before the inhabitants had celebrated the presence of Castro's army with a grand *fandango* and it was only reasonable to conclude that they were all lying abed now, half drunk and fast asleep.

So he did attack. 'The enemy were panic-stricken and fled. Seeing us coming out of the woods, they could not tell how many we were.' Unfortunately they were not nearly drunk enough to have forgotten the rules of California warfare. Presently they massed together in their flight, stopped, turned towards Sutter and his men, 'calling us thieves and all bad names,' as their martial code required. Only then did they continue their retreat. Much breath, but not a granule of powder had been wasted.

Sutter, if one may believe his word, would have liked to pursue. But his general, who had stayed far behind, sent word: 'No. Better go on all together.' 'If we had followed up our advantage,' Sutter continues in his tale, 'we could easily have routed them; but this was not the Mexican fashion. They must first have something to eat and drink.'

Quietly then, they took possession of the *pueblo*. The town band, which the night before had played for the Castro-Alvarado army, was obliging enough to furnish music also for the 'deposed' Governor-General, the hated Sutter, and the despicable foreign legion of the north. Indians with very long black hair and very short white shirts came to entertain them with their exotic dances. In the court of the San Antonio Mission stood a large cross to which, the inhabitants of the *pueblo* politely informed Sutter, he would be nailed if he were caught. And finally it was now the turn of Micheltorena's army to get drunk; with the result that during the night a great many horses were stolen.

Their next encounter, several days later, was with a woman reputed to be the mistress of Alvarado. With her was a little boy who had a lot of *tortillas* wrapped up in a cloth and he insisted on presenting them to Captain Gantt. Hidden in the *tortillas* was a cordial note from Alvarado and Castro for the foreign settlers under Gantt's command. They were invited to pay a visit to the other camp, shake hands and make friends with the Alvarado-Castro forces. Some German residents of Los Angeles sent a similar invitation to Sutter. But he declined emphatically: 'We do not serve for pay but out of conviction and free good will . . . the strangers there [in Los Angeles] make themselves guilty before the world if they take up arms against their friends and the legitimate government.' [9]

All this was part of the game.

The moment to play these cards was well chosen by the Californians. The long weary march, mostly in the cold rain, had completely demoralized the army of the north. Sutter's letter to Reading of February 15 tells a story entirely irreconcilable with the impression he later tried to convey in his Reminiscences. Here he depicts himself as the guiding spirit of the whole campaign: 'the whole responsibility fell upon me.' But in his letter:

'The General persists to attack them, and I am in a bad Situation . . . only a few will go with the General, the Forces of the Enemy are really the double of ours.' He is harassed by the fear that Castro might send some of his men north to attack New Helvetia. The increasing desertions and disobedience worry him. 'I can hardly describe you how bad I feel on account the behaviour of the Men of the camp. . . . The General was greatly deceived, but he will fight the battle and tomorrow Morning it will be done. . . . we are with the Indians about 300 Men, and the enemy have nearly or about the double strength. If I have luck to survive the day I shall endeavor to return so quick as possible.'

Such were the thoughts and feelings with which Sutter celebrated the forty-second anniversary of his birth. He was twice twenty-one now, and, indeed, the experiences of these days were to be for him a second coming-of-age. After all his boyish dreams of military glories, Sutter was now about to shake off in disillusionment some of the vestiges of an extended adolescence.

For seven weeks he and his army had now been on the road which seldom was a road. During all this time John Marsh had exercised his talents of persuasion, of gentle and ribald invective, of ridicule and satire against Sutter. Together with the weariness of the slow march and the inclemencies of the season, nothing more effective could have been devised to undermine completely the morale of the Micheltorena-Sutter forces. When, therefore, the grand moment came for putting the cards on the table, the conventional argument—who would have won if the game had been played—was quickly settled.

But this last argument, too, followed firm rules in California. The aspects of war must be preserved, though bloodshed was frowned upon. A rigid etiquette demanded that the political farce be played with the mask of tragedy or of decorous heroism.

23. *CAHUENGA*

THE tales spread in the south of the 'atrocities' of the Micheltorena-Sutter forces showed the desired result. Micheltorena aimed at nothing less than the total destruction of the *pueblo*; Sutter's ferocious Indians were granted every male scalp; to Micheltorena's *cholos* were allotted the women and maidens of the city of the angels; and Sutter himself had sworn to deliver to his general the heads of Alvarado and Castro, dead or alive, on a silver platter.[10]

So ran the tales. Almost the last man of the South able to stand on his legs joined the Alvarado-Castro army. A company of forty American mountaineers under William O'Fallon who had just arrived in Los Angeles was easily enlisted under the influence of lies, wine, food and flattery. Besides, what casual American, in those days of the Texas dispute, would not have known his place when a Mexican general was to be fought?

The date was February 19, 1845, when Micheltorena's army came again near the enemy. The place was Cahuenga, a ranch belonging to the San Fernando mission in the desolate highlands north of Los Angeles. A few miles below, the Castro camp could be seen from a near hill. Two hours after dark a messenger from Alvarado delivered the formal challenge to fight, and Micheltorena promised an answer in the morning at the point of his bayonets.

The night on these heights was distressing. The wind blew down the tents. Dust and sand provided torture. But at daybreak Micheltorena and Sutter marched with drum and fife towards the enemy—towards that region which today is known as North Hollywood and Universal City. Long before mankind dreamed of the blessings of celluloid romances, the genius loci of filmland manifested itself in a sham battle which was now to take place between exemplary stagers.

When the two armies were close enough to each other, the artillery began playing a rousing overture. The Alvarado-Castro forces had three cannon; Micheltorena four, one of which belonged to Sutter. The cannonade was perfectly harmless and did not last over two hours. Small fire-arms, too easy to aim with at any target and therefore too dangerous, were ruled out on both sides. Altogether it was a perfect *simulacro de combato*. The accidental losses amounted to one mule in Micheltorena's camp and two horses on the Californians' side. Other equally dependable statistics, however, arrived at the grand total of one broken cannon wheel and one ripped-off mule's tail.

But the pretence of battle was carefully guarded. Accordingly, Micheltorena ordered Sutter to push forward a vanguard of Americans who were to occupy a deep and winding gulch within rifle-shot of the opposing forces. No orders to open rifle fire were given.

Even in such a shadow-fight this proved a severe blunder. For no sooner did these Americans under John Gantt come near enough to the enemy's advanced lines than they discovered that the men staring at them were not Californians, but fellow-Americans at least as many in number as they were.

This was the moment 'Doctor' Marsh had been waiting for. He suggested that relations be at once established with their compatriots on the other side. No-one saw anything unusual in his advice. In fact, in a situation like this it was no doubt the thing to do.

The Americans on Castro's side had not overlooked the commotion at the upper end of the little canyon. They at once dispatched a delegation under a flag of truce, which was cheerfully received by their American brethren from the north. In an instant the pretence of battle was forgotten and the gulch was turned into a lively rialto where news and gossip were exchanged and where old friends slapped each other on the back.

Similar scenes of charming intimacy between enemies were played in other corners of the battlefield. 'Captain' Isaac Graham, a dubious and rarely sober American, was also directed by Micheltorena to occupy an advanced position, where he was caught napping by Joaquin de la Torre and a few other natives. 'Don't kill me!' Graham called out in fright. And his captor, jumping from his horse and embracing the American in martial fashion, replied graciously: 'Captain, how could I kill you? you are my friend.' 'And thus,' ends the narrator of this interlude, the captor's brother

Estaban, 'was cemented a very strong friendship between these two men.'

The Governor's Mexican dragoons, however, getting wind of the trend of the battle, began to desert in large numbers.

Micheltorena, noticing that his American riflemen were not advancing farther, sent Sutter and Bidwell after them. Sutter arrived just at the moment when Private John Marsh, practising fine eloquence, stirred the men to mutiny when the latter were democratically taking a ballot.

'What are you doing here?' Sutter shouted at Gantt. 'Why do you not advance?'

'We are voting to see who is for one side and who for the other,' Gantt replied.

Sutter, ineffectually standing on his authority, insisted angrily: 'This is the time to fight and not to vote!'

At this juncture, O'Fallon's party of American hunters came over from the Californians' side and joined in the noisy discourse, trying to dissuade Gantt's riflemen from continuing their support of Micheltorena. 'Let the Mexicans and Californians fight it out between themselves!' was soon the general opinion. Only Sutter and a few others dissented.

Meanwhile, Bidwell acted as liaison officer between this American debating club and Micheltorena. Alas, what could the general do but finally allow his Americans to withdraw from the battlefield, provided the Americans from the other side departed with them?

Just as Bidwell brought Micheltorena's message, a large group of Californians and Americans came galloping towards the little canyon. Sutter and Bidwell, therefore, who had made themselves decidedly unpopular on this rankling spot, deemed it wise to retreat towards the safer neighborhood of Micheltorena. But before their horses had carried them very far, the two saw themselves hedged in by a group of Californians demanding their surrender. 'Had they known who I was,' maintains Sutter, 'they would have cut me in small pieces.' Fortunately for him, Antonio Castro, José's brother, appeared in time. He prevented these ignoramuses from violating martial etiquette and brought the grand battle of Cahuenga to a culmination worthy of the spirit of the land.

As Sutter reports this scene:

'Antonio Castro came up and recognized me and said to the men, "I will take your prisoner." He saluted me and said, "I am very glad you are here." '

' "Yes," said I, "But I am not." '

'Then he said he should have to send to Alvarado, and accordingly he sent his *vaquero*. We rode a short distance. . . .' When Alvarado appeared, 'we dismounted and he embraced me like an old friend. Alvarado then ordered his *vaquero* to give him the bottle. He had a bottle of good *aguardiente* and we took a drink, then he sent his *vaquero* after Castro. Castro came up.

'Alvarado said to him, "Dismount and salute Captain Sutter." '

'We dismounted and there was more embracing. Then we all mounted and I rode between Castro and Alvarado in a hollow square of Californians, who looked at me as though they would like to eat me up, to the adobe at Cahuenga, where I was incarcerated in a dark room and held prisoner. I left my little double rifle before the door and this was gone forever—splendid arm.'

Men and women from the neighborhood came to stare at the big bad wolf from the Sacramento.

'I thought to myself, "this looks bad." '

Sutter also felt that his captors had not acted up to his dignity, because they had given him a guard of common *vaqueros*. When, therefore, an officer came in . . . 'I said: "You can do me a favor. Tell them they know nothing of the usages of war to put an officer of my rank under a common guard." '

The complaint was effective. Sutter was given back his sword and asked to join a group of Californian officers drinking in an adjoining room. Among these was John Rowland, a wealthy American farmer, who at once offered bond for Sutter's security and conducted him to more comfortable quarters in Los Angeles. The following morning Micheltorena, because the Americans on the opposing side broke their parole, was forced to hoist a white flag. A friendly parley ensued. The Mexican general, having to admit that he had too poor a hand to prolong the game, graciously conceded the victory to the native sons. But he was allowed to march from the battlefield and through Los Angeles with drums and music and flying colors; then, having been formally disarmed, he embarked for Monterey to fetch his wife, to clear his desk and say good-bye to his many friends.

Sutter remained imprisoned in the comfortable house of Abel Stearns, a friendly American merchant of Los Angeles, but on the second and third days was allowed to go visiting. He took walks in the yard with Juan Bandini, the Secretary of State of the new government; he was invited to play billiards with him, for which diversion, however, he was not in the proper frame of mind.

There was reason for his concern. All others, his aides, his officers and men enjoyed complete freedom. He alone was treated as a prisoner. Alarming rumors reached him. Some of the heads of the revolutionary government seemed to advocate reducing his short length by one head. Some were for fusillading him. Others proposed exile and confiscation of his property. But all such measures would have been contrary to the treaty of peace with Micheltorena.

At last Juan Bandini, a kindly, cultured man, solved the difficulty by asking Sutter for his motives in supporting Micheltorena. With naive cunning, Sutter now reared for his defence a breastwork of official ethics and of fealty. He could not but have obeyed orders from his General and his Governor! In his rambling narrative he tells how he succeeded with some difficulty in producing Micheltorena's written order to march. But these are trimmings of his virile fancy. The records clearly indicate that even when Sutter was called to defend his conduct before the heads of the new regime, he had nothing but oral explanations to offer—no lines from Micheltorena.

It is, therefore, surprising that the pasteboard ramparts behind which he took his stand were respected by his enemies—Surprising? Well, perhaps not. Here, too, the play was the thing! Sutter was now informed that his behavior had been quite correct and irreproachable, and he was asked to support the new regime with the same blind zeal. He took the oath of allegiance, was reinstated in all his offices and redecorated with his sonorous titles. A beautifully penned document resembling a diploma was given him to this effect, old grudges were temporarily washed down with plenty of *aguardiente*, 'and all of us were happy.'

Thus ended the inglorious military adventure of a man who all his life had been longing for the braided cloth, the rattling and flashing of sabres and the booming of cannon.

The peace, of course, was patchwork. Despite all the *aguardiente* in which the hostilities were drowned, Sutter remained *persona non grata*. The Californians refused to help him to get home with the men who were still with him. He had no money to buy provisions; he had no horses; he was stranded in Los Angeles.

A German cooper by the name of Mumm who, until a year before, had been in Sutter's employ and experienced much kindness at New Helvetia, finally offered him thirty horses on credit. The government, too, then relented a little and gave him an order on the San Fernando mission with which to buy a meal of mush for the Indians. For the rest, Sutter and his men depended on the horseflesh of the wild manadas of the Tulare valley.

Hunger or the fear of hunger was their constant companion on the way home. They left Los Angeles about March 18 and after two weary and dreary weeks reached New Helvetia, as Gantt says sarcastically, 'with their hearts on the ground; down tumbled all the air built castles and most dreadful was the crash.' [11]

False rumors of Sutter's death had preceded his return and the effect had not been to the best of his affairs, some of the whites at the fort having displayed great willingness to take the report as a cue to plunder New Helvetia.

So much remains true and was a supreme trump of irony that, inasmuch as Micheltorena and his army had been the answer of the Mexican Government to Sutter's threats of earlier years, he was now tossing about in the bed he had made for himself.

It was, however, left to the Californians themselves to give the finishing touch to the whole tragi-comic revolution. After having loudly proclaimed their independence from Mexico, they meekly cowered down again before the superior government as soon as they recovered from the katzenjammer of the victory celebrations.

24. ALL FOOLS' DAY

ONE of the most curious things about Sutter's life is the fact that circumstances were always ready to erect symbolical milestones along his path. January 1, the day of universal hope and optimism, he had set out on his campaign. He sneaked back into his fort on April 1—All Fools' Day.

Three months wasted; at least $8,000 thrown away; 150 horses lost in the absurd adventure! At home, meanwhile, three months had sufficed to let his empire go to seed. The home force of 15 whites and 30 Indians had turned Sutter's absence into three months of holidays with nothing to do but to defend the fort against the enemy who never came within 400 miles of it. For the first time in years the weather would have been favorable to agriculture, but not a clod had been turned, not a seed put out after Sutter's departure. Bill Daylor had meddled with his master's paramour.[12] And the tribes of the valley had reverted to savagery.

Wherever Sutter turned, whatever he saw and heard brought home to him the irony of his adventure in soldiership.

The backsliding of the Indians was the most serious of all the troubles meeting him at his gates. Two days after his return a few hundred Indigenes attacked the ranches of his far neighbors Lindsey and Gulnac, near the present town of Stockton, and drove away their cattle. Lindsey was killed. Sutter was called to help, and with a little band of twenty-two men he set out again to fight the fiercest battle of his life. No stage effects here! No drum and fife! No 'uniform coat all buttoned down below with silver eagle buttons,' but a deadly plainclothes affair. Many of Sutter's men were wounded, and Juan Vaca—the only white victim of his Indian campaigns—was killed. However, the stolen cattle were recovered and returned to the ranches.

William Gulnac, by the way, was anything but a friend of Sutter's. But when the lives and property of settlers were endangered, Sutter, this immense paradox, showed himself great enough to forget personal differences. The *soldier* Sutter remained forever a fiction in the flesh, a genteel reincarnation of the *miles gloriosus* of ancient comedy. But the *pioneer* Sutter, the reclaimer of the wilderness and tamer of Indians, had few equals.

All over the country horse- and cattle-thieving by the Indians had assumed menacing proportions during his absence. Tribes that once had been most friendly refused to return to work in Sutter's fields. It required threats and the persuasive force of lead and powder to check this serious reversal in Indian affairs.

The next incident was all the graver because signs pointed to José Castro as the power behind it. Castro, now *comandante general*, could not forgive himself and his associates in the revolt for having allowed Sutter to return to his Sacramento stronghold. He therefore turned the Mokelumne Indians under Chief Raphero against him. Sutter, as always, forestalled the attack by his sally. Raphero was made captive, court-martialled, and his scalp was nailed above the fort gate as a warning to other tribes.

Notwithstanding this threat, Chief Rufino, lieutenant of Sutter's company of Indians, avenged Raphero's execution by killing his own brother-in-law who worked for Sutter. But Rufino, too, was captured a few months later, 'tried for murder, found guilty, and executed,' according to one of the early entries of the New Helvetia Diary for September 16, 1845.

More Indian trouble swept over the country with the thieving Walla Walla tribe under Chief Elijah. This conceited young buck, whose head had been completely turned by an education received from the Methodist missionaries on the Willamette and who went about foppishly dressed in the fashion of white men, was finally shot down in self-defence by Grove Cook, whom he had threatened to murder. Now the Walla Wallas threatened an attack upon the fort. Again a campaign was quickly launched against the horse-thieves; but these preferred to be satisfied with their vain menaces and their booty and to flee to their Oregon homelands.

The result of these sundry campaigns was twofold. First, trade in Indian orphans reached a record volume this year; second, Sutter was able again to hire out the surplus of those Indians who found it wise to accept anew the yoke. On May 19, for instance, Sutter promised Suñol for delivery in three weeks '30 Indians and shall be glad to receive dried meat in payment.' Nor had he this time any difficulties in redeeming his pledge. On June 14 the Indians were shipped along with the customary note in French:

'All the Indians (Gentiles) are of the best we have, they are very willing to work, have not yet come in contact with the mission Indians and are therefore absolutely innocent, and for this reason I recommend you to keep them separate, so that they cannot learn the vices of the others.'

Apart from the sensational metamorphosis during the overland trip of the downhearted, down-at-heel and bankrupt shopkeeper to the glamorous social butterfly and ex-captain of the Swiss Guard, no achievement of Sutter's equals his success as an Indian tamer. This was the one triumph which even his bitter enemies conceded to him. And who could doubt but that here his own nature, often childlike and in many ways so naive, was his greatest help? In these difficult relations with the aborigines he was guided by an unerring instinct. He used force but as a last resort, was swift but just in the infliction of punishment, always conciliatory where he encountered a trace of goodwill, ever ready to show his faith in the good heart of a savage, and paternally kind toward those who submitted to his will.

Marsh and Gantt had at the end of the revolt signed a contract with Governor Pico for a campaign against Indian horse-thieves. As Sutter predicted, the two accomplished nothing. He, on the other hand, invited the chiefs of the thieving tribes to come like gentlemen and solemnize a treaty with him. 'And they informed me by express' he wrote with pride to Suñol, 'that they would come if I would forgive them, and I sent them the answer that I would forgive them.' He continued: 'The poor Sutter who is now so despised in the country will give proof that he is able to stop the horse-thieving *by and by*; I have always, with the greatest sacrifices, *done* and *acted* for the good of the country, but one never acknowledges that and I am paid with ingratitude.'

This last comment was not vain boasting. Indeed, at no other period of his life is Sutter to be taken more seriously than after the salubrious chastisement of the Micheltorena campaign. That the Californians were now more hostile towards Sutter than ever before was only too true, not the least reason being that, in their victory over Micheltorena and Sutter, they had inadvertently jumped from the frying pan into the fire. Their new departmental government was from its inception rotten to the core. But, unwilling to admit self-frustration, they sought relief in venomous demonstrations against the foreign settlers.

Nominally, Pio Pico was now Governor. Actually, the new *comandante general*, José Castro, a choleric drunkard to whom the hatred of foreigners was as necessary for life as *aguardiente*, had the last word. So, all considered, the Micheltorena revolt turned out to be a much more drastic defeat for the native sons than for the beaten party. They had won the battle but lost the war. California was in a quagmire. Even the foreign settlers who had joined hands or sympathized with the Californians now wailed with regrets and writhed with contrition. Charles M. Weber, war prisoner at Sutter's Fort, who had indulged in mighty gloating over the defeat of Micheltorena and Sutter, cried aloud: 'Public affairs are in the worst conditions; we are without government or justice. . . . Is there no descendant of the great Washington in the land to rouse the spirit of the freemen to claim their rights and establish peace and order? . . . My heart is bleeding to see around me a lot of men unworthy of the noble birthright of Americans.'

More and more fervently the eyes of the settlers turned east, towards the mountains from which salvation was to come. Secret efforts were made to hasten the advent of the Stars and Stripes or, failing that, of more and larger covered-wagon trains. Their coming or staying away now seemed a matter of life and death.

Even staid Thomas Oliver Larkin, the American Consul at Monterey, bestirred himself and whipped the eloquent but lazy

Marsh into writing propaganda articles for eastern papers: 'Awake, slumber not forever! All but California is going by steam and in California you appear one of the most behind, for your talent. I'm cruel but I am in earnest and hope you will attend to this.'

But there was still another reason for this spurt of propaganda: the Republic of Texas, whose example stood ever enticingly before the settlers of California, had just been invited to accept statehood in the American Union.

25. THE LIFE-BLOOD OF EMPIRE

How did these critical conditions in the land affect New Helvetia? How was Sutter able to save himself from being sunk in the mire into which the unfortunate campaign had led him?

It has already been mentioned that about the time of his forty-second birthday, even before the end, before the laughable culmination of his great martial adventure, a far-reaching change had begun in him. It was as if an icy rain-shower had startled him out of the comfortable many-colored dreams of his childhood and opened his eyes before reality. A large soap-bubble had burst. The opalescent mists of youthful romanticism had been dispersed, allowing him for the first time to see the almost hopeless state of affairs at New Helvetia stark naked.

But lo and behold! Sutter, the one most severely hit, was also one of the few who did not lament. The comical ordeal of Cahuenga had made a man of him. With his flashing tunic he also put aside most of his super-annuated boyish ostentation and with admirable poise, and full of purpose, began again from the very beginning as if nothing had happened. In Sutter's life, so full of unexpected turns, it is one of the major surprises to find at this time his vocabulary enriched by such strange phrases as 'economy,' 'great Alterations and Reformations, Rules, and a great saving System.'

In this great task of reconstruction, John Bidwell proved of inestimable help. He had long wanted to make himself independent, but now, seeing Sutter in the worst pinch, his deep affection for this captivating Swiss made him again determined to remain at New Helvetia.

To begin with, necessity made even Sutter dip his quill into the ink of propaganda. His own realm, like the country at large, needed new blood if it expected to survive the crisis. Sutter therefore sent the old trapper Caleb Greenwood across the mountains to Fort Hall, there to sing the praise of California and to divert the Oregon immigrants from their predetermined goal. But chiefly he tried to drum up enthusiasm for California among the Swiss and the Germans of the Middle-West through articles and advertisements in the *Anzeiger des Westens*,[13] the German paper of St. Louis. 'Frankly and honestly I must confess that I am writing with a view to my own advantage and that of my countrymen, and that I should deem myself fortunate if this communication should become the means of directing some of my emigrating countrymen to this place, where thousands of families can still establish happy homes.' Then he draws an enticing picture of the agricultural advantages of California and of its great future as a wineland and fruit grower's paradise. None before him had shown such farsightedness. He makes a neat point of the cheapness of Indian labor, which renders slavery quite superfluous in California. In short, 'there is here a vast field open to all who do not shun work, whatever their calling. Skilled craftsmen can earn here a particularly good living.' Indeed, 'a good German tailor ought to become wealthy here within three years.'

It was, of course, Sutter's own bitter need for experienced mechanics which inspired this propaganda. On trained craftsmen, his own capacity as an executive, and on the favors or disfavors of the weather now depended his salvation. While it is impossible to-day to gain a comprehensive picture of his intricate entanglements, the few facts known point to the worst. His chief creditors were still the Russians, on whose account, because of the failure of two crops, nothing had been paid for two years. His obligations to them had risen above $31,000. He owed about $4,000 to the Hudson's Bay Company, at least $2,000 to Thomas Oliver Larkin, and over $1,000 to the half-Dane William Leidesdorff in Yerba Buena. By the middle of 1845 the debt to Suñol was reduced to the pittance of $500. But Sutter owed similar sums of several hundred dollars to 'almost everybody.' His total obligations were probably about $80,000 or $100,000.

Within the mesh of these debts only a contortionist's agility could prevent strangulation. Sutter solved the problem by making payments only to those creditors who were willing to reward every instalment with the advance of further credit. All others were indefinitely shelved. It was good policy for any creditor to handle the Lord of New Helvetia with gloves and to let the debtor's suggestions go before his own. '*Il est beaucoup mieux s'il est possible, de pouvoir s'arranger sur une autre Manière,*' was the amusing formula by which the agile Sutter repeatedly evaded the too insistent Suñol. At Yerba Buena public sentiment was so intensely against Sutter that the Russian agent, who came to collect the wheat this year, was obliged to come up to the fort. 'I told him I consider myself not safe enough at Yerba Buena and this is Mr. Forbes own opinion.' Forbes, the British Vice-Consul and one of Sutter's creditors, belonged to the few who did not lose their patience.

Fortunately, the Russians still kept him supplied with ammunition, 'which is worth gold in such times;' for the hand of fate smote all too few of Sutter's enemies, as one is left to guess from a letter to Reading. But one was struck: 'apoplexed so that the half of his body is like dead. God the allmighty punished this Rascal, I wish he would continue and punish a few others.' And of another he wrote: '*C'était avec grand déplaisir que j'ai entendu . . . que ce bougre de Flüggé n'est pas mort.*' Did it ever occur to him that some of his enemies might feel the need of offering up similar prayers?

Often, however, Sutter now lost his old *nonchalance de grand seigneur* when seeking credit. 'I am ashamed to ask you,' he wrote to Leidesdorff on July 31, 'but at present necessity compels me to beg you once more for a favor . . . at least 6 pieces of brown *Manta* . . . for my boys and Girls of the house, about 100 who are nearly all in Rags and naked, and when strangers come here it looks very bad. . . . After having received this favor of you I will no more trouble you until I have made a good remittance, I leave [!] in hope that you will be kind enough to do me this favor and you will see that you have done it not to an ingrateful.'[14]

That this state of affairs was by no means altogether Sutter's fault may be reiterated. He had no power over the country's climate. The poor, hungry and ragged immigrants he could not allow to starve. Nor could he sell of his lands to pay his debts; for no-one would have bought what could be obtained for nothing. As yet his lands were worthless. And finally the distressing lack of good mechanics left his industrial enterprises forever in an experimental stage, financially unproductive. For it must never for a moment be forgotten that outside of cattle-ranching there was no enterprise in California which did not require a vast amount of strenuous pioneering. The country had no industries, not even crafts worth mentioning. To be sure, the boots the Californians wore were made from the hides of their own cattle—but made in Boston. They had twice been shipped around the Horn.

So with everything. Most of the simplest necessities were lacking. The pioneer's lot was never a soft berth, and Sutter was forced to pioneer in a score of fields at once. He should have undertaken less? Be satisfied with less? Fate is not arguable. The man was born with the indomitable urge to do something, to create and produce. This wilderness provoked him. He must conquer it, redeem it, even if the task seemed beyond any one man's strength!

Until now, then, all his experiments to turn to account his various industrial establishments had failed because of the lack of skilled labor. His blanket-factory, operated by Indian women, produced barely enough to suffice for the needs of the fort population. He had a hat-factory which as yet did not throw off any profits. The great hopes he had set on his distillery never materialized. Sutter fared a little better with his tannery provided that dependable labor was on hand. The utilization of the leather, however, too often remained a pious wish; for rarely was a good shoemaker or saddle-maker to be found.

Home consumption, therefore, was the end of most of Sutter's manufacturing activities. In the latter part of 1845 he had three blacksmiths at work, 'the best kind Mechaniks;' they made him twenty plows which 'look so well as ploughs made in Boston,' all for his own need. 'If I could only get iron large enough to get 20 ploughs more made. I should like to have 40 American ploughs going at once.'

Three gunsmiths were kept busy by the fort garrison, the hunters and trappers. He had now a German cartwright, two coopers, carpenters, millwrights, all working for the glory of his own domain. Nine white men and ten Indians were kept busy thirty miles away in the mountains to supply Sutter with lumber for new buildings. One of the coopers in the lumber-camp was cutting staves for brandy-barrels; also for salmon-barrels; but salmon-packing, too, was still in an experimental stage. A pump-maker built pumps to water the vegetable gardens. Still another was working on three flat boats to be used as ferries and for the minor river traffic. Nor did the physician he kept at the fort produce him any income.

Of his many craftsmen only the miller and the baker worked for a wider clientele. The mill ground wheat for most of the settlers in the valley, and from the baking-oven came ship's-bread for the Russians.

There remained, then, as potential income-producing enterprises only agriculture and trapping, both of which had been failures for the two years past. But this year, 1845, the unusual happened. His own 'great Alterations, Reformations, Rules,' and the 'great saving System' showed admirable results in the trapping expedition managed by Pierson B. Reading. Besides, the Hudson's Bay Company no longer operated in the valley. In spite of the fact that Sutter's men stopped working the moment he went forth at the head of his army, the crops were rich because of abundant rains during the winter season. For the first time the harvest was really satisfactory—'*grace à Dieu*.'

Immediately, now, this little breeze of success caused his unmoored optimism to sail off towards the *fata morgana* of a brilliant future. 'One good year more and then I shall be clear of debts!' he wrote ecstatically to Larkin in September. During the respite following the harvest, his mind grew feverish with plans. The speculative dependence on a capricious rain-maker was to become a thing of the past. An irrigation system was to become the envy of the land. He wrote about it to friends and creditors in good standing. 'I am making great preparations for raising a very large and sure crop,' he confided to Forbes. 'By all means I will have in the American Fork a Dam, so that I shall be able to water my wheat fields . . . if I succeed this time I will be out all my trouble; to conduct this business well, occupyes me often whole nights, nothing shall this time be neglected that I am once *dé*-liberated from all my trouble.'

He was most effusive in his letters to Thomas Oliver Larkin. And for good reasons: Larkin, United States Consul at Monterey, was one of the shrewdest merchants in the land and, like every other seaport trader in California, a smuggler through whose services some of the most valuable goods came into the country. Now Larkin had cleverly transferred Sutter's debt to him to one John Williams who was leaving California and therefore had to be paid at once.

And Sutter, with surprising alacrity, did pay about $2,000 in wheat and cattle to Larkin's creditor, in order not to spoil unforeseen chances with the influential consul who was well disposed toward him. But with even greater promptness he then asked Larkin to deliver an almost unending variety of goods on a new credit account. The list is remarkable for the daring it reveals as well as for the versatility of Sutter's needs:[15]

The iron for a saw Mill, saws and files
Iron of all Descriptions, particular heavy iron for making ploughs and
     wagons
Blacksmith files, all sizes (a good Supply)
One good Anvil & 1 good vice,
Some Screw plates & 5 lbs of Borax
Whipsaw & 3 square files,
woodrasps, Shoemaker rasps & shoemaker thread & *Pita*
12 American axes & 2 good Broadaxes
2 Kegs of Shingling & 2 Kegs of flooring nails,
American ploughs of the heavier *Kind*, so many as you can get, a few
     of the lighter ones.
Log, Oxen and Drag Chaines,
2 Dozen of Shovels
1 Dozen of Spates

3 Doz of strong Hows, proper for digging.

2 Crosscut saws, 3 Handsaws & 2 shingling hatchets.

12 Gimlets, Chissels, and Gauches assorted.

Iron, wire of different sizes (not to thin)

6 House Door locks,

12 chest and 12 Padlocks

6 dozen of good butcherknifes

1000 fishhooks of different Sizes

2 dozen pairs of good Woolcards

Copperas and Verdigris, Mousseline, Marrocas, Ribbons etc. for the Hat factory.

200 lbs of fine Rifle Powder

100 lbs of Musket Do

300 lbs of Lead & 400 lbs of Beaver or Duckshot

10.000 percussion caps

500 flints for shotguns & Muskets

200 lbs of white & red Beads of the right kind like I had from you a few lbs when at Monterey last time.

2 Bales of good brown *Manta*

20 Dozen of good Gotton Hdkfs

20 pieces of dark colored Calico

10 pieces of stripe Cotton or strong Shirts

6 or 8 lbs of strong Cotton or Linnen thread

1000 or 2000 Needles assorted

6 Dozen of Jackets & Pantaloons of blue Nankin & Duck

Paintbrushes assorted

1 Keg of black and one of green paint

1 do. Whitelead

1 Barril of paintoil

Rosin about 100 lbs, and lampblack for the tanyard.

1 Bolting cloth & floursifts

about 10 or 12 boxes Tin, different qualities.

He concluded magnificently: 'With this supply I could drive on my business in Style and to my great satisfaction and benefit.' Then, as he 'forgot a few of the most importantest' of the articles, he augmented the list with the following items:

1 Dreshing Machine of four horses Power
1 iron Bark Mill (cast) for the Tannyard
1 Cutting Machine for Wheat
Bagging for about 200 bags
a large well supplied Medicine Chest.

No wonder, with credit needs like these, that he used inks of the most gorgeous hues in his letters to Larkin. Indeed he went so far as to praise to heaven his incomparable Russian market, although anything he was able to deliver to the Russians could but reduce his main debt without bringing him any tangible profit for years to come. 'If I have now in time Assistance with the proper articles for an amount of 4 or 5000 Dollars worth, I am certain that in two years from now I am able to make a fortune.'

Incurable optimist: he did not know that at that very moment the Russians were planning to drive him from his empire by selling the New Helvetia mortgage to his enemies. Or did he feel that he was sitting on top of a volcano? There are tokens which might lead one to suspect it.

The conflicting figures regarding the size of his herds, for instance, invite speculation. How large were they? In his propaganda letter to the *Anzeiger des Westens* Sutter gives his animal wealth as '4000 head of cattle, 1500 mares, 200 tame horses and mules, 3000 sheep and many hogs.' Did he exaggerate? Larkin reported about the same time to Washington that Sutter's fortune in stock was fast declining. Many of Sutter's letters to creditors and court testimony given a few years later by his employees also indicate that at this time his herds were small. But most of his employees never saw more than the few heads of cattle kept at the fort; the herds themselves remained at Hock. Yet there was almost daily slaughtering at the fort, sometimes of several animals. And leather came continually from the tanning vats, sometimes in batches of 200 hides. Where did they come from?

Could it be that he was trying to keep his herds far from the eyes and reach of creditors as something that might be salvaged out of a possible new bankruptcy? Was there lurking somewhere in his mind the embryonic ogre of another catastrophe? Indeed, some of his voluble epistolary effusions might well have been Sutter's way of whistling in the dark to keep up courage.

26. *THE NOOSE*

AND still the theater of action widened. The plot of destiny— 'manifest destiny'—in which all were actors, solidified. Ever since the depression following the Micheltorena revolt, restlessness filled every heart. The atmosphere was charged with tension, particularly since it became known that Texas, that other Mexican province, was to be adopted as a State of the Union. For the settlers of California this vibrant suspense, this throbbing, meant vernal expectancy, for the native sons it meant dread of a catastrophic earthquake, and for all the certain foreknowledge of unavoidable change.

One thing, however, was already quite certain: whatever the future held in store, the settlers of California had to be prepared. But this preparedness depended chiefly on a sufficient number of immigrants. That went for the country as a whole as well as for Sutter. Inside and outside of New Helvetia, therefore, immigration now held the spotlight. Each immigrant was a foreboding, a portent. No less than for his own immediate salvation Sutter desired, nay, prayed for, large masses of immigrants for political reasons. He was convinced that as long as California remained a Mexican province it could have no future.

None saw and expressed this more clearly than Sutter. Although there were many men in California shrewder and more practical than he where private interests were concerned, with the exception of Consul Larkin, perhaps, none had at this time Sutter's breadth of vision. None was so acutely conscious of the fact that at this time California lacked even men with enough leadership to direct the impending revolution to the best interest of all. And the fact speaks eloquently for the depth of self-knowledge Sutter had gained in the Micheltorena campaign that he did not consider himself one of these leaders. All this he openly states in his propaganda letter to the *Anzeiger des Westens*.

As a first, transitory stage he foresaw an independent state: 'Jointly with Oregon a great "Pacific Republic" could be formed with unquestionable success,' he, a Mexican official, advertised in that Missouri paper. The next step after the formation of the Republic would take care of itself. He continues in his letter: 'that for such times and in view of such events men of talent and character, able jurists and statesmen would be most welcome to us, is self-evident.' What deep and tragic irony there is in these words! For he, the only one aware of the dire need for statesmanship, was later to suffer most cruelly for the country's appalling lack of it.

It is not surprising that we meet Sutter at his best in this long propaganda letter in which, for a rare change, he could express himself in his own tongue. Here he displays the mettle of the true colonizer and of the prophetic visionary. He was one of the very few, also, who tried to work for the country as a whole and not only for his own benefit. Naturally, for California and New Helvetia were, after all, inseparable. If it should come to a crisis, his fort would be the only refuge of the settlers and immigrants. Not only that. More than ever, what foreign agents had said years before was true now: he who holds Sutter's Fort has in his hands the key to California's interior, the most valuable, most fertile part of the land.

Meanwhile, before these vast, vague hopes could be fulfilled, a much greater stream of immigrants than the country had heretofore seen was required. The few hundred who had arrived since 1841 were almost lost in the immense province and among the tenfold Hispano-Californian majority.

But, alas, these immigrants never came in sufficient numbers. Always Sutter's fervent expectations were ridiculed by the realities. In April his scouts sent news from Oregon that 900 souls were getting ready to set out for California. When they arrived in July (they were the McMahon-Clyde party) they counted only 39 men, 1 woman, and 3 children. With them also came the man who, in Sutter's hand, was to become instrumental in the shaping of California's destiny: James Wilson Marshall, a New Jersey millwright, the future discoverer of gold.

Late in September, then, the caravans from Missouri began to trickle in. First the Swasey-Todd party of 12 or 13 young men, among them Dr. William B. Gildea, who became fort physician. A week later another small party of 15 arrived with William Sublette from St. Louis. At length, in the latter part of October, the 'large company,' the Grigsby-Ide party, arrived with wagons and families. But they, too, counted only about 50 men, besides an unknown number of women and children.

And finally, almost as a joke, there appeared on Christmas Day the stentorian Lansford W. Hastings who always wanted to play Santa Claus to the Pacific Coast. He had gone back east in 1843 to write a book on this promised land and to return with an army of 1,000 men. When the first news of Hastings' belated approach reached Sutter, his expectations flew off to new heights. The following day 10 miserable phantoms sneaked into the fort: that was the entire Hastings Army. Santa Claus had come with a completely empty bag. Indeed, he and his men had barely escaped starvation and if they had been but one day later they would have met certain death under twenty feet of Sierra snow.

With Hastings came a second doctor, Robert Semple, who amused everyone with his ridiculous height and pantaloons reaching just below his knees and who, when riding a mule, was forced to strap his spurs to his calves.

Now it so happened that during the latter part of October, while Sutter's Fort was bursting with immigrants and before even the last of them had arrived, José Castro began to move about the country with Don Andres Castillero, a commissioner from Mexico, and with an armed escort. At once rumors sprang up like wildfire that Castro was raising a large armed force to expel all foreigners; for only a short while before, Governor Pico had published an edict ordering all non-citizens to depart immediately, and Castro himself had followed it up with a sanguinary proclamation of his own.

John Bidwell was just then at Yerba Buena, and the thought of the unusual number of immigrants at New Helvetia sent him flying back up the river with all the speed he could command. His news threw Sutter's Fort into a panic. Soon after, bringing the excitement to a climax, came the report that Castro himself would presently appear at New Helvetia in person. This could only mean the worst, certain other rumors notwithstanding, which would have it that Castro and Castillero were coming to buy the fort from Sutter in the name of the Mexican Government.

Never before had New Helvetia witnessed such excitement. The day Castro was expected arrived and as the hours advanced, the general nervousness waxed to a frenzy. Towards evening Sutter himself sought relief in a letter to Reading, who was then in the trappers' camp. He was confirmed that Castro had 'no good intentions.' The following day, November 11, 1845, the Indian ferryman saw the approach on the other side of the Sacramento of a uniformed cavalcade. He fled in terror to the fort to announce the coming of the attackers. But observers sent down to the river under Bidwell's command soon returned with quieting intelligence, and several boats were then dispatched to ferry across the visitors. Their party consisted of José Castro, the Mexican *comisionado* Andres Castillero, Colonel Trudin, Lieutenant-Colonel Victor Prudon, Jacob P. Leese, and an escort of about fifteen men. As they galloped up the road, the Mexican flag was hoisted and a salute of twenty-one guns fired.

What had the visitors come for? There was first the matter concerning the immigrants. This was soon disposed of. Even Castro had to admit that it was impossible to send the Americans back across the mountains at this season and he was willing to tolerate them during good behavior, until spring.

Then came the great issue, solemnly put before Sutter in his primitive reception room:

Don Andres Castillero had been dispatched to California by the new Mexican government under José Herrera as a messenger of goodwill. Between him and the Californians the admission of Texas to statehood in the Union and the threat of war with the United States were the outstanding topics of discussion, and it was natural that this led to the question whether the government should not acquire Sutter's Fort for the protection of its interests in California. The old ruse, 'if you cannot beat an enemy, buy him,' had a very happy appeal to Mexicans and Californians alike. They had now come to inspect the fortress and to discuss the price.

Precisely what happened during the negotiations will probably never be known. Sutter himself maintains that Castillero had expressly 'been sent by the Mexican Government' to 'effect the purchase of my Fort, which they could then garrison and so stop immigration.' His story that his official visitors 'wished to buy the Fort with all its appurtenances for the government and were authorized to pay for it one hundred thousand dollars,' was later to become one of his favorite articles of exhibition to which, for greater dramatic effect, he added: 'I was greatly surprised. The thought of selling or moving never entered my mind.'

In reality, Sutter was neither unprepared for the offer (as witness his letters to Reading), nor was the thought of moving away from New Helvetia a stranger to his mind. Above all, the offer of $100,000 was nothing but the ardent wish-dream of a man up to his nose in debt. This was the price *he asked*, but which the Mexicans found to be far beyond their slender purse.

Nevertheless, Sutter requested a few minutes' time to reflect upon the matter. He withdrew to his private office and there discussed the situation with Bidwell, Hensley, Loker, and others, whose own interests quickly gave direction to their arguments. If Sutter sold out, what were they to do? 'What will become of all the settlers in the valley if you abandon us to the Mexicans?' they asked.

These objections, says Sutter (and here the accounts of Bidwell, Loker, and Brown support his own story) made him determined to reject the offer. But since his championing of American interests was no grounds on which he, a Mexican officer, could fittingly decline an offer of the government, he returned to his visitors saying that his contract with the Russians forbade him to sell.

But perhaps the main reason why he refused to sell was not rooted in the colonizer's idealism; for the official price offered him ($50,000 apparently was the limit beyond which the government would not and could not go) would not even have covered his debts. But there were other obstacles in the way of an agreement at this time. The Mexicans and Californians were sharply divided against themselves. Castro not only desired Sutter to yield his fort to the government; he was equally eager to enlist his help in a new attempt of the native sons to make themselves independent of Mexico. Castillero, on the other hand, was no less intent on securing Sutter's support for the central government. This Castro knew, and he therefore watched Castillero so jealously as to make it well-nigh impossible for the commissioner to have a word with Sutter in private. Jacob P. Leese, Vallejo's proxy on this occasion, also had his secret mission. He had come to inveigle the immigrants at the fort to turn against Sutter and to move out of his valley. He behaved, writes Sutter, 'very mean and miserable.'

All this made a frank discussion of the sales topic impossible, so the following morning the visitors departed, accompanied by Sutter and Bidwell for twenty miles. They were not far from the fort when, to Sutter's great surprise, they were suddenly overtaken by a cavalcade of about fifty of his men, mechanics and *vaqueros*.

'What's all this?' asked Castro.

'Only some of my men,' Sutter replied as casually as he could. 'They would have joined the escort earlier had they been able to get their horses up sooner.' But the truth was that his men had become alarmed at the thought that Sutter might be kidnapped by the Mexicans in order to allow the government to take possession of the fort on its own terms.

For some time, apparently, the door to further negotiations was left open. Behind the scene even Vallejo worked seemingly in favor of Sutter. A few days after the negotiators had been at the fort, he wrote to Mexico: 'It would be very desirable to close that door of communication [New Helvetia] even at a sacrifice. Castro and Castillero having made propositions to Sutter for the purchase of his establishment, he said he would cede it to the government for $100,000. I grant this is a high price to pay . . . but it is the security of the country that is to be bought, and that is priceless.'

Vallejo's reasoning was, of course, nothing if not hypocritical. For if New Helvetia's 'few pieces of cannon, a bastion not very scientifically constructed, some ditches or moats, ten or twelve adobe houses and some corrals of the same material' were as worthless as he represents them, it is hard to see how, in acquiring them, the Mexican government could buy security against an American invasion, no matter at what price. The truth was that Vallejo desired nothing so intensely as the removal of Sutter from his neighborhood, and he had not the slightest scruples about encouraging the government to pay, as he himself thought, exorbitantly for his own advantage.

But the hitch that definitely brought negotiations to naught lay hidden where it had least been expected. When rumors concerning the sale of New Helvetia reached the ear of the Russian agent then at Yerba Buena, he lost no time offering the California government the mortgage (on which Sutter had not even paid the interest due) for the amount of his Russian debt, namely, $31,000. This being less than one third of Sutter's price, the California government pounced upon the offer. An agreement between the two parties was at once concluded and dispatched to Mexico for ratification.

With the mortgage in the hands of his enemies, Sutter's head was as good as in the noose. Yet, until the end of his days he apparently never learned how dangerously near complete annihilation, foreclosure, eviction from his empire, he was at this time. What saved him?

In Mexico City ratification was delayed, and before the matter could be taken up in the spring of 1846 the clouds of war that had been looming long and large broke over the Rio Grande. Thus, indirectly it was the United States that saved Sutter from dispossession.

Meanwhile, during the entire winter and while, unbeknown to him, the noose lay about his neck, Sutter went on hoping vaguely but persistently that the government would yet make it possible for him to dispose of his burdensome little empire at a price high enough to expunge his debts. But this, no doubt, means nothing else but that his burden had at last become too heavy for him. The inner dissolution of New Helvetia had begun. But before the end could come, this private empire was yet to shine as a bright star in history and during one wink of an eye at least be the focus of the whole world's interest.

PART FOUR

TOOL OF DESTINY

27. PROVIDENCE AND THE DEVIL

THE individual, no matter how great or how diminutive, is often but a pawn in an irrational game played by mysterious powers. Who would say Sutter knew precisely what drew him to California? Or who would dare rationally to explain what prompted him to select for his settlement exactly that spot in the primeval wilderness which was to reveal itself as the key position of the interior and which thus made Sutter a pivotal figure in a vastly ramified tug of war between nations?

It is enough to ask these questions and with their aid hint at the formation of certain live patterns in the infinitely intricate tapestry of human history.

By the end of 1845, the time of the visit of Castro and Castillero, numerous forces were polarized in Sutter and in his fort. No matter if he himself began to tire of the role he was playing and even came dangerously close to being evicted. The strange truth is that at that precise moment the one power to which he was to prove most useful thrust its mighty arm into the game and pinned him down firmly in his place. Whether he wanted to or not, he was to continue in his curious and instrumental role and to carry on until it was played out.

Of the many straws in the wind, at least two must be mentioned.

Señor Castillero, who had made his entrance on the stage as a diplomat from Mexico, turned discoverer within a week of his departure from New Helvetia. On his way south from Sutter's,

Castillero was shown at San José a singularly heavy, reddish rock from a neighboring cave known as the Chavayas mine, the product of which had been used since time immemorial by the Indians to prepare their red war-paint. Castillero, a native of Spain familiar with the mines of Almaden, had no difficulty in identifying the raw material for the Indian red paint as *cinabrio*, quicksilver ore.

This discovery, says Bidwell, 'at this time seems providential in view of its absolute necessity to supplement the imminent discovery of gold.' Charles M. Weber, in reporting the discovery to Marsh, likewise had recourse to an irrational power. Castillero, he wrote, threw 'his important rank as high Commissionar of the glorious Mexican government to the D . . . l' and was now occupied in the search for gold, silver and quicksilver. Bidwell's 'providence' and Weber's 'D . . . l' were but two aspects of the same unknown power.

Only a month after Castillero's visit, while Sutter, under the cover of night, sneaked into hostile Yerba Buena to attend to business with the very Russians who were now clandestinely joining hands with Mexico against him, the representative of the United States, Mexico's opponent, also appeared on the scene.

John Bidwell was in charge of the fort when, unexpectedly, Frémont and his guide Kit Carson entered the gate. Unforgetful of the lordly reception afforded him on his first visit to New Helvetia, Frémont knew no modesty when he made known his immediate wants, namely, sixteen mules, six packsaddles, flour and other provisions, and the use of a blacksmith's shop to shoe the mules. Regretfully Bidwell told him that Sutter had no mules, but could leave him horses; and that the blacksmith's shop was entirely at his disposal, only there was not a lump of coal on hand. Whereupon Frémont, with some consternation, but without as much as a 'good-bye,' made about-face and departed. Mounting his horse at the gate, he was overheard saying to Carson that Bidwell was unwilling to accommodate him.

Bidwell, his American pride hurt by the report of this utterance, immediately called upon Frémont at his camp about three miles up the river. But the only reply that Frémont would make was frigid and formal: *he* was the officer of *one* government and *Sutter* that of *another*; the difficulties existing between the two were sufficient explanation of Bidwell's unwillingness to assist him. It proved utterly useless to explain to Frémont that since his last visit Sutter's circumstances had considerably changed for the worse. Frémont could not be argued with; no-one, not even a United States court-martial, ever could argue with this stubborn mind.

Still, the following morning Bidwell sent forth scouts and on the second day was able to deliver to Frémont fourteen mules. Frémont accepted them—and rancorously hung on to his ill-founded grudge and profound suspicion against Sutter. Straw in the wind: it was, alas, to be the official attitude of the coming regime towards anything remotely tinged with the hue of Mexico.

Frémont soon hurried south in an attempt to meet the main body of his command which, under Captain Walker, he had left east of the Sierras and charged with the task of finding a passable gap in the mountains said to exist in the south—Walker's Pass today.

Four days after Frémont's departure, Sutter returned from the bay. Since it was his duty as a Mexican official to keep tag on all foreign visitors coming to his settlement, he reported Frémont's brief stay at once to Vallejo, dating his report 'December 10,' the day of the arrival of Frémont. Thus, after having in his absence provoked Frémont's ill will and suspicion, he now earned a reprimand from Vallejo, who saw in the belated information a treacherous attempt on Sutter's part to cover up the movements of the American spy.

This one crisp little incident epitomizes Sutter's situation at the close of 1845. Officially, the United States' representative afforded him the treatment he thought fit for a dyed-in-the-wool Mexican, while Mexico regarded him as a treacherous ally of the United States. He stood between the devil and the deep blue sea, and there, fundamentally, destiny pinned him down.

Thus, in a few minor occurrences, ironical forebodings, symptomatic little flashes, was heralded the double conflagration that was presently to embroil Sutter more deeply in the fate of this land which, like a magnet, had drawn him over seas and continents, which had attracted him as a rare flower attracts from miles and miles beyond the insect fit to fructify it.

28. *SUBTLE CHANGES*

SINCE the youthful romantic Sutter had returned a mature man from his first, disenchanting and sobering war experience, his inmost being had not been able to withstand further change. One is tempted to say that the strongest side of his nature, his romantic ego being broken, all the destructive forces could enter through the breach. Such developments on the very eve of grave historical events give us reason for fear.

To be sure, Sutter began the new year, 1846, normally enough by writing a long letter in French to Victor Prudon. By force of habit he was brimming over with good prospects, making his New Year's letter a catalogue of prophetic signs and indications of a new era: there is hope of a thousand immigrants bringing in their ranks modern civilization. A vessel is under sail from New York with up-to-date agricultural machinery. How much that means! Moreover, the ship carries in its hold the machinery for a river steamer! The Russians, too, will soon bring a steamboat for Leidesdorff, recently appointed American Vice-consul for Yerba Buena. And finally, Sutter assures Prudon, in not more than five years there will be a railroad connecting California with the United States: '*je peu très bien voir cela.*'

But underneath this treble of high hope there is a counterpoint of grumbling bass culminating in a frank attempt to circumvent the customs. If Prudon but knew how to take advantage of his position as Vallejo's right hand, he and Sutter could both become rich quickly.

The startling thing is not so much this plot against the custom laws. Smuggling was one of the most reputable fields of business in California, the only one, in fact, according to local feeling, in which a man could 'make an honest dollar.' What is unusual is that the self-contained lord of the Sacramento began to look about for associates. The strain of carrying a little empire on his shoulders was beginning to tell on him.

For a while yet, life at New Helvetia continued at its usual staggering pace, periods of arcadian calm alternating with intervals of kaleidoscopic variety.

On January 15, 1846, there arrived from Yerba Buena two uniformed officials: Leidesdorff, the half Danish, half Mulatto American Vice-consul, and the jocose William Sturgis Hinckley, captain of the port. Although they came merely to inspect a section of land on the American River on which Leidesdorff desired to establish a ranch, they had for the naive pleasure of display donned their uniforms. That suited Sutter admirably. Since the Micheltorena campaign life had not offered him many chances to air his official deckings. He, too, now emerged in uniform, and together the three ambled forth on a fancy-dress parade in the wilderness.

It was still early in the morning. A few miles up the American River they unexpectedly came upon Frémont's camp. Frémont had arrived on that spot only the night before, after having in vain attempted to establish contact with the main body of his command. Frémont himself lay still abed; but he was roused and invited for dinner in the afternoon, on condition that he, too, appear in uniform. When the three returned from their inspection trip, Frémont joined them; in his honor a salute of nine guns was fired and a magnificent dinner served.

Frémont brought news of tremendous excitement in the United States and of a popular will to extend the frontiers of the Republic to the Pacific coast. He, too, prophesied thousands of immigrants for the latter part of the year and he knew of preparations which were made for a regular steamer service between the two coasts.

Since September 1845 a detailed record was being kept of all the events large and small. This was the New Helvetia Diary,[1] a rather amusing chronicle in telegram style, written sometimes in Sutter's own hand, or that of Bidwell or of another employee. Observations on the weather, remarks on the business on hand, on arrivals and departures stand here close together. It is a rich mine of information, sometimes not without intended or involuntary humor. But the diary is much more. It is the most significant marker indicating a vital change in Sutter's development. It is the outward expression of a new trend toward a contemplative life and a desire for order and accountability.

Nine days after the Frémont dinner, we read in the diary, Dr. William B. Gildea died and was interred with simple ceremonies. Two days later John Chamberlain, the promiscuous Irish blacksmith, was married for the nth time, now to a white girl of thirteen years named Nancy Hess. Again two days later the diary records a quilting party at Mrs. Montgomery's, the wife of one of the fort gunsmiths, to which Sutter 'let go nearly all the gentlemen,' while he himself 'kept house.'

A significant failure is recorded on February 27, on which day the unprofitable distillery was stopped for good. Henceforth Sutter ordered his stomach-comforters from Yerba Buena. He needed a great deal, for, like all men of the frontier, he drank stoutly.

But there were other changes, too subtle, too gradual, too undramatic to be caught and nailed down for posterity in any single diary entry, and of these changes, more fundamental than those the diary comments upon, Sutter's letters bear convincing testimony. The years in the vast wilderness had starved him spiritually. He was again yearning for the amenities of civilized life. He needed friends. His letters grew more personal, more numerous, and frequently he was complaining of the shortage of writing-paper. Sometimes, also, there became articulate an ardent wish for books.

He was beginning to harken back to the days of a carefree youth; which is as much as to say that he was aging, mellowing—at a most unfortunate moment. While his once gigantic stamina for defying the world in supreme unconcern was waning, the world at large was gathering a formidable array of hostile forces against him. The Promethean fire in him, that creative self-sufficiency of man which from the beginning provoked the anger of the gods, was dying. But woe upon Prometheus when he begins to weaken!

More than any other man in California, Sutter had exerted himself in sheer labor. To what avail? His achievements were often those of a man with a genius for inviting trouble. Even now this proved to be true of his immigration policy. From the beginning of his enterprise his fondest hopes had been staked on immigration from the United States. He had contracted huge debts to be a good Samaritan to these newcomers. Year after year the mere trickle of them had failed to dampen his glowing visions of thousands upon thousands bringing prosperity and progress into the country. And now he suddenly discovered that in the course of the years there had accumulated in California an execrable scum which the great waves of unrest in the east had washed over the barrier of the high sierras.

Of the hundreds that had come, says John Bidwell, there were not 'at this time (spring 1846) over twenty-one persons who had located ranches and were living on them.' There was, however, a big vagabond population born and bred of the lawless frontier and living according to the only American code of conduct known to them: the unambiguous 'the farther from the Atlantic, the farther from the law.' What else, under the demoralizing influence of an impending war, was now to be expected but that the devil took hold of this rabble?

This turn of affairs filled Sutter with a painfully bitter pessimism quite unheard-of for him. For the first time since his coming to the Sacramento his business and agricultural enterprises looked really promising. Yet the unpleasantness swept by human coyotes into the valley and within his walls now made this first success almost unpalatable for him. As the first months of the year passed by his discouragement waxed rapidly, until it culminated in a veritable outcry of spiritual pain so unlike the proud builder of a wilderness empire. All the more remarkable is this outcry because it was addressed—of all men—to John Marsh. Between Marsh and Sutter no tenderness was wasted; yet to Marsh the man of New Helvetia wrote on April 3:

It looks every where very gloomy, and I can assure you, if I could, I would leave the Country, if the Government would purchase the Establishment and pay in *Gold* and *Silver* I would sell it, pay all my debts and go some where else. I am in did very tired and weared, because a great many foreigners behave very bad, your property is no more safe like it was about 6 Months ago, no more obedience to the laws, they march with their feet on the Authority, lately by defending my rights and property 3 at once fall over me, right enraged, touched me, and I was every Minute waiting for a merciful Knife or a ball [bullet]. When with the next Emigration we get no better people, I don't know what to do. Always I keept up my good Spirit but now I am entirely discouraged.[2]

And two weeks later he wrote to Leidesdorff: 'Every body say now, a there are no laws in the Country, every body do just what they please' and 'a good many Rascals feel themselves very impudent.'[3]

But again, in the midst of this despair, there came to him a sudden ray of sunshine. He received letters from his family in Switzerland, and this joy, too, now flowed into the same letters in which he confessed his discouragement. To Marsh he wrote:

Yesterday I received at last some letters of my family and with the greatest of pleasure I see that my eldest Son, 20 Years and 6 Months old is on his way to California and will be here in about 6 or 7 Months, his education is finished, likewise his aprentisage in one of the first counting houses in Switzerland, he speaks and writes several languages, and no doubt will be an able Clerk. My Family remains in Switzerland a year or two longer till the two younger Sons have received their education complete, the second is in a celebrated Agricultural Institut, the 3th is in a Military school or Academie as Cadet. The education of my Daughter about 19 years old is completed likewise, it was a great pleasure to read all their letters out which I can judge how the received their education, and was to my greatest Satisfaction.—Excuse of giving you this News, but it is so much pleasure for me, that I cannot help it.

Are we to understand that these were the first letters he had received from his family since his departure? This is, at any rate, the first definite instance in which we hear of intelligence reaching him from Burgdorf.

But what about these children who inspired the tearful, sentimental outpours? For he wrote to others in similar words. Here is the boastful old Sutter still untouched. For what he referred to as 'one of the first counting houses in Switzerland' was in reality a firm in the townlet of Burgdorf; the 'celebrated Agricultural Institut' probably did not cast its renown far beyond the same bailiwick; and the 'Military school or Academie' in which 'the 3th' son was a cadet was precisely the kind from which old 'Captain' Sutter himself had been graduated. The genial old poseur was not yet dead, and therein lay hope.

And Frau Sutter? He did not mention her with as much as one syllable. Behind her name stark tragedy was lurking. Until towards the close of his long life he scarcely ever referred to her. For twenty years to come she was to remain the skeleton in his closet.

So much for these unusual letters, on one page pessimistic, on the next bedewed with the joyous tears of paternal sentiment. Who can fail to read in and between these lines the warnings of a precocious old age?

All about Sutter these signs now multiply. The incessant noisy traffic of the fort, the turmoil brought within its walls by the great throng of wintering immigrants, began to overtax his powers of endurance. Once upon a time he had regarded these people as his children or his wards. Now he was sick and tired of them, and the desire to get rid of them prompted him to lay out a town, Sutterville, a few miles from the fort. 'It will certainly be a great relief. . . . 5 Miles from here will make my Establishment more agreeable.' Vain hopes: in fact the town of Sutterville was destined to play a most disastrous role in the life of its founder.

Thus sign now follows sign, revealing the one same fact that Sutter was aging, mellowing, longing for peace, leisure and relaxation. His strength was ebbing away. Even his business activities now are permeated with this new gentle spirit and we become witnesses to little outbursts of sheer childlike joy. More caressingly than ever his eyes now gaze upon the vast fields through which the young crops are just pushing. He has 1,200 acres planted in wheat and 100 in barley. Yet no longer is it the mere book-keeping value of the crops which is reflected in his correspondence. The wheat is now 'growing beautifully.' Rain had fallen in gratifying profusion during and after the planting season. Then, after the beginning dry season had already threatened to curtail the harvest, more rain as late as May sent Sutter into veritable ecstasies: 'God the allmighty did send us a most splendid rain. . . . During the whole Night I could not sleep at all, so much pleasure it was for me to hear it rain; how beautiful look now the Wheatfields south of the fort. . . .' [4]

Alas, he was never to enjoy the full fruits of his labors. Directly over his lyrical mood the political skies burst, pelting him with sleety storms.

29. *PIG AND PETTICOAT*

With Frémont's second appearance on the Pacific Coast began the involvement of California in the history of the United States. On May 13, 1846, the unavoidable war between the Union and the Mexican Republic had broken out over the Texas question. In those days it took two months for the news to reach California. But the instinct of the American settlers there knew it long before that. The presence of Frémont told it to them. It was his very presence which inspired among the vagrant population the flagrant disregard of law and order which Sutter complained of so bitterly. They were all yearning for war, not the least of their reasons being that it would give them opportunity to loot and plunder. Frémont's passive presence sufficed to unleash among them the furies of revolt.

Ostensibly Frémont had again come as the leader of an exploring expedition; but his countrymen on the coast were convinced that he held himself ready for larger tasks. In his capacity as a scientific explorer he had obtained permission from Castro to winter in California and he had pledged his word of honor to respect the authorities and the laws of the country. But scarcely had he been joined by the main body of his command, when he thumbed his nose at Castro, entrenched himself on Gavilan Peak and hoisted the American flag. This was sheer childishness which had nothing to do with his official mission. Indeed, no sooner did he realize his stupid blunder than he showed his heels and fled to Oregon which had just recently become United States territory.

On this retreat Frémont again came to Sutter's Fort on March 21. Sutter was intensely puzzled by the exhibitions of Frémont's mulish traits. Nor could he, nor anyone else, divest the explorer's acts of all official significance, the result being, therefore, that the country began to squirm under the tension of uncertainty. To Sutter himself Frémont gave further cause for grave head-shaking when, at Peter Lassen's, about 120 miles north of the fort, he bought stolen horses from the Indians. As soon as Sutter heard of this he sent him an urgent request to stop this demoralizing practice. But Frémont never answered, nor ever forgave Sutter this well-deserved rebuke.

On April 28, then, another mystifying American, Archibald H. Gillespie, appeared at Sutter's Fort and asked for the whereabouts of Frémont. He was provided with a guide and soon hurried north on Sutter's favorite mule, without, however, overtaking Frémont until he had crossed the Oregon border.

Meantime, Sutter had reported these events to Castro,[5] and in such a way as to have led some to call this document an act of self-incrimination disproving his much advertised sympathies for the United States. This matter being of vital importance not only as regards Sutter's character but for the course of events as well, it becomes imperative at this turning point of history to examine more closely his political persuasion.

In his official letter to the *comandante general* Castro (about May 12, 1846) Sutter first speaks in rather helpless Spanish of Frémont's flight to Oregon and his unlawful dealings with the horse-thief Indians of the north. Only after this overture does he proceed to report on Gillespie's visit:

He [Gillespie] told me that he is traveling for his health and has letters for Captain Frémont from his family, but . . . I think that this gentleman is an officer of the United States Army (I have seen his name in a list of officers). I told him this and he replied that formerly he was, but that now he had retired from service. Who knows? It is my opinion that this Señor Gillespie is a courier for Captain Frémont and who knows but that he may have important despatches from his government . . . and it may be that he [Frémont] will return from the frontier.

Superficially regarded, this sounds indeed as if Sutter were at this moment siding with Mexico against the interests of the United States. But is this letter to be taken at its face value? As will be presently apparent, Castro himself saw through the official mask which Sutter is here wearing. His sympathies for the United States were too well known. Almost the same day, May 11, Sutter stated his true faith in a letter to Reading. He was so firmly convinced of the inevitability of the coming of the Stars and Stripes as to believe that Mexico would not even dare to fight the United States. ('Mexico would be willing to comply with every thing what the United States demanded from them.') No-one then living in California was in doubt concerning Sutter's leanings. Indeed, half a year before this incident, the United

States Consul in Monterey had officially reported to Washington that Sutter, 'too sanguine, lives but in expectation of this country belonging to the United States.'

Then why this letter to Castro? It was above all prompted by Frémont's conniving with the Indian horse-thieves. This is what determines the tone of the whole report. The elimination of horse-thieving was one of the colonizer's pet ambitions and since, at that moment, he had no other way of striking back at Frémont for his meddling, he had recourse to a symbolical retaliation. Sutter and Frémont had much in common. Both were self-willed romantics, hypersensitive and temperamentally top-heavy; both were arch civilians hungry for the glories of a military career for which they were peculiarly unfit. Frémont, Sutter's junior by ten years, was still full of the yeast of youthful irresponsibility. Sutter, however, with his *sturm und drang* over and his position in the world assured, was beginning to stand on formality, correctness, law and order. Though his sympathies were unreservedly for the United States, his duty, as long as war or secession was not declared, was toward Mexico, and until the last moment he performed it at least perfunctorily. The report on Gillespie was such an act of duty reluctantly undertaken and therefore postponed two weeks—postponed until his mounting exasperation at Frémont's activities among the horse-thieves furnished him with a deeply personal motive for writing to Castro. By that time it was perfectly safe to divulge also his opinion on Gillespie. He had waited much too long to give Castro the slightest chance to interfere in any way with the American courier's business.

Thus Sutter tried, and somehow managed, to maintain an equilibrium between his official duties and his sympathies.[6] True, in the same letter to Castro he once more offered his fort for sale to the Mexican or Californian Government and recommended that it be well garrisoned. But he probably knew only too well that at this late date nothing of the sort could be expected. He was repeating an offer long past consideration, but designed to throw dust into Castro's eyes.

The *comandante*, however, could not be hoodwinked. Sutter had delayed his report on the American messenger two whole weeks. That was sufficient for Castro. His immediate answer was to offer the Mokelumne Indians a high price for Sutter's scalp and to present to Chief Eusebio a fine new rifle for the explicit purpose of shooting Sutter with it. Then Sutter's Fort, the stronghold of the foreign settlers, was to be demolished and the wheatfields burned. The plot, however, was betrayed to Sutter by a faithful Indian.

By inciting the Indians and plotting against Sutter's life, Castro had now torn the cloth between himself and Sutter and between Sutter and Mexico. Sutter was free to follow his own sympathies. How little he hesitated and how quickly he could forget personal differences for the sake of a larger cause he demonstrated by sending a courier to warn Frémont (whose return from Oregon he definitely expected as a result of Gillespie's appearance) of the dangerous Indian situation. For Castro had dispatched his agitators to all the wild tribes of the valley in an effort to rid the country of the foreign settlers.

All this happened long before California knew anything about the Mexican War, partly even before the war was declared. Indeed, Sutter was still confident that a change of regime could be effected peacefully. One military adventure had satisfied his martial appetite for life. But events showed no regard for his personal wishes.

Castro had anticipated official hostilities by declaring war on the foreign settlers on his own hunch and banning them from the province. These, however, did not take him too seriously. They felt pretty safe in the Sacramento Valley. But when opportunity presented itself to them to answer Castro's threats, they seized it. At the beginning of June 1846 it so happened that the Mexican lieutenant Francisco Arce, en route to San José with a *caballada* of government horses, was surprised by a group of American out-laws and deprived of his animals. Sutter, still clinging to his belief of a peaceful revolution, denounced the coup sharply and with his usual frankness. But the American vagabonds were inebriated with the success of their practical joke. They were lusting for more and banded themselves, and soon enough there could be no doubt but that the uprising of the settlers had begun in earnest. At this very moment Frémont happened to return from Oregon and, never able to repress the itch to play the leading role wher-ever he was, wrote to Washington that he had resigned from the army. Then he joined his filibustering countrymen in their rov-ing expeditions. His participation lent to the cause of the revolu-tionists a semi-official touch, and when, therefore, after a little while these insurgents moved *en masse* towards the fort, Sutter, advised by his keen political weather-eye, at once opened his gates to them, thus renouncing his allegiance to Mexico.

But in so doing he was made to swallow a few very bitter pills. Even before Frémont had followed the revolutionaries to the fort, he had sent Kit Carson ahead, theatrically to demand, of all things, Sutter's immediate surrender; and to deliver the message that should Sutter still sympathize with the Mexicans, he had better vanish post-haste! It was a cowardly, abjectly treacherous maneuver inasmuch as Frémont, more than any other American, had received substantial proof of Sutter's sympathies for the United States. But gratitude could never stand in the way of Fré-mont's boundless ambitions. Nor was he a true warrior. He had been promoted to his semi-soldierly office through the patronage of his father-in-law, the famous Senator from Missouri, Thomas Benton. He was self-willed but without personal command; in theory a mathematician, in practice an incorrigible blunderer most of his life; full of arrogance, tactless, and—so many of his own men say—a coward. If not backed by actual authority (as certainly in this filibuster he was not) what else could such a man do but tyrannize and boss?

For the first time now since Frémont's flight to Oregon the two men met again, and an ill-omened meeting it was. With one fell bullying swoop Frémont came down on Sutter. Bidwell stood at some distance, too far to overhear what was being said, but close enough to be appalled by the fierceness of the encounter. A few minutes later Sutter came to him, profoundly agitated, and with tears rolling down flushed cheeks complained that Frémont had grossly insulted him, called him a Mexican, and threatened to deport him. This was Frémont's savage retort to Sutter's rebuke concerning the deal with the horse-thieving Indians.

But the worst was yet to come. With Sutter's Fort to fall back upon, the rebels had nothing more to fear. Northern California was theirs by virtue of the fort. The capture of Sonoma, perpetrated before breakfast on June 14, was nothing but another ribald practical joke, for which the honors fell again on the reassuring presence of Sutter's Fort. Sutter's Fort, indeed, was the whole revolution, and the primary cause, accordingly, of Frémont's insane jealousy. For he mistakenly took Sutter to be his most dangerous rival in the race for the laurels.

The American insurgents, meanwhile, drunk with victory after the capture of Sonoma, adopted as their emblem a lone star supplemented by a grizzly bear. William Todd, a cousin of Mrs. Abraham Lincoln, ventured to execute the design. On a piece of a discarded old petticoat furnished by an immigrant woman, the inscription *California Republic* was painted beneath the star and bear. But under Todd's inept hands the bear assumed perfectly hoggish contours, to the immense amusement of the native population, who insisted henceforth on referring to the emblem of the improvised republic as the 'pig-flag' and to its followers as the *cochinos*. And fit descriptions these were!

The Sonoma chiefs, Vallejo, his brother Salvador, Victor Prudon and Jacob P. Leese were carried off as prisoners to Sutter's Fort and their arrival was for Sutter another bad portent. In itself the removal of these worthies was a flagrant violation of the treaty of surrender signed between Vallejo and the *cochinos*. 'I thought it very wrong and unnecessary,' says Sutter. 'They were men of property and there was no danger of their attempting to escape.' Therefore 'They took their meals at my table and walked out with me in the evening. . . . I thought it wholly unnecessary to be more severe with them.'

But again his kindliness towards his former enemies led to a hot clash with Frémont, whose perverse pleasure it was to distort a temperamental difference into a deep political discrepancy. Frémont came dashing to the fort and bullyingly took Sutter to task:

' "Do you not know how to treat prisoners?"

' "Captain Frémont," said I, "I do. I have been a prisoner myself. Take care of these men yourself; I will have nothing further to do with them!" '

In the end the prisoners were given into the care of John Bidwell and Sutter continued to pay them friendly visits.

But the end was not yet. Some Americans gave him, as he relates, well-meant warnings, 'saying that if I continued visiting them [the prisoners] on such friendly terms, my house would become my prison.' The plain truth is that Sutter, whether he admitted it or not, was of all the prisoners at the fort the most closely and most jealously guarded. Frémont had imposed a garrison of his own men on him and had given them orders to arrest and fusillade Sutter if he allowed the other prisoners to go about freely. Indeed, one of Frémont's soldiers relates that his chief had threatened to hang Sutter on a branch of the oak-tree which stood in a corner of the fort.

It was an extremely uncomfortable situation for Sutter, bitterly humiliating and disillusioning thus to be repaid by Frémont for all the sacrifices, for the kindness and goodwill shown him and his men.

Frémont was wholly incalculable, his conduct disgraceful. He bullied the original leaders of the Bear Flag revolt into recognizing his authority. With his own corps, the Bears or *cochinos*, and men conscripted from Sutter's employees, he roamed about the country, ostensibly to fight Castro, but always skillfully evading him and finally demonstrating his soldierly mettle by committing cold-blooded murder on two unarmed, helpless Californians.

The Bear prisoners at the fort, meanwhile, had little cause for complaint. When Sutter decided to be kind, his kindness was so contagious that even Vallejo wrote from prison: 'Altogether we are indebted to Sutter, in whose care we remain, for a thousand domestic favors, for which he merits eternal gratitude.' Vallejo, by the way, displayed during these days a farsightedness and political sagacity not found among other Californians. 'We believe,' he wrote in the same letter, 'that our detention is purely political and indispensable for the progress of the new order of things. We believe fundamentally that this is a matter of a total change, but an orderly change founded on justice and the law, which will bring the country out of the precarious and miserable situation in which it has remained to this day.' The words 'an orderly change founded on justice and the law,' have a familiar ring. Was he not echoing the fervent prayer of his good host and former enemy Sutter?

The 'California Republic' was short-lived. Before the moon had completed one cycle, that zoological freak, the pig-bear, expired. His had not been a glorious or very savory reign. Though begun in good faith as a movement of self-defence, the revolt had quickly degenerated into a veritable hogs' holiday, the record of which was not materially bettered by the circumstance of Frémont's proclaiming himself master of the sty. ⁻

It was a happy coincidence, therefore, that only twenty-six days after the birth of the pig-flag, news reached the coast of war between the United States and Mexico. And it was an even greater piece of good luck for the country that the news was brought by American warships themselves.

30. *STARS AND STRIPES*

ON July 2, 1846, Commodore Sloat of the United States Pacific Squadron sailed into Monterey harbor, immensely perplexed because, having been sent here to conquer a Mexican province, he found that California called itself an independent republic. He could not quite understand that and required five whole days to puzzle out the situation. Then, at length, he ventured to execute his orders to raise the American flag over California. On the ninth of the month the Stars and Stripes also rose over Yerba Buena and on the eleventh or twelfth over New Helvetia.

Nothing could have been more welcome to Sutter. For the rest it remained as true as ever that he who possessed Sutter's Fort had the interior of California in his pocket. Here Sutter remained the actual conqueror, and the United States had little else to do than accept the northern half of the province from him. Castro and Pico fled at the news that the *gringos* had arrived into the haven of the province of Sonora, and thus for the time being the conquest of California meant scarcely more for the American troops than a holiday excursion. Only a few months later did some of the more valorous Californians resort to armed resistance against the intruders.

The Stars and Stripes arrived at New Helvetia during the night. 'At sunrise the next morning,' says Sutter in his Reminiscences, 'I hoisted it over my fort and began firing guns. The firing continued until nearly all the glass in the fort was broken. The Sonoma prisoners, not knowing what to make of it, greatly wondered. Then I went and told them: "Now," I said, "we are under the protection of this great flag and will not henceforth be afraid to talk to one another. Frémont is a tyrant." Glad to escape anarchy, they rejoiced with me.' Some of the Bear people then at the fort, however, 'made long faces, as they thought if the Bear Flag would remain, there would be a better chance to rob and plunder.'

In reality the hoisting of the Stars and Stripes cannot have been half as exhilarating an event as Sutter here depicted. Although it fulfilled an ardent wish of his of many years, and although his hailing of it was unreservedly wholehearted, seen at close quarters the circumstances accompanying the change of flags prove to be acutely painful. The very surroundings of the fort were a symbol of that tragic irony which always remained dominant in Sutter's life. All about the fort in the vast fields ripe golden wheat was swaying on tall stalks. Years of Herculean labor and an angel's patience were at last rewarded with the richest harvest. Alas, why exactly now? Frémont had taken away from Sutter the whole army of workers, white and Indian alike, thus leaving half of this splendid crop to perish on the stalk!

Even worse were conditions in the fort itself. We must here accuse Sutter of the pardonable insincerity of omitting from his account the one person who no doubt directed the ceremony of the flag change. This was Edward M. Kern, Frémont's topographical draftsman. With the arrival of American troops Frémont had again entered the service of his country and was now roaming about aimlessly at the head of a newly formed California battalion. For his draftsman Kern he had procured the rank of first lieutenant in this battalion, preferring, however, to leave him behind at New Helvetia as his substitute. It was Kern who now ruled at the fort. But that he was stationed there merely as the blind tool of Frémont's tyranny and not for military reasons is palpably clear, for he was a model of soldierly incompetence, so much so that beside him even Sutter appears as a martial thoroughbred. Commander Montgomery of the sloop *Portsmouth* stationed in the Bay, who kept Kern under his supervision during Frémont's absence, had to teach him the very ABC of soldiership. For instance: 'A lieutenant is a captain's substitute called upon to act during the latter's absence;' or: 'non-commissioned officers never keep sentinel duty, but are the superintendents of the duties of the soldiers.' In order to permit the garrison, which Kern commanded over as a matter of form, to function at all, another naval officer, Lieutenant Missroon, had to be dispatched to New Helvetia to organize things for Kern. And by way of making quite sure that the organization did not collapse the moment Missroon left, this officer struck upon the idea of formally asking Sutter to enter the service of the United States and to stand by as Kern's adjutant. For the garrison was composed mainly of Sutter's Indians; than which there could be no better proof of the confidence which the leaders of the occupation army had in Sutter (they were well informed on him by the War Office in Washington).

On August 16, 1846, Sutter, therefore, was created lieutenant of the United States Dragoons with a salary of $50 a month. But although he had handed over his fort to the United States of his own free will, and although without him it would have been of little use, yet he had to remain, in his own house and castle, the inferior of a perfect military nincompoop.

There can be no doubt but that it was Frémont's influence which kept the military layman Kern in New Helvetia. He needed him there as the tool of his incredibly petty revenge, in order to humiliate and tyrannize Sutter by remote control. If in spite of this situation no outburst occurred, it was only because Sutter was soldier enough to respect military discipline. But he did suffer under the humiliation. Frémont's stark ingratitude, the root of all these latest woes, rankled in his blood, and it is not surprising that throughout his life he covered up the painful ignominy of Kern's regime with a profound silence. Voluble as he could be, here, as in his unfortunate marriage, his various bankruptcies, and the ruinous conflict between him and his eldest son (of which more in its place) his reticence is more eloquent than words could ever be. Indeed, twenty years later he preferred telling untruths to the Congress of the United States rather than admit the existence of a man named Kern.

Even in his utterances during the Kern rule Sutter barely mentioned him. Once in a letter to Leidesdorff: 'I can assure you it is very unpleasant to have another as Commander in his own house and establishment.' And to the journalist Edwin Bryant who had just arrived with a small party of immigrants Sutter admitted that 'events had . . . so far deprived him of the control of his own property' that 'he did not feel authorized' to invite the newcomers into the fort, which, he said, 'was occupied by soldiers under the pay of the United States, and commanded by Mr. Kern.' *Mister* Kern!

Because of this deeply significant reticency, details concerning this Kern episode are completely lacking. But there are other examples to illustrate the indirect tyranny which Frémont exercised in New Helvetia through his tool Kern. Immediately following the hoisting of the Stars and Stripes, all the minor 'Bear prisoners' at the fort had been released, and Vallejo alone remained incarcerated. Kern kept him locked up in spite of all intervention of friendly Americans. Even to an order for Vallejo's immediate release signed by Commodore Stockton (Sloat's successor as commander-in-chief) Kern paid no heed, because Frémont's temper carried more weight with the frightened dilettante lieutenant than all the authority of the supreme officer. It took weeks until Kern in his inexorable civilian consciousness began to realize that, Major Frémont's caprice notwithstanding, orders from headquarters had to be obeyed. Then, at length, Vallejo, after a captivity of two months, was released, heart-broken, ailing, and very much impoverished. During his imprisonment the Bear men and Frémont had taken away from him all his cattle and his horses.

It is hardly overstating the case to say that Frémont's cruel hand weighed ten times more heavily on Sutter than on Vallejo. These were dark, bitter days for Sutter. Nor need we be surprised that again Sutter now clutched at the straw that once before had floated before him and vanished again: the hope of selling his fort. 'I would be able to pay all my debts and live comfortably on my farm at Hock,' he wrote to Leidesdorff. This time the United States would be the purchaser and it may be taken as an index of Sutter's eagerness to sell that he marked down the price of the establishment from the original $100,000 to $80,000.

But as usual circumstances were against him. For the time being, it is true, the fort was of great importance to the conquering army, so vital, indeed, as to cause the establishment of the first government mail service in California between it and Sonoma. Sutter's Fort allowed the United States troops to concentrate their military operations on the south of the country where, because of the lack of a similar fortified position and the far greater native population, they had a much harder stand. However, the mere occupation of the fort served as well as a purchase and in the end was much cheaper, and the burden which Sutter had taken upon his shoulders with the building of this establishment remained upon him.

Long before the resistance of southern California to the forces of the United States was broken, the civilization of the nineteenth century came striding ashore. Dr. Robert Semple, that versatile seven-foot dentist famous for wearing spurs on his calves, established the first newspaper, the *Californian*. Yerba Buena changed its name to San Francisco. And in New Helvetia Sutter himself helped introduce newfangled notions by taking the first United States census of the Sacramento valley.

But the event which perhaps did more than any other to change the atmosphere of California was the arrival on August 3, 1846, of the ship *Brooklyn* with a full cargo of Mormons under the Elder Samuel Brannan. They had hoped to escape what they called the tyranny of the United States by the initiation of a Church State of God on the 'uninhabited' Pacific Coast. While their Prophet, Brigham Young, traveled overland with his companions, Sam Brannan had chartered the *Brooklyn* for himself and as many of his fellow saints who had money to pay for passage around Cape Horn in addition to a liberal commission to Brannan for his bright idea. But they had reckoned without the host. The unexpected sight on these shores of the Stars and Stripes is said to have prompted the elder saint to exclaim: 'By God, there's that damned American flag again!' Most of these Mormons were at once pressed into the American army of occupation and formed into a Mormon battalion of their own. In Sam Brannan, however, a printer by trade, there had arrived the precursor of a class of Americans of which much more will be heard. He was the advance specimen of those devilishly shrewd and unscrupulous money-makers which were soon to swoop down on California like a plague of locusts.

Apart from the Mormons and the American troops, immigration was almost nil in 1846. Still, Sutter's informers in New York wrote of ten or twenty thousand ready to take the first news of peace as their cue for starting out west, and the intelligence that even now a few Swiss families were on their way caused Sutter to quiver mildly with a happy tremor, as he hoped to find among these countrymen a few experienced workers and dependable assistants. 'On people from Switzerland you may depend, and they are very punctually and strict honest,' he wrote to Leidesdorff, forgetting, as usual when he was excited, to mind his grammar.

But the immigration sensation of the season was the Donner party. In the autumn there came to Sutter's Fort two starving men, walking skeletons barely able to carry themselves upright, who brought news of a large company of almost 100 immigrants, men, women and children, struggling desperately, slowly and on short rations through the Nevada desert.

Irrespective of all difficulties—men, animals and provisions had largely been conscripted and requisitioned by the army—Sutter immediately had five mules loaded with victuals and sent along two of his best Indians. Not until they had crossed the entire mountain range did these rescuers finally meet the company at Truckee meadows, and they found them in such deplorable condition, sick, famished, tottering, that the provisions Sutter had sent seemed little better than a drop in a bucket. Before they reached the summit of the pass now bearing the name of the tragic party, snow had fallen in such grim mountain blizzards that further advance was impossible. Their cattle, shrunk to a pitiable herd by the hardships of the waterless desert and the ravages of thieving Indians, were lost in the first snowstorm, and with them vanished the last hope of keeping alive during the winter in the improvised high sierra camp on what is today called Donner Lake.

Now began the most horror-laden tragedy in the history of white man's conquest of this continent. Not until the whole camp was reduced to skeletons, some still able to walk, others long invalid, and some dead, did a forlorn hope of ten, including Sutter's two Indians and five women, try to struggle through the yards of snow to the summit of the pass and into the Sacramento valley, a journey which took almost a month. Long before they reached the valley, four of them died of cold and starvation, their skinny, leathery bodies furnishing a ghastly little meal to the survivors. A little later Sutter's two Indians were killed and eaten by white men become insane with hunger.

The tales of this mountain horror brought into the valley by the surviving members of the forlorn hope set the settlements gasping. As quickly as possible a second relief party was dispatched from Sutter's Fort. It succeeded in rescuing many of the snowbound. But the third, a pretentious official affair, bungled by one Midshipman Selim E. Woodworth and the dilettante Lieutenant Kern, was hardly more than a cowardly dress-parade on horseback to the edge of the snow, beyond which the precious uniforms would not allow these would-be soldiers to advance. Many of the gruesome winter's captives therefore died. The rest succeeded miraculously in clinging to the outermost fringes of life by boiling and chewing raw bullock-hides, or the remnants of their worn shoes. Some unofficial members of the third relief expedition finally attended to what rescuing there was left to be done; but two persons, too weak to be moved, had to be left behind. Of these, the last survivor, Louis Keseberg, a tall German, was not brought to the fort until late in the spring. Alone in the ghastly mountain camp, he had kept body and soul together by extricating what little nourishment he found in the frozen skeletons of the unburied victims of this tragedy.

All the pitiful human ruins surviving the demonic horrors of a foodless sierra winter were finally gathered in Sutter's Fort. Here they were sheltered and clothed, attended by the fort physician, nourished back to life and human countenance, and, wherever possible, given employment after health and strength came back to them. At no other time did the Lord of New Helvetia stand in his fortress more like a true little king of men. Without his fort, without the settlers he had brought into the valley, without his having previously tamed the Indians of those regions, without his humaneness and his readiness to make supreme sacrifices, what would have been the fate of all of the Donner party but merciless perdition to the last of them? It was owing to the fort that at least half of them could be saved. This rescue work, in truth, constituted the crowning of Sutter's pioneer work, the supreme justification of all he had tried to achieve and done as a colonizer.

It is true that he was not able, later, to pay those among the rescued whom he employed. The weight of the military occupation, superimposed upon his already overburdened state, made this impossible. This makes it none the less surprising that among those who owed their life to him there were a few who complained he did not pay them.

The war which was meanwhile waged in the south had nothing on its record half as fierce and starkly savage as the unequal fight of this ill-organized train of emigrants against snow, deadly cold and crazing hunger. For a time the Californians fought like angered beasts and succeeded in driving the Americans into an uncomfortably tight place. But at the very moment of the crisis new troops arrived from the east under General Kearney. For another month, then, a bitter fight was waged in the vicinity of Los Angeles, until the valiant Californians saw that further resistance would be sheer suicide.

In all these battles Frémont had distinguished himself by his persistent absence; but by some curiously capricious fate or his own stage-managing, he arrived at the very moment the Californians at last threw up their arms. It was he who accepted their formal surrender. Again, as in the Bear revolt, it was he, who had no merit in the victory who carried off the final honors by signing on January 13, 1847 the Treaty of Cahuenga in the name of the United States. That was the end of the war.

But not the beginning of peace. There followed an unsavory sequence of wretched quarrels revolving primarily around the question, which of the various officers was now to represent the government. General Kearney, the only one who had come with quite specific instructions, namely, to 'establish temporary civil government,' found himself confronted with Commodore Stockton's flat refusal to recognize his authority. Stockton appointed Frémont Civil Governor of California with seat in Los Angeles, while he himself returned to Monterey as military commander.

Soon more troops arrived, under Colonels Richard Mason and Stevenson, which latter came with a regiment of New York Volunteers. The instructions these army men brought made it quite clear that Washington had designated the senior land-officer, General Kearney, to govern California; so that, backed by these new forces, Kearney could at last assume actual command. He summoned Frémont to appear before him in Monterey. There, pressed to state whether he intended to obey orders or not, the mulish would-be governor walked out of General Kearney's presence without an answer, with the result that he found himself forthwith in the predicament of being indicted for gross insubordination, mutiny and other major offences.

With Frémont's fiasco, his satellite Edward M. Kern fell likewise unmercifully from the skies. In March 1847, while Kern was pretending with Midshipman Woodworth to direct the third rescue expedition for the Donner party, Kearney arrived at Sutter's Fort on an inspection trip. He could find nothing but the most ruinous criticism for all Kern had done, and the upshot was that when the latter returned from flirtation with relief-work, he found that his job at Sutter's Fort no longer existed. Sutter was again in actual command.

The nightmare was at last gone from Sutter's Fort. The Lord of the Sacramento was himself again. No longer sovereign, though, he was once more a citizen of another nation. Half-German by the accident of birth, Swiss by parentage and prefer-ence, French officer by imposture, Mexican by naturalization, he was now by conquest as well as by choice a citizen of the United States, John A. Sutter. His heart's desire of so many years was achieved. And who would deny that he himself had been one of the prime agents of the vital change? Whether he had been driven to that isolated wilderness spot in the Sacramento valley by blind instinct, guided there by his own subdued clairvoyance, or placed there by invisible hands of destiny, the fortress of New Helvetia and the little buffer state were the creations of his will and energy. He had given the United States the first firm foothold in these regions. More than any other man he had worked to populate the country with immigrants from the United States. The presence of these men, the protection they were assured of in New Hel-vetia, the circumstance that Sutter's Fort dominated the entire northern half of the land in so far as it lay beyond the reach of naval craft in the bay, all this had secured to the United States one half of the country without combat and had rendered the con-quest of the south comparatively easy. Beyond doubt there is in-herent truth in what General William T. Sherman said when he remarked of Sutter: 'To him, more than to any single person, are we indebted for the conquest of California with all its treasures.'[7]

For a short while, from June until September 1847, a new but friendly garrison of New York Volunteers under Lieutenant Anderson was stationed at the fort. And significantly enough,

Sacramento from the foot of J Street, 1849
Stokes Collection of Historical Prints, New York Public Library

San Francisco, 1849
Stokes Collection of Historical Prints, New York Public Library

Sutter, who shunned the very name of Kern as if it were poison and to the end of his days preferred telling untruths, even to the Congress of the United States, rather than admit the existence of a man by that name, the same Sutter acknowledged without a trace of shame that, while the New York Volunteers were at his fort, 'Lieut. Anderson commanded, I turned over my command to him.'

On June 1, Colonel Mason had taken over the reins as Military-Governor, and General Kearney returned east over the immigrants' trail. Following him was Frémont, a virtual prisoner, going to his court-martial in Washington. They spent the night at Sutter's Fort, and with obvious satisfaction Sutter wrote a few years later, when he compiled the brief summary of events known as the Sutter Diary: 'June 13th, arrived General Kearney with Frémont as his prisoner.'

This, probably, was ample atonement for what he had been made to suffer.

Tried by court-martial in Washington, Frémont was found guilty of gross insubordination, mutiny, and half a dozen more major offences; but in view of his services as an explorer, he was recommended to the President's clemency. From President Polk Frémont expected an annulment of the verdict; but the President confirmed it, although he stayed the punishment. Whereupon Frémont, in a fine rage, threw down before the President's feet his rank and his commission.

31. *TRANSITION*

WITH the end of the war a joyous feeling of recovery and rejuve-
nation pervaded California. The influx of new elements, of overland immigrants, Mormons, soldiers, quickened the pulse of life
and toughened every fiber. A new impetus was given to trade and
commerce. Good mechanics could at last be found.

Sutter now had the pleasure of a companionable garrison.
Visiting officers lent color and social tone to his settlement. The
swelling volume of business sometimes kept him at his desk, writing letters until four o'clock in the morning. It caused the incessant coming and going of messengers, on foot, on horseback, by
wagon, launch, and canoe. New outhouses, granaries, a new
threshing-floor were being built and a new, larger baking-oven.
Life was again replete with flavor and zest. The very air was
humming with delight.

Most urgent at this particular time, the middle of 1847, was
the need of wood, which Sutter required for a hundred purposes:
for the new buildings that were constantly being added to the
settlement, for barrels, shingles, rafts and boats, for wagons, spin-
ning-wheels and weaving-looms, for pumps to irrigate his vegetable gardens, for fences, for the making of charcoal needed in the
smithy, and the bark of the oak for the re-opened tannery. New
exploring parties were, therefore, again sent into the mountains
to locate suitable sites for lumber camps.

Yet, with all the new hustle and bustle, fundamentally the
change of regime in California can hardly be said to have brought
about a change in New Helvetia. It was essentially a case of new
wine in old skins.

As at the beginning of his enterprise, Sutter still depended for
the bulk of his labor upon the Indians, and no employer ever had

a more knotty labor problem on his hands than he. As always, only a few of the Indians were willing to work steadily, these permanent hands being either former mission Indians or orphans brought up by Sutter. During working hours the common Indian laborers had to be unrelentingly watched by mounted *vaqueros*, and to prevent desertions at night it was necessary to pen them up within the fort, where they slept huddled together in a corner of the court or locked up in a room. 'In these dormitories,' writes Heinrich Lienhard, who was for a time keeper of the keys, 'there were neither beds nor even straw, but everyone was at liberty to make himself as comfortable as he could on the bare floor. When I then opened the door in the morning, a quite particular odor oozed out towards me, for there were of course no toilets. It is not hard to imagine what these rooms looked like after two weeks, for sooner they were never cleaned.'

In general, sanitary conditions at the fort left much to be desired. No drainage system, the peculiar method of feeding the Indians, a well in the center of the court from which came all drinking water, the drowning of an occasional skunk or other creature which fell in the well, the refuse from slaughtering lying about behind the fort and attracting coyotes and other scavengers which would creep in through openings in the wall and invade the kitchen and larder if these were left unlocked—with all this it is not surprising that from time to time typhoid epidemics, then called 'mountain fever,' visited New Helvetia.

Now again, in the midst of the lusty activities and new growth at the close of the war, the blight of this fever fell upon the colony, making savage inroads especially among the Indians. Field-work, the cutting, binding, and threshing of wheat came almost to a standstill. Dr. Bates, the physician of the settlement, was kept busy almost day and night, and Sutter accompanied him on many of his visits. For despite the seemingly crude methods (which unhappily proved to be the only efficient ones) employed in marshaling Indian labor, Sutter always had a deep personal interest in the welfare of his savages and a great liking for these unspoiled and indolent, but nevertheless charming children of the wilderness. He had, moreover, been appointed Sub Indian-Agent for the Sacramento and the lower San Joaquin Valley.

The epidemic lasted all summer and far into the fall and winter. As late as September (harvesting having begun in June) one third of Sutter's wheat was still uncut and exposed to the weather. Sadly he wrote to Leidesdorff on September 10, 'I am sorry to say that I will loose at least 3000 fanegas [4800 bushels] of Wheat in the fields, on account the prevailing decease among the Indians, some weeks I had hardly from 20 to 25 Indians, and work for more as 200.' And he added: 'The time has past when it could be depended on Indians, we need now cutting and thrashing Machines.' The time had indeed passed, though in a meaning rather different from the one which Sutter here attempted to convey. The crop of this year was to be the last one harvested outside the fort, and the machines which came were made to gather a golden harvest that had not grown on the stalk but in the soil.

For the time being, however, with or without Indians, life even during the epidemic continued rich and colorful. In August a seething wave of commotion was brought to the fort by the Mormons who were on their way to the Great Salt Lake. They were only awaiting the message of their prophet before continuing their journey, meanwhile having their horses shod, buying animals and provisions and in general enlivening the commerce of the fort.

Never before had Sutter's establishment been so brimming with life and so filled with the most diverse elements and happenings. There was the garrison of New York Volunteers, there were eminent civilian and military visitors—even Vallejo. There were marriages and burials, births and court sessions. There were serio-comic incidents such as the cutting of a squaw's hair for bad be-havior or the flogging of an Indian for stealing. This latter pun-ishment was administered in maritime fashion: the culprit was tied face down to one of the large logs of fire-wood piled up in a corner of the yard, and whipped on his bare back by another na-tive with a cat-o'-nine-tails of raw hide. Then there were wild horses to be broken or wild oxen trained to the plow. There were frequent *matanzas* to provide beef for the little army of workers. Sometimes several oxen a day were killed, all of them wild beasts just in from the open range. Before they could be slaughtered, they often provided all the gory thrills of the bull-ring. These ani-mals were lassoed by the *vaqueros* and dragged into the corral adjacent to the south-east corner of the fort walls. But before they could be shot there with muskets and, with lassoes thrown around their horns, pulled into the walled-off section of the corral to be cut up, there were frequent 'scenes;' a *vaquero*'s horse would be thrown into the air or its belly ripped open by a raging 'stag,' and there were many narrow escapes for ponies and riders.

Incidents of a much lighter, if hardly less meaty kind are shielded behind the name of Lucinda, whose coming and going is twice recorded in the New Helvetia Diary; on September 21, for instance, when the entry, more eloquent than usual, goes so far as to divulge that 'Lucinda the Widdow arrived.' Lucinda was a highly professional widow. She had been married during her overland trip the year before, only to convince her young husband after ten hours of marital bliss that she was too much for him. Without delay he got himself divorced from her. An attempt upon a second potential husband in the same caravan failed; but in California she married and soon buried a boyish mate; then a sailor, who fared no better; and she is reported to have married three times within six weeks. Apparently, thereafter, she was convinced of the hopeless insufficiency of marriage and chose an itinerant living as better suited to her talents.[8] This time, alas, she missed her main chance by a day or two; for just before her arrival the garrison of New York Volunteers had been withdrawn from Sutter's Fort and removed to Sonoma.

The garrison gone, life again followed a more normal course, though as it were, through a much broader, deeper, and ever widening channel, in keeping with American tradition. Of the old employees, John Bidwell was still a frequent visitor and from time to time was engaged for various clerical tasks or as a surveyor or special agent. Pierson B. Reading was about to settle on his own ranch in the north of the valley. Samuel Hensley, the former manager of Hock, had gone east with Commodore Stockton in order to testify in Frémont's court-martial.

Prominent among the newer employees were George McKinstry, manager-general, and Dr. Bates, the fort physician. Louis Keseberg, the last survivor of the Donner party, was now captain of the launch *Sacramento*, and James Wilson Marshall, the erratic carpenter, had become Sutter's partner in the new sawmill, of which more will presently be heard.

At this time Sutter also had in his employ ten or twelve of his Swiss countrymen, some of whom held responsible positions. Samuel Kyburz, an Aargovian, had for a time been *majordomo* but was now used in other capacities. The keys of the fort were now held by Heinrich Lienhard, to whose critical observations and colorful account of his experiences in Sutter's service we are indebted for a great deal of trustworthy information. Another Helvetian, Jacob Wittmer, was presently to be thrown into unenviable relief.

Little change had occurred among the other settlers of the valley. Near Monte Diablo John Marsh was still given to misanthropy, to his squaw, and to grumbling for having been disturbed in his solitariness by his noisy American countrymen. South of the fort, on the Cosumne River, the old fort cook Bill Daylor had established himself after his meddling with Sutter's favorite paramour had made his departure unavoidable. Near him was located Perry McCoon, formerly Sutter's overseer of stock and even now husband of one of his master's discarded Indian·mistresses, a squaw called Mary.

Sutter's nearest neighbor was still John Sinclair. A little above him on the American River was Leidesdorff's farm in charge of a *majordomo*. To the north, on Bear Creek, about twenty miles from the fort, lived little Bill Johnson and Sebastian Keyser on their jointly owned farm, the former with two squaws, the latter with a white woman whom he had recently married, lost, and regained. Still further north, and east of Feather River, resided the Bavarian squaw-man Nicolaus Allgeier, while the present site of Marysville was occupied by the ranch New Mecklenburg of Theodore Cordua, also a squaw-man and ex-husband of a mulatto woman in South America. South of Cordua's farm and west of Feather River, on the spot now occupied by the village of Oswald, Sutter's Hock Farm was in charge of Kanaka Harry, now the husband of his master's ex-paramour Manaiki. Bidwell had acquired the Chico ranch near Butte Creek, but was not yet living there. Still further north, near the volcano bearing his name, was Peter Lassen's farm, and finally, northernmost of all the settlers in the valley, Pierson B. Reading was just establishing himself on Cottonwood Creek. Between these men, here and there, a few others had located farms; but, all in all, they counted barely two score, and practically all of them were squaw-men.

Here, too, then, the conquest had as yet wrought little change. In actual fact, though not yet legally, the country was now under the Stars and Stripes, the extreme fringe of an immense American territory. But the conquest itself was far from having welded this western coast to the old Atlantic states. As if by a vast uncharted ocean, the two coasts were still separated by an incredibly expansive and practically unmapped sea of deserts, half-deserts, and barren mountains. It took more than a mere military seizure to forge a link between these two remote domains, to span the gulf of sands and rocks.

And here again, destiny had fixed its gaze on Sutter as the one man to do the incredible as its blind tool, to forge the initial link of the gigantic bridge.

None but Sutter.

32. *AN INTIMATE PORTRAIT*

LITTLE seemed to have changed with Sutter apart from the undeniable fact that he was growing older. Always meticulously dressed, as befitted a man of his exalted station, he looked, to quote Edwin Bryant's description, like 'a gentleman between forty-five and fifty years of age, and in manner, dress, and general deportment, he approaches so near what we call the "old school gentleman," as to present a gulfy contrast from the rude society by which he is surrounded.' He was never seen outside his office without the silver-topped cane. With his curly blond hair, bewitching clear-blue eyes with their disarming twinkle, with his moustache and side-whiskers preciously cared for, and being the personification of courtesy and fine manners in his intercourse with even the plainest member of his colony, he appeared indeed to be a true little blue-blooded king, a bird of paradise among the crows and sparrows.

Underneath the old glittering surface, however, he was no longer quite the same. The marked change in him that began in the disillusionment of the Micheltorena campaign had steadily progressed and apparently intensified under the gnawing, the fretting, and humiliation of the Frémont-Kern tyranny.

Although the upshot of the war itself was the realization of an old cherished dream, it had actually cost Sutter more than a pretty penny and left him deeper in the rut than he had ever been before. Even with a man as habitually cheerful and optimistic as Sutter, the feeling that he was, as it were, chained to a treadmill must at length become oppressive. He might try to ignore it, but there it was nevertheless, following him like his own shadow, a paralyzing influence, and at wide intervals popping up, like a Jack-in-the-box, disguised in one of his queer, ungrammatical 'asides' in his usually straightforward, matter-of-fact business letters.

The change of flag, then, had not benefited him materially. While the war lasted, it had laid low his industrial enterprises and caused the partial loss of one year's harvest. The typhoid epidemic of 1847 was equally damaging, so that what payments in wheat he was able to make to the Russians did not materially reduce his debt to them. Moreover, in 1846 Leidesdorff at Yerba Buena had been appointed Russian agent. The moment Sutter had tried to dispose of his fort to the government of the United States, Leidesdorff had caused an attachment to be levied on the entire property. Leidesdorff, trying as he did to serve both the Russians and Sutter to the best of his abilities, found himself in a position no less difficult than Sutter's; he was hard pressed by the Russians to bring about a foreclosure of the New Helvetia mortgage and did his utmost trying to avoid that action. Did Sutter know how close he was to the abyss? Apparently he did not. As though he were a sleepwalker dancing over steep-gabled roofs he was guarded against knowledge of his danger.

Again it must be emphasized that this critical situation was not altogether Sutter's fault. Had he been able to collect from the government for rents and provisions furnished, half of his Russian debt could have been wiped out at one stroke and the danger of foreclosure would have been averted. As matters stood, he was unable to draw on the Treasury, because the garrison of the fort had been most of the time an appendage to Frémont's California Battalion, and since Frémont was now a prisoner facing court-martial for almost every major offence, it became exceedingly doubtful whether Washington would acknowledge any of Frémont's actions in California as having been performed in the service of the United States. As was so often the case, luck was against Sutter.

There seemed no remedy for these embarrassing circumstances except new and larger enterprises which would help pay off old obligations. Sutter was in harness almost day and night, planning and scheming with greater earnestness than ever, confident, tenacious, and with less vaporous enthusiasm than in his youth.

Yet the conclusion is inevitable that in his forty-fifth year, at an age when other men approach the peak of life, Sutter had definitely passed it and was on the downward path. Long as his youth had been, old age came to him equally ill-timed. He was even now 'the old man,' or 'the old gent' of New Helvetia; and these nicknames by which his employees called him were apt. He looked older than his years. The titanic strain of building up his empire in the untamed wilderness, without proper help and without resources, had sapped the roots of his strength. Though physically he was still hale, hearty and possessed of great endurance, the powers of his mind were waning.

What lifted Sutter high above the multitudes were his intuitive faculties of heart and spirit, his sparkling, bubbling, iridescent nature, his buoyant personality and truly regal presence. These are endowments very rarely coupled with a cool, trenchant, calculating intellect, or with a passion for system and order. They are gifts invaluable in social intercourse, in every function of life where direct personal contact determines everything. In the beginning of any social order it was men of Sutter's cast who, on the strength of their valor, prowess and irresistible personality, rose to be kings. But as soon as the political game becomes involved, abstract, impersonal, these kings must lose out; they become figureheads, mere symbols, ornaments, while the actual power is wielded by ministers initiated in the magic of abstract conquests, and remote control.

Sutter, king though he was, had not even such ministers. Never an efficient administrator and executive, his over-expanded realm was now quite beyond his ability to manage. He was gradually being swept from his moorings.

He had always been an easy master. Failure of crops, two wars, rescue expeditions and relief for immigrants and exploring parties had always swallowed up all his available means. And because he could but rarely pay out wages, his men did more or less as they pleased. They stole from him as much as they could or turned their positions into sinecures. In short, they gave as good as they got, or worse.

Samuel Hensley, for instance, had taken advantage of his position as manager of Hock Farm to offer hospitality at Sutter's cost to his numerous friends and to entertain them with hunting-parties and other fine pastime. Yet Sutter remembered Hensley as one of his most faithful men. Burns, who succeeded Lienhard as manager of the small Mimal ranch north of Hock, declined to accept instructions from his predecessor, because, as he stated, he had come not to work but to take it easy. Perry McCoon, when overseer of stock, branded every third newly born calf with his own iron, and when Bidwell reported this discovery to Sutter, the indulgent master merely offered the culprit a new contract, allowing him one fourth of the yearly increase of stock as his rightful pay, 'because one fourth was less than one third and he was still the winner in the bargain.' The Indians were, of course, no better. Lienhard found that the natives in charge of slaughtering systematically smuggled aside large chunks of the best meat from every animal, and that the Indian baker saved for his relatives a large flour-bag full of loaves from every batch coming from the oven.

We owe it chiefly to Henry Lienhard[9] that we possess a detailed and picturesque description of Sutter's relations with his employees and of conditions at New Helvetia about this time. This little Swiss, sound and honest to the marrow (though somewhat inclined to nagging), and one of those whose coming in 1846 had rather excited Sutter, was in charge of the little farm of Mimal for several months without receiving any wages, and finally came to the fort to have a word with Sutter. The latter, writes Lienhard, 'welcomed me more kindly than his last letter had led me to expect,' and the upshot of the interview was that Lienhard was appointed keeper of the keys at the fort.

At the fort Lienhard again worked for a long time without pay, but after repeated threats to leave succeeded in forcing a settlement on his master. This time he was to create a large fruit and vegetable plantation, for which Sutter furnished the land, tools, seeds, cuttings, labor, fences, and from which Lienhard was to obtain half of the proceeds. 'But,' he complains in his tale,

Sutter did not take any interest in my work and its results. I had to write him repeatedly, especially since he failed to deliver the promised gardening tools. My letters of complaint however, did not seem to impress him in the slightest degree. So I went to the fort in person to catch him on the hop. In spite of my complaints that he did not even fulfil the written terms of our contract, he remained calm and full of courtesy and kindness. 'Come and search the entire fort, you know best where things are to be found. Take what you need. You know we are in a new country where one cannot have everything the way one should like it.' This he said in such a fatherly fashion and he pacified me with so much friendliness that my big grudge with which I had come vanished completely, and I could not help liking him again. So I returned to my work, hoping for a turn for the better.

There were other things about Sutter which caused the little moralist to shake his head gravely, censoriously. While he still had guarded the keys of the fort, it had been part of his daily duty, after opening the gates in the morning, to betake himself to Sutter's private room, 'the office, as it was usually called,' to get the diary and receive the day's instructions, and on such occasions he discovered that 'Sutter was inclined to drink.' Several times he saw himself obliged to withdraw his master from the public gaze when he was no longer able to stand upright. 'In his room I took off his outer garments and put him on the bed. But, unfortunately, it was not long before the same thing happened again, and I was convinced now that too much drinking had become a habit with him.' One day there were not enough plates on the dinner-table, and when Lienhard took the Indian steward to task for it, he was told that Sutter, in his intoxication, had smashed the entire dinner-set. 'These discoveries were all the more painful to me,' Lienhard continues, 'as Sutter was bound to make the best impression upon every one who saw him for the first time.'

Nor did the little group of Indian women [10] who from morn till night were to be seen in Sutter's anteroom meet with Lienhard's approval. In fact he was one of the exceptional men and shocked, although the circumstances were by no means unusual in those border lands. In his exalted station, Sutter, of course, enjoyed almost Solomonic advantages which, with his sensual nature, he could not fail to turn to pleasurable account. Only the occupation of the fort by an American garrison had imposed on him the observance of a certain patriotic restraint. It was then that he had divorced himself from Manaiki and given her away in marriage to the best of his islanders, Kanaka Harry, now *majordomo* at Hock. But Sutter's interest in Manaiki persisted. While she resided at Hock, the New Helvetia Diary faithfully recorded every visit to the fort, as well as the births and death of the children she bore Harry. No doubt she continued to remain for Sutter a sentimental link with the romantic past put far behind him through the changes brought about by the American conquest.

At the time he released Manaiki, Sutter also gave away a favorite Indian girl to Perry McCoon, the overseer of stock. Since the departure of the New York Volunteers, however, he was again fully his own master, relieved of the need to keep up appearances in the presence of strangers.

Every time, every land, every newly settled region in particular, evolves its own laws. In all these amatory matters, Sutter remained entirely within the prerogatives of his lordly station and the accepted moral standards of the Indian frontier. Nevertheless, one cannot overlook the serious obverse of such regal unrestraint and indulgences. Sutter's ambitions were those of a world other than the frontier. His financial entanglements were more complex and his industrial problems more intricate than any mind resigned to frontier standards would ordinarily solve. Between his two worlds a rent was forming which allowed easy access to the sharp wedge of tragic catastrophe. It required little to widen this rent to an abyss deep enough to engorge Sutter and his whole little empire of New Helvetia, and with signs pointing distinctly towards an early old age and rapidly declining faculties of the mind, this danger could not be minimized. Was he aware of it?

With all his optimistic nature, he was, apparently, merely looking towards a golden future. Here beyond dispute lies one of the deep roots of Sutter's tragedy. It is perhaps idle at this late date to ask: whence this premature decline of a once virile mind? Was it a natural slackening due to the many years of unceasing supertension? Was it purely the upshot of his indulgences? Or must we see in it one of those freaks of fate which the one-track logic of our mind entirely fails to comprehend?

Whatever the reason, the fact of his beginning decline is undeniable. Seen at close quarters and contemplated as a factor in this drama of history, it cannot fail to impress one as a deeply tragic occurrence on the very eve of the discovery of gold and the chaotic gold-rush. It was doubly tragic in that Sutter himself was the chief agent in bringing about, although inadvertently, this revolutionary event.

33. *MILLS, MORMONS, AND ANASHE'S DAUGHTER*

IN any rural community, to be the owner of the gristmill or the lumbermill is to be king. For this reason alone it would have been incumbent upon Sutter to make himself the first man also in these matters. Indeed, as early as 1840, projects for such mills operated by water-power crop up in his correspondence, but they were invariably frustrated chiefly for the lack of credit and good mechanics.

Now, however, after the American conquest, the certainty of a rapidly increasing population (ten or twenty thousand were to come from New York and thousands from Oregon) rendered a far-sighted building program peremptory. The country must be prepared to accommodate all the newcomers. Moreover, the stringency of Sutter's financial situation made the tapping of such new lucrative sources, as gristmill and sawmill were bound to be, imperative. For, let there be no mistake, the Stars and Stripes now waving over Sutter's roof (mortgaged to the last nail and shingle) had been bought dearly.

As luck would have it now, a number of circumstances combined to make the beginning at this time of the two enterprises particularly opportune. First, Sutter had in his employ an ingenious, if cantankerous and erratic millwright and carpenter, James Wilson Marshall, who had already found what he termed an ideal location for a sawmill, some fifty miles up the American River, on its south fork. The large flourmill, five miles above the fort, was already under construction, though making little headway because of the lack of good labor.

Then something almost miraculous happened. In the latter part of August 1847 about 150 men of the disbanded Mormon battalion, en route to their new kingdom of God on the Great Salt Lake, stopped at the fort. It was on the Great Salt Lake where the news had reached the Mormon overland brigade under Brigham Young that California, too, was now in the hands of the Americans. And on the Salt Lake the Prophet had there and then decided to remain. The members of the extinct Mormon battalion, too, were now only awaiting the word of their Prophet to set out for their new home. And lo, as if coaxed out of the wings of the theater of destiny by the cue of a mysterious stage-manager, the Mormon messengers arrived forthwith, bringing the prophet's command: 'Stay! Stay where you are, until it is possible to raise food for all the saints in the new Kingdom of Utah.' What seemed even more miraculous was that there were an unusually great number of exceptionally skilled craftsmen among these Latter-day Saints of the Church of Jesus Christ. To Sutter this was a gift from heaven. It was exactly what in his heart he had been praying for these long years.

Two days after the arrival of the first large contingent of Mormons, on Friday, August 27, Sutter, according to the New

Helvetia Diary, 'made a contract and entered into partnership with Marshall for a sawmill to be built on the American fork,' and the very day after the signing of the papers Marshall departed for the mountains.

Among the members of the colony, Bidwell alone warned Sutter against this undertaking. He regarded the location selected by Marshall as utterly unsuitable, and to him there was about this project something altogether quixotic. 'It is hard to conceive,' he remarks, 'how any sane man could have selected such a site for a saw mill under the circumstances. Surely no other man than Marshall ever entertained so wild a scheme as that of rafting sawed lumber down the cañons of the American River, and no other man than Sutter would have been so confiding and credulous as to patronize him.' The site which Marshall had chosen, by the way, lay far outside Sutter's boundaries.

Bidwell's was the usual calamity howl of the sanely timid in the face of any departure from known rules of conduct. Under similar auspices Columbus had sailed forth, in the opinion of his contemporaries, to precipitate himself over the rim of the world. Not that anyone would at the time have thought of comparing Sutter's venture with that of the great discoverer. Yet, as the fates would have it, the effect of the discovery at the sawmill was no less profound, even if less permanent, than had been the discovery of Columbus on his own age. Indeed, the two events were but the beginning and the end of the same long-drawn-out adventure, considering that the ostensible purpose of the Genoese's intended shortcut to India was not fulfilled until 356 years later at Sutter's Mill.

For the time being, however, nobody in California took any particular notice of this mill, save as a laughing-stock. Like Bidwell, the rest of the country shook its head and chose to refer to Sutter's newest venture as 'another of Sutter's follies.'

For Sutter, however, there can be no doubt but that the building of these two mills was an event of paramount importance. In the middle of September the signing on *en masse* of Mormon workmen began. Sutter was overbrimming with praise for these workers, employing them in every corner of his realm. Their coming was to him a stroke of enormous good fortune, bringing to life, as if by magic, his oldest and most pious wishes. So unusual were they in their unheard-of ardor and zeal that on October 2, in the New Helvetia Diary, they are the subject of an entry of remarkable rarity in old California's annals of labor. It reads: 'A good many of the Mormons are sick on account of their working to hart.'

Once more the old Sutter awakened as he was jostled gleefully on the shoulders of this splendid young crew. Again visions arose, saner ones than before, and the reality of a future free from debts and anxieties became almost tangible. Seemingly in no time eight millstones were cut from the quarry on Stoney Creek, and without much hesitation the cautious Thomas Larkin delivered the iron for the sawmill. Acknowledging its receipt, Sutter wrote in his old optimistic vein:

The sawmill will be in operation in about 4 or 5 months and shall be able to supply the market with the finest of pine lumber the next spring or summer.—End of December my grist mill likewise will be in operation with 4 runs of 4 feet stones which will grind what the whole Sacramento Valley will be able to produce in wheat, and will be a real Marchand-Mill. Nothing is wanting now to this enterprise as the bolting clothes, and for these I take the liberty to apply to you for them as the protector of such undertakings. . . . My tannyard is now once carried on well, I have 1500 hides to tann. I have two tanneries and 3 shoemakers (Mormons) all the hands on my mills are Mormons and the best people which I has ever employed.—I hope now when the gristmill, sawmill & tannery are going well on, I will soon be out of my difficulty's.[11]

To Vallejo, whom the prison term at Sutter's Fort had converted from an enemy to a friend, he wrote: 'The Mormons are the best workers I have, without them the mills would not be made.' And to Leidesdorff he made the daring promise (actually to be fulfilled, though in a manner Sutter never dreamed of!) that within a year of beginning mill operations all his debts would be paid. The gristmill was to have a capacity of forty bushels an hour; from the sawmill he would bring on the market the finest planks California had yet seen, and 'above and below the flour Mill I can water an immense quantity of land which will be worth $25.— pr acre.'[12]

Thus, New Helvetia resounded with sheer glee, as though two mills were the millennium. The New Helvetia Diary, too, in its dry, business-like manner, shows clearly that the building of the mills dominated all activities and turned the fort into a pigeon-coop of endless arrivals and departures.

Tuesday, November 30, 1847, for instance, we read: 'A most beautiful day. . . . Went to Natoma [where the flourmill was being built] to see how they are raising the fram[e] of the Mill. 34 hands has been employed on it, and all was going on well and no accident happened. Wednesday, December 1: '. . . finished to raise the Mill house at Natoma.' Thursday, December 2: 'Despatched the Wagons with flour and Saltbeef to the Mountains [i.e., the sawmill in the mountains]. . . . Mr. Bidwell arrived from Sonoma. Preparing other Wagons which have to go to Morrow in the Mountains.—A fine day.— Henry Smith left for the Mountains.'—Friday, December 3: 'Despatched 4 Wagons with provisions to the sawmill and 4 Wagons direct to the shingel makers with provisions. . . . Gingery & Lenox has had some difficulty about the Millstones. Made a contract with Brouet & Kelly to get the necessary lumber saw yet for the mill. Mr. Bidwell surveyed a straight road to the Mill at Natoma. . . . . A fine day.'

For a brief time, then, another event typical of the new industrial age overshadowed the building activities. That was the arrival of California's first steamboat, on Saturday, December 4: 'Afternoon the little Steamboat arrived here from San Francisco having had a voyage of 7 days. Passengers Messrs McKinstry, Petit, Stevens, Edde, Scott, & Mrs. Gregson, Shaddon, Murphy, Sheldon, Saml. Smith, Daylor, Wyman, etc., etc..—A fine day.'

The little vessel belonged to William A. Leidesdorff, who had bought it from the Russians. Built in Sitka as a pleasure-craft for the Governor of the Russian-American colony, it was a small thing and the few passengers mentioned in the diary were almost more than it could carry. The voyage was the most uncomfortable anyone of them ever had, lasting six days and seven hours for about 100 miles, at about half the speed of the average pedestrian. Nevertheless, it was a memorable trip, all the more as it was the last one; for after her return to San Francisco the little steamer was sunk at its moorings during a gale.

Thus, with the nineteenth century rising with big strides towards its peak, the year 1847 drew to a close. At its end, however, there was yet another catastrophe, a little human tragedy, touching and mysterious, revealed to us only through a few semi-cryptic entries scattered over the pages of the New Helvetia Diary; but undoubtedly an event that went straight to the sentimental heart of Sutter. It concerns Anashe's daughter.

Anashe was the chief whose tribe, more than eight years before, had watched from ambush the ascent up the river of the strange white man. He had served as Sutter's pilot, rose to be supervisor of the salmon-fisheries, and although he had once participated in a conspiracy, he was in general considered one of his master's most trustworthy servants. Anashe also had a daughter, whose worth to Sutter can only be surmised from stammered utterances in his diary:

Sunday, December 19*th,* 1847.
  Visited with the Doctor Anashe's Daughter who was dieing; the Doctor bled her, and we left, and started again to bring her some remedies. . . . The boys had a dance.
Monday, December 20*th,* 1847.
  The doctor went to see Anashe's Daughter who is getting a little better.
Tuesday, December 21*st,* 1847.
  The doctor took a ride to see Anashe's Daughter who is getting well again.
Wednesday, December 22*nd.*
  Doctor Bates went to see Anashe's Daughter who is getting better. Anashe here himself getting flour.
Thursday, December 23*rd.*
  Doctor Bates visited Anashe's Daughter.
Saturday, December 25.
  A Christmas dinner in the Hatter house, given by the tanners & shoemakers. . . . Yanti arrived in the night with the news that Anashe's Daughter is death.

Behind these few staggering sentences tucked away between matter-of-fact remarks on trade, building construction and the weather, is screened a personal experience, the depth of which we cannot even approximately fathom. Indians had died by the score during the epidemic in the fall and summer; but only a few had their death recorded in the diary. Anashe's daughter alone was important enough to cause a special messenger to be dispatched to the mansion in the middle of the night. Was she another uncrowned queen of New Helvetia? Manaiki's successor? We can only guess.

No matter what her precise status, the unprecedented intrusion of such deeply personal concerns into the diary and the reiteration of those opaque utterances, outlining in the simplest gestures a little drama with its exposition of despair, the first glimmer of hope, the treacherous dawning of a new day of light and confidence, and the final inexorable darkness—all this is muteness of a touching eloquence.

But the significance of this event transcends Sutter's own feelings. We are again standing at one of those symbolical milestones. As the unique history of New Helvetia began with Chief Anashe's first friendly greetings to the white intruder, so the death of the chief's child now marks the beginning of the end. It is the end of Sutter's little Indian empire and of the Indian days of California as well.

Another month, and a new era was to be born. . . .

34. *LIGHTNING IN THE MOUNTAINS*

'The New Years day began very quiet. Invitation to dine with Mr. Sinclair, which has been accepted, remained over there till 9 o'clock in the evening. Mr. Kyburz gave a dinner to all hands remaining at the fort. 4 Guns has been fired. Despatched a Wagon for Dr. Bates & S. Norris which has missed the chance of the Launches. A fine day.'

With the day of rustic celebrations and rural calm thus recorded in the New Helvetia Diary, the year 1848, the most fateful in Sutter's life, began. The 'fine day' was not to last long.

For almost a month, though, work continued in the zestful allegro tempo struck by the arrival of the Mormons at the fort, and with one of these latter almost stealing the show from Sutter. This man was Fifield, the master blacksmith. On January 7 the diary reports: 'Today the Sawmill Crank has been commenced and will be finished tomorrow as the iron is good, this is the heaviest kind of Blacksmith work which has ever been done here, and give Fifield great credit as a good workman.' Little sparks of sentiment in this work-a-day record betray Sutter's heart. A week later the mill-irons were dispatched to the sawmill in the mountains, over a road so rain-soaked that the wagons remained rutted in the mud for several days.

Work at the sawmill had gone ahead by leaps and bounds. The dam was completed and the tail-race was dug. For the first time things progressed according to schedule, smoothly, joyfully, and in general everything looked pretty. The very name of the mountain valley seemed to have struck the keynote. The Indians called it *cul-luh-mah*, the beautiful valley, Coloma of today.

But during January the skies grew black with massive clouds spilling torrential downpours, endangering the barely finished dams of both mills and holding the last man in tremulous suspense.

Suddenly, on January 28, during one of these cloudbursts, Marshall arrived at the fort and wildly demanded the whereabouts of Sutter. Always a mysterious man, the effect of a reckless chase of fifty miles on horseback through a slashing rainstorm, his picturesque buckskin dress, his wide-brimmed hat and Mexican *serape*, all this gave him the appearance of a madman. Dripping with water, bespattered with red mud, gasping, palpitating, he entered Sutter's office next to the guard-room.

The sight of Marshall in this wild outfit and with seeming craziness in his countenance shocked Sutter. What was the meaning of the millwright's coming at this time? He had been at the fort only two weeks before, to supervise in person the transport of the mill-irons, and only the preceding day Sutter had dispatched a wagon with fresh provisions to the sawmill. Nothing could be lacking up there. Was this another Job's post? Was it the dam?

But Marshall would not answer questions. With unwarrantable rudeness he demanded to speak to Sutter in a place where they would be undisturbed and safe from eavesdropping. Sutter found the demand very strange, though not so unusual with a moonstruck fellow like Marshall, and he immediately took him into his bed-sitting-room in the main building. Yielding reluctantly to Marshall's insistent demand, he locked the door.

After the millwright was reasonably assured that they were alone and the door was locked, he demanded two bowls of water. A bell-signal brought to the door an Indian boy who was sent for the required things. Next Marshall asked for a stick of redwood, some twine and sheet-copper, and upon being asked what he intended to do with all these things he explained that he wanted to make a pair of scales.

'But I have scales enough in the apothecary's shop!' Sutter exploded and went to fetch a pair, forgetting, as he returned, to lock the door again. At length Marshall produced from the pockets of his pantaloons 'a white cotton rag which contained something rolled up in it,' some yellowish, metal-like substance. But just as he was about to unfold it, and before Sutter had had half a glimpse at the contents of the rag, the door opened and a clerk entered to ask Sutter a question about his office work. Marshall grew furious. 'How quick Mr. Marshall put the yellow metal in his pocket again can hardly be described,' says Sutter.

The clerk gone, Marshall burst out: 'There! Didn't I tell you we had listeners!' It took some time to pacify him. The door was locked anew, and Marshall at last brought forth again from his pocket his mysterious cotton rag. Unfolding it, he displayed its contents before Sutter's eyes.

'I believe that this is gold,' he said tremulously, admitting at the same time that some of the men at the mill had laughed at his notion and called him crazy.

Gold? This was unexpected, unusual.

Frantically, Sutter examined the specimens, resorting at length to the *Encyclopaedia Americana*, an old edition of which was in his library. Then, having studied the article 'Gold,' he submitted the intriguing yellow substance to all the tests that could be made in the privacy of the room.

Aqua fortis did not affect the metal. It was then balanced on the scales with an equal amount of silver (a little over two dollars' worth of silver was all that could be hunted up in Sutter's Fort!) and when the scales were dipped into water, the one containing the yellow substance sank heavily, outweighing the silver. It seemed evident that this was gold of the finest kind, at least twenty-three carat, Sutter declared.

How did Marshall find it? What had happened at the sawmill?

Today, thanks to a few diaries of Mormon workers connected with the discovery, we are accurately informed on this epoch-making event. It seems that the first trial run of the new sawmill had disclosed one very serious fault. The tail-race lacked sufficient depth at the lower end, so that the water would dam up against some gravel bars, wash back against the flutter-wheel and prevent it from turning. For a few days, therefore, all efforts were bent upon deepening the channel. The task of blasting the exposed rock was assigned to Henry Bigler, a young Mormon of Swiss ancestry. Helping him were about twenty Indians who dug up the gravel bed of the channel and with their hands lifted out the larger pieces of the blasted rock and the boulders. At night, then, when work ceased, the flood-gates were opened to allow the water to rush through freely and wash out the loosened sand and gravel. And thus, inadvertently, gold-washing in one of its primitive forms, sluicing, had been initiated.

It is claimed by some that James Wilson Marshall had an ink-ling of the existence of gold in these mountains. On January 23, we learn from the accounts of workmen, Marshall suddenly or-dered Brown, one of his Mormons, to fetch him a pan or tin plate, and with this he began to wash some of the sand from the bottom of the race. At the time, however, he merely insisted that he believed he had 'found a gold mine,' and because he had noth-ing to show for proof was freely ridiculed by his underlings. In the evening, Marshall again ordered the flood-gate opened, giv-ing special instruction to Bigler and Brown to 'shut it off again in the morning' and to 'throw in a little sawdust and rotten leaves and dirt and make it all tight.'

Early the following morning, while the crew were having breakfast in their cabin, Marshall climbed down into the tail-race after the gates had been tightly locked. And there, lying in crevices and depressions of the exposed rock, about six inches be-low the surface of the water, he found some glimmering par-ticles, which he gathered and kept in the depressed crown of his white woolen hat.

Then he went to join his workmen. Carrying his old white hat lovingly in his arms and 'looking wonderfully pleased and good-natured,' he who was otherwise inclined to be a surly man beamed: 'Boys, by God I believe I have found a gold-mine!' Setting his hat down on the workbench he displayed to the aston-ished gathering his morning's gleaning of shining granules.

The men were rather inclined to tease him for his optimism. One of them, Azariah Smith, forthwith drew from his pocket a five dollar gold-piece saved from his army pay. Held beside it, or bitten between the teeth, Marshall's mystifying flakes and grains compared favorably with the coin. One of the grains was then heated in the fire and came out bright and untarnished. Ham-mered on the anvil it flattened out to the thinness of paper. Another particle was thrown into boiling lye which Mrs. Weimar, the camp cook, happened to have ready for the making of soap. Lye, too, did not affect it.

For a few mornings the tail-race was then inspected very searchingly by all the men, and every night's sluicing laid bare another little yield. On the fourth day Marshall decided it was high time to inform Sutter and to consult his superior knowledge in an effort to dispel the last vestige of doubt. For, according to Henry Bigler, 'the fever had set in and gold was on the brain.' After each morning's gleaning the regular work continued, 'but gold was the talk.'

This, roughly, was the story which Marshall, in incoherent fragments, told Sutter while they were cloistered in his room. Marshall's report, his initial evasiveness, the discussions, interruptions, the reading up on the matter, the procuring of the many paraphernalia, and the tests, all together had consumed half a day. But at length Marshall's patience was exhausted. He wanted to return to the sawmill, although it was very late and rain was still pouring in torrents. He refused to take any nourishment. Moreover, he insisted that Sutter accompany him without delay. This Sutter could not do. The millwright then deferred his departure till the following day.

What was necessary now, above all, was strict secrecy. Sutter knew that as soon as the secret was out all work would stop. Gold is demoralizing! 'Mein Gott!' he is said to have exclaimed in his Swiss accent, 'If de boys find out dere is gold dere, dere is no more work at our mill. It will be all up—gone to the dyfel.' He admits that he 'thought a great deal during the night about the consequences which might follow such a discovery.'

Did he know that Marshall's appearance at the fort, marked as it was with every symptom of a remarkable event, had at once set the fort population puzzling? Was he aware that the strange

assortment of articles called for or fetched one after another into
the locked room and the unprecedented length of the secret meeting had given rise to guessing conferences in many nooks and corners of the workshops? That his own men came very close to hit-
ting the nail on the head? Lienhard, who was at the fort during
those hours, tells us that the guessers before long concluded that
Marshall must have discovered a quicksilver mine like the one
found near San José two years before.

Of all this excitement—soon to span the globe and to affect almost the last little hamlet of the world—the New Helvetia
Diary of January 28, 1848, reveals nothing except a few words:
'Mr. Marshall arrived from the mountains on very important
business.'

Arrangements having been completed for Sutter's absence, he,
accompanied by a *vaquero* and an Indian soldier, departed for the
sawmill in the evening of February 1, staying overnight at the
flourmill. The Diary for the next four days bears the laconic entry, 'absent.'

Now Marshall, apparently in an effort to convince Sutter that
he had not chased him into the mountains on a fool's errand, as
well as for some other reason, had planned a little practical joke
for the reception. He advised his men to sprinkle all the gold they
had collected during the last few days over the bottom of the tail-
race, 'and when the old gentleman comes down and sees, it will
so excite him that he will bring out his bottle and treat.' For Sutter always carried his brandy-bottle wherever he went.

Sutter arrived in the evening of February 2, well-dressed even
for this trip into the mountains. Early the next morning the gold
yield of the last few days was actually thrown back into the mill-
channel. Already, while the men were sitting at breakfast, they
saw Sutter coming up from Marshall's cabin, walking elegantly
between the latter and Peter Weimar, the foreman of the works.

After a cordial handshaking between master and men, Sutter invited them all to accompany him down to the mill-race. But just at this moment one of Weimar's young sons spoiled Marshall's joke. He had been in the race already and now came running, out of breath, and shouting: 'See how much gold I have found!' The men dared not say a word lest they should betray themselves and forfeit the hip-flask. But Sutter, seeing the heap of gold gleaming in the boy's hand, excitedly 'jabbed his cane into the ground, saying, "By Jo, it is rich!"'

Happily, the Weimar boy had picked up only the largest and most handy flakes and grains, so that Sutter still had the pleasure of finding gold himself in crevices and seams of the exposed rock —though not enough, apparently, to cause him to pass the flask around.

Fully aware of the potentialities behind this discovery, Sutter now made all his men promise to keep the secret for at least six weeks. And as a preliminary safeguard he leased from the Indians of the neighborhood for the duration of three years the land around the mill, as well as the neighboring wooded slopes. His main anxiety was the early beginning and the continuation of sawing operations. These he held to be paramount for the success of his business affairs, particularly for the completion of the gristmill on the lower course of the river. For in both these enterprises he had sunk much capital, $10,000 in the sawmill and $25,000 in the flourmill. His heart clung to these mills much more than to the hidden gold. Before his inner eye these mills now stood like guarantors of prosperity, of a secure and happy future, whereas this new gold (and who could tell how much or how little of this treasure there was buried in the ground?) was bound to bring disturbance.

Sutter was filled with a sudden deep distrust of this bright metal. He who had for years lived precariously and dangerously, as though he needed to keep himself steeped in an atmosphere of hazards of all sorts for his spiritual well-being, now shrank back inwardly, instinctively clutching at the clods of a reserved agrarian's life.

Was he aware that the new era which had rudely hammered on his door with Marshall's ghastly coming to the fort was something foreign and hostile, something against which he would be as helpless and vulnerable as the Indians had been against his own conquering spirit? Or was it merely because the 'old gentleman' of forty-five was so much older than his years? He was longing for the ease and comfort of a quiet old age, and yet he must, during odd moments of those fateful days, have felt the very mountains rock under his feet.

Those little sparks of gold were lightning in the mountains presaging a conflagration of the world.

35. *SECRETS WILL OUT*

SECRETS as permanent fixtures of the psyche are contrary to human nature. Like embryos whose time has arrived they must be born to the light of day. Sutter's secret was no exception, though for a while it could be guarded and business continued at New Helvetia as if nothing out of the ordinary had ever happened. After all this was by no means the first discovery of gold in California. Already in 1842 a *vaquero* named Francisco Lopez, digging out a few wild onions for his lunch, had discovered a lot of golden little particles clinging to the roots and for a few years derived a comfortable little income from his placer, which was about forty-five miles north of Los Angeles. But as the yield was rapidly declining, there was no ado about the matter.

Then, in the summer of 1843, the Swede Waseurtz de San-dels, a naturalist who had gained some mining experience in South America, had told Sutter that there was gold in the soil of the upper Sacramento, although he did not believe the deposits rich enough to warrant exploitation.

A year later, in 1844, Sutter's Mexican servant, Pablo Gut-ierez, pointed out to Bidwell certain deposits of quartz sand on Bear Creek which, he insisted, contained gold. The two resolved to make the best of the find as soon as possible, but not long there-after the Micheltorena revolt broke out and Pablo, sent to Mon-terey with confidential messages, was hanged on a tree by José Castro. Sutter knew this secret too, but was not particularly in-terested in the prospects.

Even now, apparently, he tried to coddle himself in the belief that what his partner had struck up at the sawmill was merely an isolated, though evidently rich placer. For if gold were really widespread in the mountains, the Indians, diggers all, could not have failed to have discovered it long before. Sutter had often asked them to bring him any curiosity which they might find. What he received were 'animals, birds, plants, young trees, wild fruits, pipe clay, stones, red ochre, etc., but never a piece of gold.'

Yet, though this was by no means the first gold discovery, there was about it something which set it off from all the previous ones. There was here a dramatic combination of diverse circum-stances giving the event a meaning far beyond its personal and local import. Coming right on top of the military occupation, the discovery appeared like a significant phase of the American con-quest itself and therefore something which sooner or later was bound to concern the whole nation. Indeed, it was the very seal upon the conquest; for (though the men in California could not yet know this) at that very moment, on February 2, 1848, the day Sutter visited the sawmill, there was signed the Treaty of

Guadalupe Hidalgo, through which California was formally
ceded to the United States.

Although everyone connected with the discovery tried for a
while to be casual and nonchalant, the general suspicion of its
deeper implications and potentialities made the secret hard to
bear. Above all Sutter himself did not guard the mystery as closely
as would have befitted him. Naturally: on men with conversa-
tional proclivities secrets are particularly burdensome. Where the
secret touches upon pride, as in Sutter's lowly origin and deplorable past, it can at least be paraded under the palliative of an iridescent fable. But what if it would enhance one's pride, if in
itself it is a thing of such perfection as to outshine the most glittering fiction? Then it becomes an urge, a craving that finally
must be satisfied. Such a case, no doubt, is a rich gold-find.

Need one be surprised, then, that Sutter, from the very day of
his visit at the mill, committed a series of indiscretions and blun-
ders? The first was probably the grossest error, even if it was intended to be a safeguard. Sutter at once applied to Governor
Mason for a formal grant of the mill-site and the surrounding
lands, indicating in rather vague and therefore suspicious terms
that there might be minerals in the soil. So far, so good. But it
was downright foolish to select as the messenger to Monterey one
of the Mormons who knew about the gold. This man, Charles
Bennett, sailed as a passenger on the *Sacramento* down to the
Bay, carrying with him not only Sutter's letter to the Governor,
but also the little heap of gold which he had gathered. The story
goes that during a stop of the launch at Benicia, Bennett listened
to the excited discussion started among a group of men by rumors
that coal deposits had been found near Monte Diablo. So much
ado over such a ridiculous matter as coal was too much for the
good Mormon. Coal! And probably before he knew what he was
doing, his little bag of gold-dust was the focus of all eyes. Thus

Bennett's trip in a double sense turned out to be a fool's errand. While failing in his main purpose—the interim governor had no right to make land-grants—Sutter's messenger left behind him, here and there along his spoor, whispers of gold.

But this was not enough. Even before Sutter undertook his inspection trip into the mountains, he confided to his countryman Henry Lienhard that 'something had transpired at the sawmill which, should it prove to be what it was supposed, would be apt to create a kind of a revolution.' And after his return from the mountains he 'appeared to be in quite a peculiar humor, talking about his secret a great deal.'

Then came a third transgression. Only five days after his return from the sawmill, Sutter could not refrain from inserting into a letter to his friend and former enemy Vallejo a remark that 'there has been the discovery of a gold-mine which, as we have since experienced, is extraordinarily rich.' Moreover, Bidwell, who seems to have carried the letter to Sonoma, was already within the secret and when he enlarged upon Sutter's laconic hint, Vallejo replied gracefully: 'As the water flows through Sutter's mill-race, may the gold flow into Sutter's purse.'

In still another way did Sutter relax in his vigilance over the explosive secret. On February 9 he dispatched two wagons with provisions to the sawmill and with the wagons he sent along his head teamster and fellow-Swiss Jacob Wittmer. At the mill, Wittmer was at once met by one of the little Weimar boys who was enthusiastically proclaiming 'we have found gold up here.' The teamster, of course, merely scoffed at the startling pronouncement, and at that moment the inevitable woman appeared on the scene: Mrs. Weimar. Indignant at hearing her offspring called a liar, she forthwith brought out of hiding some of the gold dust and showed it to Wittmer; indeed, she gave him some!

Now Jacob Wittmer was a good-natured and usually abstemious fellow, although a loquacious braggart. But when he was back at the fort, the devil plagued him for once to treat himself to a hearty swill of liquor, his new lore being very well worth it. Soon he entered the store of Brannan & Smith, recently opened in one of the outhouses, and asked for a bottle of brandy. This article, being non-recoverable, was never sold on time. So it was not unnatural that when Wittmer proudly put down on the counter his gold-dust as proof of his capacity to pay, George Smith felt very much insulted. Did the fool of a teamster think he could trick a Mormon out of a bottle of liquor? Wittmer insisted that it was gold, adding finally that if Smith would not believe him, he had but to ask the old gentleman. Smith ran to Sutter's office 'in hot haste,' still denouncing Wittmer as a rascally trickster. 'Nevertheless,' Sutter now saw himself obliged to confess, 'it is gold.'

Then Wittmer mingled with the mechanics of the colony and, encouraged by his liquor, boasted that there was so much gold in the mountains that a man could collect a quart of it in a single day. They laughed at him, they said he was a brazen liar and at length demanded proof. Wittmer actually showed them 'eighteen specks of yellow metal, the largest about the size of a small pinhead,' according to Lienhard's account. The men were nonplussed. Quickly, in the smithy, Fifield subjected one of the pieces to the hammering test. As it spread out to the size of a silver five-cent coin, a roaring shout resembling an Indian warwhoop arose and 'a kind of wild war dance was carried on around the anvil, over iron tongs, hammers, and old iron,' amid laughing and singing, whistling and shouting and yodeling. Shouts of 'Gold! Gold! Gold!' shook up the entire fort and soon brought Sutter out on the stair-landing. Seeing Lienhard among the men, he called him inside, saying: 'I see my secret is out; now let us go and drink a bottle of wine and let us hope that we shall all be rich.'

Nor had the Mormons at the sawmill remained tight-lipped. At first they were quite willing to live up to their promise of secrecy, gathering only what gold accidentally came their way in the mill-race. But since, as Bigler wrote into his diary six days after the discovery, they had already 'pict up more than a hundred dollars worth,' the lure of the gold became irresistible. They began prospecting in their free time and on ostensible hunting-trips. There was gold everywhere! In some places large nuggets could be pried out of fissures in the rock with a knife. Now, in the face of such miraculous abundance, treachery, in the guise of a very pious thought, crept upon Henry Bigler's mind. Since God Almighty had showered such favors upon him and his five fellow-saints, it would be mean and wicked not to let the Mormons working on the gristmill receive their share. He wrote a letter to them. On the Sunday following, several Mormons from below answered with a personal visit, staying three days and piously partaking of the heavenly gift. And was it not natural that, after their return to the gristmill, their former work seemed to them wholly devoid of interest? An alluvial deposit a few miles above the mill caught their attention, and from them the second place where gold was found in large quantities received the name of Mormon Island.

Three weeks after Jacob Wittmer had spread the news at the fort, the first men definitely threw up their jobs: Hudson, one of the fort blacksmiths, and Willis, one of the men at the gristmill, both Mormons. Their going set in motion that up-hill avalanche of fortune-hunters and the spring-tide of demoralization. Two days later there was an orgy of drinking at the fort, to which a session of the court of justice gave the ulterior pretext. The same day a man fell from his horse and was robbed of $300. In this style things continued.

From now on men left Sutter's service almost daily. By the middle of March the first notice of the gold discovery appeared in the California press; a tame notice, to be sure, creating no excitement, as the rumors of gold were as yet perniciously interpreted as a shrewd maneuver of Sutter's to bolster up his credit.

On March 20 a great many of the Mormons from the gristmill thronged Sutter's office, demanding their pay and their release. Of course he could not or would not pay them because they broke their contracts. And this only gave momentum to the general desertion. Thus the contagion spread furiously, with the Mormons always serving as the spearheads of this revolution. Without them, the mills would not have been built; without them, they could not now be finished. Once again, therefore, Sutter's story ran true to his peculiar pattern: bad luck in the guise of good fortune.

It was a Mormon, also, who became the determining force in advertising to the country at large the newly discovered gold and who thus quickened the onset of Sutter's doom. This man was Elder Samuel Brannan of San Francisco. He arrived at the fort on April 7 and from there took a flying trip into the mountains, a few days only after the editor of his paper, the *California Star*, had also taken a leisurely excursion among the miners, without apparently becoming convinced that there was much substance behind the persistent rumors. But Elder Sam Brannan, like most professed saints and piety-mongers, had his eyes on earthly as well as heavenly rewards. No sooner had he landed at San Francisco upon his return from the mines than he ran up the street, braying as though he were the trumpet of Judgment Day and holding aloft a bottle filled with the precious metal: 'Gold! Gold! Gold! From the American River!'

Frenzy seized the town. Gold as free and as plentiful as air! It seemed impossible. Whatever skepticism and aloofness had hitherto held back the men of San Francisco was now blasted by the shrieks of Sam Brannan. By the middle of May, Brannan himself was back again at the fort, on his way to the mines, and soon he was followed by every man in San Francisco, Sonoma, San José, and Monterey who was not quite chained fast to his house.

Daily, henceforth, there are entries like the following in the New Helvetia Diary: 'Some people going and coming from the Mountains. . . . A small launch arrived with a many passengers. . . . Continually new arrivals from Sonoma. . . . Messrs Brannan & Ward left for the Mountains. . . . Continually people arriving from below. . . . Continually people arriving by water & by land & going up to the gold regions. . . . More and more people coming bound for the Mountains.' The entry of Thursday, May 25, reads: 'A number of people continually travelling to the Mountains. Pablino & other Indians of the Walagumne tribe came on a visit from the pueblo de San José.—A very warm day.'

Then, apparently, there came such an avalanche of people that it was impossible to keep a record of events. It was the last day for the diary.

Four days later the offices of the *Californian*, the first newspaper in the country, were forced to close down for lack of labor and of readers. After a fortnight, the *California Star*, Sam Brannan's mouthpiece, likewise had to suspend publication.

In May, it was believed, 800 men were already washing gold along the streams of the Sierras. In the first half of June their number was estimated at 2,000.

The gold-rush was on in earnest.

36. ORGIES OF DRUNKENNESS

In troublous times most lives lose their individual meaning. What counts is the sweep of the mass and its direction. Even those who, by virtue of their buoyancy, ride the crests of the waves are not always too visible; they, too, are apt to be engulfed by the moiling floods.

As yet, during these early months of the gold-rush, it is possible to keep track of events, the fever having ravaged California alone and not the whole continent, not the entire world. But in California everything went topsy-turvy. Within a few days of the close of May, San Francisco lost one fourth of its inhabitants; by the middle of June three fourths of all the men were in the mines or on the way to the mountains. Land values suddenly plunged fifty per cent as a result of this exodus. All towns became the abodes of women, infants and old men. The rest of the population was mining.

In Monterey, the capital, Governor Mason was deserted by most of his soldiers. Fifteen minutes after he had planted a sentry anywhere, the man was usually gone—and so were those sent to apprehend him. The fever spared no class of the male population. The blacksmith dropped his hammer, the farmhand his reaping-tool. Fields of ripe wheat and corn were left to be trampled down by roving cattle no longer guarded by a *vaquero*. Some traders boarded up their shops; others thought time too precious to lock even their doors. Doctors left their patients to die unattended. The clergy deserted their parishes, the sheriffs their prisoners, judges their courts. Masters and servants, teachers and students, whites and Indians, Negroes and Kanakas alike were drawn into the 'mountains of gold.'

At Sutter's Fort the change was even more dramatic and radical. First all hands struck for higher wages; but soon no wages were enough to tie a man to his post. The looms in the blanket-factory were abandoned to the spiders. The tanners ran away, leaving over 1,000 unfinished hides to rot in the vats. The fire in the smithy went out for good. The Mormons at the gristmill deserted *en masse*, and the mill, on which Sutter had already spent some $20,000, was never finished. The hatters, coopers, carpenters, the blacksmiths and gunsmiths, the clerks and cartwrights, saddlers and shoemakers, the shipbuilders and supervisors—all were gone like water through a sieve. The time came when Sutter was even his own gate-keeper. The fort itself, once the pride of the valley, degenerated into a wayside station for transient miners and a trading-post for miners' supplies.

Because of his sway over the Indians, Sutter still succeeded in cutting most of the year's wheat, about 40,000 bushels. But when it was cut, it had to be left stacked up in the fields. It could not be carted to the fort; it could not be threshed for lack of men and animals; it could not be put into the granaries, because they were packed every night with crowds of miners. And as it lay in the open fields, it became an easy prey to the gold-rushers, who fed it to their mules and horses.

Fabulous tales of overnight fortunes now began to echo out of the mountains. All of Sutter's neighbors had rushed there, taking their Indians along to work for them. In a few weeks John Sinclair had gathered $16,000 on the South Fork of the American River. In Auburn, then called the Dry Diggings, a Frenchman mined as much out of five cartloads of dirt. In a little ravine south of Sutter's Mill, Bill Daylor and Perry McCoon, working together, had realized $17,000 within a week, and Weber, on the creek now named after him, had found a nugget which alone weighed ten and one half pounds. Still others claimed to have made from $8,000 to $15,000 in a single day.

These tales were maddening, they were intoxicants; they destroyed all former standards of commerce, fairness, morals, decency, justice, right and wrong. There was no man made of a mettle that could resist the pressure and the heat of this new wind blowing down from the mountains and singeing the country.

The incessant rush of would-be miners coming from the towns and those returning from the mountains with something to show quickly transformed the fort into an inferno. Gone was what now appeared to have been the easy tranquillity of 'the old days,' the almost idyllic charm of the prairie fortress. Where once all had been welcomed with a friendly handshake, some now had not even time to stop. They came lunging headlong, their own and their horses' tongues hanging out; they shouted hoarsely, asking for the way to the mines, they dug their spurs into the animals' flanks so that they almost collapsed, and off they flew, vanishing in a cloud of dust, their paraphernalia, pans, basins, picks and shovels, clanking devilishly.

Those who stayed overnight stole what was not nailed and bolted tight—spades, picks and shovels, provisions, boards, axes, even the fort bell—anything that might be of some use in the mines. But the worst were those who came back after a week or two in the mines. They came to re-provision and to recompense themselves for hardships and deprivations suffered; they came to revel, to wallow in all excesses, chiefly to swill and guzzle. Empty and broken bottles now littered the court and piled up fast in the corners, bottles littered the whole neighborhood. Gambling dens were opened in the fort. Opportunity made crooks, and many a man who, the night before, had arrived with a few thousand dollars in gold-dust, woke up in the morning from his drunkenness without a penny's worth of anything in his pockets, and even his horse gone.

'In and around my fort things look as at a fair,' Sutter wrote on

July 25 to a distant relative, Herr Haas in Darmstadt. A score of merchants now operated at the fort, paying $100 rent a month for a single room. Kyburz had turned the main building into a hotel and paid a monthly rent of $500. All in all Sutter collected $2,000 a month in rent alone. Prices of everything had risen fantastically. By July, two months after the outbreak of the rush, flour was $36 a barrel. The principal store alone, that of Brannan & Smith in the old hospital building, took in $36,000 in gold-dust between May 1 and July 10. It was estimated by Governor Mason, who at this time undertook an inspection trip through the mining districts, that in the few mines then existing from $30,000 to $50,000 in gold was produced daily.

The golden age was come: people were wading in gold. From years and decades of scarcity they soared into superabundance, and few were the heads that survived the flight unscathed. Not only at Sutter's Fort, but everywhere riots of indulgence were the order of the day. And why not, since during those very days news reached the Coast that it had legally and formally become United States territory?

Came the Fourth of July, the first of its kind in the Golden Era, and the first of the American era. Governor Mason, who arrived at the fort at the beginning of the month, accompanied by Captain Folsom and Lieutenant William T. Sherman, was urged to stay for the celebration and delay his inspection-trip of the mines. The day turned out to be one of powder-smoke and liquor fumes. A large supply of wines and liqueurs had been acquired from a trading-ship at San Francisco. The dinner, says William T. Sherman,[13] 'would have done credit to any frontier town.' Sutter presided at the head of the table, the Governor on his right and Sherman on his left. Toasts and after-dinner speeches eulogized Sutter in every possible tune, and everyone indulged in everything at the top of his bent. 'Before the celebration was over,' writes Sherman in his memoirs, 'Sutter was very tight and many others showed the effect of the *aguardiente*.' To which Sutter replied in his own Reminiscences: 'I was no more tight than he [Sherman] was.'

But whether with liquor or otherwise, all California was excessively intoxicated. For Sutter, too, these feverish summer days of 1848 were days of soaking and wading, of wallowing, of guzzling and gorging in these new riches and the new fame and glory. Although not the actual discoverer of the gold, yet the man whose initiative in the face of ridicule had led to the opening of the undreamed-of veins of fortune, it was naturally he who was hailed as the colossus of the day, the bringer of light, John the Baptist heralding the Golden Age. Captain Sutter, Sutter's Mill, and Sutter's Fort, these were the units of a new trinity whose splendor was liable to increase in direct ratio of the distance the name traveled.

Sutter's name, long known to thousands in the east as that of the man who had pushed the American frontier from the Missouri to the Sacramento, as the protector and father of the immigrants, now seemed at long distance to spread a dazzling glamor about him. The first thought of almost everyone now coming to the country was to see this miracle man who, single-handedly, had done so much. Particularly men coming from distant parts now sought the honor of knowing him. These men came singly, in pairs and in little groups, with letters of introduction or without, waiting sometimes in queues before his door and making him the busiest handshaker in all America.

The man they found within was still beyond all doubt a man of regal presence, if in his best shoes. Even Sherman, who had seen him in his cups, was impressed by his personality and thought that he was 'likely to continue his onward career.' But the critical, argus-eyed Henry Lienhard, that accurate reporter and paragon of self-righteousness, drew Sutter's portrait from another side. In his memoirs he sets down a number of conversations between Sutter and strange callers, and although he does not claim that these are verbatim accounts, he maintains that they represent the gist of all such interviews. His closing comment on the strange pageant of soft-soapers reads as follows:[14]

Again there is a knock on the door, and upon his 'Come in,' it opens, this time to let in two gentlemen, while Major X withdraws with a courtesy. From the latter the fine new gentlemen have heard his [Sutter's] name, which facilitates their approach.

'Captain Sutter, if we understand correctly?'

'Indeed, gentlemen; what can I do for you?'

'We must apologize for calling on you without a formal introduction. We have only just arrived and do not know anybody here, but it was quite out of question to pass your world-famous fort without paying our personal tribute to Your Honor. Permit us, for want of a formal mediator, to introduce ourselves. Captain, this is Judge A.B. of C.'

They both bow to each other with much dignity and then Judge A.B. makes use of a slight pause to introduce also his old friend, Colonel D.E. of F.

Both these gentlemen are, as they maintain, of prominent families and consequently men of eminence themselves. Sutter, therefore, is full of courtesy toward his new acquaintances of the Elite. His head is probably a little befuddled from the various drinks which he took in the company of the numerous earlier callers. But to dismiss these two, probably the most fashionable visitors, without treating them to a glass of his Extra French Brandy, would in his eyes have been an offense against good form and custom. Sutter, therefore, has again filled three glasses and they are raised to the lips, not without the judge's proposing a high-sounding toast to the most venerable Captain Sutter, and not without the colonel's adding his most sincere wishes for the prosperity of the noble discoverer of the gold and benefactor to the entire civilized world.

Already Sutter, to judge by his eyes and the fervor of his loquacity, is in the initial stage of intoxication. The gentlemen seem to notice that and perhaps are themselves familiar with this experience; they therefore retire, happy in the hope further to cultivate Sutter's acquaintance.

The door is closed. Sutter, elated by the unending tributes seemingly paid to him by all the world, is swaying towards his broad curtained bed, into which he half drops, half scrambles.—Curtain!

During the first summer after the gold discovery, this kind of scene could be observed at the fort almost every day. He entered into a number of partnerships with several of these gentlemen and was almost invariably swindled.

Though sketched with a certain contemptuous restraint, Lienhard's picture is fairly realistic and by no means overdrawn. And it cannot help raising the question: was this man, as Sherman thought, 'likely to continue his onward career?' What were the prospects for such a spineless parcel of humanity to survive the landslide which he himself had invited? Many have felt that his misfortune was due entirely to dissipation and riotous living. That is true only in the most superficial sense. But even if there is no denying that his fondness for drink quickened his catastrophe, a man's fate, nevertheless, is not reducible to a formula.

With Sutter, too, the roots of the evil lay much deeper, perhaps went back to his very first years or even further. He was an only child until his sixth year and, according to the nature of such children, subconsciously tried all his life to remain an 'only child' and mother's darling. Seen at close quarters, however, this only child was really a double or split personality, a most palpable case of spiritual Siamese twinship.

One partner in this fatal duality was August, the brilliant cherubic youngster craving congenial company, by which alone he was spiritually nourished, through which alone his particular genius was brought to flower. The other partner was Johann, a plain businessman, awkward, and utterly helpless in competition. In Burgdorf as in Missouri August had tried to live the life of a gentleman on the puny income of Johann the shopkeeper. The

upshot had in each case been a catastrophic collapse which un-
ceremoniously had propelled the pair across the Atlantic or the
great prairies. Once more, then, August had revolted and lunged
into a riot of indulgence, a grand carnival in the role of Captain
Sutter, 'lately of the Royal Swiss Guards of France.' Then, his
social stature securely forged, his genius proven, he had wisely
betaken himself, his impressive array of fancy-dress and fig-
ments, and his wretched twin Johann, into the starkest wilderness solitude. There the genius among the twins was for a time
to have renounced his butterfly-existence and to have given the
backward Johann the benefit of his tuition. But the valorous
scheme had one big twin flaw: genius cannot teach, even as kin
will not learn from kin. Thus, always fighting a tug of war, the
Siamese twins had trudged through the years, with August, in
order to compensate himself for his noble sacrifice, beginning to
dissipate his genius in drink and in the arms of dusky belles. On
one point only did the two finally agree: since they could not
carry their common kingdom among the people, they had to
bring the people to their kingdom. And in the united effort of ac-
commodating the masses they had called for to sustain Johann's
business credit and rescue August from the boredom of the wilderness, they had unwittingly invited the deluge.

Now if one considers the positive accomplishments which
Sutter had attained within nine years and the conditions under
which he had wrenched his successes from the raw wilderness,
can one be surprised that at the age of forty-five he was an old
man? He felt old. His life-task was done. The Stars and Stripes
waved over the land which he had opened single-handedly, in
which he had been the main tool of destiny. And right now he
had accomplished his greatest feat. Through the gold discovery,
in which he was more instrumental than the actual and accidental discoverer, he had bridged the vast gulf separating this

remote and insular territory from the main body of the nation. An indestructible tie had thereby been woven between the two coasts of the continent. No-one could deny that he had served magnificently in the hand of fate. Inasmuch as he had been an instrument he could now be discarded.

But individually, could he indulge in rest now, relaxation? It was a tragic error, if a venial one, that he believed the gold discovery enabled him to repose on his laurels. By nature this 'only child' and mother's darling was inclined to seem instead of to be. Though brilliant within his limitations, he often coveted the trifling rather than the worthy things. At heart life had fashioned him to be a movie idol rather than a hero of history. Extremely handsome, gracious and graceful, it always cost him less to conquer with the host of his charms than through the marshalling of all his energies. He may have possessed the might of a Titan, as at times he did, yet a certain levity was always apt to outbalance it. And often enough sporting the uniform or ceremonial robe meant more to him than actual conquests and the exercise of lordly power.

In all this lay his fatal constitutional weakness. Playing the grandseigneur was now a thing of the past—or ought to have been. For these new Americans in California cared not for regal grace and the paraphernalia of ceremonial life, except inasmuch as these could be turned into weapons against him. They would not give a penny for achievements of the past; they lived only for the day. And they were shrewd, with senses sharpened to a razor-edge on the grindstone of competition; graduates most of them of the university of sharp practices, past masters in the art of finding out a man's weak spot, and unscrupulous in the surgery of pockets. He was old and they were young; he a spendthrift, they greedy. They were in their own country, he was a foreigner and an exotic curiosity. They were adaptable and pliable, he was no longer. Dazzled by the flood of gold now trickling through his fingers and unaware that not an ounce of it remained in his hand, he spent more liberally than ever.

What chances to survive were left to John A. Sutter?

PART FIVE

TRAGIC DAWN

37. *FATHER AND SON*

ON May 20, 1848, just before the New Helvetia Diary was swept aside by the torrent of events, it still contained an extraordinary entry. It records the receipt of 'a letter from the French Consul and from Europe.' Since it was never Sutter's custom to enter the arrival of letters in the diary, this one 'from Europe' must have been of quite unusual importance. As a matter of fact, circumstantial evidence allows us to state with certainty that on that day he received the news that his eldest son would soon be with him.[1]

And with that beginning and end join hands to close the circle.

Sutter had a son? Yes. Thousands of miles away he had a wife and family whom he had not seen for fourteen years. In one of his genial flings of post-adolescence, August Sutter had begotten a son whom he had made legitimate a few hours before birth. This was the son who, he had written boastfully to John Marsh, spoke and wrote several languages and no doubt would make an able clerk. And who, at this critical juncture, could have been more welcome to Sutter? He was in dire need of an efficient and trustworthy manager of his complex affairs. Only such a man could save the little empire of New Helvetia from destruction. In California such men were not to be found, all being in the throes of the gold-rush. All the more miraculous would seem to be the appearance of this son, at the very moment when the father was writhing in the claws of the monster. He came as on the magic carpet. As so often before in Sutter's life, things 'clicked' again.

This son seemed sent as his saving destiny. He was shrewd, fearless, intelligent, energetic, level-headed, though as nervous as a blooded racehorse. In later years he proved to be a most successful businessman. In brief, he was the very man whom Sutter needed.

But what happened?

Until now Sutter had fought against the current, resisted the temptation of the mines, and tried to stem the mass-flight of employees. He boasted that for him there was no need to go into the mountains to make his pile of gold.[2] Gold flowed to him. He paraded his conviction that he had but to stick to his agriculture, his herds, and his fort, in order to get richer than any miner. And although he had already become a silent partner in several mining enterprises, yet nothing had been able to coax him away from New Helvetia.

But then, in August, he unaccountably fell a victim to the general mining fever. Lienhard,[3] who until this moment had stayed with him and tended his gardens, says that Sutter's abrupt about-face was very perplexing. What was responsible? Why now this sudden craving for the gold-fields? It was by no means the usual gold-fever, for Sutter mined very little gold. It was a mere excuse for getting away from the fort. Why?

His son was drawing near! The mainspring of this flight was a deep fear of his son, a feeling of shame perhaps, a profound dismay rooted in the very circumstances of his son's birth.

So now, at the worst conceivable moment, during the very orgies of drunkenness brought about by the gold-craze, Johann August the Younger stood suddenly in the fort, hearing to his amazement that his father had but recently departed for the mines. No words could come as close to the reality of young August's feelings on his arrival as his own confession. Apparently brought up in the belief that the one we called Johann was his father, he could have no idea who his true father was and it was inevitable, therefore, that the shock he was now about to receive should leave its mark for life upon the impressionable young man. He writes (in his own English): [4]

I arrived in California in the month of August 1848; the gold had been discovered only a few weeks previously. Already in Sanfrancisco I had heard some very strange reports and altogether contradictory rumors about my father and the state of his affairs. Some said he was the richest man on earth and did not know himself his wealth; others in the contrary told me in confidence that my father on account of his dreadfully loose and careless way of doing every business transaction was on the brink of ruin and that instead of having in his employ good and trustworthy men he was surrounded by a parcel of rogues and immoral men, which instead of helping him, only would accelerate and in a short period accomplish his utter moral, physical, and financial ruin. . . .

It is impossible for anybody to imagine with what contradictory feelings I set out for Sacramento, the next day after my arrival at Sanfrancisco in the schooner of my father, which had happened to be there. All these contradictory reports had made a dreadful impression upon my mind. Having never before heard that my father was affected with the dreadful vice of drinking and other disorderly habits, I really could not and would not believe it until further proof. Arriving at Sacramento the first people I met with, were Mr. George McDougall's clerks and men on board his vessel, Robert Ridley (now dead), a German by the name of Hahn, an American Lang, which latter three were pointed out to me as my father's business men. . . .

Hahn and Lang I saw drunk the first day I was at the fort. My father had gone to the mines and was only expected to be back in some days, so that I was left alone with my reflections about the rumors I had heard in Sanfrancisco and moreover everything not only was confirmed, but painted to me in stronger and more vivid colors than before.

I saw myself how everything went on. Anything belonging to my father was at everybody's disposal. The traders at the fort (Brannan, Ellis, Pettit, Dr. McKic, Capt. Dring, Pickett a.s.f.) furnished anybody who wanted it with enormous bills for my father's account. Indians, Negroes, Kanakas and white men of any nation indiscriminately by applying to my father, easily obtained letters of credit from him to any amount for any stores then existing in or about the fort. . . .

From the books I received from Hahn, I never could obtain any knowledge of the state of affairs on account of their dreadful confusion; also they had been neglected for about six months. As a proof of the confusion of things, I will only state, that I found the now so important original map of Capt. Vioget in an open drawer, as also the contract with the russian american company and acknoledged bills and accounts of Col. Frémont.

At last after a week of terrible excitement and anguish, my father, whom I had not seen for fifteen years, arrived. Our first meeting after such a long separation was as affectionate and sincere, as ever meeting ought to be between father and son on such an occasion. We both wept. Seeing my father so kind, so affectionate, I soon forgot all I had heard and was as happy of having met with him as I could be. We spoke a long time of my mother, my brothers and sister, family matters and times long gone by; my father very often was moved to tears; then we commenced to converse on his present state of affairs; he would soothe all my fears, telling me of his plans for the time to come, of his hopes to be soon out of all difficulties a.s.f. . . . I was quite happy. . . .

His happiness was short-lived. The squall that now approached and which was to pitch son against father and father against son, blew from its habitual quarter: the Russian purchase. Leidesdorff had died. A new Russian consul, Colonel Steward, had been appointed. Much more intent upon his own enrichment than on serving the Russians, he now threatened to dispossess Sutter.

To prevent the execution of Steward's schemes, George McKinstry urged upon Sutter the plan of transferring all his property on his son's name. To this Sutter finally consented and on October 14, 1848, the transfer took place.[5] It was, as the younger Sutter frankly admits, an act which would have been impossible under the laws of any nation; but under the hopelessly muddled legal status of California's interregnum, such things could be done. Congress had failed to extend over California the laws of the United States, and none of the Americans charged with the administration of the Spanish law, which theoretically still continued to be in force, pretended to know anything about it.

However illegal, the transfer was a desperate act of self-defence, perpetrated merely to prevent the scheming agent of the Russians from pocketing Sutter's entire realm to the detriment of all other creditors, even of the very Russians in whose name he was ostensibly acting.

Once more, then, by this illegal expedient, Sutter was saved from total ruin, from being driven from his possessions, though saved, as it were, through the unpalatable medicine of abdicating. Again, on the face of things, one might presume that nothing could have been more welcome to him. He had long been yearning for leisure and relaxation, and shortly before the arrival of his son he had written to Herr Haas in Darmstadt: 'I have no other desire but to conclude my so troublesome life surrounded by fine and noble men, and once the burden of my extended affairs shall have been taken off my shoulders by my sons, I want to live retiredly . . . either on the coast or in the mountains, and devote the remainder of my life to scientific reading.'

More speedily and more beautifully this dream could not have become actuality. But alas, at this very moment mysterious powers awakened in unfathomable depths, ruining everything.

It is easy to see that those initial hours of tearful reveling in filio-paternal sentiments could not be prolonged by any means. For that the younger Sutter had heard too much even before the *wiedersehen*, and saw too much during the short period for which his father consented to remain at the fort in his honor. 'Hardly a day passed,' young Sutter writes, 'on which he [old Sutter] himself and his clerks, partners, Indians, etc., were not on a general frolic intoxicated.'

August was a youth with a remarkable temper, but with determination and will-power, even a certain grimness, which was partly his maternal heritage and partly the fruition of the shadow of poverty under which he had grown up. Since he was seeing and hearing the things he was now daily forced to see and hear, was it not inevitable that his filial love should rapidly be galled into hatred? By natural law his sympathies attached him to his mother, with whom he had shared sufferings and misery. His father was less than a stranger to him. This Lord of New Helvetia, whom he knew chiefly as a drunkard and cock-of-the-walk of squaws was not the man he had been hoping to find—and yet the very man who had abandoned wife and children to stark poverty in order that he might live lavishly and court luxury. Unjust, one-sided, and distorted as this view was, it was the only one the young man could gain under the circumstances. Of all the distressingly unfortunate coincidences of Sutter's life the most tragic one was that son should meet father under the worst auspices imaginable.

Nor was the growing asperity all on the son's side. Things were bound to look even worse to the father. Instead of enjoying the long-hoped-for relief from his burdens, he, a second King Lear, only noticed that he was discarded, that the scepter had passed out of his hand. He had become the ward of his son, conscious only that a guardian had been set above him. To the Lord of New Helvetia any such state of affairs must be intolerable. But what, under the pressure of circumstances, could he do except impotently fume and fret? Thus it came about that the very instrument of the transfer, which had averted financial ruin, became a wedge thrust between father and son and distending day by day the rent between them to an abyss past repair.

Not enough! Sutter senior had primordial grounds for resenting his spawn. Was it not this threatening conflict, this brewing tragedy, manifesting itself in a fear, as yet unconscious, of this fateful child which had caused him to save himself in the mountains? Even before the arrival of the son, the aboriginal filio-paternal conflict, long dormant in the elder Sutter, had been re-awakened. For was not this the child whose impending birth had caught the father in the detested slings of matrimony? This was a filial sin for which the father knew no forgiveness. Here a gulf was gaping which not even Sutter could bridge. Here were roots ineradicable of an enmity from which naught but evil could spring.

And now again, almost from the first moment of their reunion, the hand of this fateful youngster loomed unmercifully over the aging father, making him subservient to him with whom he was least acquainted of all the men about him. Though his intellect saw the necessity of his submission, his stronger nature, his passionate temper, his blood began to revolt.

Immediately after having signed over his tottering little empire to his son, old Sutter fled back into the mines, a crazy man. People thought the gold had turned his head. In reality it was the head-on collision with his son which for a few months bereft him of all reason. And though by sheer force of habit he filled the mountains for a while with a reverberating hue and cry about the marvelous progeny he was capable of having (his old trick of raving about heavenly nectar when pride forbade admitting it was wormwood), his general behavior belied the wagging of his tongue.

Wherever men are flung out of their orbits, grow deranged in their minds permanently or temporarily, there are deep powerful conflicts at work. So here with Sutter. The spectacle he now gave to a miners' audience was not mere sinful profligacy, it was the stench and roar of a battle raging in an old man's heart, the heart of a fallen king. King Lear of the Heath!

> The tempest in my mind
> Doth from my senses take all feeling else
> Save what beats there: filial ingratitude.

If not as starkly grotesque as King Lear's, Sutter's conduct was nevertheless scandalous. Only topographically he was in the mines, spiritually he indulged in a most disorderly rampage, a walk-out of protest against his son. While others made fortunes in the mountains, old Sutter squandered. They sought gold. He sought oblivion, by day in drink, by night in the embrace of his favorite paramour of the moment.

In his Reminiscences Sutter lays the blame for his failure in the mines on the 'travelling grog-shops' which now pervaded the camps and where his Indians and Kanakas spent all the gold mined at his cost. Beyond doubt there is much truth in this. But what was to be expected of Indians and Kanakas and many of the white employees, if their overlord was the best customer of his own liquor-store? Sometimes he was soused for days on end, spinning blustering yarns about his experiences in the Royal Swiss Guard of France, reveling in sublime drunkenness or raging like an angered devil.[6]

His bed-mate who, with her native husband, had been dragged by Sutter into the mountain camp was the squaw named Mary, once before discarded and married to Perry McCoon (who now had a white wife). However, Sutter had promised to set her free for good and leave her to her latest husband. But when the day on which he had arranged to bring her back to the fort in person arrived, he seemed completely to have forgotten his pledge, no doubt because at heart he felt no desire to see his son again. Instead he withdrew into his cups. At night the storm broke. Squaw Mary, infuriated because her release from bondage had come to naught, struck openly in her capacity as his fallen lordship's concubine. Like a furious bull, Sutter, with the vilest curses, pursued her through the bush, while the awakened sleepers in the camp raised their heads from the blankets and snickered expectantly. But Mary escaped. Two miles down the

valley was the camp of Perry McCoon, and as the thought came
to the foaming Sutter that she might be seeking shelter with her
former husband, he went into his tent, emerging again into the
moonlight with his double-barreled shotgun. 'He carried it
shouldered,' writes Lienhard, 'and with his lips was drumming a
sort of march, "drum-di-dum, drum-di-dum, drum-didi, drum-
didi, drum-didum," wheeling left and right several times, though
unable to keep straight. . . . When at last he stopped, he declared he was going to the camp of the goddamn Perry McCoon
to shoot Mary and Perry.' An Englishman in the camp had the
courage to take hold of him and shove him into his tent, 'but far
into the night Sutter continued to curse Mary and Perry.'

Such was Sutter's impotent raging against destiny which, in
the person of his own son, had now taken him into its cruel hand.

His conduct as a businessman was scarcely more commendable
during these days of inner crisis. At Coloma he had established a
trading-post and the offices of the mining firm of Sutter, Hastings & Co. 'Without exaggeration each of us shall have made
100.000 Dollars within six months,' we read in that letter to
Haas in Darmstadt. Some say that the profits of the firm actually
were enormous; however, only so much is certain that in the end
Sutter had to share in the company's debts, real or fictitious, to
the tune of about $10,000. According to his son, Sutter fur-
nished Indians, outfits, provisions, and other supplies for other
entrepreneurs, he always receiving the bills, the others the profits.
Such paying enterprises of his own as were still left at the fort
were held in virtual confiscation by some of the traders there, as
security against goods furnished him at gargantuan prices.[7]

Yet there were still a few people in the mines who had confidence enough in Sutter to entrust their stores of gold to his care,
and these, admits his son, 'could very often not obtain it back
from him, when he used to give them orders on me to pay them

as well and as fast as I could.' What became of that gold, no-one has ever tried to explain, and young Sutter himself saw 'very little' of it.

August Sutter, meanwhile, was expected to save money in this deluge, under the incessant demands upon him from all sides, to send to his mother, his sister and his brothers, who 'were anxiously waiting in Europe, and I can assure you not in brilliant circumstances, for me to send them news from my father and from me, as also pecuniary aid. I knew they depended on me to send them the means to come here. What favorable news, what consolation, could I send my poor mother, as a compensation of so many years of toiling and suffering?'[8]

Thus it came about that day by day, with every little incident, with every bit of friction, after every provocation but one thing happened: the painful wedge already lodged fast between father and son was driven deeper and deeper. And presently, before the son had been in California half a year, father and son were the most bitter enemies.

38. *A SAGA OF TWO CITIES*

IF one tries to find a motto or *leitmotiv* for Sutter's life, one must inevitably arrive at the formula: ill fortune in the guise of good luck. It was always this one theme in countless variations, just as if the old Sutter coat of arms—a field of gold across which a fess falls like a heavy black shadow—was always trying to become flesh and blood.

Always Sutter's future had stood before his inner eye radiant, sparkling, handsome like himself, but pernicious deviltry had invariably 'behexed' the alluring phantom and made it behave like a bewitching female who, when in his arms, became abhorrent. It had been that way from the very beginning. Born amidst the fanfares of *Liberté! Egalité! Fraternité!* he had grown up as a disfranchised semi-serf. Then came the seductive Annette Dübeld, whom he was forced to marry, from whom he escaped, and whose name remained taboo almost until the close of his life. Next the allurements of California, whose people turned against him no sooner had he reached that goal. Then the enticing possessions of Ross and Bodega, which became a millstone around his neck. The desire for military glories for which he suffered punishment in the Micheltorena campaign. Even the Stars and Stripes brought him naught but sorrow. The treacherous gold of the sierras was to become the prime agent of his misfortune. And finally also his eldest son. Above all this son!

With unprecedented velocity the conflict between them now soared to its tragic climax, and as clashes between two rulers are apt to draw two people into the hell-fire of war, so the strife between the deposed and the actual ruler of New-Helvetia-Over-the-Abyss now evolved into a war between two towns.

Since 1845 Sutter had been writing to his friends of the great new town he had founded. It was in the first line to relieve him of the human traffic at the fort and for that reason was in itself a symptom of his declining powers, a monument to a dying man. Its name was Sutterville. From the outset Grandseigneur Sutter had with a lavish hand signed away to friends large sections of the town. Its location, three miles below the Embarcadero, was generally pronounced ideal, for there the banks of the Sacramento lay far above high-water level, so that, while the rest of the valley was exposed during the rainy season to regular brutal inundations, Sutterville was assured serene aloofness from all perils. Gently moulded hills gave picturesqueness to the terrain and groves of live oaks and sycamores lent to the whole a particular charm. But then, who had ever doubted that Sutter had an eye for beauty? A map, too, was drafted in such elegant fashion as to convince a visiting countryman from Switzerland that the magnitude and splendor of this new town on paper could have been inspired only by Captain Sutter's memories of gorgeous vistas from the walls of Paris.

But again this great plan contained the germ of starkest misfortune. And here, too, there was something of the woeful and compelling necessity of ancient tragedy in that the little Titan's last and most magnificent scheme was to become a colossal symbol of that conflict whose seeds lay in his first creation, his first-begotten son.

Sutter had gone back to the mines in the latter part of October, a very strange time, when the majority of fortune-diggers came back again, because all the untapped reservoirs of gold could not bring them to face the hardships of a sierra winter. Only Sutter was evidently glad to become snow-bound at Coloma, while his son was left to wrestle with the octopus of debts at the fort. A youngster of only twenty-two knowing little English and less of the ways and conditions of this new land, as yet bewildered by all he saw, doubly bewildered spiritually by the discovery of who his father was, August was now called upon to clean out the Augean stables at the fort—an almost superhuman task! But the young man, having taken upon himself the obligation, was intent on fulfilling it.

At this time and under these conditions one of the most unscrupulous of schemers became aware of the golden opportunity of arrogating to himself a goodly portion of Sutter's tottering little empire. This man was Sam Brannan, ex-saint of the Church of Jesus Christ of the Latter-day who now carefully and cunningly pursued the Almighty Dollar. When still a Mormon elder, Brannan, as soon as his lesser saints had engaged in washing gold at Mormon Island, had begun to collect 'the Lord's tithe' from them, ostensibly for a tabernacle building-fund. He had kept up this levy until one of the suspicious young saints asked Governor Mason what right Elder Brannan had to collect from them. Mason had answered that he had a perfect right as long as they were fools enough to pay. When Brigham Young at Salt Lake heard of the collection, he summoned Brannan to deliver the tithes to him; Brannan, however, merely sent the envoy back with the reply that he would deliver the Lord's Money against a receipt signed by the Lord, but no sooner, and thus he brought about his excommunication.

Now, two years after his arrival in California, Sam Brannan had his finger in every pie. It was Brannan who had largely financed the building of Sutter's mills; it was he who had roused the country to the full realization of the importance of the gold discovery and given the impetus for the gold-rush. It was now Brannan who quickened the onset of New Helvetia's doom.

This astute fallen angel of the Latter-day Kingdom of Jesus Christ was now the chief trader at Sutter's Fort, quick to perceive in the strained relations between father and son magnificent opportunities for fishing in troubled waters. He had bills against Sutter amounting to about $16,000, and it was probably his anxiety to collect the last cent of it which gave birth to his scheme and led him to suggest to young Sutter to found a city between the fort and the Sacramento River—a rival city to the old captain's Sutterville.[9]

Brannan's arguments were invincible. Young Sutter needed ready money to pay off his father's debts. The sheriff and the marshal were now forever at Sutter's door. But here, too, were a hundred traders wanting to erect miners' supply stores and not finding any room in the fort. For miles and miles the land about the fort was Sutter's. Nobody wanted to go to Sutterville, for it lay three miles off the well-established trade-route. A new city, on the other hand, bedded between the fort and the Embarcadero, would make an ideal trading-center. Lots would sell like hot cakes. The value of the land would multiply. In no time Sutter would be out of the morass of debts!

There was no objection young Sutter could raise to which Sam Brannan had not a ready and practical answer. He suggested the surveyor. The survey would cost money? Brannan would advance it. Brannan even had a name ready for the new town: Sacramento City. Everything was ready, everybody was helpful. Sam Brannan had the very devil on his side.

Which means that the weather, too, connived. A normally wet winter would have drowned Sutterville's rival under several feet of water before a dozen lots could have been sold or tents erected. But as things were, the customers, newcomers all, remained completely ignorant of the fact that they were buying temporarily dessicated fragments of a big swamp. Old Sutter, meanwhile, was snow-bound in the mountains and for that matter might have been on the moon.

Peter H. Burnett, a lawyer who had just come from Oregon, was engaged as young Sutter's general manager and land-agent. The first lots were sold in January 1849; they lay in the vicinity of the fort. But within a month the river-end of the long straight road between the fort and the Embarcadero gained an outright preponderance over the fort-end, and with the mushroom city shooting up beside the river, Sutter's Fort was quickly pushed far out 'into the country.'

During all this time the weight of old debts upon young Sutter had increased. The Russian-American Fur Company, whose president was the Czar, had at length resorted to diplomatic representations in Washington, the upshot of which was that not only the Russian Consul in San Francisco, but also Governor

Mason began to exert the strongest pressure. In January, at last, Steward appeared in person at the fort to collect the purchase price for Ross and Bodega, about $31,000. He was paid $10,000 in gold-dust, the remainder in notes obtained from the sale of Sacramento City lots. Fortunately for the Sutters, Steward left a receipt; for no sooner had he converted the notes into cash than he vanished with his loot, leaving the Russian-American Fur Company minus the cash he had collected in its name and the Czar minus one consul.

In the same month the Hudson's Bay Company also presented its old claim of $7,000, and James Douglas came to collect in person. A bill of $3,000 was presented by Mr. French, supposedly for the loan of the ship with which Sutter, in 1839, had sailed from Honolulu to Sitka and Monterey, for trade goods supplied him at that time and on later occasions. Antonio Suñol had a bill for $3,000 and countless other creditors swarmed after him to get their dues or what they pretended that Sutter owed them. There were even claims dating back to Sutter's Missouri years. Because of the indescribable confusion in the books, there was no way of verifying all the bills; but all those with a semblance of merit were paid as rapidly as the sale of city lots put money into the till.

The instantaneous success of Sacramento City in a trice blew itself up to the dizzy heights of speculative mania. The sight of young Sutter paying off ancient debts at breath-taking speed led some of the speculators to believe that the son could be as easily bamboozled as his father into lavishly distributing regal favors. But when George McDougall, one of the traders at the fort, made an effort to secure for a song the entire river-front and met with a rebuttal, brigandage broke loose. McDougall had been mistaken in his estimate of the son, but he knew the father only too well. The angry speculator, who until now had shown every readiness to sacrifice the old gentleman's Sutterville to the son's Sacramento, now betook himself to Coloma. With him went George McKinstry, Sutter's former general manager. At Coloma, the two first bought most of Lansford Hastings' Sutterville acres; then they informed old Sutter what his son, the rascal, had started during his absence! This was at the end of January.

The news of a rival city to his beloved Sutterville immediately brought Sutter down from the mines. He came accompanied by George McDougall, McKinstry, and Hastings. So infuriated was he, and to such an extent had his scheming cronies already succeeded in turning father against son, that Sutter even refused to see young August at the fort. Instead, the three wolves carried off the old ram to San Francisco, where, after having given him his fill, they began the grand feast. Over his cups they made him sign a bond which committed him to obtain from his son a deed in their favor for one square mile of Sutterville land, free of charge.

The moment this document was in the rascals' hands, they started boosting Sutterville. Presently all others who had already bought, or obtained as presents, lots in Sutterville joined in the raucous exodus of protest from the upstart city of Sacramento.

The first course of the wolves' feast was over and the second could be served without delay. Nor was it to be avoided that the biggest of the wolves now invited himself to the table. It was now, after McDougall, Hastings and McKinstry had rowdily withdrawn from Sacramento to Sutterville, that Sam Brannan, the master mind, the fallen angel, Sutter's evil spirit, perceived his greatest opportunity. Already, Sutter senior, because of his lavishness, his foolishness and the rascality of his friends, had forfeited most of his original interests in Sutterville. Sacramento, on the other hand, had made a very promising start, with clapboard shacks and canvas booths rising in proud display along the river-front and J Street. Most of the Sacramento land still did belong to Sutter, even if temporarily his son controlled it. Whether Sutter liked it or not, his fortune was now tied up with his son's city, not with Sutterville.

Sam Brannan was the first to see that, and it inspired him to an act of the most fiendish roguery. Getting in touch with the Sutterville clique, he induced these fellows to make a fraudulent public offer of free building-lots to all merchants willing to remove to Sutterville. At once, then, Brannan and his accomplices (among whom young Sutter mentions George McDougall's brother John, McKinstry, Hastings, Cordua, and others) threatened to make use of this offer unless Sutter deeded to each of them 200 Sacramento lots free. Two hundred lots to each! And Sutter, afraid now that he might forfeit Sacramento too, pledged himself, against his son's protest, to this supreme sacrifice. Thus it came about that, even before the great hordes of lawless squatters came from the East, Sutter's empire began to be devoured.

About this time the fort itself was sold for $40,000. Since its abandonment to the drunken excesses of the miners, its clay walls had become rapidly dilapidated; roofs had remained unrepaired, because no lumber could be obtained for less than a dollar a foot. Quite fittingly, the symbol of Sutter's empire now passed out of his hands. The personal property still belonging to him was removed to Hock Farm, and Augustus, Jr., himself took up his quarters there.

After the second course of the wolves' banquet there was a long, pleasant pause. The bitter warfare between Sutter and son, kept alive by rapacious 'friends' of the old madman, was now well launched. Calumniators, blackmailers, lickspittles and trouble-feasters were busily widening the gulf between the two. Sutter *père* was said to have sworn he would send Sutter *fils* back to Switzerland in chains. Lienhard, who for some time in the spring of 1849 slept on the floor of old Sutter's room in the fort, was sometimes peppered with the curses the father aimed at the son. In vain did Lienhard try to make it clear to the old man that his friends' tales about his son were naught but calculating lies. Sutter would not listen to good advice; he cursed and swore that he would kill his offspring.

'I asked him,' writes Lienhard, 'how he could possibly use such language in speaking of his son? "I tell you I would never have expected that of you." Whereupon Sutter, with one leap, was at his bureau and opened a big case, out of which he took a pair of double-barreled pistols, saying, "I will shoot myself." Like lightning the thought came to me that if he killed himself, I would be taken for the murderer. No sooner had Sutter taken the pistol in his hand than I wrenched it from him.' The pistol was unloaded. . . .[10]

Nothing could explain the savage and ruinous ugliness of this family feud, nor Sutter's rage over the attack upon the city of his hopes, nor the rascality of all his cronies, if there had not always been buried deep down in his soul the seed of paternal hatred of the child who, even before his birth, had made himself the master of his father's fate.

As yet the breach between father and son was not quite complete. Contacts could not always be avoided. Moreover, experience had bought Sutter one costly ounce of wit; he could almost count in square miles the penalty he had paid for trusting scheming friends more than his own flesh and blood. He therefore withdrew from all partnerships in mining ventures and trading-stores, spending an occasional day himself up at Hock Farm, which was being prepared for the reception of the family.

In April 1849, Augustus completed arrangements to send Lienhard to Switzerland and escort Frau Sutter and the younger children to California. Their presence, he hoped, would have a beneficial influence on his father and 'detain him from committing any more excesses.' [11] Old Sutter himself, as was almost to be expected, raised not a finger to bring about a reunion of the family; he confined himself to giving his passive consent to his son's measures. On June 20, Lienhard embarked for Panama.

By the middle of the year, the aim of the temporary transfer of all property and powers on Sutter, Jr., was achieved. The unforeseen success of Sacramento City had made it possible to remove within half a year the gigantic mountain of debts. The danger of dispossession and collapse was passed, or so it seemed, and the elder Sutter, therefore, left nothing undone to regain control of his empire.

On July 11, while they were both at Hock Farm and the son was stricken with a mysterious fever, the latter was forced to return to his father all lands, moneys, bonds, notes and other security derived from the sale of Sacramento property. Old Sutter had taken along with him two acquaintances, Archibald Peachy and Henry Schoolcraft, who had drawn up the re-transfer, witnessed it, and were then appointed Sutter's agents, the first for San Francisco, the second for Sacramento. Peter H. Burnett, the son's manager, was then informed by Sutter that his services were no longer required.

Young Sutter was profoundly convinced that in dismissing Burnett his father committed one of his gravest mistakes. 'I have the firm belief,' he wrote in 1855, 'that if Judge Burnett could have been retained for the management of our affairs up to the present date, my father would now be the richest man in California.' In truth, a man like Burnett had now become the tender thread on which depended salvation, for Augustus himself, severely shaken by the savage conflict, was no longer able to attend to business. [12]

One is strongly inclined to side with young Sutter's judgment of Burnett if one reads the favorable account his agent gave in later years of Sutter the pioneer. A quotation from Burnett's Recollections and Opinions will not be amiss here, if only to illustrate the depth of Sutter's fall:

> His [Sutter's] heavy expenditure of capital and labor was made before he could realize any returns. . . . I hesitate not to give it as my decided opinion that no man could, under the exact circumstances in which Captain Sutter was placed, have paid those debts before the discovery of gold. . . . How could any pioneer refuse aid to a poor comrade who would fight and die for him when occasion required? The circumstances of a new country are so different from those of an old one that a different law of social life must prevail. . . . This is the reason why so few pioneers ever become rich, and remain so. Besides, Capt. Sutter had a nobler object in view than the accumulation of a fortune for himself. His purpose was to colonize the great valley of the Sacramento.

Such fair words, indeed, lend weight to young Sutter's wish that this man could have been retained as his father's right hand. And yet it will be doubted whether even Burnett could have successfully weathered the riot of the years that lay ahead, those Saturnalia unparalleled in the history of public vice, from which not even men more staunch of heart survived.

The bitter truth is that the only man who might have saved what was still left of Sutter's realm was Sutter's son. He was later to prove himself one of the staunchest, shrewdest, most fearless men. But therein looms tragedy again: one so indomitable lay even now half broken, uprooted, almost deranged by the savage brutality of a psychic conflict.

Old Sutter, meanwhile, seemed to have regained his equilibrium with his crumbling empire. But, as if to indicate that all was not as it ought to be between the Sutters, the war of jealousy between Sacramento and Sutterville was to rage for years.

39. *THE PEAK OF LIFE*

HISTORY can never be explained; it can only be experienced and retold, even as we cannot explain why our hearts beat, though we feel the pulsations and count them. Or how should we explain that, for better or worse, events always 'clicked' in Sutter's life? He was born the day the American West was born. The Mormons had been halted on their way to the Great Salt Lake at the very moment when skilled workmen were most urgently needed at New Helvetia. As on a magic carpet Sutter's son had arrived at the most crucial moment, meaning the last hour at which the complete collapse of the little empire could still be forestalled, meaning also the worst possible moment for his decisive first impression of his father. But perhaps the most important of these coincidences is this: at the very time that Sutter signed the contract for the building of his sawmill, three contracts were also signed in Washington as if in anticipation of the gold discovery. They were for steamship lines, one between New York and Liverpool, another between New York and Chagres in Panama, the third between Panama City, California and Oregon.

In this way a relay mechanism had been created to span half the globe. Seemingly independent centers of action on the Atlantic and the Pacific were now so attuned to each other that it required but the cue-word 'Gold' to release the mechanism and hurl a barrage of humanity towards that magic target, Sutter's Mill.

The first Pacific steamer, the *California*, was already on her way around the Horn when, in November 1848, the news of the gold-discovery reached New York. Two more Pacific liners were ready for their maiden voyages. Others that could be made available were quickly pressed into service to rush the first forty-niners down to Chagres. By the time the *California* had made her way around Cape Horn, she found the landing at Panama City crammed with prospective passengers, and though she was built for a capacity accommodation of but seventy-five, she carried between four and five hundred to San Francisco, dumping them on February 28, 1849. A month later the *Oregon* arrived, and thereafter boat followed boat.

Never before had the world witnessed a similar voluntary migration. Never before had the entire population of the globe held itself so instinctively ready to spurt forward at the sound of a starting signal not consciously expected. 'Gold! Gold! Gold! Gold for the asking! At Sutter's Mill in California!' Never before had one locality become so vibrantly the center of the whole world's attention, an eddy sucking in all the ships afloat on all oceans. But wherever boats came from, once they had entered the Golden Gate they were compelled to stay. Crews invariably deserted and the captains themselves went to the gold-mines. By the middle of 1849 more than 600 deserted ships, which had discharged some 40,000 men, were anchored in the Bay of San Francisco, a swaying forest of masts. At the close of 1848 the city had counted 250 inhabitants. In February 1849 there were 2,000, and by winter 20,000.

Sacramento City drew its share of the newcomers, and Sutter had, instead of rain from heaven, the deluge. Most of these forty-niners arrived with tragically erroneous conceptions, so that trouble was afoot at once. For these newcomers, chiefly a shrewd eastern city crop, the only way of looking at an Indian was down the barrel of a rifle or pistol, and in a trice, therefore, a new war between whites and Indians was raging. There were no more troops. There was no law, because Congress had not yet recognized California. And so the freedom to kill and scalp with impunity combined with the demoralizing effect of the gold epidemic to precipitate the country into an orgy of depravity, the like of which few countries had witnessed.

While in the mines a primitive sort of self-government was maintained, the rest of the land was soon exposed to complete anarchy. The ablest men were in the mines or in trade, and only the basest scamps accepted office. There was at Sutter's Fort an *alcalde* who was also a silent partner in a horse-thieving band; his sheriff was the chief of the gang. There was another *alcalde* at the fort whose favorite verdict was a fine of from 6 to 12 bottles of beer (costing $48–50) which was then guzzled by the court and its friends in open session. One of the traders at the fort, Charles E. Pickett, shot a man in cold blood for disagreeing with him; but the first and second *alcaldes* and the sheriff resigned rather than take part in a hearing. Finally Sam Brannan conducted the trial in the double role of judge and prosecutor; but because of the inertia of the new sheriff, the murderer walked about happily ever after.

In every respect, after Sutter and son had abandoned it, the fort was the very picture of depravity, its crumbling walls the haunts of rats and every other kind of vermin, its court obstructed with piles of 'broken champagne, claret, and brown stout bottles, bullock's heads with horns on 'em, fly-blown and decaying.' It was a disreputable boarding-house, a liquor-shop, criminals' hide-out, and a hospital for miners in which, on about thirty cots, the sick, the dying and the dead lay side by side in unspeakable squalor.

At last, when news arrived that Congress had again adjourned without giving a thought to conditions in California, General Riley, Mason's successor as Governor-Military, took matters in his own hands and convoked a State Constitutional Convention at Monterey. Sutter, Brannan, Burnett and John McDougall were delegates from the Sacramento District. Of Sutter, a

trustworthy fellow-member reports that he was only 'a sort of ornamental appendage to the convention . . . without much force
and very little influence.' [13] But as the Grand Old Man of California he was respected and contributed much towards the convention's atmosphere and general amusement by the sheer presence of his colorful personality and his gentlemanly manners.

The convention, however, was not to pass into history without
becoming one of the most signal events in Sutter's life. Because of
the illness of Chairman Robert Semple, Sutter was called upon to
preside on the last day, October 13, when the only business on
hand was the affixing of the signatures to the constitution. To relieve the tedium of pen-scratching and to enhance the solemnity,
Governor Riley had ordered a salute of thirty-one guns to be
fired from the presidio. It was a momentous occasion. As gun
after gun boomed from the bay, the acting chairman, emotional
old Captain Sutter suddenly fell victim to a fit of boyish enthusiasm for military pomp. Casting to the winds the dignity of the
chair, he stumbled to his feet, frantically waved his hand over his
head and roared at the convention: 'Gentlemen! This is the happiest day of my life! It does my heart good to hear these cannon;
they remind me of the time when I was a soldier. Yes, I am glad
to hear them!' Tears glittered on his ruddy cheeks. His mind became confused with excitement and tremblingly he sank into his
chair, while the cynical convention cheered raucously.

That night there was a banquet and ball. Since there were but
11 ladies to 120 gentlemen, a young poet and correspondent for
the *New York Tribune*, Bayard Taylor, selected the good-look-
ing Captain Sutter as his lady and was surprised to find himself
whirled about by his fair partner of twice his own age until he
was completely out of breath. While Sutter's mental powers were
fast deteriorating, his physical stamina was still unbroken.

Again, the following day, the honor devolved on Sutter to

head the solemn procession to the gubernatorial residence and to commit to the hands of Governor Riley the constitution as signed by its makers. Called upon to deliver an address before the Governor, emotion again wrought havoc with poor Sutter. His large child's eyes filled with tears of joy, his lips trembled, his body shook, but words failed him completely.

Yet, this was the man who, ten years before, had shaken up the sleepers and idle dreamers of the land, who had bossed and bullied the native sons, built a fortress against them and a buffer state between their settlements and the wild Indians. He had opened the large interior valley to civilization; he had by his pioneering practically made a present of northern California to the United States and finally had unlocked the golden treasures of the sierras—a record few could equal in ten years. And now, in the touching episode blended of the tears of second childhood and high official honors, Sutter's public life reached its bizarre culmination. In this brief scene became epitomized the heights of grandeur and a precipitous fall.

As rapidly as he had risen from unknown depths, as rapidly he was to sink again. He had served well in the mysterious hands of destiny, as a torch to illumine for a moment and to ignite the world. The match was now burnt out and could be thrown away.

In yet another way, in a much deeper and more tragic sense, the peak of Sutter's life summed up his rise and fall, linked past and future. While the glamorous Captain Sutter stood before Governor Riley as the embodiment of California, looking through tear-filled eyes on the scroll of the California constitution trembling in his hand, while he was in vain fumbling for a few simple words, something again mysteriously clicked. That moment his unglamorous past began to encroach upon him: on that very day, 7,000 miles away, his abandoned family was about to leave, or had already left Switzerland.[14]

40. A PEER'S BOURGEOIS FAMILY

By the token of external circumstances, Sutter was never such a carefree man as at the time before and during the Constitutional Convention. He was restored to power, and with the guardianship over him removed, the spell of madness vanished. The almost visionary future about which, during his years of struggle, he had written so hopefully had now evolved into the tangible present. He was relieved of all debts. At last he could live fully according to his worth; he could afford again to be generous.

He was at the fort when the first great armies of overland immigrants arrived. Most of them were penniless or became so after a day or two in the new land, prices of everything having risen to dizzy heights. For a tiny room and single bed, for instance, $150 a month was asked by hotels and boarding-houses which were nothing but the flimsiest shacks of clapboard with muslin partitions. But no appeal to Sutter was in vain. He was now the Grand Old Man of California; he 'benignly governed the motley race, dispensing favors with open hand.' One of this colorful crowd has left us a charming little sketch:

On the 4th of September, which was a Sunday, as we were nearing Sacramento, we fell in with a stranger, who appeared to be a pleasant, genial man. He addressed us in broken English, saying: 'How do you do, shentlemens; gum into the ford and make yourselves at home.' We went into the fort and were right royally entertained by the stranger, who was no other than the noble gentleman. . . .

Perhaps, after the Constitutional Convention, Sutter hoped for some return for such favors, having been weak enough to let himself be drawn into the first gubernatorial race. But in the ballot he came out only third; the choice of the people fell on Peter H. Burnett, his dismissed agent.

With this defeat there began for Sutter another series of trials and tribulations. Already his family was crossing the Isthmus of Panama, and with them old misfortune came from the old country.

Just before Christmas, 1849, Sacramento was visited by the worst floods the valley had ever known. Two weeks later matters became even worse. The river spread to a width of many miles, so that Sacramento City stood under water up to twenty feet, save for those parts nearest the old fort. Schooners, beside which only the roofs and upper stories of the tallest buildings were visible, cruised through its main thoroughfares. Thousands of boxes, bales and barrels, and the stacks of costly lumber, tons of tobacco, tea and cotton were washed down the valley on the crests of the waves. A few miles below, Sutterville on its serene heights roared with laughter at the supposed end of its upstart rival. This was reason enough for Sutter to fume again over the scoundrelly intrigue against his own Sutterville, yet not reason enough to join in its wanton jubilation; for by now his connection with Sutterville had shrunk almost to the dead letter of the name.

Up the valley cattle drowned by thousands or fell a prey to organized freebooting butchers who went out in boats and slaughtered enough of them to supply whole cities with beef at Sutter's cost. 'Some of these butchers,' says he, 'cleared sixty thousand dollars and then left. We had no law then to protect us.'

It was during the last week of January 1850, while part of the town lay still under water and Sutter was sitting in the City Hotel over a real-estate transaction, that Lienhard entered, bringing the tidings of the safe arrival of Sutter's family in San Francisco. The City Hotel, by the way, was nothing else than Sutter's gristmill, dismantled, removed, and re-erected in Sacramento. Sutter and Lienhard spent the night in the hotel warehouse among the rats (unknown in California before the gold-rush) and the following morning took passage on the steamer *Eldorado* for San Francisco. But since Lienhard tactfully left himself out of the intimate scene between the old pioneer and his family, nothing has ever become known regarding this strange *wiedersehen*.

The family stayed at Graham House, San Francisco's fashionable board-and-canvas shack, standing in a swamp and surrounded by the charred ruins of the metropolis which had recently gone up in flames. Was the ominous sign-language of these ruins intelligible to one or the other member of the little gathering? Did it dawn upon any of them, who had traveled 12,000 miles to sun themselves in father's magnificence, that actually they had come merely to witness the collapse of his kingdom?

This much is certain, that the arrival of the family at Hock Farm during the first days of February brought to a new head the conflict between Sutter and his son August. The latter, to whom alone his mother, brothers and sister owed it that they were now in California, unbalanced through the harrassing experiences of the past eighteen months, flew into a towering rage because his father had snatched from him the honor of receiving the family at the seaport. Son accused father of having designedly left him out of the reception lest he, the son, inform his mother of what he knew of Sutter's ways of life at the fort.[15]

Who were the members of this family from whom the troubled shopkeeper of Burgdorf had escaped sixteen years before and who now had caught up with him?

Frau Sutter, once the alluring belle of Burgdorf, had become a self-effacing *hausfrau*, much taller than her husband, rather haggard, with deep-set, shortsighted eyes spreading gloom from under horizontal brows, her grim, thin mouth bending down at the corners like an Indian bow. She seemed the personification of ill fate; a sibyl exhaling an atmosphere in which naught could prosper; the most abysmal contrast imaginable to her handsome, genial mate.

After Augustus, Jr., there came a daughter, Elise, the apple of her father's eye, now renamed Eliza for greater sonority. She was in her twenty-second year and had inherited some of her father's good looks, his *joie de vivre*, and the facility of making human contacts; but she was rude, boorish, and filled with boundless conceit.

Next was Emil Victor, just twenty years of age, he who was supposed to have been educated at a famous agricultural institute, but whom Lienhard had found acquiring a very badly needed last-minute polish in the private school of Herr Haas at Darmstadt. Emil was a rather quiet and introspective young man, inclined like his mother to deafness.

The last one (the youngest having died three years after his father's escape) was Alfons Wilhelm, a boy not yet eighteen, already eager for martial fame. Sutter, almost four years previously, had written that Alfons was being educated at a famous military academy. But the truth was that he, too, before coming to America, had been sent to Darmstadt, there to receive an all too thin educational varnish.

For a brief while, the presence of his children detained, as the eldest son had hoped, their father 'from committing any more excesses.' While Frau Sutter ensconced herself in the sombre role of her husband's closet skeleton, the younger generation broke into this new life zestfully, enjoying themselves on hunting-parties and excursions on horseback, which were to familiarize them with their father's little kingdom. In honor of his daughter the proud father immediately laid out a new town, Eliza City; but it became at once apparent that the neighboring Marysville on the site of old Cordua's farm had already made too prosperous a start to allow the younger Eliza a chance to grow. Eliza, therefore, quickly became a ghost town.

Nor was this the only sorrow Eliza brought her father. Before many weeks had passed, he discovered a love affair between his daughter and a young Swiss, George David Engler, whom he employed as secretary and as piano-teacher to his youngest son. Though Engler came of a good family, he was yet held to be far beneath the dignity of Sutter's wealth and station. The discovery brought down upon the would-be son-in-law the old gentleman's wrath and the young man was straightaway discharged and banished from the realm.

The main exterior change, however, brought by the coming of the family, was the erection of a residence spacious and stately enough for the representative life of the country squire. John Bidwell was the builder. The land belonging to Hock Farm embraced excellent grazing country, with wide bands of extremely fertile grain and garden soil beside placid Feather River and its willows and cottonwoods.[16] The banks of the river were high enough to protect the farmlands from the hibernal floods. Magnificent old groves gave to the estate the aspect of a park, out of which the imposing pyramids of Los Tres Picos, now known as Sutter's Buttes, rose like friendly guardians adding immensely to the picturesqueness of the scenery.

The old uncomfortable farm buildings, standing a few hundred feet away from the river, were now augmented by new outhouses and a new large residence so as to form a large quadrangular court, in the center of which there was a well under an old sycamore. The residence, half frame, half adobe building was a two story house, facing east towards the river and with a wide piazza in the New England style. A few poplar trees, planted so as to emphasize the formal but friendly symmetry of the front of the residence, stood in line with the flagstaff on which on festive occasions the Stars and Stripes was hoisted amid the boom of a cannon brought up from the old fort and fired by Alfons, the would-be young soldier.

In that vast and now so turbulent valley dotted with tents, canvas booths and other improvised habitations, Sutter once more became a pioneer of civilized living. How strangely everything was changed! Was all this true? Were these the blessings of his regained family? Amid a hundred thousand fortune-hunting adventurers, had the oldest and greatest adventurer indeed turned into the epitome of that stability inherent in the very soil? And while the gold-fever putrified the country, had old Sutter in earnest turned his devotion to the fertile soil in order again to point out the way California must later go? So it seemed.

Sutter became the pioneer of California's fruit industry. As he had proved to the sceptical Mexicans that it was possible to live in the interior and to grow wheat there, so now he took singular pride in demonstrating to a gold-crazed world that, with proper care, it was possible to grow almost every species of fruit and vegetable. He laid out a large-scale experimental plantation and had seeds and cuttings, particularly fruit and vine cuttings, sent him, irrespective of cost, from all over the world.

This was the life that suited Squire Sutter; to plant, to grow, to experiment without having to worry about profits and losses. As was presaged in one of his letters to Leidesdorff, he did not now 'trouble much his head about growing wheat,' or other staple produce, for the market. He could afford to do whatever he liked for the sheer pleasure of doing it.

Yet it is remarkable that even in his declining state this man's hobby took on the garb of practical idealism, remarkable that even now he wanted to guide and to explore, to find new paths leading to happiness and prosperity for all. The best that was in Sutter was not yet dead. Indeed, Hock Farm before long was recognized as a 'model farm, a normal school where one can come and study the special acclimatization processes in order to avoid the importation of foreign trials and errors.'[17]

Thus, ever changing and ever the same, this strange man Sutter now seemed to pave the way even for Luther Burbank.

41. *SHORTCUTS TO RUIN*

As yet Sutter's star stood high in the firmament of fame, guiding hundreds upon hundreds of celebrity-hunters to Hock Farm.

The eminence to whom these curious folk were introduced was a man of barely medium height, stoutish, and with the typical round head of the Alpine race. The color of his face, framed between fast greying side whiskers, was a healthy, bronzed ruddiness. His baldness, which had reached the top of his crown, lent to his forehead a suggestion of great mental powers. He wore a neatly trimmed moustache and underlip tuft. A straight and finely modeled nose divided two somewhat unequal halves of an unusually handsome face. This asymmetry, enhancing the vividness of his mobile features, was noticeable chiefly in his eyes: the left was a little lower than the right. Although underlined with baggy little 'sausages,' his wide-open eyes were a clear, sparkling blue, and they retained until his very end some of their old fire.

But what impressed visitors even more than his appearance was the extraordinary refinement of his manners. 'Courteous as a prince,' says Bidwell of him; 'one more polished in his deportment I have never seen.' Even the arch-critical Lienhard wrote: 'He made such a favorable impression on one that it took a long time and many disappointments before this fascination vanished.' Others saw in him the perfect 'gentleman of the old European military school,' possessed of all its civility, ease, and dignity, but without any of its snobbish hauteur. [18]

With his high-collared dark blue frock-coat with wide lapels, he would, when out of doors, wear a peaked cap which added the finishing touch to his military air. In this attire he would take visitors on a tour of his extensive gardens, orchards and vineyards. Then, back in his study in the new residence, among a large collection of books, drawings, etchings, paintings, cabinet specimens of minerals and Indian handiwork, they would settle down to the host's greatest pleasure: the sampling of the choicest vintages of the world's most famous vineyards. Ambitious as Sutter was to make his own plantations the best in California, as a connoisseur he depended for his own delectation on the vineyards of France and the Rhineland. Pierre Charles de Saint-Amand, who visited Sutter in 1850, found that 'nowhere can one enjoy in better quality and greater abundance the *mousse pétillante* of the slopes of Rheims and of Aï. Indeed, one even has to guard oneself against a liberality pushed to excesses in the most sympathetic of toasts.'

Few visitors were refused a friendly handshake and kind word. But the guests after Sutter's heart were the men of title, worldly position and achievement. Next to himself it was for these that he bought up what almost seem to have been shiploads of the rarest wines, and from Havana the most expensive cigars. Only when he was enlivened by imported wines, by tinkling glasses and eager listeners, would Sutter drop his mask of dignity, and then emerge a hale and hearty fellow disporting himself in his element.

Then Sutter was 'the happiest of the happy and full of good spirits,' as Lienhard once described him. Of stories of his fictitious service in the Swiss Guard of Charles X of France there would then be no end, and they must have been so accurate in detail that not one Frenchman ever suspected that he was listening to a genteel Rabelais. Sometimes he ventured to declare that he was really of noble blood.[19] He would talk of his 'fellow cadet' and 'bosom friend' Louis Napoleon, now Emperor Napoleon III, whom he would visit again at Versailles as soon as conditions in California were settled enough to allow him to take a trip to Europe. Then he would also call on Queen Victoria. . . .

Famous visitors from the four corners of the earth flocked to Sutter, writers, painters, scholars, statesmen, noblemen. Most flattering was perhaps the visit of Prince Paul of Würtemberg, a scholarly and widely-traveled young giant who, with a few officers, was his guest during a ten days' Bacchanal in San Francisco, Sacramento and Hock Farm.

Before long, countless stories, true and false, of Sutter's extravagance were afloat: A doctor who had attended Sutter's family during their voyage from Panama to San Francisco and refused to send Sutter a bill was finally coaxed into accepting an invitation to Hock Farm. When the guest unfolded his napkin, he found in his plate a little heap of gold nuggets of the most curious shapes. Their value by weight was $700, but their collector's value much more, as curiosity nuggets fetched unusual prices. Touched by Sutter's ruse, the physician at last consented to accept his fee. Thus ran one of the tales.

On one occasion, credible rumors have it, Sutter spent $15,000 on a little group of friends during a four weeks' spree in San Francisco. Then, to return home, he had to borrow $1,000 more. Back at Hock Farm he offered a note due in two weeks and worth $10,000 for half its face value, preferring to have the cash at once rather than wait a fortnight. During his frequent sprees in the cities it was nothing unusual for him to throw out $1,000 a night for his and his friends' champagnes, liqueurs and cigars.

Nor was such spendthrift extravagance confined to pleasure-trips. On numerous weekends during the fair season the grounds of Hock Farm were overrun with guests.[20] No invitation was necessary. You went and took your friends, and when you had introduced them to the host they were as welcome as old acquaintances. On Sundays, the river-boats from Sacramento were usually crowded with such visitors. Sometimes, knowing Sutter's extreme weakness for music, they took a band. Then, while the large company disembarked to the tunes of the band and the booming of cannon, the host sauntered elegantly down to the garden gate, within which, in his meticulous attire, he would receive his old acquaintances with his most graceful and kindly civilities.

Soon the company rambled all over the place, after a while to gather again at long tables set up under shady trees. 'At times,' says one of the frequent visitors, 'as many as three hundred guests were gathered at his board, they were treated to the most cheer that the land could raise, and the costliest wines flowed freely as water.' Instead of rare bread and jerked meat once given out to starving, ragged immigrants, he now lavished expensive luxuries on just as motley a crowd, most of whom had no other reason to be present except to indulge in extravagances they could not themselves afford. Among these revelers were also those who, between symposia, spirited away section after section of Sutter's empire. The third act of the great partition was in full swing.

It must at first glance appear paradoxical that a man who had gained his start on the strength of an ingenious fable could become so trusting, so credulous. Apparently, in his beginning second childhood, it was Sutter the 'only child' and darling of his mother who seemed to be reclaiming his birthright, which was to be coddled tenderly, to be the recipient of all attention. Alas, this state could not but quicken his disaster. For as he was ready to accept such crude idolatry he was himself making advances to his humbuggers. Unfortunately he was too thoroughbred an actor not to take himself seriously in any role. The sweet honey of self-approbation, therefore, was bound to attract a whole swarm of parasitic wasps. But who was there to save him? Among his children none but the eldest amounted to anything, and the eldest now needed a savior himself.

Ever since old Sutter had regained control of his estate, Augustus Jr. had lived at Hock Farm, a decrepit young man, suffering from what today would undoubtedly be diagnosed as a severe neurosis. It was the upshot of the conflict with his father, a breakdown manifesting itself in attempts of an oversensitive soul to escape from an unbearable reality in fits of blindness, swoons and delirious fevers. In spite of these afflictions, the father, as soon as the family had arrived, had tried to remove the son from Hock Farm. For this purpose he established him in business in Sacramento with three gentlemen from Germany, Dr. Brandes (the physician who attended Augustus in his illness), and two friends of this man, the brothers Wetzlar. It was typical of Sutter's lavishness to furnish the capital and make the three outsiders equal partners of his son, although they contributed practically nothing to the firm's assets.

Augustus, however, was incapable of attending to business either because of his afflictions or, as he believed, because Dr. Brandes designedly kept him drugged. The young firm had barely been launched when Augustus's troubles became so acute as to make it imperative for him to escape from all the nightmares of California. He left on July 1, 1850, intending to make his home in the eastern United States; but in Acapulco, Mexico, he fell in love with a young Spanish-woman, married, and stayed in Acapulco. In his place the inevitable Sam Brannan entered the young firm, and under Brannan's genius the large part of Sacramento City which old Sutter had deeded to his son as backing for the business, was elegantly hocussed away during the young man's absence.[21]

Old Sutter had meanwhile become the helpless victim of his designing friends and agents. It is impossible today to conjure up a convincing picture of the fetid chaos that pervaded California with the gold-rushers. The hundreds of thousands lured into the country by the gold came with but one object: to get fabulously rich by fair means or foul. Politics obeyed the same wolfish spirit. While a man was still at liberty to go before the law, the delay, the litigation, the unavoidable extortionate bribes on every side, and the lawyers' fees were such as to recommend the simple act of being publicly stripped of all he had as a very pleasant and much the cheaper way to ruin than the law.

Under careful and efficient management (of which John A. Sutter Jr. would have been capable had his relations with his father been friendlier), it would have mattered little if old Sutter had squandered $1,000 a night quite frequently. It is almost unthinkable that any man could dissipate the wealth which the gold-rush and the rise of Sacramento City created for Sutter. But the hair-raising truth is that twelve months after he had again taken things 'in his own hand,' he found himself virtually stripped of all income-producing property.

By whom? And how? The men who did it were the same who swilled and guzzled and fawned upon him most at his banquets. These men he trusted while his curses had driven from the country the son who once had saved him and conceivably could have saved him again.

Of this last shearing of the sheep, details are lacking, except those furnished by Sutter and his eldest son. However, since the results of the gigantic pillage are amply verified, there is no reason to doubt even old Sutter's indictments. 'I was so foolish,' he wailed in his old age. 'I understood so little about business. I gave men powers of attorney to sign deeds and they swindled me on every side. . . . I was the victim of every swindler that came along.'

Of Sutter's first two agents, Schoolcraft soon returned east, after having made his quick pile, and died of cholera. 'Peachy,' says Sutter, 'made a fortune out of me in a short time.' A favorite trick of all the agents was to sell the same lot several times, keep their multiple commissions, and let Sutter pay for their 'mistake.'

About June 1, 1850, Sutter revoked the power of attorney granted Peachy and transferred it to Albert Winn. This fellow had his entire family portrayed in oils by an expensive artist and paid the painter in city lots at Sutter's expense. Winn, says Sutter, 'sold lots, a great many, and never accounted for them.' Moreover, he borrowed money at ten per cent *a month* on Sutter's account, and Sutter did not learn about this loan until the debt had risen to $35,000 and the sheriff appeared at Hock to levy an attachment on the farm.

A sorry detail, which Sutter conscientiously omits from his accounts, is that all these schemers and swindlers continued the lucrative practice of pushing yards of treacherous legal verbiage under his nose for signature, when, at the height of revelry, he did not trouble to read what he would not have understood had he been sober. Later he was to find out that he had again signed away a fat parcel of his empire.

Such, briefly, were the shortcuts to his ruin. Only half a year had passed since Frau Sutter and the younger children had entered upon the scene. Already, unforgetful of the hard school of penury she had gone through, Frau Sutter was compelled to resort again to her accustomed penny-splitting. The two remaining sons, Emil and Alfons, were obliged to labor in the fields and gardens; the daughter Eliza attended to the household and kitchen with the help of three Indian girls and a French girl. And as in the old New Helvetia days, the embarrassed squire of Hock now hired a young relative to work for him without a more definite promise than that he would 'certainly pay' him 'well.'

This young man, Gustav Schläfli,[22] was a son of Frau Sutter's eldest sister. At the end of 1850 he wrote to his mother: 'Uncle is still fairly wealthy in cattle and land and could own much more if not almost everybody who deals with him were trying to defraud him; bad experience has made him a little wiser.' And his moral judgment of the family he put into these words: 'Auntie and the children have become stingy and haughty beyond all words. Uncle is respected and beloved by everybody; but about the family people talk only with deprecation.' Lienhard, too, describes them as petty, coarse, conceited, without a trace of their father's many virtues.

Nine months only after he had stood on the summit of his life, six months after his family had caught up with him, Sutter was facing evil days again. Fantastic as this might seem, it was the bitter truth. The Frenchman Ernest de Massey who came to California at this time and wanted to visit Sutter, like every other prominent Frenchman before him, changed his mind when he heard of the old pioneer's plight. His words may here stand in testimony of what was even then public knowledge:

If he [Sutter] had more of the Yankee in him, he would today be one of the richest capitalists in the whole world; but unfortunately much of the vast fortune that seems to have turned his head got away from him. His followers have tricked, deceived, and plundered him; taking advantage of his weakness for drink, they have cajoled him into making transactions involving land concessions which contain clauses so cunningly worded that they brought ruinous and endless litigation. According to local opinion he will be completely ruined within a few years by those whom he formerly aided.

Sutter himself, in 1866, confessed in his petition to Congress that 'since 1850 all his resources have been cut off, save a small mortgaged remnant of Hock Farm.'

The richest man in California was now Sam Brannan, who every Sunday preached a fine layman's sermon in San Francisco, who organized Sunday schools and in every other way indulged in exemplary observance of the Lord's Day after each week's painstaking devotion to God Mammon.

42. *THE SPIRIT OF CONQUEST*

IT must now be said that if Sutter was stripped of most of his income-producing property, these lands were not, as yet, irrevocably lost to him; some of his assets were simply 'frozen.' In fairness to Sutter it must be added that if he was now at the mercy of commercial and legal cut-throats, he was so not merely by reason of his own deplorable weakness. In fact, first among those whom he formerly aided and who now did their utmost to ruin him was the United States.

Amid the topsyturvydom and the deluge of the gold-rush one of the most important facts is easily overlooked: namely, that these years were a post-war period as chaotic and demoralized as any other. To understand what happened, it must never for a moment be forgotten that California was a conquered Mexican province now to be penalized, according to age-old martial tradition, for the capital crime of having been possessed by another master.

Much of the agitation preceding the Mexican war had been fed by the demagogic bait of untold square miles of uninhabited land to be added to the public domain.[23] The fallacious belief that all lands of California were still free was especially rampant among the backwoodsmen from the former frontier, now become the Middle-West. Because where they came from all unoccupied land did belong to the Government and the squatter's right did obtain, these greedy and narrow-minded Middle-Westerners could scarcely believe other than that gigantic frauds were perpetrated. Could these Spanish-Mexican land-grants be genuine? And had not that fellow Sutter alone—a foreigner to boot—claimed 229 square miles under his grants?

The rather vague character of the Spanish-Mexican grants made matters worse. Under the Spanish tradition exact surveys were neither necessary nor possible. Now ill-luck would have it that Sutter's New Helvetia grant, which he had received from Alvarado on June 18, 1841, gave as the southern boundary line the parallel of 38°, 49′, 32″ of north latitude, a designation which August Sutter had made public in a standing advertisement of the *Placer Times*, in which he warned against squatting. But when it was discovered that the parallel of 38°, 49′, 32″ ran several miles north of the fort, and therefore excluded Sacramento City, Sutterville, and all the surrounding lands, hell broke loose. To the squatters this was palpable evidence of an attempted huge swindle.

Now there can be no doubt but that New Helvetia's southern limit was fixed at 38°, 49′, 32″ only because of the inaccuracy of J.J. Vioget's instruments. For in the sketch of the survey accompanying the application for the grant, the line of this parallel is clearly drawn a few miles south of the fort. However, these inaccuracies afforded the squatters a convenient point of attack. They forthwith ensconced themselves behind the position that, as long as the Spanish-Mexican grants were not confirmed by a law court, they had as much right as anyone to occupy a piece of land, whether it was covered by a grant or not. The landowners on their part employed every means to drive away the squatters.

Under the hot breezes of the dog days of 1850 a bloody revolt broke out, during which the Mayor, the Sheriff and a number of other persons were killed. The greedy and misled squatters raised the war-cries of 'human rights,' 'natural rights,' and of the 'American tradition;' the equally unscrupulous land speculators who, through frauds and swindles, had by this time gained control of most of the Sacramento City lands, stood upon the sacrosanctity of ancient titles, international law, and the Treaty of Guadalupe Hidalgo which guaranteed the rights of property in conquered Mexican territories.

At this juncture the United States joined hands with the lawless squatters. For a long time after the conquest the government in Washington had left California to its own devices. Not until September 9, 1850, did the Senate formally admit California into the Union, and not until March 3, 1851, did Congress pass a law, 'to settle private land claims in California.' Since no man was more profoundly affected by this legislation than Sutter, a few words must here be devoted to this rather amazing subject.

In its 'Act to settle private land claims in California,' Congress simply tore to pieces all international agreements touching upon the question of private property in conquered territories and dragged every holder of a Spanish or a Mexican grant into the law courts. Moreover, the law was so designed that automatically every case won by a grant-holder in the lower courts stood appealed, and, though it was the government which appealed, the defendant had to bear all costs. In short, it was the kind of victor's legislation which all vanquished lands fall heir to and which invariably proves more destructive, more apt to make the blood boil than war itself.

By virtue of this legislation, Sutter now found himself virtually indicted for trying to defraud the United States of 146,454 acres, or 229 square miles of land. At a time when his assets had vanished or were 'frozen,' he was forced to employ legal counsel at a cost which few in the country could afford. He was no longer the man to stand the financial or mental pressure of such litigation. Although only forty-eight years of age, his singular destiny, the trials and tribulations of his ten years of pioneering, and to some degree, perhaps, his excesses, had definitely made him an old man who, according to his own admission, was 'incapacitated for business' and reduced to a 'retiring disposition.'

Already the legal tussle with individual squatters in the improvised local courts was too great a strain for him and caused him, in July 1850, to dispose of all his holdings outside Hock Farm to a real estate concern for the shameful pittance of $6,000 and a right to one sixth of the proceeds from the sale, lease, or other use of the land. With the stroke of the pen that signed that conveyance, the Sutters had practically divested themselves of all their property, since John A. Sutter, Jr., leaving for Mexico, had likewise disposed of his part of these lands. And the pitiful down payments were all the cash that father and son were ever to receive for these immense tracts.

For the effect on conditions in general of the 'Act to settle land claims' and its retroaction on individual affairs was ruthlessly severe. The attitude taken by Congress was equal to a *prima facie* recognition of the squatters' claims. It therefore encouraged squatting and paralyzed all honest marketing in land values since it did not cost the squatters anything to occupy another man's land as long as his title had not been confirmed by the Supreme Court in Washington. Not the gold-fever, but this Act of Congress was accountable for the blocking of all paths towards the attainment of settled conditions in the new state.

The market being paralyzed by virtue of the Land Claims Act, there was nothing left to the landowner but to borrow money at sinful rates of interest to defend himself against the government, or to shorten the torture by disposing of his title for a pittance to a group of speculating loan-sharks, among whom Sam Brannan now ranked uppermost. The situation opened an enormous field for every shyster lawyer in the United States. And on top of it all, the holders of grants were forced to pay taxes, exorbitant taxes, whereas the squatters paid nothing.

It must be evident that where the law encourages corruption the millennium of depravity is at hand. 'In God's name,' writes Judge Elisha Crosby, who for many years sat over disputes arising out of this congressional legislation, 'what sense of right was there on the part of the Government of the United States in putting these claimants to the enormous expense of carrying the litigation of their claims to Washington? . . . I have no hesitation in saying that the course of legislation on the part of the United States and the litigation they have forced upon the original claimants was a very great injustice.'

Under such circumstances it was of course not given to Sutter to find peace in his retirement at Hock. For soon enough the squatters were not only occupying valuable city property and preventing its sale, they swooped down on the old ranches as well like swarms of locusts. As their ranks were swelled from month to month through the continually rising stream of immigrants, increasing their political influence, the time soon came when a squatter could without fear of consequences permit himself anything short of murder against a title-holder. The squatters took hold of any land that pleased them; they drove away or killed the owner's cattle, cut down and sold his trees, fenced in his springs; they enjoyed all the benefits of ownership without paying rent or taxes, but through their political influence they had it in their power to force the owner to pay exorbitant taxes on the property which they occupied. And with the tax money thus obtained the squatter communities paid lawyers to appear in the name of the United States, to contest the owner's title and delay decision. Then, when a decision had been reached, they got up a new contest about the survey and delayed as long as possible the settlement of the boundaries.

Here, then, was re-enacted the war of conquest on a civil basis and in a spirit of savage vindictiveness, compared with which the professional war of soldiers had been a placid gentlemen's game. One may propound the question of legal philosophy whether, in thus pressing towards a more equal distribution of land, Congress did not act in the best interest of democratic principles? With such a tenet, had it existed, there could be no quarrel. But the philosophic principles of law and democracy were the last things to guide congressional reasoning. What was to be achieved here was simply the final and complete purging of the conquered province of the remains of the Mexican regime. And that, to those who, like Sutter, had done their utmost to quicken the advent of the Stars and Stripes in California, was an event ineffably cruel and tragic.

43. *THE SQUIRE OF HOCK*

THE years of Sutter's life spent under the shadow of lawsuits imposed on him by Washington can be accounted for in few words. From being the strong arm and hammer he had become the anvil; from being a man of destiny he was become the shackled victim on whom the shame of his own time was most cruelly and most indelibly branded.

In January 1851 Peter H. Burnett resigned from the governorship and Lieutenant-Governor John McDougall automatically became his successor, so that the ship of state was now guided by one of the unconscionable old Fort Sutter traders. John McDougall was a partner in the firm of Robinson, Fowler, Gillespie & McDougall—Sutter's agents. He was one of the original blackmailers in the Sacramento-Sutterville feud, one of those who had made irreparable the rent between Sutter father and Sutter son. Augustus, Jr., called him the curse of his life. Very characteristically, McDougall, immediately upon his inauguration, offered to send Sutter to the World's Fair in London as California's official delegate. And what could have been his purpose except to despoil his victim of the last foot of land during his long absence? This would have been an easy matter and one of countless precedents. But Sutter apparently did smell a rat, for he declined the offer.

How did he succeed in weathering the tornado of corruption of these years? According to his nephew Schläfli, *vaquero* at Hock, Sutter, at this time 'was not exactly in bad circumstances but only suffering from a dire shortage of cash.' Not a cent came in from the last vast stretch of land which he had put on the market through Messrs. Robinson, Fowler, Gillespie & McDougall. The upshot was that he found himself deprived not only of all resources but also of friends.

Adversity had driven away the crowds of frivolous revelers and left the old pioneer to solitude and his uncongenial consort. Where were they whose laughter and acclaim had once echoed the popping of champagne bottles? What had become of the idolatrous burners of Havana incense? And what of the hordes of claques? Gone were the last of them. The desolation of a cemetery now prevailed at Hock.

Need one be surprised that Eliza Sutter, despite the distressing shortage of women in the country, was still unmarried? Was it in despair, for reasons of pecuniary stringency, or out of a longing for a son whom he could trust, that in March 1851 the proud father went to the length of urging John Bidwell to marry Eliza? Bidwell, however polite and uncomfortable, declined in a pathetic, long letter. A little later Sutter found a fiancé for Eliza in a portrait-painter named William Shaw. But a few days before the wedding it was discovered that the groom had sought out his role for no other purpose than to swindle Sutter out of the small remainder of his fortune and the bride out of an estate in San José settled on her soon after her arrival in the country. The wedding, therefore, was canceled.

In the summer of 1851 Sutter's eldest son returned temporarily from Mexico in order to collect the balance of $100,000 of the $125,000 for which he had disposed of his interest in Sacramento property to Messrs. Bruce, Brannan, Graham & Wetzlar. But these rogues and others who in the meantime had bought shares in the bounty, the lawyers of San Francisco and of Sacramento, the judges and the juries, presented a solid grinning front, extracted fees and fines from the seeker of justice, found fictitious debts of his, or paid pittances in notes on which he found it impossible to collect. Young Sutter was publicly pillaged. Some of these practitioners, like Sam Brannan, were signers of the Vigilante Proclamation, men who wore the mask of Puritanism and of patriotism to wage war upon the small-fry bandits and were themselves wholesale robbers and despoilers of the law. To read of their tactics against Augustus Sutter is enough to make one cry aloud with pain even today. The young man, not yet cured of the afflictions which were the upshot of the conflict with his father, was forced to leave the country again, poorer in health and money. Driven to the verge of insanity by the diabolical conspiracy against him, victim of a persecution mania, he strayed into the deserts of Mexico and lived for a long time among the Indians, until solitude and desert peace restored his equilibrium.

The case of the Sutters, the most spectacular and most tragic, was only one among a thousand. Few of those who had owned anything before the gold-rush and whose mode of living was geared to the gentler pace of the previous era could survive the cut-throat methods of the California swindlers. The plight of these old settlers is illuminatingly summed up in a letter George McKinstry, Sutter's former manager, wrote in 1851 to Edward M. Kern (one time fort commander) in Philadelphia:

Our old friend Capt. Sutter has fitten up the Hock buildings in fine style, and I regret to say is bursten all to flinders; old Cordua *tom bien*; Daylor and Shelden estates both said to be insolvent . . . old Kitnor [Kyburz] is Major Domo at Hock, made a fortune and bust. . . . Old Keseburg the Man-eater, has made a fortune and is now keeping a Restaurant in K.St., Sac City. . . . I could fill a fools cap sheet with the names of the old guard bust community, including your humble servant.

Not until January 1852 did the United States Land Commission for California take up its duties as an investigating body and the lowest land tribunal. Fortunately they were men of honor and integrity, themselves severely upset over the unpardonable, but quite irremediable, congressional blunder. Nor could their presence prevent the soaring of swindling and speculating to new heights. Now was the time when grant-holders needed lawyers to defend themselves against the government, and money with which to pay extortionate lawyers' fees. And between the onslaught of scheming lawyers, the bleedings of money-lenders, the tricks of speculators and the law's delay, the chances for survival were as good as nil. In order to defray the cost of these lawsuits, Sutter mortgaged piece after piece of his Hock estate, or the income he was to derive from the land in the hands of his agents, and within two years spent $100,000 on lawyers, scribes, witnesses, interest on mortgages, and taxes on the land held and exploited by squatters.

One more brisk party lightened the gloom of these years when, on March 21, 1852, Eliza Sutter finally married. Who was the happy groom? The very George David Engler whom, two years before, Sutter had angrily driven from his house for daring to love as exalted a person as Princess Eliza. So low had fortune sunk at Hock that the same man had now been received back into grace. Once more a steamship load of 200 invited guests came up Feather River as Sutter opened wide the gates of his retreat. Once more a band played, the Indians entertained the crowds with their exotic dances, and the more intimate circle of friends spun out the revelry into the small hours of the following day. Sir Henry Huntley, who happened to call on Sutter the morning after the wedding found him 'sitting at a table amongst bottles half and quite empty, wine glasses and tumblers showing what once had filled them, and stumps of half-used cigars, the floor covered with all the debris of a supper, the captain scarcely recovered from his indulgences.'

The year 1853 began with the most devastating floods Sutter had ever seen in the valley. All buildings stood in several feet of water; old adobe walls were dissolved or yielded to the pressure of the current and caved in. Only with the utmost exertion could Alfons save the cattle, driving them in the middle of the night to the top of a hill, while his father and mother fled in terror from one building to another.

Now Sutter was ready to call 'Enough!' Determined to seek peace of mind on the Sandwich Islands, he entered into a provisional agreement for the sale of Hock Farm with one J. B. Steinberger, another rogue, of course. Fortunately, Sutter had had the presence of mind to make the transaction contingent upon a very substantial down payment which, it became presently apparent, the prospective buyer could not afford. For once, thus, Sutter had saved himself by his own wits.

Now, while his material fortune continually declined, his fame strangely began again to rise. His plight, well known throughout the country, elicited much sincere pity. His glamorous name could not be kept out of the news. A figure like his began to answer a more and more pressing need of the young state: the need, namely, for historic background and prestige. These Sutter was able to provide like no-one else. Already his severe retirement had cast about him the cloak of mystery, and presently he found himself a legendary figure, the living embodiment of by-gone days, whose rare public appearances were accompanied by spontaneous outbursts of popular acclaim.

On February 8, 1853, for instance, a concert was given in Sacramento by two famous operatic artists of the day, Kate Hayes and Sutter's countryman Joseph Mengis. It was the first recital in the city by such celebrities and the occasion was not to be allowed to pass without appropriate festivities. The first tickets were therefore sold at auction, and the Sutter Rifles of Sacramento, a unit of the State Militia, brought down the hammer on their bid of $1,200 for the very first ticket. They presented it to their great patron and went *en masse* to Hock Farm to escort him to Sacramento. Thus, followed by the officers of the corps, the stout, affable pioneer made his showy entrance at the concert-hall to the wild applause of the whole audience. He was ushered to the seat of honor, a wide commodious sofa of green plush standing in the vacant space between the stage and the stalls.

On the sixteenth of the same month an even greater public honor befell Sutter. He was created Major-General of the California Militia, a decorative and representative post which, however, had its severe drawbacks. The office carried with it no remuneration but rather forced the impoverished grandseigneur into new extravagances, in order that he might live up to his splendid title. It called for brilliant uniforms, for occasional lavish display. It had to be paid for with new champagne and cigars exorbitantly priced. But rarely was an honor received more deeply or more proudly appreciated. Even his most retiring spouse became filled with inordinate conceit in her new role of Frau Generalin, and the two inconspicuous sons Emil and Alfons stuck out their chins again.

About a year after these glamorous events Sutter's affairs were in a new pit of depression. Twice the cycle of the seasons had revolved in its course since the Land Commission had begun its investigations, and still the end was not in sight. During all this time Sutter, because of his agents' fraud and because the Land Claims Act was an effective deterrent to land sales, derived no income from the 200 square miles of property in the hands of his agents. Schläfli, who meantime had left Sutter's employ, summed up the situation at Hock Farm in the following words: 'Although Herr General Sutter owes me 400 dollars, it was impossible for me to get as little as 5 dollars out of him, because the innumerable Champagne bottles which he emptied with his friends (but his enemies behind his back) have swallowed up his entire substance. . . . All his land, including Hock Farm, is attached, his credit is altogether gone, and only with the greatest difficulties can he even procure enough food for his family.' Yet even this young man's scorn becomes mellowed by profound pity: 'What he squandered in former years is irretrievable, and for all he gave away to comparative strangers he earns little gratitude and sometimes sorrow. There was a time when Captain Sutter was everything, that is, as long as he had anything left; but now they let him stick in the mud.'

More trouble visited Hock Farm this same year when Eliza was divorced from George David Engler. Evil tongues would have it that the son-in-law was simply thrown into the street in order to reduce the number of mouths to be fed. But these are rumors; nothing definite is known. However, the foundering of

Eliza's marriage remained a secret for a long time closely guarded by the family, until at a much later date it seemed safe to refer to the unfortunate child as to a 'widowed daughter.'

Good fortune had completely forsaken the pioneer and his family.

It was a bizarre life that Sutter was now living. In this last act of the strange pageant of Hock he had arrived at doubling as Prince and Pauper. An aging country squire in vain trying to make ends meet, he was on the other hand becoming the hero of a saga who had done fabulous things in a far distant age and who occasionally was celebrated like a dragon-slayer. But such duplicity of fate is starkly tragic. To be drawn again and again from his loneliness at Hock Farm, to be paraded, a living mascot, before the great world, officially or semi-officially glorified for a day, only to be rejected into the cesspool of old misery, that was suffering the torments of Tantalus.

For thirty years, to the very end of his span of life, this was his lot. These public celebrations were all the more cruel in that they were not altogether born of sincerity and veneration. They were shrewdly contrived and staged by the calculating 'Sutter interests,' those operators of dubious integrity who by now had staked more on the two Sutter grants than Sutter himself. These celebrations were an ingenious ruse to drum up public opinion and public sentiment opposed to the 'squatter interests.' The 'Sutter interests' succeeded in having Sutter's portrait, as that of a founding father of the state, hung in the Assembly Room of the State Capitol, even as the likeness of George Washington graced the Senate Chamber. And why not? Measured by his positive accomplishments, he was a hero as good as most who have been dubbed that, the difference being only that our modern passion for full, unsparing, realistic detail tends to become a drag on the primeval urge for building up superhuman heroes on the foundation of one or two selected traits or deeds. Yet, conscious of this difference, can we not all the more readily agree with Joseph Warren Revere, scion of Paul Revere, when he says about Sutter: 'In times past men have been deified on slighter grounds?'

An almost orgiastic celebration took place on the fourth anniversary of California's statehood, September 9, 1854, in San Francisco. Amidst the din of brass bands and the roar of cannon, Major-General Sutter, the embodiment of the state and genius of the golden era, rode on a splendid charger at the head of California's first regiment, its artillery and cavalry, through the beflagged and begarlanded streets of the large city which, fifteen years before, he had first seen as a puny hamlet. At the Metropolitan Theater, where the final solemnity took place, Sutter's name was celebrated with some of the most famous names in history as the immortal name that would outshine and outlast all others once the historians of the future would settle down to limn in full the rise of the great Empire of the West. Today we differ somewhat from this opinion. Yet we remember: 'In times past men have been deified on slighter grounds.'

Notwithstanding this, it was a cruel and unconscionable game that was thus played with Sutter. In spite of these periodic waves lifting him for a moment from the rocks of despondency, his tide was receding, and no optimism could reverse its course.

Another such wave occurred on May 15, 1855, when the United States Land Commission for California at last handed down its decision in the Sutter Case and confirmed both the New Helvetia grant and the Sobrante grant. Sutter improvidently responded by giving another of his elaborate state celebrations at Hock Farm in the presence of several hundred guests and a brass band. But what reasons had he to celebrate? What did he hope for after this decision? Only an infinitesimal fraction of the original empire could still be said to belong to him, and even that was mortgaged. The only benefit he could possibly derive from the decision was a little easing up of his stringency of credit. For the rest, by virtue of the operation of the Land Claims Act, his case stood automatically appealed, imposing on him new heavy financial burdens.

In the privacy of Hock Farm, this legend-in-the-making presented a picture differing pitifully from the glamorous idol which the crowds revered on festive occasions.[24] Here he was living under the sword of Damocles which Washington had hung over his head, even though, sucking sustenance from every deceptive sign of hope, he succeeded in keeping up appearances. As yet the over-mortgaged estate showed no sign of the impending ruin. The orchards and vineyards which he had planted had grown magnificently. Everything was kept scrupulously clean. The English garden between the residence and the river was lush with a rich variety of green shrubs and flower-borders. Farthest up the river was the famous peach-orchard, Sutter's pride, covering three acres and inspiring the improvident old lover of things good and beautiful to talk of planting another twenty thousand young trees. On the south side of the houses there was an avenue of vigorously growing peach-trees 300 yards in length dividing the acres of vineyard to the right from the strawberry patch to the left. Two entire acres of the gardens were given over to every kind of rose which it had been possible to obtain; scattered among every other species of garden plant that thrived in the soil were found forty varieties of cacti. Sutter was still building fences to protect his plantations from the inroads of wild animals and of his own cattle.

All this was maintained by very few hands. Sutter's own sons had by now deserted him. Emil had taken to the mines, the conceited Alfons had found nothing better to do than to go filibustering with Walker in Nicaragua. Work on the farm was attended to by the remaining few of those Indians whom Sutter had brought up at the fort, who still clung to him as to their protector in the greatly changed land of their ancestors. Frau Sutter and Eliza did all the housework with the assistance of an Indian girl, and the master himself was forced to work in the garden.

But outside the narrowest confines of Hock terror reigned. The confirmation of Sutter's grants by the Land Commission had only served to spur the wantonness of the squatters. To the continuous killing and stealing of cattle, of horses, sheep and pigs, the squatters now added the cutting down of the valuable timber, chiefly oaks and sycamores, the numerous groves of which had added immensely to the charm of the estate and which, moreover, represented the most valuable asset still left to Sutter.

Before his eyes the squatters cut down these magnificent old trees by the thousand and sold the wood. When Sutter finally tried to salvage some of the fortune in trees and had expended several thousand dollars in labor, the squatters, wrathful at Sutter's competition, set fire to his wood-stacks. Their insolence knew no bounds, their greed no check. They maintained a lumberyard on his very grounds and hauled their bounty down to the river under his very nose. They called him a goddam foreigner and told him to go before the law if he wanted to stop them, knowing full well that he had not the money to do so and that, even if he tried, he had no chance of finding justice in the local courts because they controlled them.

Such occurrences were to Sutter a Chinese torture-of-a-thousand-wounds, under which his spirit was grievously bent, his pride mortified, his soul humiliated.

The presence of his wife made things no easier. With her grim face and her increasing deafness she must at times have been a nightmare to him from which he was glad occasionally to flee. She rarely showed herself to any visitor, save to the few with whom she could converse in her Swiss dialect; for she never learned to speak English.

Still Sutter hoped and in his better moments would express his firm belief in a day when justice would be obtainable even in California. Actually, on January 14, 1857, both his grants were confirmed by the United States District Court for Northern California. But again, by virtue of a perfidious law, his case was automatically appealed at his expense, thus turning his second victory into a crushing penalty. Meanwhile, the squatter interests continually gained in strength. Every legal victory of the grantholders enhanced the blood-thirstiness of the *canaille* of this revolution. The municipal government of Sacramento, maintained by taxes levied on property under the Sutter grants, appropriated $5,000 to send an attorney to Washington to contest the Sutter title before the highest court. This was but one of the many signs of the constantly rising squatter strength and a political omen foreboding no good.

In May of the same year, 1857—one misfortune never coming alone—Hock Farm was sold by the sheriff for the ridiculous sum of $14,000. But somehow Sutter managed again to redeem it. His plight elicited much pitying comment. Hutchings' *California Magazine*, for instance, in whose November issue Sutter published his own account of the gold-discovery, wrote: 'The men who shared most largely in his princely hospitality and possessions were the first to take advantage of it by stealing away his possessions. . . . May God forgive us Californians for our shameful indifference to the Old Pioneer.'

44. THE LUXURY OF JUSTICE

THE year 1858 at last brought the final decision of the United
States vs. Sutter. And a crushing blow it was for the poor old
man. While the court condescendingly confirmed the New Helvetia grant, it unanimously reversed the lower courts' decisions
on the Sobrante grant which Sutter had received during the
Micheltorena campaign. In other words, the court declared that
two thirds of the lands claimed by Sutter had never belonged
to him.

It was a crushing blow. Today, one may be amazed at the
twists and turns whereby the court arrived at such a decision. But
considering the circumstances, one must recognize that not much
else was possible. It must be borne in mind that this lawsuit, like a
thousand others of its kind, was merely a continuation of the
Mexican War. But war and justice are like oil and water: they
will not mix. In more than one way Washington of 1858 was
like Versailles of 1919. In those turbulent days, the nation had
not yet purged its system of the toxic waste-products of the Mexican War and yet was already headed for the Civil War. Two
wars, two conflicts bore upon the outcome of the Sutter case, and
in both Sutter had the ill fortune to stand on the wrong side.

Concerning the Mexican War, we must remember that from
the outset it was the purpose of the California Land Claims Act
to assert the rights of the victor. This is quite evident even in the
first part of the Supreme Court decision, the one favorable to
Sutter. In it two of the judges held that the New Helvetia grant
was invalid despite the eloquent testimony of the Mexican Government which, in 1846, wanted to buy Sutter's Sacramento
possessions. What better proof could there have been of the legal-
ity of his grants under the former regime? Considering, then,

that under the international law in general and the Treaty of Guadalupe Hidalgo in particular, the United States was obliged to respect private property in the conquered territory, there is no other way of looking at these two minority opinions, save as victors' opinions, attempts to let selfish interests precede the dictates of justice.

But if such a thing was possible in the face of the clearest proof of legal possession, what was likely to happen where evidence was not quite perfect according to American law? In view of the haphazard ways of making legal grants under Spanish-Mexican tradition, it was the easiest thing for the court in Washington to relieve a former citizen of the vanquished nation of what was rightfully his under the defeated government. This the Supreme Court did in the second part of its decision in the Sutter case, the part concerning the Sobrante grant.

Had this decision rested squarely on the technical deficiency of the grant itself, at least the semblance of right would be on the court's side.[25] Characteristically, however, the court found it necessary to have recourse to the most appalling legal captiousness with which to buttress its opinion. It maintained, for instance, that Governor Micheltorena had already 'abandoned his capital' before signing the Sobrante grant. One wonders whether there could possibly be found a similar distortion of historic truth as a means of arriving at a preconceived 'conclusion.' Micheltorena having been both civil Governor and Commander-in-Chief of the army, was it not perverse sophistry to assert that the Governor had 'abandoned his capital,' i.e., abdicated when, in his capacity as commander of the army he set out to save the department for his superior government?

Furthermore, the court argued that the signing of the Sobrante grant by Micheltorena was 'not an act of civil administration or had any reference to the law of colonization and settlement,' because it happened 'at a distance from his capital, in the prosecution of an intestine war against a band of insurgents,' and because it was an act of 'compensation for service.' Again it is hard to see why an act of the civil governor should be illegal simply because the gentleman happened to wear the uniform of the commander-in-chief for the occasion. Or why a grant should be void which was made in return for services to the nation. Such a grant would have been doubly valid under the government from which it had been derived, and the United States itself had made promises of land to all its soldiers fighting in California.

And here, of course, is the salient point of the argument: precisely *because* this grant was received in compensation for service to Mexico, the vanquishers of Mexico could not and would not recognize it.

However, if it is easy today to lay one's finger upon the main flaws of the court's reasoning, one must nevertheless concede the presence of extenuating circumstances which relieved the court of some of its onus. In the violent turmoil of 1858, how could any man, even a supreme court justice, have impartial opinions? The nation was torn in factions. Civil war was imminent; the controversy over the slavery question was nearing white heat and there was then no issue, no matter how remote from and alien to the 'irrepressible conflict,' which remained undistorted.

In 1858 the Democrats were entrenched in the seat of power and had been so for almost three decades. The Democrats, however, were dominated by the southern planters and slave-owners. It was these 'minority stockholders under the Constitution' who bullied the nation, and the overwhelmingly democratic Supreme Court was their legal megaphone. The most burning side of the dominant issue was the status of the territories with regard to slavery, the slave interests proving by the Bible and the Constitution that the vast new territories of the West were pre-ordained to be exploited under the slave labor system by southern gentlemen. But California, the first and as yet the only state of the New West, had outlawed slavery by a unanimous decision of its constitution makers—Sutter among them. Considering the passion of those days, was it so strange that the High Priests of slave-owning orthodoxy welcomed an opportunity to retaliate against an anti-slavery heretic? It was only human.

For nothing, absolutely nothing remained untouched by this one issue. Indeed, one could almost quote the Supreme Court's decision in the outstanding slavery case as psychological proof of its biased attitude in the Sutter case. Only a year previously the court had declared in the famous Dred Scott case that a 'man of color' had 'no rights which the white man was bound to respect.' One need but substitute 'Mexican' for 'man of color,' and 'the United States' for 'white man' (a device eminently justified by the national psychology of those days) and one arrives at the formula which consciously or unconsciously must have influenced the same judges in their handling of many of the claims arising out of the conquest of Mexican provinces.

Quite clearly, then, the annulment of Sutter's Sobrante grant was decreed by a frankly partial tribunal. On the one hand it represented the decision of a quasi court-martial, a piece of the victor's mind; on the other hand the opinion of a prejudiced caste threatened in its very existence. Victory has always put itself above the law, even as prejudice has always undermined it.

Yet, seen from a higher plane, there was logic and justice in the fact that a man who all his life had flirted with the martial spirit was now made to taste the bitter fruits of war-like defeat. And so the fundamental irony, the innate rhythm of Sutter's life had once more asserted itself: ill fate in the guise of good fortune. The thing that had so long beckoned to him as the most glorious future, American rule in California, in the end became the cause of his greatest downfall. It was his habitual bad luck that his law case was decided at the very moment when justice, as far as man can dispense it, was simply not to be expected.

As a result of the adverse decision of the court, Sutter literally lost his last foothold. It now became apparent that he had deeded away by grant, sale or otherwise, vastly more land than the decision of the court allowed to have been his. Moreover, he was forced to make good in money or otherwise the deeds he had conveyed over and above the eleven square leagues of the confirmed grant.

According to figures which Sutter in later years submitted to Congress, his bill for the kind of justice he had been able to obtain amounted to $325,000 which, measured by today's standards, would probably be $1,000,000. It was luxurious justice!

Meanwhile the Civil War broke out. By 1862 the old Sutter couple were living alone at Hock Farm with their eldest grandchild, the son of John A. Sutter, Jr., who had separated from his Mexican wife. Sutter himself was forced to perform daily labor in the fields and his infirm wife cooked his meals. For connection with the outside world they were entirely dependent on the teams of charitable neighbors. So much in need[26] was Sutter that the Society of California Pioneers (with Sam Brannan on the special committee) organized a state-wide subscription for the relief of 'California's Almoner in earlier days.'

In 1863 Sutter's youngest son and favorite, Alfons, died at Nevada City of a tropical disease contracted during the Walker Nicaragua campaign. He left a wife and child. Emil, still unmarried, lived in San Francisco as a notary public. The eldest son was still in Acapulco, Mexico, whither Eliza and her second husband, Dr. Franz Xaver Link, a refugee of 1848 from Wurtemberg, whom she married about 1860, had also moved.

At the close of the California legislative session, on April 4,

1864, a bill was adopted which provided for an appropriation of $15,000 for Sutter's relief, to be paid in monthly stipends of $250 over a period of five years. This 'pension,' however, was by no means an act of state charity; it was merely a refund in disguise of the taxes he had paid on the lands taken from him by the Supreme Court. For years Sutter had neglected to claim this refund, because he knew that whatever lawyer he might engage for the purpose would inevitably swindle him out of every dollar of this money. Not till he was in dire need did he dare address himself to friends in the legislature, and these finally succeeded in having a bill passed which converted the tax refund into a pension.

From now on the years rolled on in uneventful drabness. A year after he had been granted his 'pension,' the Civil War ended, on the outcome of which, more than is apparent at first glance, his life also had its important bearing. During the war alone one hundred and eighty-six million dollars' worth of gold came from the mines of California, one fourth the amount which during the same period Washington had managed to raise by taxation. It was largely this gold which paid for army supplies and maintained the credit of the Union Government. Thus, in still another way was Sutter an instrument in the hands of fate, a tool for the attainment of an end which had long before been written in the horoscope of national statistics. And again it was the tragic irony of his personal fate that, just as this aim was achieved, he himself was hopelessly crushed.

As usual, an external event now provided a striking symbol for the end, the last flicker of this straw fire of adventurous imperialism. On June 21, 1865, Hock Farm was set on fire by a vagrant, it was believed, who, a few days before, had been caught stealing and was whipped. The fire occurred early in the morning. Sutter and his wife barely escaped with their lives. With the

residence of Hock there vanished in the heat of the flames innumerable valuable records of Sutter's pioneer days, his correspondence, the memoirs he had begun to write, his library, his
pictures and his wardrobe. A month later fire also consumed
large sections of the town of Burgdorf, including the house Sutter had lived in and conducted his drygoods store.

The last feeble link between Sutter and California was now
destroyed. Assured of a living for the next few years he turned
his face away from the summits to which fame and fortune had
once carried him. The years directly behind him were the black-
est of his life. He had witnessed the triumph of the greedy, lawless
squatters, speculators, and legal gangsters over the old pioneers.
From California's first citizen he had been degraded to an alms-
receiver. After wallowing in riches he had tasted the bitter dregs
of poverty and utter mortification. He had experienced the ingratitude of the nation to whose enrichment he had contributed
so much. And he who once had written 'Hope not to have found
a friend, save in him who has found one in thee,' had been betrayed by most of those whom he had endowed with the trust of
friendship.

And he was ailing also, often being confined to bed for weeks
at a time.

During these last dark years in the Sacramento valley the man
who had the reputation of writing letters to his creditors for a
pastime had rarely touched the pen. Poverty had thrust him into
the vacuum of loneliness. In every respect his contact had ceased
with the state whose driving power he once had been. The flames
which devoured Hock Farm had wiped out everything.

45. *A NEW CAMPAIGN*

Where should he go now?

He decided to invade Washington and to seek redress from the representatives of the nation for the injustice done to him by the Supreme Court. In December 1865 Sutter and Mrs. Sutter arrived at the national capital,[27] scarcely realizing, of course, what the long trip they had undertaken would lead to. For he had stepped from the frying-pan into the fire.

Washington in 1865: the Civil War had only just ended, yet already it was only too apparent that the ugly aftermath of the strife was to surpass the preceding turmoil. The intense hatred of narrowminded politicians who had fought Lincoln's humane moderation and patriotic wisdom now became rampant under the weak leadership of President Andrew Johnson, presently to be impeached.

The years ahead were the vilest in the hectic history of the country. They have been rightly called the 'dreadful era' and the 'tragic era.' The atmosphere in Washington was nauseating with the stench of corruption. These were 'years of revolutionary turmoil, with the elemental passions predominant, and with broken bones and bloody noses among the fighting factionalists,' as a recent historian describes them. 'Never have American public men in representative positions, directing the destiny of the Nation, been so brutal, hypocritical, and corrupt.'

Were these auspices favorable to a penniless one-man lobby, a 'foreigner' to boot? Was not this man coming to Washington again the 'only child' and pampered darling of his mother, clamoring for a slice of the moon?

To be sure, he had not failed to fall back upon that old device that used to work miracles for him, the weighty introduction—

notably one from Governor Lowe of California. Equitably considered, he had indeed a worthy case. The wrong done him by the Supreme Court had evoked a good deal of public comment favorable to Sutter. He could proudly point to his pioneering achievements. The very outcome of the Civil War, which had launched Washington on its orgiastic revelries, seemed to be grist to his mill; for the California gold had been an important factor in the balance-sheet of victory. Beyond the slightest doubt, blind justice would have been on Sutter's side.

Beyond question, no less, stern realities were preponderantly against him. What hope was there for him of wrenching recognition, by means of a mere petition with no golden strings attached to it, from congressmen accustomed to having their pockets well stuffed with railway bonds and stocks in return for parceling out gigantic strips of the public domain to railroad companies? In his optimistically personal views, Sutter was bound to leave out of his reckoning such decisive realities. Moreover, between the Supreme Court decision and Sutter's coming to Washington lay the whole pandemonium of a four years' war. To him the war meant nothing, to Washington everything. How could he, living as he did narcistically in the memory of his vanished glories, realize that to Washington the events preceding the Civil War were almost prehistoric? The war had made chopped straw of memory.

Early in 1866 Sutter presented his case to Congress in the form of a petition. In this document he tries to show 'without any vain boast, that he has been the agent in developing to this country the mineral and agricultural wealth of California.' He pleads 'that his second grant has been unjustly rejected . . . that these things, while they have led to his great embarrassment and complete ruin, have greatly increased the national wealth and that of many thousands of individuals.' In short, that he has 'an equitable claim, founded in justice and right, against the United

States, for some indemnity and relief, which he is now constrained to ask.' The petition was ordered printed and referred to the Senate Committee on Claims.

Meanwhile Sutter's pension kept him from monetary worries. He made numerous friends. His name, of course, was well known to all, and as everybody seemed at first delighted to press the hand of a man of his affable conviviality, his early stay in Washington was like a tonic bath, imparting new glamor, new vigor and buoyancy to the wilted spirits of the old pioneer. Certainly his intent to affect the will of Congress—and such a one as was the thirty-ninth!—was not the least daring of his many gigantic schemes.

By a very happy coincidence, in the summer of 1866 one of the foremost Swiss artists of the time was in Washington: Frank Buchser, master of the *genre*, romantic realist and very much a man of Sutter's own cast. During July and August Sutter was a frequent visitor at Buchser's studio, and it was there that the best likeness of the Grand Old Man of California originated. [28]

Against a vast blue California sky and a glimpse of the snow-capped sierras rises the monumental figure of the pioneer with his wide-brimmed hat. It is a portrait both flattering and unsparing in its character delineation. Here is the inveterate actor in his *rôle de grand seigneur*. With his studiously careful make-up of fuzzy side whiskers, moustache, and underlip tuft, he is straining at the ultimate in ornamental effects. In the genial round face of this precious old beau, meticulously attired, is still detectable the cherubic, spoiled and naughty little darling of his mother; the sweeping brim of his Panama graphically suggests the far-flung schemes that were hatched beneath it. For the last time we meet here the charming roguery of that sparkling pair of clear-blue eyes, apparently still telling those tall tales which once netted him a kingdom in royalties. But in the vertical fold between the eyebrows and half hidden under the moustache is lurking restrained grief.

Sutter had originally planned to stay in Washington only for the brief time which he imagined would be required to convey his case successfully through the congressional mill; then he would go back to Switzerland to visit old friends, relatives, and the charming scenes of his youth. But for a long time Congress had more pressing business to attend to.

The second session of the thirty-ninth congress got under way and ended; the fortieth congress moved into Washington, and still Sutter's petition was gathering dust on the committee shelf. Meanwhile his advancing age brought him increasing physical discomforts, so that, during the winter months, he suffered acutely from attacks of rheumatic fever and was confined to bed for long periods. In summer, when Congress was not in session, he began to flee the distressing heat of the small town calling itself the capital. City life did not agree with him and the cost of living in Washington dismayed him. He was glad, finally, to move to a new address, 'about ten minutes outside the city which is as good as in the country,' even though the house stands 'just opposite the Department of State.'

As for his daily life, he wrote in May 1868 to his sister-in-law, Frau Schläfli in Burgdorf:

I move in the best society and have to be at the Capitol every day, where I must call upon the senators and members of congress etc., and you can imagine that I have to be elegantly dressed and that it costs money. . . . Otherwise we economize as much as possible, we very rarely drink wine, because wine is very expensive here, only occasionally we take a little sherry for medicine. I frequent no public houses, that would be too vulgar; I drink no more beer, and wine very sparingly, and thus we manage to keep hale and well. At 9 o'clock in the evening we go to bed, never go to the theatre, and get up again at 5 in the morning, read, and write, etc. . . .[29]

In November 1868 Ulysses S. Grant was elected President of the United States. Sutter was among the notables who arrived first to offer their congratulations, and he did not fail to point out in another letter to his sister-in-law in Burgdorf that the Washington papers mentioned him 'together with 5 other generals.'

But the change in the White House, although Sutter was proud to count Grant among his friends, had no influence on his case, and dust continued to accumulate on his petition. Only during the second term of the forty-first congress a 'Bill for the Relief of John A. Sutter' was at length introduced in the Senate, but adversely reported upon from the committee, so that the settling of the case was again indefinitely postponed. [30]

After more than four fruitless years of dancing attendance upon a thousand persons, the vague fear began to creep upon Sutter that his time of waiting might never come to an end. As he was now nearing the three-score-and-ten, he definitely gave up the plan of visiting again the scenes of his youth. For five years he and his wife had been homeless boarders, wintering at the national capital and spending their summers in New England or Pennsylvania. They were thoroughly weary of this gipsy life, and at the end of the congressional session of 1870–1 therefore returned to Lititz, Pennsylvania, where they had spent several summers, and where now they decided to establish a last permanent home of their own.

46. *THE LAST RETREAT*

LITITZ, the little hamlet, had a population almost purely German-speaking, with dialects ranging from Pennsylvania Dutch to German Swiss. The inhabitants were almost to a man members of the Moravian Brotherhood, whose traditional atmosphere of the most genteel piousness inspired the old heathen sinner and adventurer with paradoxical confidence. Two daughters of Augustus Sutter Jr., now United States Consul at Acapulco, Mexico, were being educated at the Brotherhood's Lindenhall Seminary of Lititz, because their father, separated from their mother and unable to obtain a divorce from her, had begun a new 'lefthanded' family in Mexico.

Upon his return to Lititz in the spring of 1871, Sutter began building himself a house, or rather, Mrs. Sutter built it with the help of a local contractor, while Sutter was confined to bed for more than two months with a severe attack of rheumatic fever. Once more, now, he was to live in style, his house being the only one besides the hotel which was built of brick, the only one equipped with the latest modern conveniences. Once more, owner's pride furnished the stimulus for one of his utterly rare letters of these last years, a letter again addressed to his wife's sister in Burgdorf.[31]

He describes to her the house in all details and measurements, from the 'solid foundations . . . masoned of limestone' up to the roof 'covered with slate.' The red bricks, 'having in addition received a coat of red paint, the pointings white,' seem to have a particular appeal to him. The house has a front of 30 feet and a depth of 42; the ground-floor is 12 feet high, the rooms on the upstairs floor 14. 'The windows are 8 feet high, with only 4 panes, each of which is 2 feet and 4 inches high and 1 foot and 5 inches wide; the outside shutters are a nice green, the inner ones are of walnut, the window frames are white. . . .' In short, everything 'looks very well, especially as we touch upon only one neighbor from whom we are still separated by a vacant lot of about 20 feet, the house faces the beautiful hotel: towards the West we have a free view and can see everything that goes on along two roads. . . .'

We have one of the most beautiful locations in Lititz and only one among the houses is as beautiful as ours and so well built; everything has been firmly made because built on a daily wage basis, and the inside is nice, too; simply, but tastefully furnished. . . .

The house cost us more than we intended to spend on it, but that always happens if one builds and now we have it the way we wanted it and we are again 'at home.' We were terribly tired of hotel life, it will also be better for our health because now we can again live to suit ourselves; moreover, we shall be better off during days of illness, and finally we should not exactly care to die in a hotel. . . .

Our maid is from here; Mama is rather satisfied with her, although she speaks Pennsylvania Dutch to which one has to get used first, because the uneducated address everybody with 'Du' just as in the Tyrol; she will say, e.g., 'Mrs. Sutter willst du mir erlauben nach hause zu gehen'; or 'General, es ist ein gentleman da der dich sehen will', and they say 'Du' to the minister and to everybody, even the rich farmers don't know better.

But the pride of the house seems to be a cooking-range of the most modern type, 'so built as to furnish hot and cold water day and night, and in the bathroom there are two faucets for hot and cold water at any time, the same in the kitchen above the sink.— This installation is still rather expensive. . . .'

Thus the letter shuffles on, a touching self-revelation, a pathetic old-age self-portrait, so to say, clad in the description of a house. Was this the scintillating personality whom, only five years previously, Frank Buchser had painted? Or the fascinating martial blue-blood sketched by Surgeon Wood of the frigate *Savannah*? The man who once had impressed Lieutenant Emmons of the Navy as looking like 'Cortez in his palmiest days?' Barely a shadow of these. Rather is one forced to think of the obverse of the Sutter portrait as adumbrated by Wood: that head 'flat and wall-shaped behind.' This is a poignant formula·for certain of Sutter's shortcomings, which increased as his glamor paled and which also determined the tone of this letter: an actor long past his prime, with a wealth of rather faltering and vacant gestures predominating. But had not the empire of New Helvetia itself been little more than a gesture? A magnificent gesture, to be sure, never-to-be-forgotten, such as only a few divinely gifted mimics on the stage of history can produce, but as a gesture bound to be ephemeral, written into the wind; and yet a thing compelling our admiration.

And is this letter the evanescence of a mind from whom a horde of· self-seeking politicians would accept directions? Anything but that: it is the prattling of gentle senility. Sutter himself had begun to realize the extreme difficulty of his undertaking. With profound misgivings he was now preparing to spend his seventh winter in the frigid atmosphere of Washington, a beggar on the doormats of congressional offices. 'The prospect is rather poor for one who has not a pocket full of money in Washington, only with that justice can be bought,' he wrote a week later, December 18, 1871, to Thomas Shannon, Speaker of the California Assembly, when seeking a renewal of his pension. But in this epistle he remains the mime that he was; with this difference, that whereas in his letter to his sister-in-law he fondly dwells upon the niceties of a retired general's life, in the one to Shannon he penned his role of martyr to a great national cause:

I am now sixty-nine years old and my wife sixty-six years; I will have to live only a few years longer, as I am subject to inflammatory rheumatism and have to suffer very severely every year. I am confined to my bed for months, and have to walk on crutches for weeks, and so I begin to feel the hardships of my pioneer life. Everybody who knows my history know[s] that I have no other resources to depend on, having been swindled and robbed in every way and shape.

Twice the State of California extended Sutter's pension for periods of two years. In 1875, however, this subsidy was definitely stopped. What, henceforth, furnished him the means of existence it is impossible to ascertain. Probably it was the eldest son, the United States Consul in Acapulco, whose children of the first marriage had been brought up at Lititz, who now kept his parents in funds. He had accumulated considerable wealth in the import and export trade and as a wine-merchant. After all these years the father's tragedy had apparently narrowed, if not quite closed, the ruinous breach between the two. There are strong reasons to believe that it was Augustus, Jr., who had made possible the building of the house in Lititz (which also would explain why the house belonged to Mrs. Sutter, not to her husband). Even Sutter himself admits that 'naturally' Augustus paid for the piano, which may very well be taken to mean that 'naturally' everything as far as the piano could be heard ('it has a strong tone, one can hear it throughout the house') derived its *raison d'être* from the eldest son.

Why mention all this? Because from Sutter's own time down to ours it has been a favorite and stereotyped trick of journalists, novelists, playwrights and scenarists to reduce old Sutter to a ragged, shabby tin-mug handler and park-bench squatter in the twilight daze of dementia. Which is as far from truth as it could be. Until his very end he was mentally alert enough to react violently against the falsehoods of such scribblers. Nor was he ever in want during his last years. Even a fortnight before his death he wrote to J.J.Jenny-Roth, an old boyhood friend in Basle: 'It is scandalous the way those little German papers have decried us, as if we were living in the most bitter poverty. . . . If occasionally the American papers state that I am now poor, they do not mean it in the German sense of the word, for today they call anybody here who has not $100.000 a poor man.' He was poor only when appearing in his role of petitioner and supplicant; before the rest of the world he kept up appearances until his last breath.

Regularly, during the winter months, he beleaguered the Capitol in Washington, always with the same negative result. But when back again at Lititz, he lived in almost monastic retirement, shame and wounded pride keeping him from the gaze of his fellow villagers. Save for a privileged few of these, his life remained, according to the parish pastor, 'a sealed book, a volume, chaptered, illustrated, costly and rare, but of which, beyond its title, little was known.'

Today there are still living in that neighborhood one or two old men who in their youth have seen and spoken to him. Until his very last days the old general kept up his habit of meticulous dressing and never was seen without his cane. His favorite place in good weather was in his back-yard garden. There, whenever the sun was out, he could be seen sitting in a grandfather's chair among his dearly beloved peach-trees. But Mrs. Sutter remained completely invisible and among the people of Lititz was believed to have died long ago.

Very rarely was the monotony of Lititz broken. In 1876 Sutter permitted himself to be drawn into the world once more in order to preside at the Swiss Day of the Philadelphia Centennial Celebration. In the same year, also, the California historical industrialist H.H.Bancroft sought out Sutter in his retreat for the purpose of having his reminiscences dictated. He had been warned that Sutter was ill and that even if he were not it would be impossible to gain access to the forbidding house. But the collector of memoirs was not to be discouraged:

After knocking loudly at the portal three several times, the door was slowly, silently opened a little way, and the head of an old woman appeared at the aperture.

'This is Mrs. Sutter?' I asked.

No response.

'May I speak with you a moment in the hall?'

Still no response, and no encouragement for me to enter. There she stood, the guardian of apparently as impregnable a fortress as ever was Fort Sutter in its palmiest days. I must gain admission; retreat now might be fatal. Stepping toward the small opening as if there were no obstacle whatever to my entering, and as the door swung back a little at my approach I slipped into the hall.

Once within, no ogress was there. Mrs. Sutter was a tall, thin, intelligent Swiss plainly dressed, and having a shawl thrown over her shoulders. Her English was scarcely intelligible, but she easily understood me, and her deafness was not at all troublesome.

Handing her my card, I asked to see General Sutter. 'I know he is ill,' said I, 'but I must see him.' Taking my card, she showed me into a back parlor and then withdrew. From Mrs. Sutter's manner, no less than from what had been told me at the hotel, I was extremely fearful that I had come too late, and that all of the history that house contained was in the fevered brain of a dying man.

But presently, to my great astonishment and delight, the door opened, and the general himself entered at a brisk pace. He appeared neither very old nor very feeble. . . . He was rather below medium height, and stout. His step was firm, his bearing soldierly, and in his younger days he must have been a man of much endurance, with a remarkably fine physique. His features were of the German cast, broad, full face, fairly intelligent forehead, with white hair, bald on top of the head, white side whiskers, moustache, an imperial, a deep, clear, earnest eye met ours truthfully. Seventy-five years, apparently, sat upon him not heavily. He was suffering severely from rheumatism, and he used a cane to assist him in walking about the house. He complained of failing memory, but I saw no indication of it in the five days dictating which followed.

No one could be in General Sutter's presence long without feeling satisfied that, if not the shrewdest, he was an inborn gentleman. He had more the manners of a courtier than those of a backwoodsman, with this difference: his speech and bearing were the promptings of a kind heart, unaffected and sincere. He received me courteously, and listened with deep attention to my plan for a history of the Pacific States as I laid it before him. . . .

'You fill an important niche in the history of the western coast. Of certain events you are the embodiment—the living, walking history of a certain time and locality. Often in my labors I have encountered your name, your deeds, and let me say that I have never yet heard the former mentioned but in kindness, nor the latter except in praise.'

Tears came into the old man's eyes, and his utterance was choked, as he signified his willingness to relate to me all he knew. . . .

'Come as early as you like in the morning, but we must rest at six o'clock. I retire early.'

47. *THE SHADOW OF THE CAPITOL*

As year after year passed uneventfully, between the austere solitude of summers in Lititz and winters of the mortifying existence of a charity-seeker before a cynical Congress, Sutter's vitality was slowly whittled away. Ten winters he had already exposed himself to the chilly grins, insincere promises, and haughty, patronizing airs of congressmen.

Ten years after his first fruitless petition, Sutter, in 1876, addressed to the Congress another, more urgent in tone and dominated by a pathetic note of self-pity. He lays stress upon 'his old age,' his 'state of absolute penury,' insisting again, a little later, that 'he is now old and poor.'

At the end of the same session, the House Private Land Claims Committee voted to recommend the passage of a bill

granting him $50,000 in consideration of his services to the im-
migrants, his losses for want of legal protection, and the injury
received because of the adverse Supreme Court decision on his
Sobrante grant.

The action of the committee had a tonic effect upon the old
man; it revitalized his sinking hope, it saved his self-respect and
his countenance before the world. He began showing himself
more often in public, attending, whenever his health permitted,
the yearly reunions of the Associated Pioneers of the Territorial
Days of California. Here he found an admiring and sympathetic
circle, whose atmosphere was balm to his wounded heart. Many
of the members had once, as pitiful immigrants, enjoyed the
boundless benevolence of the Lord of the Sacramento, and some
were now men stationed high in life, generals, admirals, govern-
ors and mayors. Among these men, who understood better than
congressmen the true meaning of the word pioneer, there was no
snickering as in the officious atmosphere of Washington and no
haughty condescension for him. On the contrary. Here 'every
one of his tremulous and embarrassed utterances' was received
with thunderous acclaim, and men like Mark Twain and General Sherman, when they could not attend the meetings, wrote to
express their regrets to be unable again to press the hand of the
venerable Grand Old Man of California.

But despite the favorable action of a House committee, Sutter's case still made no real progress in the national capital. At this
time, if not subject to his frequently recurring attacks of rheumatic fever, he still looked 'as hale and hearty as many of his com-
rades a score of years younger.' Still, as again session after session
passed and nothing was done for him in congress, the severity of
old age became rapidly unbearable, and he was ravished with a
corroding bitterness at the heartlessness and ingratitude of his
adopted nation. A telegram which, on January 20, 1879, he sent

Sutter in his early seventies. The signature, that of a proud broken man, is from the end of the 'Reminiscences' which Sutter dictated in 1876 to Hubert Howe Bancroft. Photo by permission of the Lancaster County, Pa., Historical Society.

to the Associated Pioneers (whose president he was since 1877) on the occasion of their annual banquet in New York, reads like an outcry of profound despair:

> Sick in heart and body, in vain appealing to Congress to do me justice, and to return only part of what was wrongly taken from me, and with little hope of success this session, unless you, my friends, by your influence will aid me, I could not feel cheerful as your guest at table to-night, and did not want to mar your pleasure by my presence. Remember old times without me.

Immediately the Associated Pioneers began an agitation, declaring it to be a 'duty that was imposed upon them all to use their personal influence to induce Congress by all honorable means to repay the old pioneer, and thus to contribute to his comfort and smooth the pathway of his declining years.' This charitable propaganda was not without effect. In January 1880 a new memorial was submitted to Congress, and Sutter now seemed to have sufficient assurance of the success of his case to reduce his presence in Washington to five short stays between January and June. Towards spring, however, his rheumatism and chronic kidney-troubles assailed him with new vigor, making his sojourn at the capital almost unbearable. 'Getting sick here in Washington is the worst of all. My last attack was so violent as to cause Col. Schaefer (formerly of my staff) to sleep in my room and nurse me during four nights,' he wrote in May to his niece in Burgdorf. And two days previously, in another letter to the editor of *Der Deutsche Pionier* in Cincinnati: 'I am now so far restored that I can be dragged to the Capitol at the arm of a friend, in order to exert my entire personal influence to get my claim acknowledged.'

He seemed to have reasons for renewed hopefulness, even though most congressmen would no doubt have horse-laughed at Sutter's 'entire personal influence.' Still, on April 8, a bill for his relief had been favorably reported from the House Committee.

On April 30, a similar bill was brought up in the Senate, whose Committee on Claims, on June 11, introduced through Senator Voorhees a joint resolution to compensate Sutter for his losses and services to the country. Says the Senate Report, in part: 'It is scarcely to be doubted, that under Mexican government Sutter's Sobrante grant would have been confirmed, while under ours the spirit of the pre-emption and homestead laws produced such a popular feeling against large grants of land, that even the administration of justice by the courts seems to have been brought insensibly . . . under its control.'

In other words, even the Senate Committee hinted at the truth that in its decision on the Sobrante grant the Supreme Court had simply 'cringed before the clamor of the mob,' in disregard of all solemn international treaties under which the case was to be adjudicated. The committee estimated the damage thus done to Sutter at a minimum of $1,000,000 and recommended the appropriation of $50,000 for his relief.

As an indemnity the sum was a mere pittance; but as a token of justice, after Sutter's grueling quest of fifteen years, it was most gratifying. Any crumb was now acceptable to him if it would satisfy his wounded honor and 'as long as I don't have to come here any more.' But until that was achieved, his presence at the capital seemed imperative, 'to keep my lawyers and friends in Congress busy.'

There is noticeable in all these utterances a vibrant intensity and anxiety to be done with the affair. He felt that success would come now or never. His solicitude during these critical days was enhanced by thoughts of his wife's loneliness in Lititz. It is one of the most touching sides of Sutter's story that old age, common suffering and humiliation had at last succeeded in welding unbreakably his marriage to the grim sibyl to whom fate had chained him in a few moments of youthfully sensual enjoyment, whom he had once deserted for sixteen years, and from whom a thousand infidelities had separated him. Only during the nine years of severe retirement at Lititz did the mother of his children become his wife spiritually. Not until these last years do his references to her go beyond the perfunctory meaninglessness of the two words 'my wife.' Not till now did she cease to be the skeleton in his closet and became even in his letters a living human being (though still rather sphinx-like), something to which his heart clung. 'I am so glad,' he wrote to her niece in Burgdorf, 'to be able soon to return home, auntie is so lonely and good maids are not to be had in Lititz. For the last three years a girl has been coming every morning at seven and stays until nine or ten and sometimes longer, then again at six o'clock in the evening. . . . At night, then, a German woman comes to sleep in the house, because something might happen to auntie, or somebody might break into the house; at any rate, it is better so; and we have also two good watchful little dogs. . . .'

Until the last days of the congressional session, Sutter was confident that a final settlement would be reached. In his letter (probably his last save one) of May 31, 1880, to the friend in Basle, he expressed his belief that in two weeks he would be able to journey home to Lititz for the last time, 'satisfied to be done with the whole affair.' He spoke prophetically.

It seems that the gentlemen who had taken it upon themselves to pilot Sutter's little ship of hope through the turbulent waters of Congress had definitely promised him the passage of the bill for his relief at this session. In the House the bill lay on the table and a recognition on the part of Speaker Randall would have admitted it to a vote, although its passage was in no way assured. For the 'Bill for the Relief of John A. Sutter' was only one among a car-load of 1,400 bills and joint resolutions cluttering the congressional calendar.

Came the month of June. 1880 was an election year. The party conventions, which the members of Congress were eager to attend, were scheduled to open by the middle of the month in Cleveland and Chicago. Pre-election congresses have never been known to accomplish much good, and on June 16, 1880, the forty-sixth congress, too, abruptly adjourned *sine die*, leaving the Sutter bill buried under the mountain of other unfinished business.

Sutter was hopelessly crushed.[32] His friend Colonel Schaefer immediately called upon Senator Voorhees, who had charge of the bill, to inform him of the critical effect of the adjournment upon the old petitioner, and asked him to come and talk to Sutter himself in order to comfort him. The Senator promised that he would bring up the bill again on the first day of the next session and to see that it was passed without delay. He promised, furthermore, to come and have breakfast with Sutter the following morning and to bring him assurance in person. But a more pressing engagement prevented him from keeping his promise to Sutter, and when he called a day later, he found that Sutter was dead.

He had died on June 18, about 1.30 in the afternoon, two days after the shock of the adjournment. On his table in the plain hotel room was an unfinished letter to his wife, in which he tried to tell her of his defeat and of his return, presently, to Lititz. Over the strain of this severe task his broken heart had given out.

Colonel Frank Schaefer who thus found him, stretched out on his bed, completed the distressing message to Mrs. Sutter by adding the few words necessary to explain the strange signature at the end.

After a funeral service at Mades' Hotel, where he had died, Sutter's body, bedded in California flowers from the Botanical Garden in Washington, was brought to Lititz. At two o'clock of Thursday, June 24, the embalmed remains were carried out of the house and to the little Moravian church, where the Reverend Charles Nagle officiated over the rites. Then, headed by a band and followed by the entire village and numerous visitors of note, he was brought to the quaint Moravian cemetery. Generals Hugh G. Gibson and John C. Frémont, his former enemy, delivered touching eulogies. Said Frémont: 'He died under the shadow of the Capitol of the people whom he had served so well. Looking upon him lying here, the uppermost feeling in my mind is one of surprise and regret that such a life—a life so filled with kindly acts, so valuable, so honorable, and so signalized by services to the country, should have met such cruel neglect and such harsh injustice.'

Half a year later, on January 19, 1881, Sutter's widow followed him to the final resting-place given her and her husband as a token of honor and compassion by the Moravian Brotherhood. They lie apart from the Moravians in a secluded corner. An aisle runs through the regular cemetery, separating even in death the brethren from the sisters. But the two who have been separated, physically or spiritually, most of their lives, now may rest side by side under the same large marble slab.

Thus ended the terrestrial adventures of one of the most colorful men this continent has seen. Even though he squandered a large part of his energies in charmingly futile impersonations of an eighteenth century ideal, his life, nevertheless, assumed a peculiarly representative meaning in that it was the very epitome of certain nineteenth century trends: its romanticism and its worldwide struggle for colonial possessions. With him passed away the last great romanticist and the last great colonial pioneer of America. It was his unreserved abandonment to these trends that made him the typical embodiment of his time. What he represented, however, had its roots sunk deep in former ages, and he was but the curious fruit, the end of a long process. In that there was little or nothing in him pointing to the century ahead, perhaps, was conditioned his tragic defeat by forces beyond his comprehension.

And yet in essence Sutter was completely ageless, simply and luxuriantly human, kaleidoscopic and self-contradictory. He was in one peasant and grandseigneur, trader and *chevalier d'industrie*; Indian-tamer and roving Münchhausen; spellbinder in high society and Mexican Robin Hood; sabre-rattling imperialist and torch-bearer of civilization; a deserter of his family and father to a thousand adopted charges; constant husband and sultan of squaws; a modern Midas and petitioner for relief; the perfect (though self-made) gentleman and an endearing liar; a voluptuary and lover of simplicity; a fabulist and naive believer in other men's tall tales; a boaster and man of unassuming modesty; one often accused of greed and an incurable philanthropist and spendthrift; a one-man lobby in Washington and quiet recluse in a Pennsylvania hamlet.

All this was Sutter. And yet not a desultory, but an impressive personality, always plastic, fascinating, affable, dynamic, eminently and intensely human.

He has received the most fitting monument in the reconstruction of his fort, which today is a museum dedicated to Sutter's age of pioneering, of conquests and of gold.

NOTES

In undertaking the task of writing this biography of an extraordinary life it has been the author's aim above all to produce a readable account, as accurate and complete as possible without the burden of too much extraneous detail. However, scholars and those already more or less familiar with Sutter's life may welcome a few notes on certain episodes, particularly on the new material, and the points in which this biography differs from earlier ones.

The first attempt to survey Sutter's life was made by a contemporary, Edward E. Dunbar (*The Romance of the Age*, New York, 1867), who, of course, had much of his material from Sutter himself, some from hearsay and from newspapers. None of these sources stand up too well under investigation. Still, it is Dunbar's merit first to have sensed the grandiose line of Sutter's development and the irrational forces whose playball Sutter was. He saw with the eyes of the artist.

T.J.Schoonover's *Life and Times of General John A. Sutter* (1907), written with love and admiration, still accepts uncritically all the fables of Sutter's early life, and for the California phase chiefly presents a digest of newspaper items and of a few memoirs which had meanwhile been published (Bidwell's, e.g.). On the whole it is a scrap-book rather than a biography.

Although Blaise Cendrars' *L'or, ou la merveilleuse histoire du Général Johann August Sutter* (Paris, 1925) has very little relation to the facts, at least it served to awaken interest in Sutter all over the world. In Europe it was accepted as documentary evidence and re-hashed by such writers as Stefan Zweig and Francis Gribble.

Julian Dana's *Sutter of California* (1934) calls itself 'a biography.' But even though Dana undoubtedly made use of some of the 'more than twelve thousand manuscripts' and the 'hundred books' referred to in his foreword, he used them rather as material for fiction. Judging by his account, Dana, like all his predecessors, apparently did not trouble to find out what Sutter did before he reached California. His book presents Sutter's life in California as a native son must wish that that life had been.

Erwin G. Gudde's edition of *Sutter's Own Story* (1936) comes much nearer the truth as far as his commentary and interpolations go. The facts of Sutter's life in Switzerland, which had meanwhile been made public by R.Bigler and the author of this book, enabled him to give a rather correct sketch of the early years. But since as a whole the very readable volume remains Sutter's

343

own version of his life-story, it cannot, valuable though it is as a document, take the place of a biography. Too many gaps remain. In line, coloring and composition Sutter the fabulist prevails, and Sutter's own stories cannot be viewed too critically.

Most of the source material is probably well-known to those who have previously occupied themselves with Sutter's life. The following notes are therefore designed chiefly to document and augment new material, or to stress a viewpoint which differs from that of earlier interpreters.

Part I: One of God's Gentlemen

1. The house shown on page 14 of Gudde's *Sutter's Own Story* was not the residence of the Sutters, but that of another Suter family. See the following note.

2. Attempts have often been made by various Sutter or Suter families in Europe and the United States to establish a relationship with Johann August Sutter. The invented link is usually a 'brother' or 'step-brother' of the general. But Sutter's only brother, Jakob Friedrich, died without issue in 1844. His alleged 'twin-brother' Johann Heinrich, mentioned by Gudde (p.3), and by Dana (p.2 etc.), never existed. It appears from the archives of the *Landeskanzlei Liestal*, Baselland, Switzerland, that the attempt to graft this Joh. Heinrich upon the Sutter family tree was assisted by a former *Justizsekretär* of Kandern, and this was confirmed to the author by authorities in Kandern itself. Joh.Heinrich was born exactly nine months before Jak. Friedrich. This fact alone indicates that he was the child of another mother. Moreover, he spelled his name 'Suter,' belonged to a family originating from Opfikon, and his name is never mentioned by the birth-registers of Rünenberg, where the Sutters were citizens. One forged document trying to link an unrelated family with John A. Sutter was published in the *Pacific Unitarian*, VOL.XXVI, no.10, Sept.1917, in the form of a 'letter of Sutter's to his brother Andrew in Chur, Switzerland,' and Dana, pp.287,288, reprints it with a few inventions of his own.

3. See Zollinger, 'John Augustus Sutter's European Background,' Calif. Hist. Soc. *Quarterly*, XIV,1, p.36, and the authorities cited ibid.p.44.

4. Bigler. *Burgdorfer Jahrbuch*, 1935, p.9.

5. The writings of Laufkötter are not unknown to historians and others who have looked into the sources of information for Sutter's life, but until now no-one apparently used them because, being rather isolated, their authenticity remained very doubtful. But the new material which has come to light in Missouri, particularly the statements by Friedrich Muench, the columns of the *Anzeiger des Westens*, and other descriptions of life among those Missouri Germans, show that much of what Laufkötter has to say is

creditable. The tone in which he tells his story usually indicates whether or not he speaks the truth.

6. Laufkötter's declaration, sworn to in the County Court of St. Charles, Mo., (Circuit Clerk's office) is dated October 12, 1835. It states that he was born in Wünnenberg, Prussia, in 1812 and landed at Baltimore on November 29, 1834. The store of Wiese & Laufkötter was licensed by the St. Charles County Court on May 28, 1835. L's doubt as to Sutter's declaration of intention is expressed in his *John A. Sutter*, p.26.

7. *Der Deutsche Pionier*, 1872, No.IV, p.2.

8. Laufkötter, *John A. Sutter*, p.6.

9. *Anzeiger*, December 17 and 24, 1835: '*Ein Handelszug nach Santa Fe.*' It is evident from many parts of this report that the writer ('E') could not have been Sutter himself. The German is better than Sutter's would have been and free from the traits which usually crept into Sutter's German writings. Moreover, 'E' was one of the 'runners,' the fast riding vanguard of the caravan, and Sutter always was a bad horseman, so bad that, according to Laufkötter (op.cit.p.9), he refrained from participating in the daily cavalry drill with which the men tried to break the monotony of the long trip. Unfortunately, 'E' has abstained from all personal references, so that neither Sutter nor any of the participants is directly mentioned.

10. Robidoux, *Memorial*, 174. Coman, II,87. *Anzeiger*, Dec.24,1836.

11. Laufkötter, op.cit.p.13.

12. *Der Deutsche Pionier*, IV,2–3.

13. According to correspondence in the *New York Herald Tribune*, May 26, 1929 his store was at Main Street and Westport Avenue.

14. Without exception Beaubien's name has hitherto been given as *Popian*, because Hubert Howe Bancroft, to whom Sutter dictated his memoirs in 1876, wrote it that way. Bancroft's spelling is remarkable in that it is a very accurate phonetic rendering of Sutter's French pronunciation, which was very close to Alsatian French.

15. Personal communication to the author from one of the McCoy descendants. Also R.M.Snyder, in *Syat*, Nov.7,1926.

16. Sutter himself never mentioned the man's name but stated that he was 'a German cabinet-maker.' *Der Deutsche Pionier*, XII,5,204 mentions one Joseph Koch who traveled with Sutter from Missouri to Honolulu and California. But *Deutsch-Amerikanische Geschichts-Blaetter*, II,2,21 gives the same man's name as Joh. Bernhard Koch and knows nothing of his travels with Sutter.

17. Eells, Myron, *Father Eells*, 58.

18. Eells, *Journal*, Aug.17,1838: 'Mr. Payton [Payette] and Capt. Sutter take tea with us.'

19. *Oregon Mission Record Book*, 263.

20. *Der Deutsche Pionier*, XII,5,202 (1880).

Part II : The Empire-Builder

1. In speaking of Sutter's cattle, earlier writers have developed the habit of casting about with surprising figures even in the beginning of Sutter's enterprise. Sutter himself states in his *Petition to Congress* that in the fall of 1839 he 'purchased of Señor Martinez who resided below 300 head of cattle, 30 horses and 30 mares.' The Martinez correspondence proves these figures to be misleading. The account current of Sutter and Martinez of Nov.14,1839 (Vallejo, *Documents*, XXV,231) amounts to only 455 pesos and includes various other items beside cattle and the unspecified ones for food and seed supplies. At prevailing prices the number of cattle mentioned by Sutter in his Petition would have cost him about 1,200 pesos.

2. Even for this time no reliable figures are available. Sutter in his *Petition to Congress* states that in the fall of 1840 he 'purchased 1000 more head of cattle and 75 horses and mares.' But we are probably on safer ground if we make a good discount. Possibly the figures here given represent his total animal wealth for that time.

3. These last two quotations from *De Mofras*, unpublished parts 95ff. The naivete of De Mofras is best apparent when he writes (*Exploration*, 1,466): 'We believe it would be very useful for M.Sutter to realize the wish which he has often expressed to us of having about him French Missionaries to civilize the Indian tribes of his neighborhood.' This credulity is one of the major larks of minor diplomacy, for no one would have been less welcome to Sutter than French missionaries, whom he knew from his stay at Honolulu as unpleasant meddlers. According to Laufkötter (op.cit.p.16) Sutter wrote about these missionaries in a letter from Honolulu to his friends in St. Charles and St. Louis. Laufkötter (*Sacramento Bee*, Dec.20,'84,1-4) further remarks that this letter was published in the *Anzeiger des Westens*, and also in a German newspaper of Cincinnati. Unfortunately all efforts to locate copies of these newspapers have failed. The available sets of the *Anzeiger* of 1840 are incomplete and the one last complete set of the Cincinnati *Volksblatt* was sold for old paper in 1920. A search for files in the libraries of Germany has also remained fruitless.

4. These figures are a compromise between those given by Wilkes, *Narrative*, v,190 and De Mofras, *Exploration*, 1,457-60. Wilkes says 2,500 head of cattle, 1,000 horses, 1,000 sheep; De Mofras 4,000 oxen, 1,200 cows, 1,500 horses, 2,000 sheep. Wilkes' estimate was probably made before the acquisition of the Russian cattle; De Mofras' may already include the Russian stock.

5. In similar terms Sutter wrote to Alvarado on Nov.4,1841: 'Some very curious Rapports come to me, which made me first a little afraid, but after two hours I get over the fit.' (*Century Magazine*, Jan.1891,p.470.) Sutter

to Marsh, Nov.12: 'I am in a State of War here.' Nov.20: 'In case of hostility I am able to do a great deal.' (*Marsh collection*, MS.) The letter to
Leese is dated Nov.8 (Vallejo, *Doc*.xxxiii,250, copy by Prudon. Another
copy, ibid.x,332, and Vallejo, *Historia*, iv,170. MSS.)

6. Alvarado, *Hist*.,iv,221,iv,234, says: 'It remained to the Swiss Don Juan
   Augusto Sutter, that poor adventurer . . . to break the crystal which
   contained my good fortune.' And again he states that the Russian deal
   proves 'that this gentleman [Sutter], although he had served in the guard
   of honor of King Charles X, possessed no honor.'

7. Lienhard, MS., 118,3b.

8. S. to Hartnell, Dec.13,1844. Vallejo, *Doc*.xxxiv,81. MS. This is one of the
   few German letters Sutter wrote in California. He complains particularly
   of the Secretary of State Jimeno Casarin, Hartnell's brother-in-law: 'Da
   Sie sein Schwager sind so möchte ich Sie bitten ihm zu sagen, dass es bes-
   ser für ihn sein würde, ein wenig mehr nach Recht als nur Gunst zu verfahren, sonst dürfte er sein Verfahren bereuen, denn es wird eine Zeit
   kommen und ist sicher schon ganz nahe, wo Hr Jimeno froh sein wird
   wann ich ihn in Schutz nehmen werde. . . .'

Part III : Arms and the Man

1. Gudde. *Sutter's Own Story*, 101. S. to Larkin, Aug.7,1844. Larkin, *Doc*.ii,
   157,MS.

2. S. to Hartnell, Dec.13,1844, Vallejo, *Doc*.xxxiv,81. MS.

3. Reading Coll., Oct.19,1844: 'Mr. Forbes told me, that the best for us up
   there would be, to remain neutral,—perhaps it will.—In all Case, I shall
   endeavour to get so many Armes, Ammunition etc. as possible, but what
   for a Vessel will transport them? . . . O that the party's don't arrive so
   long time not from the U.S!!! . . .' And on Oct.20: 'The political Hori-
   zont looks very gloomy.'

4. Reading Coll., Oct.30,1844. Concerning the clothes he bought he writes:
   'All your Clothes will be ready in about 3 Weeks. I bought black Clothe so
   fine as possible for you, for a frock Coat & Pantaloons, the same time you
   will receive a fine West.'

5. Reading Coll., Jan.1,3,5,1845. These letters of S. to Reading have apparently never been consulted by any previous Sutter biographer. Yet they
   belong to the most important personal documents.

6. Marsh Coll., July 16,26, 1844. MS.

7. S. to Reading, Jan.15,1845, Reading Coll. MS: 'I am in great favor by the
   General, he gives me every proof of high esteeme, which causes some jal-
   ousie in our Camp, particularly since we have D^r· Marsh amongs us, who
   use all his influence to act against me, the Conseil was disolved, and another elected, disolved again, now exist a Comite of 3 Capt Gantt, Dickey

& McIntosh Marshes secretary. They say the will act with me, but it is not true, they are just contrary and want to use me only for a tool, because the General agree to everything what I propose.'

8. It was probably for reasons of political expediency, if not only because of the absence of the Secretary of State, that Micheltorena had not conferred the grant when Sutter was at Monterey in October. Sutter himself accused Jimeno Casarin of obstructionist tactics: 'which document [his petition] was misled or destroyed by D^n· Manuel Jimeno.' Sutter, *Diary*, 26,27. His suspicion was unfounded, for his petition was 'referred to the Secretary [Casarin] for further information' and Casarin 'reported there was no objection.' Howard's *Reports*, XXI,178,179.

9. Beckwourth, 469,470. Sutter to Gessen (fragmentary Spanish translation) Dept. State Papers, VI,140-1. He adds: 'the strangers there in Los Angeles make themselves guilty before the world if they take up arms against their friends and the legitimate government.' Suspicion has sometimes been cast on Sutter that he did not really mean to support Micheltorena after he had the Sobrante grant in his pocket. The letters to Gessen and Reading (Reading Coll., Feb.15,1845) prove that even in these discouraging moments he was absolutely loyal to his governor. In the letter to Reading he says: 'So far as we are now here, we have by all means to safe the honor of the foreigners, the General never had gone so far if he would not have depended on us, and now 2/3 of the Men leave him, he told me that it had been better when they had never come to join him.'

10. Alvarado, *Historia*, IV,235 (MS.), renders this promise in what is supposed to be Sutter's own broken Spanish: '. . . en primera oportunidad vea el enemigo mi toma prisionero a Castro y Alvarado, y despues trae a ti sus cabezas sobre una bandeja de plate.' But the fact that Alvarado makes Sutter speak in the second person singular (typical of the broken Spanish of Americans) seems to prove that he made up the speech himself. Sutter was perfectly familiar with the polite form of address.

11. Gantt to Marsh, March 11, 1845, Marsh Coll., MS.

12. Lienhard, MS.,118,4a. He was not at the fort at this time. The story was told him about a year later. According to him Daylor was imprisoned for his offence.

13. *Anzeiger*, Sept.23,25,27,1845. The letter is dated '*Neu Helvetien*, 14.May, 1845.' The advertisement, ibid.Sept.30, Oct.2,4,7, reads: 'Nach Californien! J.A.Sutter in Neu Helvetien am Sacramento Fluss in Ober Californien wünscht unter vorteilhaften Bedingungen anzustellen: einen Oekonomen welcher die Landwirtschaft gründlich versteht, einen guten Schäfer, einen Bierbrauer, einen Müller, einen Gärtner, einen Lohgerber, einen Zimmermann, zwei gute Schmiede, einen Waffenschmied, zwei Schuhmacher, und einen Wollenweber. Nähere Auskunft wird die Redaktion geben.'

14. Leidesdorff Papers, No.58 (MS.).

15. Larkin Docs., III,232,234.

Part IV : Tool of Destiny

1. The *New Helvetia Diary* was kept Sept.9–27,1845, by Bidwell; Sept.28–Oct.25 by Swasey; Oct.26–Nov.6 by Bidwell; Nov.7–8 by Swasey; Nov. 9–17 by Bidwell; Dec.1 by Swasey (who was discharged Dec.31); Dec.2, 1845 to April 4,1846 by Bidwell; April 5 to June 21 by Loker; June 22 by Bidwell; June 29 by Bidwell. Then follows a long interruption caused by the American occupation. Dec.9,1846 to Dec.9,1847 by Sutter; Dec.10–21 by Bidwell; Dec.22,1847 to May 25,1848 by Sutter. Then the gold-rush closed it forever.

2. Marsh Coll., MS.

3. Leidesdorff Papers, No.122,MS.

4. Reading Coll., May 11, 1846. MS. Similarly to Leidesdorff, Leidesdorff Papers, 119, 'on the 5th inst. we had an 11 hour long good rain, which make a great alteration in my Crops, God thank in heaven for this rain.'

5. Castro, *Doc.*, II,98,MS.

6. No less a person than Consul Larkin, one of the shrewdest judges of men in California, tactfully made allowances for Sutter's difficult position. On the occasion of Gillespie's visit he had asked Sutter to assist any courier that he might have to send overland. 'But,' he then wrote to Vice-Consul Leidesdorff, 'on second thought—he [Sutter] being a Mexican officer—I thought I ought not to require him to do it as he may dislike it, although be willing to oblige me.' June 22, 1846. Leidesdorff Papers 185,MS.

7. In later years even Frémont admitted that Sutter's 'fortress became the point of support and point of departure for the military operations which resulted in the occupation of California.' And he admitted that Sutter's 'far-reaching intelligence saw in its [California's] occupation by Americans the great development of that rich coast.' *A Nation's Benefactor*, 19.

8. Lienhard, *Californien*, 15,18,21,22,73,82. Compare Dana, *Sutter of California*, 275.

9. Lienhard's *Memoirs* are largely based on diaries, some of which, however, he admits to have lost before he wrote his reminiscences. As a rule his statements are corroborated by others. He is a keen observer and writes well for a man with little or no education. Only when he becomes personal it is probably safe to make discounts. His book, *Californien*, is a very much edited and abridged version of his manuscript. It has apparently never been used by any earlier writer on Sutter.

10. Lienhard, MS.118,3b, states that there were 'a large number of Indian girls constantly at his beck and call.'

11. Larkin, *Docs.*, v,319. MS.

12. Leidesdorff Papers, 321.

13. Sherman, *Letters*, 44,45. *Memoirs*, II,49.

14. Lienhard, *Californien*, 222–4.

Part V : Tragic Dawn

1. In a letter to H.Thommen (Cal.Hist.Soc. *Quarterly*, XI,1,p.42) dated May 4, 1848, Sutter says 'I expect my family to be here in about five months.' In another of May 28, 1848, to Herr Haas in Darmstadt (*Der Deutsche Auswanderer*, III, 1849) he also speaks of his sons, by whom he expects to be relieved of many duties in the near future.

2. Sutter to Haas, May 28, 1848.

3. Lienhard, *The Early Days*, 1,2; *Californien*, 216.

4. J.A.Sutter, Jr., *Statement*, 1ff.,MS.

5. California Supreme Court, Sac.No.4732; Appendix, Exhibit 1. J.A.Sutter, Jr., Statement, 5,6.

6. This and the following mainly after Lienhard, *Californien*, 224,225; *Memoiren*, 140,4–141,1; J.A.Sutter, Jr., Statement 8. Lienhard renders one of Sutter's stories about his service under Charles X as follows: 'Ja, meine Herren, in der Schlacht von Grenoble . . . erhielt ich einen Bayonetstich in den einen meiner Schenkel. Unser Major, welcher zufällig in meiner Nähe sich befand, hatte dieses bemerkt, wie mir das Blut über die weissen Hosen hinabfloss; er rief "Capitän Sutter ist verwundet, nehmt ihn zurück, damit man ihn verbinde," aber ich sagte "No, no. Vorwärts" und ich hieb mit meinem Säbel tüchtig umher.' Then he adds: 'They say if a man lies, he tells the same story differently every time. But Sutter had told the story of this battle at different times in pretty much the same words.' Laufkötter, *Sacramento Bee*, March 28, 1885, 7–3.

7. J.A.Sutter, Jr., op.cit.8.

8. Ibid.8,9.

9. Ibid.10.

10. Lienhard, *Memoiren* (MS.) 159,4; J.A.Sutter, Jr., *Statement*, 13.

11. J.A.Sutter, Jr., op.cit.16,17. It is interesting to note that young Sutter had to borrow money to make Lienhard's mission possible. He borrowed $6,000 from Bill Daylor 'with great difficulty.'

12. Ibid.17. Be it said that young Sutter's *Statement* has the ring of veracity. He himself concludes the first part of it (written at San Francisco, Feb.25, 1855); 'I declare once more solemnly that anything I state here, is the whole naked truth, as far as I recollect, and has been brought to paper by me after due reflections and in an altogether quiet state of my mind.'

13. Crosby, *Events*, 37.

14. Lienhard, *Memoiren*, 179,4 says that he arrived at Basle Oct.16 and learned that Sutter's family had started for Darmstadt and on their way to America two days before.

15. J.A.Sutter, Jr., op.cit.23; Lienhard, *Californien*, 295.

16. In figures of the U.S.Census of 1850, Hock Farm presents itself as follows: Improved acres of land 200. Unimproved 1,000. Cash value of farm

$100,000. Farming implements and machinery $10,000. Horses 1,000. Asses and mules 25. Milch cows 300. Working oxen 50. Other cattle 600. Sheep 500. Swine 60. Value of live-stock $46,000. Bushels of wheat 200. Bushels of Indian corn 50.

17. Saint-Amand, 555.

18. A few of the notable descriptions of Sutter's appearance are by J.C.Ward, *Placer County History*, 46. Bayard Taylor, *El Dorado*, 158. St. Field, *Personal Reminiscences*, 27. T.T.Johnson, *California and Oregon*, 139,140. Saint-Amand,557.

19. Lienhard, *Memoiren*, repeatedly mentions that even Sutter's children began to allude to their 'noble' blood, particularly Eliza.

20. Upham, *Notes*, 323–5 describes one of these parties held on June 2, 1850.

21. J.A.Sutter, Jr., op.cit. Engler, Sutter's son-in-law, in a letter to his father, May 1, 1852, writes: 'Wetzlar and his partner Brandes robbed Captain Sutter of about 100.000 Dollars and the eldest son, Augustus, during a journey which he undertook, of his entire fortune.'

22. *Burgdorfer Jahrbuch*, 1935, p.30.

23. For the historical background of this chapter the following sources have been used: Bancroft, *History*, vi,535–50,635ff.; Blackmer, ch.III; Hoit; Jones; New Helvetia; Morrow; Plumb; Royce; Crosby. (For complete titles see list of sources.)

24. Steamer Union, Aug.15,1854 and San Francisco Chronicle, June 5, 1856, 1–2.

25. Howard, *Reports*, xxi,170ff.

26. *Alta Californian*, Sept.9,1862. Circular, Soc.Cal. Pioneers of Sept.15,1862. *Sacramento Union*, Oct.3,1862.

27. Sutter's note to Bidwell of Dec.16,1865 (Bidwell Coll.), gives his address as 'Corner of E and 10th St., Mrs. Graves.'

28. Original in the Städtisches Museum, Solothurn, Switzerland. An excellent color reproduction is to be found on the jacket of the Swiss edition of this biography: J.P.Zollinger, *Johann August Sutter, Der König von Neu-Helvetien*, Zürich, 1938. (The frontispiece, also in color, is not so good.)

29. *Burgdorfer Jahrbuch*, 59–62.

30. The following are the entries concerning Sutter in the Congressional publications: *Congr. Globe*, 41st Congr., 2nd sess., March 22, 1870, 3rd sess., part 3, 1871, Feb.27. *Congr. Record*: 44th Congr., 1st sess., vol.4/1,487, Jan.19,1876; vol.4/5, p.4287, June 3, 1876. 45th Congr., 1st sess., vol.6,134, Oct.22,1877; 2nd sess., vol.7/2, p.1960, March 21, 1878. 46th Congr., 1st sess., vol.9/2, p.1351, May 15, 1879; 2nd sess., vol.10/1, p.311, Jan.13, 1880; vol.10/3, p.2903, April 30, 1880, and p.2228; vol.10/5, p.4402. *Senate Journal*, 44th Congr., 1st sess., p.118, Jan.19,1876. 46th Congr., 2nd sess., p.499, April 30, 1880; p.716, June 11, 1880. *House Journal*, 44th Congr., 1st sess., p.244, Jan.24,1876; p.1188, June 30, 1876. 46th Congr., 2nd sess., pp.211,977. *House Reports*, 44th Congr., 1st sess., vol.5, no.718, June 30,

1876. 46th Congr., 2nd sess., vol.3, no.867. *Senate Misc.*, 39th Congr., 1st sess., no.38.

31. *Burgdorfer Jahrbuch*, 66–70.

32. *A Nation's Benefactor*, 19ff.

SOURCES

MANUSCRIPTS, BOOKS, NEWSPAPERS, PAMPHLETS, PERIODICALS,
AND PUBLIC DOCUMENTS CONSULTED AND QUOTED

Manuscripts

(Abbreviations: BL: Bancroft Library, University of California, Berkeley, Calif. CSL: California State Library, Sacramento, Calif. HL: Henry E. Huntington Library, San Marino, Calif.)

Alvarado, Juan Bautista. *Historia de California.* 5 vols. BL.

Arce, Francisco. *Memorias historicas y documentos originales.* 1877. 71 pp., 30 docs. BL.

Archive der Landeskanzlei Liestal, Baselland.

Archives of the Society of California Pioneers. Copy for BL., 243 pp.

Avila, Maria Inocente Pico. *Cosas de California.* 1878, 31 pp. BL.

Baldridge, William. *The days of* 1846. 1877, 36 pp. BL.

Bandini, Juan. *Documentos para la historia de California* 1776–1864. 159 docs. BL.

——. *Historia de la Alta California* 1769–1845. 482 pp. BL.

Belden, Josiah. *Statement of historical facts on California.* 1878, 70 pp. BL.

Bear Flag Papers. A collection of statements. BL.

Berreyesa, Antonio. *Memoir.* 1877, 21 pp. BL.

Bidwell, John. *California* 1841–1848. 221 pp. BL.

——. *Journey to California in* 1841, 17 pp. BL.

Bidwell Collection. Original Correspondence. 7 boxes. CSL.

Bigler, Rudolf. *J.A.Sutter in Burgdorf.* (Collection of the author.)

Bigler, Henry. *Diary of a Mormon in California.* 1872, 98 pp. BL.

Burnett, Peter H. *Recollections of the past.* 2 vols. BL.

Carrillo, Domingo. *Documentos para la historia de California.* 127 pp. BL.

Carrillo, Julio. *Narrative.* 11 pp. BL.

Castro, Manuel. *Documentos para la historia de California. Papeles originales.* 2 vols. BL.

——. *Relacion sobre acontecimientos de la Alta California.* 206 pp. BL.

Chamberlain, John. *Memoirs of California since* 1840. 20 pp. BL.

Chiles, Joseph B. *A visit to California in early times.* 1878, 12 pp. BL.

Clyman, James. *Diary* 1836–1848. 148 pp. BL.

——. *Notebook* 1844–1846. 27 pp. BL.

Crosby, Elisha O. *Statement of events in California.* 1878, 132 pp. BL.

Davis, Wm. H. *Glimpses of the past in California.* 396 pp. BL.

Departmental Records. Excerpts from the archives of California. 14 vols. in 4. BL.

Departmental State Papers. 20 vols. in 7. BL.

——. *Benicia.* 5 vols. in 2. BL.

——. *Benicia Military.* 36 vols. in 3. BL.

Documentos de la historia de California. 4 vols. BL.

Douglas, James. *Journal* 1840–41, *Fort Vancouver and the northwest coast.* 128 pp. (Copy.) BL.

Eaton, Henry. *A pioneer of* 1838. 8 pp. BL.

Estudillo Documents. 2 vols. BL.

Fay, Caleb. *Statement of historical facts.* 1878, 44 pp. BL.

Fernandez, Juan. *Documentos para la historia de California* (MS. copy), 65 pp. BL.

Fitch, Josefa C. de. *Documentos para la historia de California* 1827–1856. 624 docs., fol. BL.

Geldstagrodel betreffend den Geldstag des Joh. Aug. Sutter. 1834. Gerichtskanzlei Burgdorf. 262 pp. foolsc.

Gomez, Vicente P. *Lo que sabe sobre las cosas de California,* 1876. 427 pp., foolsc. BL.

Gonzalez, Mauricio. *Memorias dadas en* 1877. 52 pp. BL.

Graham and Sutter, some facts about, by a pioneer of 1841. 1877, 7 pp. BL.

Green, Alfred A. *Life and adventures of a 47er in California.* 1878, 86 pp. BL.

Guerra y Norriega, José de la. *Documentos*. 7 vols. BL.

Gwin, Wm. M. *Memoirs on the history of the United States, Mexico and California*. 1878, 265 pp. BL.

Hargrave, Wm. H. *Statement on the Bear Flag Operations in '46*. 1886, 7 pp. BL.

Hopper, Charles. *Narrative of a pioneer of 1841*. 1871, 14 pp. BL.

Hyde, George. *Statement of historical facts on California*. 26 pp. BL.

Janssens, Agustin. *Vida y aventuras*. 223 pp. BL.

Juarez, Cayetano. *Narracion*. 12 pp. BL.

Kirchenbücher Liestal.

Kirchenbuch II *Kandern*.

Knight, Thomas. *Recollections*. In California MSS. BL.

Larkin, Thomas Oliver. *Documents for the history of California*. Papers of the Consul of the U.S. in California before the conquest. 1839–56, 9 vols., 3,408 docs. BL.

——. *Official Correspondence as U.S.Consul and Navy Agent* 1844–49. 2 vols. in 1., fol. BL.

——. *Notes on the personal character of Californians* (in *Official Correspondence*) 9 pp. BL.

Leese, Jacob P. *Memoir on the Bear Flag* (in *Bear Flag Papers*).

Leese, [Mrs.] Rosalia. *Narrative of the Bear Party*. 6 pp. BL.

Legislative Records (California Archives), VOL.III, 1836–40, 4 vols. in 3. BL.

Leidesdorff, Wm. A. *Leidesdorff Papers* 1844–1855. HL.

Lienhard, J. Heinrich. *Memoiren*. 1,000 pp. foolsc. Property of Mr. A.H.Lienhard, Minneapolis, Minn.

Marsh, John. *The Marsh Collection of correspondence*. CSL.

——. *Letter to Commodore Thomas Ap Catesby Jones containing information on California*. Nov.25,1842 (copy of 1843), 19 pp. BL.

Martin, Thomas S. *Narrative of Frémont's expedition* 1845–47. 58 pp. BL.

McChristian, Pat. *Narrative*. 13 pp. BL.

McKinstry, George. *Documents for the history of California* 1846–49. 57 docs. fol. BL.

Marshall, Henry. *Statement*. 5 pp. BL.

Monterey Archives, 16 vols. in 1. (copy) BL.

Nidever, George. *Life and adventures since 1834*. 165 pp. BL.

Pierce, Henry A. *Rough sketch of life and experiences.* BL.

Pico, José de Jesus. *Acontecimientos en California.* 1878, 78 pp. BL.

Pico, Pio. *Documentos para la historia de California.* 2 vols. BL.

Pico, Ramon José. *Documentos 1781–1850.* 3 vols. BL.

Pinto, Rafael. *Documentos para la historia de California 1823–1847,* 2 vols. BL.

Reading, Pierson B. *The Reading Collection of Correspondence* 1843–1868. CSL.

——. *Diary of an overland trip, June 28 to Nov.10,* 1843. CSL.

Russian America (translations from various Russian sources), VOL.VI, *Reports on Colonies,* Parts I & II, 1758–1852, 942 pp. BL.

St. Charles, Mo., Archives: 1.County Records. 2.Tax Collectors' Records. 3.Deeds of Trust. 4.Naturalization Records.

San Jose Archives. Copies and extracts, 6 vols. in 1. BL.

Savage, Thomas. *Documentos para la historia de California.* 1877. 4 vols. BL.

Sketches of California Pioneers, written or dictated by themselves for Bancroft's Pacific Library. BL.

Staatsarchiv Baselland, Liestal. Akten Joh. Aug. Sutter betreffend.

State Papers, *Missions and Colonization,* 2 vols. BL.

Streeter, Wm. A. *Recollection of historical events in California* 1843–1878. 245 pp. BL.

Sutter, John Augustus. *Personal Reminiscences* 1876. 206 pp. BL.

——. *Letters to Antonio Suñol and others* [in French] 1841–1846. Sutter Collection, CSL.

Sutter, Bidwell and Loker. *New Helvetia Diary of Events,* 1845–1848. Society of California Pioneers, San Francisco. Also copy, BL.

Sutter, John A. Jr. *Statement regarding early California experiences,* 1855. CSL.

Swasey, Wm. F. *California in* 1845–46. 27 pp. BL.

Torre, Estavan de la. *Peripecias de la vida Californiana* 1843–1850. 150 pp. BL.

——. *Reminiscencias* 1877. 234 pp. BL.

Unbound Documents (Archives of California, copy) 1846–1850. 1 vol. BL.

Vallejo, Mariano Guadalupe. *Documentos para la historia de California, 1769–1850. Archivo particular del Sr Don M.G.V.* 36 vols., 11,172 docs., fol. BL.

——. *Historia de California.* 5 vols. BL.

——. *Correspondencia historica.* 193 pp. BL.

——. *The Vallejo Papers,* 1844. HL.

Vallejo, Salvador. *Notas historicas sobre California.* 157 pp. BL.

Vincent, George. *Dictation.* 11 pp. BL.

Watson, Frank. *Narrative.* 7 pp. BL.

Wiggins, William. *Reminiscences.* 1877, 23 pp. BL.

Wilson, Benjamin D. *Observations on early days in California and New Mexico.* 1877, 113 pp., foolsc. BL.

Winans, J.W. *The days of* 1849. 24 pp. BL.

Yates, John. *Sketch of a journey in* 1842 *from Sacramento through the valley.* 35 pp. BL.

*Books, newspapers, pamphlets,
periodicals, public documents*

Alta Californian, The (Sacramento).

A Nation's Benefactor, General John A. Sutter. New York, 1880.

Abbot's National Digest of reports of the U.S.Courts.

Angell, Myron. *History of Placer County, Calif.* Oakland, 1882.

Anzeiger des Westens (St. Louis, Mo.) 1836–45.

Associated Pioneers of the Territorial Days of California. *Report of* 1876.

Bancroft, Hubert Howe. *History of California.* 7 vols., San Francisco, 1886.

——. *California inter pocula.* San Francisco, 1888.

——. *Literary Industries.* Works, VOL.XXXIX. San Francisco, 1890.

Bari, Valska. *The course of empire.* New York, 1931.

Basellandschaftliche Zeitung (Liestal, Switzerland).

Beckwourth, James P. *Life and adventures.* New York, 1858.

Bekeart, Phil. B. 'James Wilson Marshall.' *Quarterly,* Society of Calif. Pioneers, VOL.I,no.3, pp. 1–95.

Bidwell, John. *Echoes of the past in California.* Chicago, 1928.

——. 'Life in California before the gold discovery.' *Century Magazine,* VOL.XLI,no.12,163–183. Dec.1890.

——. 'Frémont in the conquest of California.' Ibid., no.4,518–25.

Bigler, Rudolf. '*General Johann August Sutter und seine Beziehungen zu Burgdorf.*' *Burgdorfer Jahrbuch*, 1935, 7–20.

Birmann, Martin. '*General Joh. Aug. Suter.*' *Gute Schriften Basel*, no. 73.

Blackmer, Frank W. *The life of Charles Robinson.* Topeka, 1902.

Bonney, B.F. *Across the plains by prairie schooner to Sutter's Fort.* Eugene, Or., [1924?].

——. 'Recollections.' Oregon Hist. Soc. *Quarterly*, XXIV, 46–50.

Bowers, Claude G. *The tragic era.* New York, 1929.

Brown, James S. *California gold.* Oakland, Calif., 1894.

Bryant, Edwin. *What I saw in California.* New York, 1848.

Burgdorfer Jahrbuch, 1935. Burgdorf, 1934.

Burnett, Peter H. *Recollections and opinions of an old pioneer.* New York, 1880.

California Assembly Journal.

California Historical Society, *Quarterly*.

Chittenden, Hiram M. *The American fur trade of the Far West.* New York, 1902.

Clyman, James. *American frontiersman*, 1792–1882. Ed. by C.L.Camp. San Francisco, California Historical Society, 1928.

Coan, Charles F. *A history of New Mexico*, VOL.I. Chicago, 1925.

Colton, Walter. *Three years in California.* New York, 1852.

Coman, Katharine. *Economic beginnings of the Far West.* 2 vols. New York, 1922.

Conard, Howard. *Encyclopaedia of the history of Missouri.* VOL.VI.

Congressional Globe and Record (see *United States*).

Cordua, Theodor. 'Memoirs.' Ed. and trans. by E.G.Gudde. Calif. Hist. Soc. *Quarterly*, XII, no.4, 279–311, Dec.1933.

Coy, Owen C. *Gold Days.* San Francisco, 1929.

Davis, William H. *Seventy-five years in California.* San Francisco, 1929.

Dellenbaugh, F.S. *Frémont and '49.* New York, 1914.

Denys, M. Ferdinand. *L'univers pittoresque.* Paris,1849.

Deutsch-Amerikanische Geschichtsblätter. Herausgegeben von der Deutsch-Amerikanischen Historischen Gesellschaft von Illinois. Chicago, 1901 ff.

Der Deutsche Auswanderer. VOL.III, no.32. 1849.

Der Deutsche Pionier. Monatsschrift für Erinnerungen aus dem deutschen Pionierleben in den Vereinigten Staaten. Cincinnati, 1869–85.

Duden, Gottfried. *Bericht über eine Reise nach den westlichen Vereinigten Staaten,* etc. St. Gallen, 1832.

Dufour, Clarence J. 'The Russian withdrawal from California.' Calif. Hist. Soc. *Quarterly,* xii,3,240–276.

Dunbar, Edward E. *The romance of the age.* New York, 1867.

Dunbar, Seymour [Ed.]. *Fort Sutter Papers.* [20 copies privately printed. MS. in the Huntington Library.]

Dye, Eva Emma. *McLoughlin and Oregon.* Chicago, 1900.

Eells, Myra. 'Journal.' *Transactions,* Oregon Pioneer Soc., 1889, 54–88.

Eells, Myron. *Father Eells.* Boston, 1894.

Eisele, Albert. *Die Entwicklung der Papierfabrikation in Kandern.* Freiburg, 1928.

Eldorado County (Calif.) History. Sacramento, 1915.

Essig, E.O. 'The Russian settlements at Ross.' Calif. Hist. Soc. *Quarterly,* xii,3,191–209.

Farnham, Th. *Travels in the great western prairies.* New York, 1843.

Ferry, Hypolite. *Description de la Nouvelle Californie.* Paris, 1850.

Field, Stephen J. *Personal reminiscences of early days in California.* [Privately printed, 1880.]

Frémont, John C. *Exploring expedition to the Rocky Mountains, Oregon, and California.* Buffalo, 1849.

———. *Memoirs of my life.* Chicago and New York, 1887.

Gauss, Karl. '*Herkunft und Familie des Generals Joh. Aug. Suter.' Basellandschaftliche Zeitung* [Liestal, Switzerland], Jan.26,28, 1931.

Gray, William H. *A history of Oregon* 1792–1849. Portland, 1870.

———. Journal. [In Gray's *History of Oregon,* privately printed for Mrs. Jacob Kamm. No date.]

Gregg, Josiah. *Commerce of the prairies.* 2 vols. New York, 1844.

Harris, Nellie McCoy. 'Memoirs of Old Westport.' *The Annals of Kansas City,* 1,4,472–4.

Hastings, Lansford W. *The emigrant's guide to Oregon and California.* Cincinnati, 1845.

Historisch-Biographisches Lexikon der Schweiz. 7 vols. Neuenburg, 1921–34.

Hittel, John S. *The resources of California*. San Francisco, 1863.

Hittell, Theodore. *History of California*. San Francisco, 1885.

Hoit, C.W. *Fraudulent Mexican land claims and the false location of the Sutter grant*. Sacramento, 1869.

Howard, Benjamin. *Reports* on the cases before the U.S.Supreme Court, xxi,170ff.

Huntley, Henry V. *California, its gold and its inhabitants*. 2 vols. London, 1856.

Jackson County (Mo.) *History*. Kansas City, Mo., 1881.

Johnson, Theodore T. *California and Oregon*. Philadelphia, 1851.

Jones, William C. *Report on the subject of land titles in California, made in pursuance of instructions from the Secretary of State*, etc. Washington, 1850.

Kelly, Hall J. *On Oregon*. A collection of five of his published works. Ed. by F.W.Powell. Princeton University Press, 1932.

Koerner, Gustav Phil. *Das deutsche Element in den Vereinigten Staaten*. Cincinnati, 1880.

Kotzebue, Otto von. *Neue Reise um die Welt*. 2 vols. Weimar, 1830.

Lancaster Daily Examiner. Lancaster, Pa.

Laufkötter, John A. *John A. Sutter and his grants*. Sacramento, 1867.

——. Letters to the *Sacramento Bee* (Oct.3,1884), and the *Sacramento Union* (June 2, July 21, 1889).

Lee, D., and Frost., J.H. *Ten years in Oregon*. New York,1844.

Lienhard, Heinrich. *Californien unmittelbar vor und nach der Entdeckung des Goldes*. Zürich,1898.

——. 'The early days.' *San Francisco Daily Examiner*, March 8, 1885.

Loeher, Franz. *Geschichte und Zustände der Deutschen in Amerika*. Cincinnati and Leipzig, 1847. Second edition, Göttingen, 1855.

Lyman, George D. *John Marsh, pioneer*. New York, 1931.

McGlashen, C.F. *History of the Donner party*. Sacramento, 1907.

McGroarty, John S. *California*. Los Angeles, 1926.

Massey, Ernest de. 'A Frenchman in the goldrush.' Transl. by Marguerite Eyer Wilbur. Calif. Hist. Soc. *Quarterly*, v,3–43,139–77, 219–54,342–77; vi,37–57.

Meyer, Carl. *Nach dem Sacramento*. Aarau,1855.

Moerenhout, J.A. *The inside story of the gold rush*. Transl. by A.P.Nasatir. San Francisco, Calif. Hist. Soc., 1935.

Mofras, Eugène Duflot de. *Exploration du territoire de l'Orégon, des Californies et de la mer vermeille.* 2 vols. Paris, 1844.

——. 'The unpublished parts of Mofras' work.' Transl. by A.P.Nasatir. *Proceedings,* Pacific Coast Br., Amer. Hist. Ass., 1928, 95–102.

Morrow, William W. *Spanish and Mexican land grants.* San Francisco, 1923.

Muench, Friedrich. '*Berichtigung und Ergänzung Johann A. Sutter betreffend.*' *Der Deutsche Pionier,* 1872, IV,2,3.

Nasatir, A.P. 'French activities in California before statehood.' *Proceedings,* Pacific Coast Br., Amer. Hist. Ass., 1928,76–88.

Nevins, Allan. *Frémont. The West's greatest adventurer.* 2 vols. New York and London, 1928.

New Helvetia. The United States vs. John A. Sutter. Testimony taken in behalf of the U.S. in the U.S.District Court of Northern California. San Francisco, 1861.

Oregon Mission Record Book. Or. Hist. Soc. *Quarterly,* XXIII, 263ff.

Parsons, George F. *The Life and adventures of James Wilson Marshall.* Sacramento, 1870.

Phelps,W.D. *Fore and aft.* Boston,1871.

Plumbe, John. *The settlers and land speculators of Sacramento. An open letter to James Gordon Bennett, Esq.* Pamphlet, 1850.

Reading, Pierson B. *Journal.* Soc. Calif. Pioneers *Quarterly,* VII,3,148ff.

Report of the Attorney General on California land claims etc. Washington, 1860.

Report of the Committee of the U.S.Senate on the claim of General John A. Sutter and bill for his relief. Washington, 1880.

Revere, Joseph W. *A tour of duty in California.* New York and Boston, 1849.

Rickard, T.A. 'The discovery of gold in California.' *University of California Chronicle,* 1928.

Robinson, Alfred. *Life in California.* New York, 1846.

Royce, Josiah. *California from the conquest in 1846 to the second vigilance committee in San Francisco.* Boston, 1886.

——. 'Squatter riots of '50 in Sacramento.' *Overland Monthly,* VI (second series), 237ff.

Sacramento Bee (Sacramento, Calif.).

Sacramento Union (Sacramento, Calif.).

Saint-Amant, Pierre Charles de. *Voyages en Californie et dans l'Orégon.* Paris, 1854.

Sandels, G.M. Waseurtz de (the 'King's Orphan'). 'Memoir of California in 1843.' Soc. Calif. Pioneers *Quarterly*, III, 56–98.

Sandwich Island Gazette, Honolulu, Oahu, 1838, 1839.

San Francisco Chronicle.

San Francisco Daily Examiner.

Schlagintweit, Robert von. *Californien, Land und Leute.* Cöln, 1871.

Schoonover, T.J. *The life and times of Gen. J.A. Sutter.* Sacramento, 1907.

Sherman, William T. *Memoirs.* 2 vols. New York, 1875.

——. *The Sherman Letters.* New York, 1894.

Sherwood, Ely. *California, her wealth and her resources.* New York, 1848.

Simpson, George. *Narrative of a journey round the world.* London, 1847.

Society of California Pioneers, *Quarterly.*

Sutter, John A. *The Diary of Johann August Sutter.* With an introduction by Douglas S. Watson. The Grabhorn Press. San Francisco, 1932.

——. *Petition to the Senate and House of Representatives of the U.S. 39th Congress,* 1st sess., Sen. Misc. Doc. No. 38 (1866).

——. *Memorial to the Senate and House of Representatives of the U.S.* Washington, D.C., 1876.

——. 'Statement regarding the discovery of gold.' *Hutchings' Illustrated California Magazine,* II, 5, Nov. 1857. Reprinted: Coy, 335–42.

Swasey, William F. *Early days and men of California.* Oakland, 1891.

Taylor, Bayard. *El Dorado.* 2 vols. New York, 1850.

Treaty Stipulations between Mexico and the United States. . . . Instructions of the Department of the Interior to the commissioners. Regulations to the commissioners for the prosecution of land claims. San Francisco, 1852.

Tuthill, F. *History of California.* San Francisco, 1866.

Twitchell, Ralph E. *Old Santa Fe.* Santa Fe, N.M., 1925.

United States Congress: *Congressional Globe; Congressional Record; Senate Journal; Senate Miscellaneous Documents; House Journal; House Reports; Congressional Directory.*

Upham, Samuel C. *Notes on a voyage to California* 1849–50. Philadelphia, 1878.

Wallace's *Reports* on cases in the U.S. Supreme Court. VOL.III, 1864.

Wilkes, Charles. *Narrative of the U.S. Exploring Expedition*. Philadelphia, 1845.

Wood, William Maxwell. *Wandering sketches of people and things*. Philadelphia, 1849.

Zollinger, James Peter. 'John Augustus Sutter's European background,' Calif. Hist. Soc. *Quarterly*, XIV, March 1935, 1, 28–46.

INDEX

Aarburg, 9.
Acacio, Chief, 76.
Acapulco, Mex., 296,329,332.
Aeschlimann, Salzfaktor, 9,10.
Agriculture (see also Cattle, Horti-
culture), 82,104–106,108,111,
123,124,137,166,188,191,212,214,
249.
Allgeier, Nicolaus, 41,77,111,121,
123,217.
Almaden, 182.
Alvarado, Juan Bautista, 51–55,57,
71,79–81,86,89,93,95,96,100,102,
103,109,110,144–156,301,347,
348.
American Civil War, 317,319,321,
322–325.
American Creek, 95.
American Fur Company, 39,41.
American Immigrants in California
(see Immigration).
American River, 63,65,66,78,82,
130,185,217,226,227,246–249.
Americans in California, 80,81,138,
150–152,154,191,196–200,256.
Anashe (Chief), 65,84,230.
Anashe's Daughter, 230–232.
Anderson, Lt., 210,211.
Anzeiger des Westens, 27,31–33,162,
169,171,344–346.
Apaches, 31.
Arce, Francisco, Lt., 196.
Arkansas River, 30.
Assoc. Pioneers of Territorial Days,
336,337.
Auburn, 249.
Austria, 5.

Baden, Margravate, 4,5.
Bakery, Sutter's,166.
Bancroft, Hubert Howe, 333–335,
345.
Bandini, Juan, 154.

Bartleson Party, 91,103.
Basle, 4,6–8,332,339.
Bates, Dr., 213,216,231,232.
Bear Creek, 217,241.
Bear Flag Prisoners, 198,199,201,
203.
Bear Flag Revolt, 191–201.
Beaubien, Charles, 36,345.
Belcher (Sir), Edward, 53,63.
Benicia, 242.
Benitz, William, 123.
Bennett, Charles, 242.
Benton, Thomas, 196.
Bernal Bros., 107,136.
Berne, Military Academy, 6,8.
Berne, Police, 15.
Berreyesa, Rudesindo, 102.
Bidwell, John, 103,105,113,123,
124,133,136,152,162,173–176,
182,183,186,188,197,198,216,
217,221,227,229,230,241,243,
290,307.
Bigler, Henry, 235–237,245.
Bigler, Rudolf, 343.
Blacksmiths, Sutter's, 115,165,232,
233.
Blue Mountains, 43.
Bodega (see also Ross and Bodega),
52,57,94–100,125,133.
Boise, Fort, 42,43.
Bolivar (Ship), 46.
Boston, 59,118,165.
Brandes, Dr., 296,351.
Brannan, Samuel, 205,246,247,263,
272–274,276,277,283,296,300,
304.
Brannan & Smith, 244,251.
Brooklyn (Ship), 205.
Brouett, 229.
Brown, Charles, 175.
Brown, James S., 236.
Bruce, Brannan, Graham & Wetz-
lar, 307.

Bryant, Edwin, 203,218.
Buchser, Frank, 326,327,330,351.
Buena Ventura, 146,147.
Buffalo, 30,40,43.
Burbank, Luther, 292.
Burgdorf, 9–16,19,20,35,37,38,44,
    69,189,190,254,323,329,339.
Burnett, Peter H., 274,279,280,
    283,286,305.
Burns, William, 221.
Burrows, Bill, 41.
Butte Creek, 217.

Cabinet-maker, Sutter's (see Wet-
    ler).
Cahuenga, Battle of, 149–156,161.
Cahuenga, Treaty of, 209.
California (American period), 200–
    211,248–251,264,265,281,283,
    297,302.
California (Mexican period), 28,36,
    37,44,46–52,72,85,86,88,102,132,
    133,145,164,165,170,171,271 (see
    also Bear Flag Revolt).
California (Ship), 281,282.
California Assembly, 312.
California Constitution, 320.
—— Constitutional Convention,
    283–286.
—— Land Claims Act, 302,304,
    311,314,317.
—— Legislature, 321,322,332.
California missions, 49,50.
California Republic,197–200.
—— State Capitol, 312.
—— State Militia, 310.
—— Statehood, 302.
Californian (newspaper), 205,247.
Californian Star, 246,247.
Californians, 50,51,70,72,80,83,88,
    89,91,92,100,108,109,132,133
    (see also Micheltorena War, 133–
    156), 160,174,201,209.
Camino Real, 49.
Canada, 87,118.
Canadian River, 30.
Cape Horn, 118,282.
Cape Mendocino, 95.
Carpenters, Sutter's, 165.
Carquinez Straits, 63.
Carr, Capt., 29.
Carson, Kit, 41,129,182,196.
Cartwrights, Sutter's, 165.
Casarin, Jimeno, 80,347,348.
Castillero, Andres,173–176,181,182.

Castro, Antonio, 153.
Castro, José, 89,100,101,136,140,
    141,143–156,158,160,173–176,
    181,192–195,199,200,241.
Cattle, Sutter's, 67,82,83,99,106–
    108,134,157,169,170,215,221,
    287,309,346.
Célis, Eulojio, 107,125.
Cendrars, Blaise, 343.
Chagres, 281,282.
Chamberlain, John, 78,121,186.
Charles X of France (see Swiss
    Guard).
Chavayas Mines, 182.
Chico ranch, 217.
Chiles, Joseph B., 106,111.
Chiles-Walker Party, 111.
Cholos, 133,137,149.
Cimarron, 30.
Cincinnati, 20,337,346.
City Hotel, Sacramento, 287.
Clementine (Ship), 46,48,53,54,56.
Clyman, James, 116,117.
Cochinos, 198.
Coloma, 233,269,272,276 (see also
    Sawmill).
'Colonel' of Prairie du Chien, 22,25.
Columbia River, 80,87,101.
Columbia (Ship), 45.
Columbus, Christopher, 26,227.
Cook, Grove, 158.
Coopers, Sutter's, 165.
Cordua, Theodore, 111,123,217,
    277,289,308.
Cosumnes River, 74,217.
Cottonwood Creek, 217.
Council Grove, 28.
Creditors, Sutter's (see also Debts),
    108,119.
Crosby, Elisha, 304.
Custot, Octave, 68,71,72,74,78,86.

Dalles Mission, 43.
Dana, Julian, 343,344.
Davis, Wm. H., 66,117.
Daylor, William, 78,157,217,230,
    249,308,348.
Debts, Sutter's (see also Russian
    debt), 16,36–38,106,107,123–
    126,136,138,163,166,170,219,
    220,224,272,274,275,279.
Defensores de la Patria, 131,137,
    140,143.
Delaware Indians, 35,39,65,101.
Democrats, 319.

Der Deutsche Pionier, 337.
Diamond Springs, 29.
Distillery, Sutter's, 82,104,106,115, 120,165,187.
Don Quixote (Ship), 136.
Donner Lake, 206.
Donner Party, 206–209.
Douglas, James, 44,45,47,85–87, 275.
Dring, Capt., 263.
Drips, Capt., 39,41.
Dry Diggings, 249.
Dübeld, Annette (see also Sutter, Mrs. John A.), 9,10,18,27,271.
Dübeld, Marie Sophie, 13.
Dübeld, Rosina, Frau, 10,11.
Dübeld, Samuel, 10.
Dubosc, Pierre, 86.
Duden Gottfried, 18–22,25.
Dunbar, Edwin, 343.
Dürr, Jacob, 131,142.
Dutton, David, 111.

' E ' (Engelmann?), 27.
Edde, 230.
Eells, Myra, 39,40,42,43.
Eldorado (Ship), 288.
Elijah (Chief), 158.
Eliza City, 289,290.
Ellis, 263.
Embarcadero, 115,271,274.
Emmons, George F., 87,91,112,130, 331.
England, 86,118.
Engler, George David, 290,309,311, 312.
Erasmus of Rotterdam, 7.
Ermatinger, Francis, 42.
Estrada, Capt., 146.

Feather River (see also Hock Farm), 65,108,123,217,290,309.
Fifield, 232,233,244.
Fleas, 117.
Flourmill, Sutter's, 106,115,118, 166,225,230,238,239,246,249, 273,287.
Flügge, Charles A., 104,107,110, 123,164.
Folsom, Capt., 251.
Forbes, James Alexander, 134,144, 163,347.
Foreigners in California (see also Americans, Settlers, Immigration), 81,87,100,131,160,188,189.

Fort Sutter (see New Helvetia, buildings, political importance).
France, 1,46,87,88,101,102,110, 293.
Frémont, John Charles, 129–131, 182,183,186,191–204,208,209, 211,216,219,220,264,341,349.
French, William, 46,56,275.
French & Co., 56.
French-Canadians, 85,87.
Frenchmen, 24.
Fur trade (see Trapping).

Gantt, John, 142,143,146,148,151, 152,159,347.
Gavilan Peak, 192.
Geneva, 13.
German Club, St. Louis, 21.
Germans, 19,23,26,27,31–33,101, 119,162,333,344.
Germans in California (see also Cordua, Flügge, Huber, Mumm), 148,207.
Germany, 5,19,118.
Gibson, Hugh G., 341.
Giessen Emigration Society, 22.
Gildea, William B., 172,186.
Gillespie, Archibald H., 192–194.
Gingery, 229.
Gold Discoveries before 1848, 240, 241.
Gold Discovery of 1848, 232–257, 271,281.
Gold rush, 245–252.
Golden Gate, 48,282.
Graham House, San Francisco, 288.
Graham, Isaac, 151.
Grant, Ulysses S., 328.
Gray, William Henry, 39,42,46.
Great Salt Lake, 214,226,273,281.
Green, Jacob (see Dürr).
Green River, 41.
Greenwood, Caleb, 162.
Gregson, Mrs., 230.
Grigsby-Ide Party, 172.
Grimes, Eliab, 78.
Gristmill, Sutter's (see Flourmill).
Guadalupe Hidalgo, Treaty of, 242,302,318.
Gudde, Erwin G., 343,344.
Gulnac, William, 157.
Gunsmiths, Sutter's, 165.
Gutierez, Pablo, 33,41,43,77,123, 141,241.

Haas, 251,265,269,289.
Hahn, 263,264.
Hall, Fort, 42,140,162.
Harris, Nellie M., 36.
Hartnell, W.E.P., 347.
Hastings, Lansford W., 111,132, 172,173,269,276,277.
Hat factory, Sutter's, 115,165,231.
Häussler family, 4.
Havana, 293.
Hawaiian Islands (see Sandwich Islands).
Hawaiian Spectator, 46.
Hayes, Kate, 310.
Hebel, J.P., 5.
Helena (Ship), 99.
Hensley, Samuel J., 111,175,216, 221.
Hernandez brothers, 141.
Herrera José, 174.
Hess, Nancy, 186.
Hinckley, William S., 58,59,185.
Hock Farm, 108,123,204,216,217, 221,224,277-279,288,290-292, 294,295-300,303,304,306,308- 316,321-323,350,351.
Hollywood, 150.
Homestead laws, 338.
Honolulu, 45,46,48,56,118,275,346.
Horticulture (see also Agriculture), 165,212,291,292.
Hospital, New Helvetia, 251.
Huber, Henry, 104.
Hudson, 245.
Hudson's Bay Company, 39,41,44, 85,86,93,102,106,118,124,163, 166,275.
Hügel, Friedrich, 67.
Humphreys, Capt., 45.
Huntley, Sir Henry, 309.
Hutchings California Magazine, 316.

Immigration, California, 91,100, 102,103,110-114,132,140,162, 164,170-173,175,184,185,187, 188,190,206,212,281,282,286, 304.
Impostors, 25.
Independence, Mo., 28,35,78.
Indian boy servant, Sutter's, 41,67.
Indian children, 108,126,158,164.
Indian frontier, 224.
Indian labor, 104,105,108,126,158, 159,162,165,212-214,235,249.

Indian trouble, 74-77,81,84,157, 158,195.
Indians, 35,45,307.
Indians, California (see also Squaws), 55,69,74-77,147,158, 192,232,239,249,282.
Indians, Sutter's, 73,101,102,116, 117,119-121,126,142,146,149, 173,174,206-208,212-214,222, 230-232,241,247,263,268,269, 298,309,314.
Industries, New Helvetia (see also Labor), 90,115,119,122,162,164- 166,212,224,225.
Isabella (Ship), 58,65,66.

Jäggi, Samuel, 9,10.
Jefferson, Thomas, 2.
Jenny-Roth, J.J., 332,333.
John, James, 91.
Johnson, Andrew, 324.
Johnson, William, 217.
Jones, John C., 45,54.
Julian, 76,77.

Kalb de, General, 26.
Kamehameha III, 46.
Kanaka Harry, 217,224.
Kanaka women (see also Manaiki), 47,67,88,120.
Kanakas, 47,53,63-65,67,73,79, 120,263,268.
Kandern, 4-6.
Kandern papermill, 4,7.
Kansas City, 35.
Kearney, Gen., 208,209,211.
Kelly, 229.
Kelsey Party, 132.
Kern, Edward M., 201-204,207, 209,210,211,219,308.
Keseberg, Louis, 207,216,308.
Keyser, Sebastian, 41,77,111,123, 217.
King Cotton, 17.
King, Henry, 67.
Koerner, Gustav Ph., 21.
Kostromitinoff, Peter, 94-96.
Kouprianoff, Gov., 47,48,53,96.
Kyburz, Samuel, 216,232,251, 308.

Labor problems, Sutter's (see also Indian labor), 106,132,134,135, 162,163,221,222,245,246.
Lake Tahoe, 129.

Land grants (see also New Helvetia grant, *Sobrante* grant, Squatters), 301–305,313,317–320.
Land speculators, 275,304,308,312, 323.
Lang, 263.
Laramie Fort, 40.
Larkin, Thomas Oliver, 55,130,160, 161,163,167–169,171,228,349.
Lassen, Peter, 77,134,192,217.
Laufkötter, Johann August, 20,21, 23–27,29,32,33,35,36,344–346.
Lausanne (Ship), 77,94.
Lee, D., 43.
Leese, Jacob P., 99,101,174,176, 198,347.
Leidesdorff, William A., 163,164, 185,189,203,204,206,214,217, 219,229,230,264,271,349.
Leipzig, Battle of, 5.
Lenox, 229.
Lienhard, J. Heinrich, 14,213,216, 221–223,238,243,244,252–254, 262,269,277–279,287–289,293, 299,349,350.
Liestal, *Landeskanzlei*, 344.
Lincoln, Abraham, 21,344.
Lincoln, Mrs. A., 197.
Lindenhall Seminary, Lititz, 329.
Lindsey, 157.
Link, Franz Xaver, 321.
Lititz, Pa., 328–335,338–341.
Little Arkansas River, 29.
Livermore, Robert, 107.
Liverpool, 281.
Livingston, Robert R., 2.
Loker, Wm., 175.
London, World's Fair, 306.
Lopez, Francisco, 240.
Los Angeles, 91,144,145,148–150, 154–156,208,240.
Los Tres Picos, 290.
Louis Napoleon (see Napoleon III).
Louis Philippe, 25.
Louisiana Purchase, 1,2,21.
Louisiana Territory, 1,17.
Lowe, Governor, 325.
Lucas & Cavenaugh, 35,37.
Lucinda, 215,216.
Lumber, 82,98,165,212,315.

McCoon, Perry, 78,217,221,224, 249,268,269.
McCoy, John Calvin, 36–38.

McDougall, George, 263,275,276.
McDougall, John, 277,283,305,306.
McGee, Allen, 37.
McKic, Dr., 263.
McKinstry, George, 216,230,264, 276,277,308.
McMahon-Clyde Party, 172.
McVickers, 106.
Mades' Hotel, Washington, 340.
Madison, James, 2.
Manaiki, 67,122,142,143,157,217, 224,231.
Marsh, John, 78,83,91,108,113,143, 144,149,151,152,159,161,182, 188,189,216,217.
Marshall, James Wilson, 172,216, 226,227,233–240.
Martinez, Ygnacio, 64,67,70,73,74, 78,79,83,346.
Mary, Squaw, 217,268.
Marysville, 217,289.
Mason, Richard B., 209,211,241, 248,251,273,275,283.
Massey, Ernest de, 299.
Matanzas, 215.
Meiggs, Capt., 63.
Mengis, Joseph, 310.
Menschikoff, Princess, 47.
Mexican citizenship, Sutter's, 79, 80.
Mexican Dragoons, 152.
Mexican Government (see also Mexico), 49,50,52,93,96,109,156, 173–178.
Mexican War, 177,200–211,217–219,241,300,317–320.
Mexico, 49,51,95,96,109,131,143, 156,173–176,181–184,191,193–195,307,317,319,337.
Micheltorena, Manuel, 109,110, 131–136,144,318,348.
Micheltorena War, 132–156,170, 185,191,219,241,271,317.
Miller, Sutter's 166.
Millwrights, Sutter's (see also Marshall), 165.
Mimal Ranch, 221.
Mission Indians, 50,159.
Missionaries, 39,40,42,43.
Missions, California, 49,50.
Mississippi, 18,23.
Missouri, 7,18,24,35,91,92,101,102, 252,254,275,344.
Missouri Republican, 32.
Missroon, Lieut., 202.

Mofras, Eugène Duflot de, 87,88, 92,346.
Mokelumne Indians, 74,142, 158.
Monroe, James, 2.
Monte Diablo, 64,242.
Monterey, 51,54,55,79,86,89,125, 133-137,200,247,248,275,283, 284.
Montgomery, Allan, 186,187.
Montgomery, Commander, 202.
Montgomery, Mrs., 186.
Moravian Brotherhood, 329,341.
Mormon Battalion, 205.
Mormon Island, 245,273.
Mormons, 205,212,214,226-229, 232-240,242,244,246,249,272, 273,281.
Morstein, Louis, 67.
Mumm, 155.
Münch, Friedrich, 25,26,34,344.
Münchhausen, 5.
Munsoon (Ship), 59,63.
Murphy, 230.

Nagle, Charles, Rev., 341.
Napoleon Bonaparte, 1,2,5,119.
Napoleon III, 6,8,294.
Narciso, Chief, 68.
Natoma, 229,230.
Navaho Indians, 31.
Negroes, 120,134.
Neuchâtel, 6.
Nevada, 206.
Nevada City, 321.
New England, 328.
New Helvetia. First settlement, 67-69,71,72,82,83; fort, 89,90,101, 103,115-117,119,212,251,277, 331; historic importance, 91,92, 171,174-177,181-184,191-197, 204,205,210; manner of life, 117-122,161-166,212-217; After the gold-discovery, 248-252,271,283; transferred to John A. Sutter, Jr., 264,266,279; collapse of the empire, 251-257,261,264-280, 295-300.
New Helvetia Army, 138,140,142, 145,148.
New Helvetia Diary, 158,186,215, 224,227,228-232,238,247,261, 349.
New Helvetia Garrison, 90,101, 116,119,142.

New Helvetia Grant (see also *Sobrante* grant), 89,103,110,133, 146,301,313,317.
New Helvetia Mortgage, 97,98, 169,177,178,219,220,264.
New Helvetia Population, 77,78, 91,237,238.
New Mecklenburg, 111,217.
New Mexico (see Santa Fe).
New Orleans, 1,2.
New York, 17,118,184,206,225, 281,337.
New York Tribune, 284.
New York Volunteers, 209-211, 214,216,223,224.
Nicolas (launch), 59,65.
Norris, S., 232.
North Platte River, 40.

Oahu, 45,46.
Ochecame Indians, 68.
O'Fallon, William, 150,152.
Ohio, 20.
Oregon, 39,40,45,77,87,91,111,112, 132,158,162,171,172,192,193, 196,225,274,281.
Oregon (Steamship), 282.
Oswald, 217.

Pablino, 247.
'Pacific Republic,' 171.
Pacific Steamship Lines, 281,282.
Panama, 279,281,282,287,294.
Paris, 272.
Paris July Revolution, 11,25.
Paul, Prince of Würtemberg, 294.
Pawnee Rock, 29.
Payette, Capt., 43.
Peachy, Archibald, 279,298.
Pelly, Lord, 45.
Pennsylvania, 19,328.
Pennsylvania Dutch, 329.
Perkins & Lee, 43.
Pettit, 230,263.
Philadelphia Centennial Celebration, 333.
Physician, Sutter's, 166,172,208, 213,216,231.
Pickett, Charles E., 263,283.
Pico, Pio, 145,159,160,173,200.
Placer Times, 301.
Platte River, 40.
Polk, President, 211.
Polynesian, The, 118.
Popian (see Beaubien).

Popoazua, Popoagie River, 40, 42.
Portsmouth (Ship), 202.
Prudon, Victor, 56,109,174,184, 185,198.
Pumpmaker, Sutter's, 166.

Queen Victoria, 294.

Rae, William G., 124.
Randall, Speaker, 339.
Raphero, Chief, 158.
Reading, Pierson B., 111–114,116, 134,135,142,143,148,164,166, 173,175,193,216,217.
Revere, Joseph Warren, 313.
Revere, Paul, 313.
Richardson, William A., 56.
Ridley, Robert, 78,81,263.
Riley, Gov., 283–285.
Ringgold, Lieut., 87,96.
Rio Grande, 129.
Robinson, Fowler, Gillespie & Mc-Dougall, 306.
Rocky Mountains, 39,71.
Ross and Bodega (see also Bodega), 56–58,77,93–100,103,108,110, 123,271,275.
Rotscheff, Alexander, 58,93,96,98, 125.
Rousseau, Jean Jacques, 18.
Rowland, John, 154.
Rufino, Chief, 142,158.
Rufus, Ernst, 131,142,144.
Rünenberg, 3,4,10,13,344.
Russia, 5.
Russian Alaska (see Sitka).
Russian America, 93.
Russian American Fur Company, 52,95–100,274,275 (see also Russians).
Russian debt, Sutter's, 103,106, 123–125,163,169,219,220.
Russian Purchase, 58,95–100,103, 108,123–125,175,264.
Russians, 58,95–100,119,125,163, 166,169,177,183,185,219,230,265.

Sacramento (launch), 99,106,119, 124,125,142,216.
Sacramento City, 64,67,273–277, 279,280,282,283,286,287,294, 297,301,307,310,316.
Sacramento River, 55,64,99,115, 174,271,287,295,309.

Sacramento Valley, 49,56,63,195, 214,241,252,283,323.
Saint-Amand, Pierre Charles de, 293.
Salinas, 144.
Salinez, 144.
Salmon fisheries, 84,230.
Salmon packing, 165,166.
San Antonio Mission, 147.
San Diego, 49.
San Fernando Mission, 150,155.
San Francisco (see also Yerba Buena), 53,86,92,94,230,246–248,276,279,282,287,288,294.
San Jacinto, 92.
San Joaquin, 49,64,76,142–144, 214.
San José, 80,133,140,141,182,196, 238,247,307.
Sandwich Island Gazette, 46.
Sandwich Islands, 45,46,56,110, 119,309.
Santa Barbara, 145.
Santa Fe, 23,24,26–33,69,345.
Santa Fe trade, 28.
Santa Teresa, Treaty of, 137.
Savannah (frigate), 135,136,331.
Sawmill, Sutter's, 216,225–230,273, 281,282.
Schaefer, Frank, Col., 337,340.
Schläfli, Frau, 327,329–330.
Schläfli, Gustav, 299,306,311.
Schnell, Carl, 10.
Schoolcraft, Henry A., 279,298.
Schoonover, T.J., 343.
Scott, 230.
Scott (Dred Scott case), 320.
Scott, Walter, 13.
Seelhofer, Benedikt, 11,12,13.
Semple, Robert, 173,205,284.
Settlers in California (see also Americans, Foreigners, Immigration), 81,122,132,138,161,170, 171,188,195.
Shaddon, Thomas, 230,331.
Shaw, William, 307.
Shawnee Indians, 35,101.
Sheldon, Jared, 230,308.
Sherman, William T., 210,251,252, 254,336.
Sierras, 183,247,271.
Simpson, Sir George, 86,87,92.
Sinclair, John, 78,117,122,217,232, 249.
Sioux Indians, 46.

Sitka, 46–48,63,93,118,119,124, 230,275.
Slavery Question, 319,320.
Sloat, Commodore, 200.
Smith, Azariah, 236.
Smith, George, 244.
Smith, Henry, 229.
Smith, John, 123.
Smith, Samuel, 230.
Smith, Stephen, Capt., 125.
Smuggling, 52,167,185.
Snake River, 42.
Sobrante Grant, 133,134,146,313, 317–320,336,338 (see also New Helvetia grant, Land grants, Squatters).
Society of California Pioneers, 321.
Sonoma, 49,52,56,86,102,110,138, 140,197,204,216,247.
Sonoma Prisoners (see Bear Flag prisoners).
Sonoma Valley, 57.
Sonora, 200.
South America, 119,217,241.
Spain, 1.
Spaulding, Josiah, 77,94.
Spear, Nathan, 56,68.
Spear & Hinckley, 56,58,59.
Spence, David, 54,55,79,135.
Spinning, 212.
Squatter Revolt, Sacramento, 302.
Squatters, 301–305,308,315,316, 323.
Squaw-men, 111,120,122,217.
Squaws, 111,120,122,217,223,224, 268.
St. Blaise, 6.
St. Charles, Mo., 23–25,30,34,345.
St. Louis, Mo., 17,20–23,26,28,31, 34,162.
St. Petersburg, 119.
Stars and Stripes, 160,200,271.
Steamships in California, 230.
Stearns, Abel, 154.
Steinberger, J.B., 309.
Sterling (Ship), 136.
Steuben, General, 26.
Stevens, 230.
Stevens, Elisha, 140.
Stevens' Party, 140.
Stevenson, Col., 209.
Steward, Col., 264,265,274.
Steward, Sir William Drummond, 39,45.

Stober, Christine Wilhelmine, 4.
Stober, Johann Adolf, 4.
Stockton, Commodore, 204,209, 216.
Stockton (town), 111,157.
Stoney Creek, 228.
Sublette, William, 172.
Suisun Bay, 63,64.
Suisun Indians, 86.
Suñol, Antonio, 80–83,94,96,107, 126,133,136,144,158,159,163, 275.
Suter, Capt., 44,45.
Suter, Johann Heinrich, 344.
Sutter, Alfons Wilhelm, 189,190, 289,290,298,309,311,314,321.
Sutter, Anna Elise, 189,289,290, 298,306,309,311,312,315,321.
Sutter, Emil Victor, 189,190,289, 298,311,314,321.
Sutter Genealogy, 3,344.
Sutter, Hastings & Co., 269.
Sutter, Jakob Friedrich, 4,11,13, 344.
Sutter, John Augustus. Name and family, 3,4; birth, 4; childhood and youth, 4–8; apprenticeship in Basle, 6,7; in Burgdorf, 9,10; flight to America, 15,16; St. Louis, Mo., 20–26; St. Charles, 23–26; first trip to Santa Fe, 24; second Santa Fe trip, 27–34; at Westport, 35–38; overland trip, 39–45; explores the Sacramento, 63–68; establishes New Helvetia, 67ff.; receives New Helvetia Grant, 89; buys Ross and Bodega, 93–102; builds Fort New Helvetia, 89,90; alliance with Micheltorena, 134; Sutter and U.S.A., 191–196; Sutter and Frémont, 192–204; raises U.S. Flag over fort, 201; Sutter and Donner Party, 206–208; sawmill and gristmill, 225–230; discovery of gold, 233–245; effects of discovery, 246–257; arrival of his eldest son, 261–264; conflict between father and son, 265–270, 275–280; delegate at Constitutional Convention, 283–285; gubernatorial candidate, 286; arrival of the family from Switzerland, 287–290; his extravagance, 293–295, 297–300; influence of national

legislation on Sutter, 300–305, 308; Major-General of the California Militia, 310; his grants confirmed by U.S. Land Commission, 313; by U.S. District Court for Northern California, 316; *Sobrante* Grant rejected by U.S. Supreme Court, 317–321; removes to Washington, D.C., 324; Petition to Congress, 325; establishes residence in Lititz, Pa., 328, 329; Memorial to Congress, 335; his affairs before Congress, 335–340; death and burial, 340–341.

Sutter Bill (bill for the relief of J.A.S.), 328, 335–337, 339.

Sutter Diary, 211.

Sutter Family, 13, 16, 118, 133, 188–190, 264, 265, 270, 278, 279; arrive in California, 287–289, 294, 296, 298, 299, 351.

Sutter Memorial, 337.

Sutter Petition, 325, 328, 335.

Sutter, John A., Jr., 10, 14, 189, 190, 261–281, 288, 296, 301, 303, 306, 307, 321, 325, 332, 350.

Sutter, Mrs. John Augustus (see also Dübeld, Anna), 9, 13, 16, 190, 264, 278, 287, 288, 298, 299, 311, 315, 316, 324, 329–334, 338–340, 341.

Sutter, Johann Jakob, 4.

Sutter's Buttes, 290.

Sutter's Fort (see New Helvetia, Fort).

Sutterville, 190, 271–277, 280, 287, 301.

Swasey-Todd party, 172.

Sweetwater River, 40.

Swiss Army, 6, 8.

Swiss Emigration Society, 19.

Swiss Guard of Charles X of France, 25, 35, 38, 44, 46, 87, 116, 131, 159, 255, 268, 293.

Swiss in California, 119, 206, 216, 272; in U.S.A., 20, 162.

Switzerland, 1–16, 44, 118, 277, 278, 285.

Tannery, Sutter's, 83, 106, 115, 126, 165, 169, 212, 327.

Taos, N. M., 36.

Taylor, Bayard, 284.

Telles, Rafael, 131.

Texas, 31, 92, 111, 131, 150, 161, 170, 174, 191.

Thurneysen, Emanuel, 7.

Todd, William, 197.

Torre, Estaban de la, 151, 152.

Torre, Joaquin de la, 151.

Trappers, 71, 102, 165.

Trapping, 73, 80, 82, 85, 86, 106, 166.

Trechsel-Grimm, Widow, 11.

Truckee, 206.

Trudin, Col., 174.

Tulare Valley, 155.

Twain, Mark, 336.

Typhoid epidemics, 213, 214, 219, 231.

United States, 1, 2, 86, 87, 89, 131, 161, 174, 178, 182, 184, 185, 191–193, 200–211, 219, 220, 242, 285, 300–305, 317–319.

—— Census for California, 204.

—— Congress, 5, 6, 27, 131, 203, 264, 265, 282, 300, 302, 305, 321, 325–328, 335–340, 351.

—— House of Representatives, 1, 335, 337, 339.

—— Senate, 302, 326, 328, 338.

—— District Court, North Calif., 316.

—— Land Commission for California, 308, 311, 313, 315.

—— Supreme Court, 27, 303, 317–320, 322, 324, 325, 336, 338.

—— Topographical Bureau, 130.

Universal City, 150.

Vaca, Juan, 157.

Valdez, Capt., 146.

Vallejo, José Jesus, 72, 77.

Vallejo, Mariano Guadalupe, 52, 54–58, 71–73, 77, 80, 81, 93–95, 98, 100–102, 108–110, 125, 138–141, 176, 177, 183, 185, 198, 199, 203, 204, 229, 243.

Vallejo, Salvador, 198.

Vancouver, 44, 45, 63.

Vera Cruz, Mex., 28.

Victoria, Queen, 294.

Vigilante Proclamation, 307.

Vioget, Jean-Jacques, 89, 99, 107, 264, 301.

Voorhees, Senator, 338, 340.

Walagumne Indians, 65, 247.

Walker, Capt., 183.

Walker, Joseph R., 111.
Walker Nicaragua Campaign, 314, 321.
Walker Pass, 183.
Walla Walla, Fort, 43,46.
Walla Walla Indians, 158.
Ward, 247.
Warren County, Mo., 19.
Waseurtz, G. M. de Sandels, 116, 241.
Washington, George, 26,312.
Washington (see also United States), 47,274,281,304,316,317, 322,336.
Weaving shops, Sutter's, 115,212, 249.
Weber, Charles M., 141,144,160, 182,249.
Weber, Johann Jakob, 6-8.
Weimar boy, 239,243.
Weimar, Peter, 237,238.
Weimar, Mrs. P., 237,243.
Westport, Mo., 28,35-39,48,73.
Wetler, 37,41.
Wetzlar Bros., 297,307,351.

Whitworth, Lord, 2.
Wiese & Laufkötter, 26,345.
Wiggins, William, 77.
Wilkes Exploring Expedition, 87, 96,112,346.
Willamette Mission, 43,158.
Willamette Valley, 43,44,92,101.
Williams, John, 167.
Willis, 245.
Wilson, Capt., John, 56,57,67.
Wind River Rendezvous, 40-42,45, 67,77.
Winn, Albert, 298.
Wittmer, Jacob, 216,243-245.
Wood, William Maxwell, 135,331.
Woodworth, Selim E., 207,209.
Wyman, 230.

Yalesumnes, 76.
Yanti, 231.
Yerba Buena, 49,53-56,66,73,77, 85,86,119,121,124,125,130,136, 163,183,187,200,205.
Young, Brigham, 205,214,226,273.
Yuba River, 111.

CALVIN T. RYAN LIBRARY
KEARNEY STATE COLLEGE
KEARNEY, NEBRASKA